# CONFLICT IN CHRISTOLOGY

# CONFLICT IN CHRISTOLOGY

A STUDY OF BRITISH AND AMERICAN CHRISTOLOGY, FROM 1889—1914

*By*

JOHN STEWART LAWTON

M.A., B.D., Oxon.

WIPF & STOCK · Eugene, Oregon

Wipf and Stock Publishers
199 W 8th Ave, Suite 3
Eugene, OR 97401

Conflict in Christology
A Study of British and American Christology, From 1889 - 1914
By Lawton, John Stewart
Copyright©1947 SPCK
ISBN 13: 978-1-60899-833-3
Publication date 7/15/2010
Previously published by SPCK, 1947

# CONTENTS

| CHAP. | | PAGE |
|---|---|---|
| | INTRODUCTION | vii |
| 1. | PRESUPPOSITIONS AND INFLUENCES | 1 |
| 2. | THE COLLISION AND COLLAPSE OF ORTHODOXY | 23 |
| 3. | THE GOSPEL EVIDENCE FOR THE KNOWLEDGE OF OUR LORD | 44 |
| 4. | CONCERNING CHRIST'S KNOWLEDGE AND AUTHORITY | 74 |
| 5. | THE KENOTIC THEORY | 111 |
| 6. | THE CONSCIOUSNESS OF JESUS | 165 |
| 7. | THE DIVORCE OF THEOLOGY FROM HISTORY | 189 |
| 8. | IMMANENTISM, IDEALISM, AND "THE NEW THEOLOGY" | 223 |
| 9. | PERSONALITY AND INDIVIDUALITY | 251 |
| 10. | THE THEOCENTRIC SOLUTION | 271 |
| 11. | THE ANTHROPOCENTRIC SOLUTION | 284 |
| 12. | THE NEO-ANTIOCHENE SOLUTION | 302 |
| | BIBLIOGRAPHY | 325 |

# INTRODUCTION

THE Lady Margaret Professor of Divinity at Oxford, Dr. F. L. Cross, whilst engaged upon his researches into the life of the late Dr. Darwell Stone, suggested to the present writer that a detailed enquiry into the course of English Christology during the years succeeding 1889 might be of considerable interest. And such, in fact, it has proved to be. Dr. Cross himself has subsequently devoted some pages of his *Darwell Stone* to this very subject: for as is shown, especially by his anonymous reviews, Dr. Stone was keenly alive to the momentous import of the discussions then taking place to the truth of the Christian Faith.

The period of British and American Theology from the publication of *Lux Mundi* to the outbreak of the first world war will probably come to be known as the "liberal" era of English-spoken Theology. Though some may demur, wishing to extend the boundaries in either direction, it remains true that the period in fact represents a unique epoch in the religious thought of these lands.

In the first place, it marks the beginning and the virtual conclusion of the struggle for the recognition of the rights of higher criticism in the English-speaking world. At the outset of the period, the methods of that science were but feebly struggling to gain a foothold in the great centres of learning (see e.g. the Introduction to T. K. Cheyne's Bampton Lectures), whilst, by its close, the rights of the historical method were almost universally recognized. Then again, the period marks the introduction and assimilation of new methods in the study of both dogmatic and apologetic theology. The mood of the age is even more characteristic, for the uneasiness detectable in *Lux Mundi* has settled into unbroken gloom in *Foundations* (1912)—a despair of ever again being able to convince modern man of the truth or relevance of the dogmas of traditional Christianity; and the course of the numerous newspaper controversies upon religious topics, which were carried on in the years immediately preceding the first world war also testify to the same situation—the trial and breakdown through inadequacy of a whole cycle of theological thought, and the insufficiency of a new interpretation of the Christian faith.

It is surely not unfair to enquire into the inmost nature of—and even perhaps to pass final judgment upon—a movement in Christian thought on the basis of the question, "What think ye of Christ?" Here then is our justification for venturing to examine English liberal theology from the specifically Christological angle. This procedure is particularly justifiable in the present subject since the doctrine of the Person of Christ was itself in the very forefront of discussion for much of the period. No judgment is offered in these pages upon the relative adequacy of liberal theology or its fidelity to the facts of the eternal Gospel. Our purpose is historical and descriptive. The new theories and systems are, as far as possible, merely contrasted with traditional orthodoxy in order to exhibit their own characteristics.

It remains simply to delineate the subject more precisely and to offer an explanation of some of the expressions employed in this volume. The voluminous and diffuse character of the material makes it imperative to confine our enquiry to the realm of Christology, strictly so-called, that is, the relation of the Deity and humanity in Christ. Even such closely cognate subjects as soteriology can be alluded to only in passing.

Little distinction in broad character can be drawn with any value between writings produced on either side of the Atlantic. The protagonists of traditional orthodoxy in all the Protestant traditions in America were on the whole more thoroughgoing and dogmatic—to say nothing of being voluminous—than their British brethren. At the other end of the scale, the enthusiasts for the new liberalism were in America perhaps more hasty in the assimilation of Teutonic systems of thought than were English scholars. Hence as this thesis deals with the development of Christology in the Anglo-Saxon world—as opposed to German thought—the word "English" will for the sake of brevity be generally substituted for the expression "British and American".

Only at one point will anything need to be said concerning Roman Catholic theology, since the intellectual life of that communion was left largely unaffected by the stirring events without. Among Protestant writers a bewildering variety may be discovered, which makes it necessary to restrict our enquiry to that sphere of thought which for want of a better word we may describe as Trinitarian Protestantism, confining ourselves to the representatives of those Churches which embodied the three main Protestant traditions, Anglican, Reformed, and Lutheran. Though

INTRODUCTION ix

it should be noted that at this time certain Unitarian writers, such as Martineau and Drumond, were exercising an influence far beyond the bounds of their own confession.

It has already been said that the period was one of conflict between the exponents of new methods, critical, dogmatic, and apologetic, and those who desired to retain the older ways of thought—one could scarcely have a greater contrast than that between the two major theological works which appeared in 1889, the book already referred to, written to "succour a distressed faith", and W. G. Shedd's uncompromising *Dogmatic Theology*. It will therefore be convenient to designate theologians of the former leanings as "Liberals", distinguishing between "Moderates" and "Radicals", whilst describing the latter class as "Conservatives".

My thanks are due to the University of Oxford for the degree of B.D. conferred in respect of this thesis. My gratitude is also due to my mother and to Mr. G. H. Witcomb, whose patient assistance made this work possible, also to Canon A. E. Simpson for correcting the proofs and for valuable suggestions.

Hooton, Cheshire.
1944.

# CONFLICT IN CHRISTOLOGY

# 1

## PRESUPPOSITIONS AND INFLUENCES

### (a) *"a priori"* and *"a posteriori"*

IN the history of human culture, there can scarcely be imagined a more radical change in the method of acquiring and interpreting knowledge than that which took place when the *a priori* method gave place to the *a posteriori*. In olden times, the scientist would sit in his study, and with no instruments other than Aristotelian logic, and no text books or records other than his volumes of Greek philosophy, would write his treatise on the course of the stars and the composition of matter. The whole of reality was covered by this same *a priori* method of study.

By the close of the Middle Ages, however, it was becoming increasingly clear to the most far-sighted of men that such a method is inadequate for the proper understanding of the natural world. If, for example, you begin your study of astrophysics with some such teleological assumption as that the sun rotates around the earth, then no progress in knowledge can possibly take place; since any observed facts which come to light subsequently will be manipulated so as to fit in to the original assumption. No natural science that begins with assumptions about what is or what ought to be—from which deductions are made, which in their turn form the basis of further *a priori* assumptions—no science based upon such principles could ever have discovered the properties of ether waves or the circulation of the blood.

Only an inductive method could be legitimate for learning about the world around us—a method based upon experiment, hypothesis, further experiment, and conclusion, each step dependent upon the previous one, and open to modification by the succeeding step.

Theology, the queen of the sciences, had naturally been treated in exactly the same manner of old as the rest of man's knowledge. It had been confidently assumed that man's God-given reason was itself capable of arriving at ultimate truths or even new truths by its own unaided deductive powers, whether working upon the data of revelation or not. In the first part of the *Summa*, for instance, St. Thomas deduces the various attributes of God one from the other by the all-compelling force of reason—and he naturally applies precisely the same method to the interpretation of the Person of Christ.

This method was still the predominant mould for theological thought long after the natural sciences had discarded it. The Reformation demanded freedom of thought, but no new method was introduced, and the writings of Luther and Calvin differ little in their type of argumentation from those scholastic writers whom they replaced. The Deists, too, showed little advance on this: works such as *Christianity as old as the Creation* and *Christianity not Mysterious* attempted to show that all the truths of religion could be demonstrated and deduced from the facts of existence by reason alone.

With the nineteenth century there came a change. The natural sciences, which for long had enjoyed emancipation from their former fetters, suddenly sprang into unprecedented prominence in the industrial revolution. Science, its inventions, its material progress, and its methods, came to touch men at every point in their lives.

It was therefore inevitable that methods of research which man had found so eminently successful in respect of his study of the physical world should be applied to other regions of thought—to history, to philosophy, and to theology.

The reliability of historical events—even belief in God—must ultimately stand at the bar of inductive reasoning.

Waiving the thorny question how far, if at all, the methods appropriate to an empirical science are applicable to theology or to any of the fields of speculative, ethical, or æsthetic regions of thought—though attempts were made to apply them in all these departments, with very definite results—there is one aspect of the situation which at once characterises it. Christianity *in its traditional form* has never been regarded as merely a cycle of moral or metaphysical conceptions, it has always professed to be a historical religion. This was not the case because it made its appearance in the world at a given point in history and owed its foundation to a historical figure, but because the articles of its

## PRESUPPOSITIONS AND INFLUENCES

belief are largely concerned with a certain interpretation of a series of historic events: Jesus Christ is not simply the founder of the Christian religion, he *is* the Christian religion, and the events connected with his life are believed by Christians to have a vital importance for the life and eternal well-being of every human being. Christianity is therefore inextricably bound up with certain events which took place in Palestine two millennia ago; but to a lesser degree, it is also concerned with the long history of the people in whose midst the religion ultimately took its rise—since as the preparation for that religion, this people was believed to have been the peculiar object of divine providence and revelation.

It was thus that it came about that the application of the new scientific methods first impinged upon Christian interests, not in the realm of pure dogmatics, but in the department of history.

A whole science of history was developed, in regard to the study of ancient documents. There was the textual criticism which attempted by the comparison and adjudication of manuscripts to ascertain the correct original versions. Even more characteristic, however, was the higher criticism, which essayed to discover the original meaning intended by the authors of given documents. By comparing various writings, with one another and with what was known of the times in which they purported to have been written, such a criticism was believed to be competent to pronounce upon the authenticity or spuriousness of any piece of ancient writing, and to assess the date at which it came into being.

No one to-day in his senses would challenge the rights of scientific historical investigation. Like the science of physics or astronomy, the science of history deals with empirical facts. Its mode of approach, as its scope of operation, is very different from that of any of the natural sciences, but the principles underlying its study must be the same. Just as it was illegitimate for the ancient scholars to declare that planets moved in circles, so it is equally illegitimate for one to declare that such and such an event *must* have taken place in history: the only adequate method is experiment—in the case of history this will be investigation of known facts—followed by hypothesis and further corroborative investigation. In this sense, historical criticism has as much right to its own methods as botany. Unfortunately, this science was not confined within its proper limits. It was all too easy for the science of criticism to slip back into older ways of thought, and for its investigations and findings to be coloured by predelictions and presuppositions of an equally *a priori* character to those displaced.

Yet what had Christianity to fear from such research? The primary object of the application of the new methods was the establishment of truth. If all that Christianity had said with regard to its historic origins was true, then the scientific verdict could only redound to its further establishment. Yet Christianity is not all history: that history is interpreted by it in terms of certain theological and philosophical tenets. The application of the critical methods might fall into the hands of men who did not hold those tenets—and in fact it did, with very alarming results for Christian thinkers. It is this which so largely accounts for the long and fanatical opposition to higher criticism in Britain and America; it was not that men feared the truth, but they did fear the purely negative criticism that had sprung up in Germany under the inspiration of men who did not share their own beliefs and philosophical background.

Thus it came about that every detail of the Bible was placed beneath the microscope. The application of higher criticism to the Old Testament was itself to lead to a peculiar Christological crisis, but for the general appreciation of the changed outlook brought about by the method it is of greater importance to consider the effect which was produced by it upon the study of Christ's own life and person. Hitherto, the Christologian, like the student of any other branch of theology, had employed the New Testament and particularly the Gospels as an armoury of prooftexts and pictorial illustrations in support of his doctrinal disquisitions. Such a scholar would begin his labours with the assumptions that Jesus Christ was God and man, and from what his metaphysics taught him of the nature of two such beings he could theorize at will upon the precise manner of their union in Christ: for such a study, the inductive scrutiny of the Gospel evidences was generally regarded as affording little assistance, at any rate, in the formulation of exact theories. It would have been argued that the New Testament was written when faith was at a white heat, and when men had as yet been given little time to think out the theoretical implications of those facts of faith which they had grasped, and that it was now the business of the Church's thinkers to elaborate the fuller meanings enshrined in those facts, at first apprehended in a pneumatic rather than an intellectual form.

## PRESUPPOSITIONS AND INFLUENCES

It was against such an approach to Christology as this that the men of our period were in such earnest revolt. "The *a priori* method is utterly illegitimate, and issues in a perverted exegesis" writes one Christologian of the time.[1] That only may legitimately be believed of Christ which is based upon a study of the actual evidences of his life. If Christ was a historical figure, it was argued, he cannot be simply theorized about—any more than the course of the planets—he must stand at the bar of historical criticism and his Person and work be estimated in precisely the same manner as that of any other historic individual. The documents relating to his life must be scrutinized in exactly the same way as those relating, say, to the life of the Buddha; the estimate of his character and the content of his consciousness must be ascertained in exactly the same way as one would appraise the personality of Mr. Gladstone; and the significance and importance for history of the events of his life must be weighed with the same impartial exactness as one would discuss the reign of Alexander the Great or Lord Melbourne's ministry.

It is in this context that we meet with the concept of the "Jesus of history" or "the historical Jesus"—terms that are used to distinguish the Figure depicted by the students of higher criticism from the Christ of traditional Christian dogmatics.

It is, of course, inherent in the fact of Incarnation that this should be so. The taking of flesh by God made him an empirical figure, as such capable of being judged by historians, and of being photographed by press-men—had any such been present—and even made his existence necessarily a subject of doubt. Such is the inevitable and obvious consequence of entry upon the historical stage. The historian in demanding the right to examine the authenticity of the Gospel narrative, and to criticise the Person therein represented—without having first to be told by a theologian what he must or must not therein discover—secured a prize which was his by right, and one which no one to-day would wish to deny to him. This controversy concerning the rights of historical investigation was, however, grossly confused with another quite different issue during the period. It is one thing to admit the historian's right to free investigation with the methods proper to his science; it is quite another matter to deny the theologian his right to deduce dogmatic conclusions from his data with methods appropriate to his own domain. Christianity is more

[1] Forrest, *The Christ of History*, p. 104.

than history, hence no complete account of it can be given simply with the tools employable within the sphere of a science that relates only to happenings within time and space. To appeal to what was called the "verdict of history" in order to explain fully every aspect of reality is like trying to persuade a monkey to solve a quadratic equation. When once certain facts are granted—the evangelic truths as to the Deity and humanity of Christ—then these facts become the rightful *a priori* assumptions upon which the theologian may deduce his conclusions—provided always that such results be checked with reference to the tradition of the Church, as primarily embodied in the New Testament. Thus, the scholar of an older generation, having established the Divinity of Christ by the aid of the customary apologetics, could then deduce all that he required to know of his person simply from this one proven fact. In such a way, the doctrines of Christ's hypostatic union, his two wills, his impersonal humanity, his impeccability, and even his omniscience had been deduced. Whatever criticism may be offered in regard to any or all of these doctrines—and at this time there was voluble criticism of them all—the method itself is at bottom justifiable; for to deny the rights of such a method is virtually to exclude from acceptance a whole area of man's mental activity.

There was none the less a genuine grievance against the ancient theological apparatus. The Christ of traditional dogmatic theology appeared to many to be a figure remote alike from the Jesus of the Gospels and from the sufferings and temptations of ordinary men. Such a criticism may indeed have much to commend it, but it was taken as the *reductio ad absurdum* of the whole system and method, and consequently the edifice of doctrine regarding the Person of Christ was to be rejected *en bloc* as unhistorical and unscientific. Naturally, such a labour of demolition was not effected in a day; but we are here concerned with the forces at work rather than with the way in which their purposes were brought into effect.

Thus, reason was dethroned, to be superseded by history. The method of deduction from *a priori* assumptions was abandoned for a method which, it was claimed, began solely with the scientific examination of historical materials—without preconceived beliefs—and which even then did not proceed to make unjustifiable deductions from its own findings. In the forthcoming chapters, it is hoped that two facts will emerge: first, that an

## PRESUPPOSITIONS AND INFLUENCES

*a posteriori* method of theologizing, which relies solely upon inductions from historical, or for that matter from psychological data—whether of Christ or of ourselves—is inadequate as an intellectual creation to bear upon its shoulders the weight of the evangelic truths and all that they must imply.

Secondly, it will appear time and again that such an *a posteriori* method as is envisaged is not in fact being applied as it should according to strict scientific principles. A man may be able to begin the investigation of a newly discovered plant or microbe without any preconceived beliefs about it, and thus to carry out an enquiry which is strictly scientific. But when he comes to the examination of things that pertain to the meaning of existence and his own spiritual well-being, it turns out to be virtually impossible for him to carry on an investigation that is free from beliefs and prejudices, however unconscious those influences may be. In the second part of this chapter, it will be our task to examine certain of the most obvious of those influences which became the substitutes in theology for the *a priori* assumptions of an earlier time.

For the moment, it will suffice to allude to several other effects of the historical method itself.

It must never be forgotten that behind Anglo-Saxon liberal Christology lay more than a century of highly concentrated German criticism. The English scholars were not, therefore, innovators; on the contrary, in so far as they accepted the critical method, they were forced to accept its already established findings—the paths had already been to a great extent marked out: and criticism on the continent had been and was in the hands of men who embraced very definite philosophical and theological biases. That English theologians never, as a whole, took kindly to those multifarious and radical theories which the German critics elaborated is itself a fact of great significance for our present contention.

If higher criticism had been purely a matter of impartial science, then in the long-run the findings of scholars at Oxford and at Tübingen should have been in substantial agreement. The fact that they were not leads, in the end, to the conclusion that the *a priori* method had been abandoned by neither side. The German scholars were working upon a set of principles completely at variance with the presuppositions of traditional Christianity, whilst their British and American brethren were still to a considerable extent influenced by the predilections of their traditional faith.

However diverse the results of the application of the historical method to the Person of Christ might be, one presupposition, already alluded to, was common to all, and affected Christology in two ways. We have seen how it was demanded—and rightly so—that Christ should be studied as a historic person. Students of Christ's life might conclude—as they did—that he was an Essene propagandist, a sentimental moralist, an eschatological fanatic, or the Lord of heaven and earth, but they all agreed that first and foremost he was a historic figure, a man who must first be understood in terms of the historical environment in which he had lived. A vast amount of knowledge had been accumulated regarding Christ's environment. The language he spoke, the customs of the people at that time, and above all, the religious outlook of the Palestinian Jews of that time, were now largely opened up to the student. Every word or action of Christ was interpreted with reference to its setting in the cultural background of his times. The net result of all this was that Christ was regarded first and foremost as a man, a historic man. Whatever else theologians might subsequently say about him, his humanity was what first caught the scholar's eye. The following section of the chapter will supply additional reason for this primary emphasis upon the humanity of Christ. It became the watchword of all liberal Christology—Christ's real humanity. A second, and similar, presupposition is this: If Christ is first to be understood as a historic figure, for such he was, his personality must be such as can be examined and understood like that of any other historic person; in other words his being and Person must be a psychological unity. No dogmatic fiction of one who appeared to act now with one personality—the divine—and now with another—the human—could ever serve as the basis for genuine critical study. The importance attached to Christ's unity will appear shortly. The simultaneous emphasis of these two premises produced a Christological crisis unparalleled in the history of Christian thought. For the moment, however, it will suffice to urge that the taking of such an attribute of Christ as his humanity as the starting-point for the reconstruction of Christology holds consequences which could scarcely have been foreseen at the time. It has a radical effect upon the systems which may be elaborated. Equally striking is the change which such a major premise has upon apologetics. A new starting-point required the creation of new systems in which the argument had to be developed upwards from the acceptance of a virtually humanitarian picture of Christ—this will appear in the seventh chapter.

In short, the rejection of the *a priori* method of theology was a clarion call to a re-examination of the Gospel evidences for the life of Christ with a view to the formulation of a doctrine of his Person that would be strictly consonant with what was therein written, and attested by the spiritual experience of believers.

(b) *Evolution and Immanence*

A factor of equally immense importance for the theology of the time, itself a product of the scientific and historical spirit, was evolution. It is difficult for us to-day to measure or realize the impact made upon western thought by the researches of Charles Darwin. His theory came to imply infinitely more than the supposition that men descend from monkeys. Beginning as a scientific hypothesis in the study of biology, the theory of evolution was extended into what was virtually a working principle for the interpretation of the whole universe, and it became the leading category in practically every branch of human research. As J. R. Illingworth writes in *Lux Mundi*: "Organisms, nations, languages, institutions, customs, creeds, have all come to be regarded in the light of their development, and we feel that to understand what a thing really is, we must examine how it came to be. Evolution is in the air. It is the category of the age; a 'Partus temporis'; a necessary consequence of our wider field of comparison."[1]

In the field of history, evolution assumed the form of a theory of the gradual and almost inevitable development of human relationships and culture. The doctrine of human "Progress" was by no means a new idea, but it received an enormous stimulus from the new scientific theories: if natural organisms tended to develop themselves by the workings of a law inherent in their constitution, why not human society and its various organisms?

It may not be out of place here to point out that although in the case of the growth of an empirical science there may be something akin to the evolution of a natural species, wherein the knowledge of the past experiments is built upon as the basis for new experiment and knowledge; such an idea of organic growth

[1] *Lux Mundi*, 10th ed., p. 182.

scarcely applies at all to man's more abstract pursuits; for in art, philosophy, and natural religion too, there is in history a more wave-like motion, in which the only change is in the fashion of the time, or the appreciation or obscuration of truths. This, of course, was vigorously denied at the time.

The immediate reaction of religious thought to evolution, as everyone knows, was one of terror. Hitherto it had been believed that God Almighty created the universe, sun, stars, animals and men, within the space of six days in the year 4004 B.C. The word of God vouched for this. Higher criticism was soon to assure men that such a proposition was not essential to a right appreciation of the Old Testament; but the reconciliation between religion and science needed far more than this to take place.

There were many difficulties besides the question of the simultaneous creation of the universe—which in any case the science of geology had for some time been undermining. Evolution appeared at first to destroy the belief that man was a unique creation of God, by making him the mere product of a long line of development, and reducing the idea of his dignity—so called—to the working out of the apparently blind forces of natural selection: did not his mental make-up differ from that of the animals merely in the stage of its growth, not in any fundamental distinction of nature? Evolution, to some thinkers, even appeared to militate against the ordinary conception of final causation. For the interdependence of all natural phenomena, and the fact that all variations, and new forms of life, arise not by the creating hand of God directly at work, but by processes springing from within the constitution of nature itself, seemed to be ruling out the divine activity in the world. Such an attitude to the world lent colour to the automaton view of nature; for it was becoming no longer possible to regard the world as a doll's house, replete with men and animals once placed there, much as we now see them, by the hand of their Creator. The "Creation" was now seen as not one single act of once-upon-a-time, but a continuous process going on inside nature. The life that throbbed with ever-unfolding energy upon the face of the earth was no mere array of clock-work mice, once wound up in the beginning of time, a set of constant categories obeying each its eternal laws of motion; nature was a far deeper and more vital thing than this. It was not some machine, obeying some monotonous operation; it was itself a living organism. The whole conception of teleology even was displaced: it was no longer possible to point to a cat and say, How thoughtful of God to give it whiskers, and eyes with which to see in the dark; when all the time the members of the feline species had developed such faculties through the springs of their own nature out of an original puny protoplasm. To such a living, creating, and infinitely resourceful being as nature was shown to be, the idea of a far-off Deity who set it in motion seemed scarcely relevant. If a first cause was indeed a logical necessity, what a minute portion of the life-story of the world that was—if God made the protoplasm, and the protoplasm made the man!

It was to bridge this seeming incongruity and inadequacy of the old doctrine of God and his creation that the conception of divine immanence was invoked. If God himself indwelt his whole creation, gave it life and energy at every point and every moment, then his part in the workings of nature was not confined to some long past fiat by which the surging life of nature first came into existence, but himself was the ever-present and constant life of nature, the vital power by which it assumed its manifold forms and developments.

Immanence is therefore appealed to by many writers of our period as a new apologetic not only for the nature of God but also for the Incarnation. The two writers, Aubrey Moore and J. R. Illingworth, in *Lux Mundi*, for example, make such an appeal. God is to be looked upon as the active principle in the world. Some writers point out that God as transcendent is not even knowable by man, but only in his immanent relations to the world. The Incarnation is pointed to as a demonstration of God's intimacy with his world. This topic of divine immanence, introduced here for the sake of completeness, will be returned to again more than once—it proved to be a good servant but in the long run a very bad master.

For the moment it is necessary to describe two most important ways in which the theory of evolution affected men's attitude towards the Person of Christ—influences of a lasting and a radical nature.

There was first of all the place of Christ in history to be considered. The principle of evolution had already been applied to the question of religion. Like every other department of man's thought, it was believed that his religious ideas had undergone a long course of development; beginning with primitive forms such as animism or totemism, and growing by degrees into monotheism or some purely ethical system of belief. Thus, the method of higher criticism having been applied to the writings of the Old Testament with this view in mind, it had come to be the accepted theory among liberal scholars that the Jewish religion, like every other, had undergone such a growth—taking its rise amid the animism of the primitive Semites, and culminating in the ethical monotheism of the canonical prophets. This theory itself was to occasion certain difficulties with regard to the teaching of Christ, but the point here is that such was the accepted view with regard to the evolution of religion in general—a gradual unfolding of truth.

Now according to the traditional view, Christ had entered the more or less static creation from outside. He was, however, regarded as the absolute perfection of humanity, the crowning point, nay more, the perfect representative of what humanity had been intended to attain, but now, because of its fall, could not attain—a perfect being to whom not only all past history had looked forward, but one to whom all posterity must look back as its Ideal and perfection: and he had come, it was believed, to teach and reveal to men all that they needed to know, or could know, about God and man, relevant to their salvation.

The doctrine of the Fall was itself a very grave scandal in the light of the new theories: it was commonly said by its opponents that when man fell he fell upwards. But far more serious were the questions that it raised in connection with this doctrine about Christ. How was the Christian view of Christ's Person to be reconciled with the new attitude towards the world, with a belief in evolution and progress, not merely biological, but cultural, moral, and religious? According to the evolutionary view, the climax of human life and character is to be looked for in the future: according to the Christian view, that summit was reached two thousand years ago; present endeavour was but a pale imitation of what had once and for all been realized. It was not enough to argue on behalf of the Christian view that the process of evolution operates in the realm of human personality by a series of waves—geniuses being precipitated here and there, who far outstrip the development of the whole mass of humanity. The teaching of the Church about Christ appeared to be the absolute negation of the evolutionary principle; and much of the theology of the time consisted in the attempts to make the Christian doctrine palatable to an age which held to the theory of evolution as the first article of its creed—by no means an easy task. Many of

## PRESUPPOSITIONS AND INFLUENCES

the attempts to effect such a reconciliation, as will appear, were quite futile, and resulted only in depicting a Christ who was something totally different from that figure presented in the Creeds. Christ was sometimes spoken of as the highest manifestation of divine immanence, or as the one who possesses for men the value of God; but as will be seen, such attempts to fit the Person of Christ into the evolutionary scheme either amount to the same as what the Creeds say of him, or else mean nothing at all, save that he was a rather exceptional human figure. Some theologians attempted to gloss over the problem, pretending that there is no contradiction between the Christ of Christian dogma and a human figure produced by the processes of natural evolution. Dr. Gore, for example, speaks of Christ as "the climax of natural development",[1] "the consummation of nature's order",[2] "the crown of natural development in the universe".[3] On the other hand, Principal Forsyth frankly faces the problem which beset theology. In the first chapter of his volume, *The Person and Place of Jesus Christ*, he writes: "To say that evolution is God's supreme method with the world is to rule out Christ as his final revelation".[4] If it be allowed that the natural processes were the only sphere of God's activity, then Christ could never be assigned more than a merely relative position in the story of man's apotheosis—and it was exceedingly difficult in an age dominated by natural science for men to accept a belief that entailed the admission of something totally foreign to nature itself. It may be observed that, had it been clearly stated by the theologians of the time that the coming of Christ was primarily an incursion from without nature, and not part of nature's internal development, the Incarnation could scarcely be affected by what was said with regard to the laws of progress proper to nature. Such, however, could not be accepted as a rationale of the central doctrine of the Faith, if only because of the fact discussed already, that Christ was primarily looked upon as an historic figure, intelligible only as such—he could not be thought of as essentially outside the realm of nature.

The whole tone and outlook of the age was anthropocentric; that is to say, it began not with God and what he had done, but

[1] Bampton Lectures, p. 18.
[2] *ibid.*, p. 29.
[3] *ibid.*, p. 43.
[4] P. T. Forsyth, *The Person and Place of Jesus Christ*, p. 11.

with man, and what man felt. The self-centredness of man, and his preoccupation with the things pertaining to his own condition—and not with realms outside himself—is writ large in every page of theological writing produced at this time, and the species of humanism that it produced led to this result, that even if natural science was not competent to explain the whole of reality—and many were those who thought it was—at the very least, nothing could be tolerated as decisive for man's life which came from without nature or could not be explained in terms of nature's laws.

Much will be heard in later chapters of the attitude of liberalism to the miraculous, and to the controversy regarding the place of miracles in religion. Here it is necessary to point to the source of the ever-growing antipathy to such an element. The antimiraculous movement was perhaps the most immediate, and in the end most destructive, effect of the new scientific outlook. The whole basis of natural science is the assumption of the universality and constancy of the sequence of natural phenomena. That water boiled at one hundred degrees centigrade in 1914 as it did in 1889 is as necessary a prerequisite for human science and industry as the rising of the sun. Hence, men had learned to look upon the world as being ruled by rigid laws inherent in its constitution, presided over by a God who, whether he be thought of as outside or inside nature, never violates those laws which it was his pleasure to create—he is a God of order and not of confusion. The critical study of history, itself a by-product of the scientific spirit, had aided in this respect by dissolving the miracle stories of the past; and rationalism was not slow to discover natural explanations for those miracles in holy Scripture which literary criticism by itself had failed to dispel. From the religious side, too, the mounting prestige of the doctrine of divine immanence had canonized the belief in the fixity and propriety of the laws in the natural order. It came openly to be taught by theologians that the majesty of God is surely more fully to be seen in the wonderful orderliness of nature than in any set of sporadic miracles in violation of that order within which God was pleased to work and dwell—quite apart from the question of the ethical impropriety of miracles, ever a favourite argument of the humanist writer.

Thus we arrive at the second difficulty in the way of reconciling the Christian doctrine of Incarnation with the new theories regarding natural evolution. We have seen how the doctrine of

Christ's uniqueness appears to fit in ill with the evolutionary view of the world: even harder does it fit in with that rejection of extra-natural activity of God which sprang from the theories of internal organic progress. And now, the humanism and consequent antipathy towards the miraculous was actually a far more serious attack upon traditional Christianity than if it had been a question merely whether or not Jesus cleansed lepers or walked on the sea of Galilee: for the Incarnation itself had been conceived and defined in terms of the miraculous—it was the miracle of miracles. Not only was it, therefore, a scandal to those who envisaged nature and the history of mankind as an oscillating yet steadily progressing development towards its own self-perfection. It was an even greater absurdity to those who rejected any other mode of divine operation than in and through nature as unworthy of God's majesty. The Incarnation of the Son of God in its orthodox presentation appeared not simply as a tall story but verging even upon the mythological. It appeared to be a flat contradiction of all that we otherwise know about God and the mode in which he operates. It was possible for the theologians to leave this challenge as it stood; or on the other hand to offer some compromise solution, as, for instance, the idea that God indwelt Christ in the same manner as he indwells the rest of the creation, only in a higher degree.

The Incarnation, therefore, was a scandal to the doctrine of progress, and a contradiction to the now accepted view of God's universal operation; but the scandal appeared from yet one further angle. In a world only six thousand years old with but a short future before it, situated like some small islet between the waters, the centre of its universe of sky and stars, with the localized heaven where God dwelt not far above the clouds, a world of fixed forms and laws that were none the less capable of being deflected here and there by the Creator, in such a world—the world of the old cosmogony—the idea of a cataclysmic intervention by God in the affairs of men in the manner of Incarnation would incur no very great surprise, once the metaphysical difficulties were overcome, and without any undue strain on human credulity could be accepted as the first dogma of religion. This was possible because the idea of divine Incarnation was in keeping with that very Lilliputian cosmogony, in which the specific or miraculous intervention of the Deity was not out of keeping or incongruous. For when God wished to reveal his activity in his little world between the firmaments it was normally by the exhibition of the extraordinary. Just as the Roman Catholic authorities look for miracles in the lives of prospective candidates for canonization, so men were accustomed to look for the abnormal, the startling, as the sign of God's presence and activity among them. Now, however, the cosmogony had entirely changed. The idea of the little flat world between the firmaments, with the localized heaven above, had vanished. The earth, far from being the centre, was merely one member of a planetary family which itself was a mere speck in an interminable ocean of stars, each obeying its laws of motion, stretching over distances which the mind is unable to grasp. The time factor too had altered: instead of the earth's life being thought of as a few milennia, even the laying down of rock strata and the natural development of living species is measured in millions of years. And even upon this single planet that we know, the life of plant and animal appears to be part of a measured progress and self-unfolding according to the same laws of the whole universe, stretching over vast ages of time—in which process, the production of man is but a single item in a stupendous programme of organic evolution.

In such a setting, the idea of a personal Incarnation of the God of such a universe, and under such circumstances as those in which it is supposed to have taken place, seems quite grotesque. That one minute speck in that vast universe, and one moment in that eternal motion and unfolding, should be specially favoured with the unique presence of God was something that might well stand beyond the pale of cultured credibility. Many even of the bitterest opponents of the Faith in ancient and comparatively modern times had been unable to contradict it on the grounds that it was incongruous with the manner of God's operation elsewhere and with the immensity of the natural order, for they themselves had shared with Christians the same circumscribed cosmogony.

But now the scandal of revelation was increased a thousandfold.

Such were a few of the direct problems which the scientific method and especially the theory of evolution posed for the Christologian. But the new humanism had indirect influences of a no less telling consequence; and the first of these which we may notice was the demand for the removal of the science of metaphysics.

Historically speaking, no doubt, this reaction has its genesis in Kant's searching criticism of the whole system of metaphysics, but in greater measure, the turning away from it was the symptom of a far more fundamental shifting in the intellectual outlook of western culture. Man, to begin with, was almost wholly preoccupied with the study of the natural world; he was far too busily engaged with the physical to trouble himself with what was beyond the physical. And how much more profitable physics was than metaphysics: a few months' work in a laboratory might produce some new method of locomotion or the cure for some deadly disease; whereas philosophers and metaphysicians never seemed to produce anything but books. The one was infinitely more knowable and manageable too. The laws of physical science might be known, tested and verified, and put to use. Metaphysics, on the other hand, appeared to work wholly in the dark, with neither intelligible laws, tangible results, nor verifiable conclusions.

Such a frame of mind had a profound effect upon man's attitude, not simply to particular regions of thought, but upon his whole attitude to reality. Anthropology was virtually substituted for theology. Instead of beginning one's study of the meaning of life with God, with an examination of his nature and attributes, his Person and purpose for the world and for man in particular, the new age began from precisely the other end. It began with nature, and with man, who seemed to contain and involve the only categories that are intelligible to us, from whence the study would proceed upwards and outwards to the meaning of things as a whole. We have already noted how such a method as this became the accepted mode of apologetics for the Divinity of Christ—that is an example of the direction of the current which surged through all departments of human thought at the time.

Upon the doctrine of God itself, this change from a theocentric to an anthropocentric outlook had a direct effect. The elaboration of God's eternal attributes was looked upon as a positive hindrance to religion rather than an aid to the appreciation of the nature of the Deity. The labours of the metaphysician, it was felt, always tended to place God farther than ever out of man's reach. If God was to be fully understood, he must be defined in terms that would be intelligible to men. Now man shares with God an ethical nature; hence to describe the nature of God by the use of ethical categories was at once to make him a being intelligible and knowable to man. It also had the effect, it was believed, of facilitating a true understanding of the possibility and the nature of the Incarnation.

The doctrine of the Person of Christ was likewise affected by this abandonment of metaphysics. Whereas such a study had formally begun with the delineation of the nature of God the Son who became man, and with a portrait of his eternal character and attributes and the life he had formerly lived in the glory of heaven, the doctrine must now begin with the attempt to understand the human Person of Jesus, and only afterwards may an attempt be made to relate this Person to the life of God.

For such a study of Christ's Person from the point of view of anthropology there were two principal vehicles; these were psychology, and ethics. Christ was examined in the light of these two subjects first in order that the true content of his mind, intellect, and soul might be appreciated, and in the second place in order that a possible basis might be found upon which to construct a doctrine of his union with the Person of God. In the early part of the period, Christology was largely concerned with the questions of how much knowledge Christ's mind possessed, and of the nature of his authority as a teacher, his infallibility and sinlessness; whilst the latter part of the period reveals more attempts towards tentative reconstructions of belief. But in either case, it is the humanity of Christ that is primarily being studied and taken as the starting-point for all doctrine about him—a starting-point which will be seen to have many grave handicaps for the Christologian.

Psychology—as old as the hills—was at the time being put forward almost as though it were a new discovery. What in fact was new about it was that, whilst hitherto it had been studied as a purely abstract branch of philosophy, it was now put upon the same basis as all the other inductive sciences, and had consequently undergone a sudden revitalization. At the time, it was passing through a highly subjectivist phase, in which consciousness and experience were the elements in the mental processes of man upon which attention was most concentrated; hence it appeared peculiarly suited to the elucidation of problems relating to the interior life of Christ. Like many another great discovery, psychology was hailed with high hopes of solving every problem, and it was indeed a great deal to expect from it that it would solve the major difficulties involved in the union of God and man in one Person—its success or failure will not only be noted in those sections which will deal with specifically psychological Christologies, but also in the course of the controversy over Christ's knowledge and authority.

By focusing attention upon consciousness as the decisive constituent of human personality, the new psychology emphasized in even greater relief certain difficulties in the way of accepting the hypostatic union that had already become apparent through the common acceptance of the idealistic attitude towards personality; but it also made men see the greater complexity of the problem before them. Psychology had opened up the regions of hidden thought below the waking consciousness, and had thus shown that human personality is a far more complex thing than a mere sense of selfhood or a chain of memories. It also provided a vast storehouse of materials for the understanding of the life and words of Christ as presented in the Gospels. If Christ were a truly human figure, his humanity must extend to his mind as well as his body, and hence it was possible with the aid of the new psychology lavishly to paint the picture of his mental and spiritual development.

Ethics, on the other hand, supplied that element which psychology lacked. It might be possible to trace the growth of Christ's thoughts and aspirations through his words and actions, but psychology as a purely empirical science would not of itself ascribe any absolute meaning or value to the Person thus portrayed. That a man once lived his life with a consciousness of being without sin and of being specially the son of God is by itself a merely scientific specimen; it needs the ethical evaluation of it to give it meaning and significance for us.

Ethics had virtually been Kant's own substitute for metaphysics, and in the present circumstances it had a considerable rôle to play, since it was regarded as that which alone gave dignity to human personality, meaning to human life and relationships, and, hence, content to religious ideas—the nature of God and of Christ's Deity. Note even here the anthropocentric touch: the human is placed first.

It may be noted in passing that the work of Kant, whose name heads the preceding paragraph, had a profound effect upon modern theology. The English idealists had in their day made virtually no impression upon theology; that science was as yet dominated by forms of thought which left no room for newer interpretations. The influence, however, of Kant's thought upon German, and hence upon English, theology is constantly to be seen. The substitution of ethical for metaphysical categories in respect of the being of God, issuing in the idea of the natural affinity of God and man, eventually made possible the Kenotic Christologies, and the immanentist interpretation of the Lord's Person; whilst the subjectivist view of personality led to the complete breakdown of the Patristic formula of one Person and two Natures as an intelligible rationale of the Incarnation, perhaps the most striking feature of the period under review.

Returning, then, to the place accorded to ethics: To envisage, in ethical categories, the various relationships between men, and hence those which pertain to God, and to God and man in Christ, appeared to be far more realistic and dynamic, more appealing and intelligible, to human ideals and understanding than to do so in terms of nature, substance, and physical attributes. There was at this time a very heart-felt reaction against the terminology of Patristic and Scholastic theology. Those systems of theology had been conceived in their every detail upon a metaphysic, derived from Plato and Aristotle, and applied by succeeding ages of scholars to every detail of the Christian faith with increasing thoroughness. It was argued that this system was materialistic in tone; that its definitions of man and God, rather than declaring their spiritual affinity, placed them poles apart; but above all, as will be seen, the real objection to the ancient system was that it proposed a view of the human personality which was now rejected as irrelevant to that subject.

If ethics was called upon to explain the union of the human Christ with the Father—for, on the above premises, such is the only final type of union—it was called upon to play an even greater part in the assessment of Christ's Person and work in the inductive study of the Gospel evidences. Christ's moral teaching and sinless life, his impact upon the personalities of other men, and the change wrought upon them, his witness to his own vocation, and to his special relationship with the Father: these formed the subject matter for the application of ethical judgments. Ethically interpreted, such facts of the Lord's life could be made the basis of an objective dogma of his Deity, whilst to the thoroughgoing disciples of the Ritschlian school—comparatively few in number—the attitude of the subject or believer was itself the sole demonstration of Christ's Divinity. But even to those who did not countenance such extreme theories, the ethical evaluation of Christ's life and Person played an increasingly important rôle, especially when the miraculous demonstrations of his claims came in question.

The anthropological approach to Christ's Person, then, was carried out through the medium of these two systems, psychology and ethics. A student who approached this period straight from the study of the fifth or the thirteenth century, and who did not realize this fact, would be totally at sea and would never grasp the intent of what was being said; for the ends in view, the presuppositions, the point of departure, and the tools employed would be quite foreign to him. Ethics and psychology together, reinforced by the tendencies and presuppositions of idealism, together provided the doctrine of personality, the highest category which critical theologians could conceive, and which became the principal constituent in all theological reconstruction at the time. The two together provided that ideal of the perfect ethical consciousness: psychology supplied the bones and flesh, and ethics breathed into it the spirit. This idea of moral consciousness as the highest possible category of human, and natural, evolution was a refrain which the liberal theologians never tired of repeating. When, from an inductive study of the Gospels, it could be said of the human Christ that he possessed a perfect ethical consciousness, they believed that they had mounted the final step in the argument prior to the specific assertion of his Godhead. It will therefore be clear that to one whose outlook upon the world was dominated by the idea of evolution from within, by the unfolding of the riches of God from inside nature rather than by his miraculous intervention from without; to one who thence began his theorizing from the side of man and not of God, who replaced metaphysics by psychology and ethics; for such a one, the first datum must be the human Jesus, our brother, essentially of our nature, and as such capable of examination: the only possible basis for a living Christology.

We conclude with a quotation from Rashdall that illustrates some of these latter thoughts. "We can assign no real meaning to the idea of the Divine Sonship of Jesus unless we recognize that it contains a truth about human nature in general and its relation to God. . . . In the reason and the will and the conscience of every man there is contained a real revelation of God, and a progressive revelation—growing as man's reason and will and conscience grow, and in a still higher sense grow in proportion as man responds in act to the demands which this rational and moral nature makes upon him. . . . Only if we believe that God has something in him in common with the nature of man . . . can we understand how he can be in any sense revealed in man. Only if we believe that he is in some measure revealed in every man can we attach any intelligible meaning to the assertion that to one man his spirit was given not by measure".[1]

[1] *Doctrine and Development*, p. 100.

# 2

## THE COLLISION AND COLLAPSE OF ORTHODOXY

In the preceding chapter, some of the roots of English liberal Christology were traced in the current trends of thought at large. Above and behind the constant and direct influence of German theology—in which those influences were already crystallized into theological shapes—together with the emotional strata of romanticism, there loomed in the intellectual sphere the massive form of the scientific way of thinking. Rational and scientific methods produced the science of history, whilst the preponderatingly naturalistic attitude towards the whole of life, strenuously impelled by the theory of evolution, led to the demand for the total explanation of all phenomena (in the widest sense of that word) in terms of the natural order. Naturally enough, this double influence had a profound effect upon the methods by which Christology was studied, as also upon the interests on behalf of which such investigations and reconstructions were carried out. In the main, it may be said, these methods and interests gathered around two magnetic poles. Two interests became predominant in Christology; twin postulates became the virtual centres of all activity. The satisfaction of these twin postulates was the necessary prerequisite of any proposed Christological reconstruction or reinterpretation—by which, too, every system, modern and ancient, was judged either successful or inadequate. To meet the needs of the age, satisfaction of them was essential—compliance with these twin postulates had to be satisfied: the touchstone by which any proposal was proved acceptable was indeed whether it complied with and satisfied them. At the close of the first section of the preceding chapter it was stated that the historical method demanded that in order for the Person of Christ to be studied at all intelligibly as an historic figure—and studied as such he must be—his person, his personality, must be a psychological unity, like the being of all other men: that is the first postulate.

Furthermore, in the course of the second part of the chapter it was concluded from the premises of the time, as then understood, that Christ in order to be understood as an historic Person—understood at all, for that matter—must have been first and foremost a human being, possessing human nature in its entirety, a man, recognizable as such, whatever else might afterwards be concluded to be contained in his personality. To be accepted as a saviour, to be followed as an example, to be recognized as the summit of every known or knowable categories, Christ must be a human Person, whose nature was not vitiated by the intrusion of incompatible attributes. Christ must be truly one, and truly human.

It was, however, by no means the first time in the long history of Christian doctrine that theologians had espoused these two causes. Many hard battles had already been fought on behalf of each of them: councils had been summoned, bishops had been deposed, and definitions had been framed in order to protect each of these truths. What, then, was new and peculiar to the present age in such demands? It was their combination in a single background of thought. Hitherto, they had been championed separately—often, even, the one at the expense of the other: now they were the inseparable requisites in the modern Christology. It has already been said that the liberal period was one of revolt against the classical systems of Christian theology, and the new situation can, in fact, best be seen when contrasted and compared with what had gone before in the history of doctrine.

In ancient times, the two most celebrated schools of Greek theology had each been the ardent protagonist of one of our two propositions.

In the fourth and fifth centuries—and we should probably include the third as well—the school of Antioch, numbering especially such figures as Diodore of Tarsus, his two pupils Chrysostom and Theodore of Mopsuestia, and, later, Nestorius, strongly upheld the doctrine of Christ's true humanity—the reality of his human will, and the genuine character of his moral victory. As they were equally concerned with the preservation of Christ's Deity—his Deity unmutilated and unmodified by the Incarnation—this also has an interesting bearing upon the modern situation; but what is even more striking is the Antiochene insistence upon the literal exegesis of the Gospel narrative.

If it was recorded that Christ had been hungry, weary, sad, weak, and ignorant too, then, to be sure, these symptoms were no mere simulation of a supernatural being acting a part, but factual statements relating to the man Christ Jesus, and as Theodore urges, these were not merely bodily, but psychological and spiritual traits of humanity. Here indeed was a system whose aims the modern students of the New Testament could not but regard with approbation.

At the same epoch, the school of Alexandria, under Apollinarius, Cyril, and later, Eutyches and the Monophysites, was brilliantly championing the unity of Christ's Person. By its presentation of the Incarnation as a complete union, or even fusion, of the two natures, human and divine, and the concept of the circumscription of God within the limits prescribed by congruity with true humanity, this school presented a Christ whose every thought, word, and deed, was immediately related to the same personal subject—God living as man—and not at any time or in any fashion to God or man, operating in any sense separately from one another within the same Person. Here too was a modern aim in an old-fashioned dress. For such a Christ as was presented by the Alexandrines was surely the most perfectly unified subject that could be conceived.

The modern writers, then, espoused the aims of both the great rival schools of Patristic times. Unfortunately, however, both those ancient schools, in the eyes of modern theology, had cut their own throats; for each, in asserting the one principle, had virtually denied the other.

The methods which each school had employed in the effort to establish the proposition in which it was particularly interested had led in the long run to a negation of the other: hence, of course, the reason for the protracted struggle which took place between the two schools. Therefore, although each of the Patristic schools has in turn enjoyed a certain amount of praise and popularity within our period, yet for this very reason neither of their systems could ever serve as a basis which all, or even most, scholars could accept for a reconstructed Christology. Antioch asserted Christ's true humanity, but failed to do justice to the unity of his Person, whilst Alexandria stressed his unity but did not appear to leave room for his real humanity.

Much of the thought and writing of our period does in fact

take its rise from the reaction against what were considered to be these two ancient errors.[1]

## The Reaction against Antioch

In order that the manhood of Christ should be complete, and his Deity remain unlimited and uncircumscribed, the Antiochene teachers had described the manner in which the two natures subsisted in one Person after the fashion of a moral union, one of purpose or good-pleasure rather than of nature. We need not enter into the now hoary dispute about what exactly Nestorius meant by πρόσωπον οὐχ οὐσιώδης, ἀλλὰ κατὰ ποιότητα—one of quality and not of essence—as the opponents of Paul of Samossata correctly described that bishop's teaching.

Theodore of Mopsuestia, it is true, employs such words as συνάφεια and ἕνωσις, but a more favourite word of this school to describe the way in which Christ's Deity is present to him is ἐνοίκησις—indwelling: and in one place, Theodore discusses three modes in which this indwelling might have taken place— κατ' οὐσίαν, κατ' ἐνέργειαν, or κατ' εὐδοκίαν, and concludes that the last could have been the only appropriate manner, since the first relates to the being of God alone, and the second to the way in which God indwells nature at large. Such theorising is typical of Antiochene Christology.

From this it followed, and for the purposes of safeguarding the majesty of God it was insisted upon, that a clear distinction could and should be drawn between Christ's divinity and humanity and his divine and human activity. The Antiochene writers constantly emphasize that the Word of God and Jesus are ἄλλος καὶ ἄλλος. Diodore constantly distinguishes the Son of God from the Son of David, and, of course, Nestorius' refusal to call the Blessed Virgin θεοτόκος, and his plea that he could not call a baby of two or three months old "God", illustrate the same manner of approach. The two natures within Christ were quite distinct.

On such a basis as this, it had been found possible to distinguish

[1] A proviso should here be added: certain of the tenets of the Antiochene Christology could well serve as a basis for a purely humanitarian view of our Lord's Person, in which there is no semblance or equivalent of the hypostatic union envisaged, but only the creaturely relationship of a good man to God; the Antiochenes themselves certainly meant much more than this—so much is obvious.

within the life of Christ the operations proper to natures so different and so well marked. Since Persons are known by their deeds and words, it was surely possible to discriminate between utterances and actions which are attributable solely to the Son of David and those which belonged to the Son of God, acting through this human nature which he had assumed. And such in fact was done.

Now there had existed already in the Church a well-established method of studying the life of Christ. It was the method employed by Irenaeus—following, indeed, the usage of the New Testament itself—and in our own period represented by no less illustrious persons than William Bright and Bishop Stubbs. Such writers as these take those incidents in the recorded life of Christ which exhibit his supernatural powers and place them alongside those which depict his human limitations. Thus: Christ suffered hunger, yet he satisfied a multitude with bread; he knew of the death of Lazarus, yet asked where they had laid him. Thus proceeds the juxtapositing of seemingly contradictory episodes and statements. The eleventh chapter of the Fourth Gospel, for example, affords a very striking example of the way in which a New Testament writer can without the slightest embarrassment set down side by side the most glaringly opposed inferences. It is a dialectical method that seeks to represent faithfully the double-sidedness of the impression which the Person of Christ made upon men, whilst avoiding all questions of which it is considered impossible for us to know the answer. The two elements are merely stated and contrasted, without any irreverent or unprofitable enquiries into, or rationalizations of, the relation of the Deity and humanity within Christ's Person. Such an attitude of reverent agnosticism towards the mystery of the Incarnation has attained to a new lease of life at the present day through the influence of the new dialectical theology which has sprung up within continental Protestantism: it is vigorously advocated, for instance, by Emil Brunner in his monumental monograph on Christology, *The Mediator*.

To collect together the two sets of impressions and to lay them side by side without further speculation is one thing: it is a laudable method of approach. It is quite another thing to take the two sets, collecting together the recorded utterances and actions of Christ, but, instead of laying them side by side, as it were, to gather them into two heaps, and then to ascribe the one set to Christ's divine nature and the other to his human. Such a procedure would seem to require considerably more authority behind it than is forthcoming from the Scriptures; yet to the Antiochenes, with their conception of the two natures so distinct as ἄλλος καὶ ἄλλος, it appeared to be the most natural and logical thing to say, not simply that Christ was hungry and yet fed a multitude, but that, as man he was hungry, as God he fed a multitude; in his human nature he thirsted, in his divine nature he turned water into wine. Antiochene writers freely indulged themselves in lenghty enumerations of the properties and the works of Christ's two natures in such a manner. One of the best examples of such writing is to be found in the Eucharistic anaphora of Narsai.[1] The plain meaning of such a method would appear to be that the life of Christ was governed by a dual control, as though his divinity and humanity operated separately or in turn. There would be two centres of motivation, two intelligences, and two sets of reactions to outward circumstances. There would be duality in practically everything.

The great and overriding objection to such a Christology from the modern point of view will be considered in a moment. There was a secondary objection which should not be forgotten. The Antiochene view had not merely been framed to protect Christ's humanity, it had also been constructed with a view to hedging about his Divinity. In Platonic thought, the Deity is the immutable and impassible one. It was difficult for men brought up with such a background to accept the literal truth of the doctrine that the Son of God suffered. It was felt by liberal scholars that the Antiochene distinction between acts and experiences of Christ proper to separate natures was partly a subterfuge to escape the ascription of real participation in sorrow and suffering by God the Son. With God defined in ethical rather than metaphysical terms, little place was being left for doctrines of divine impassibility: rather was it coming to be regarded as essential to the nature of God that he should feel as we do, and share in our love, pain, and sorrow—the Incarnation was believed to demonstrate this fact.

Much of the fury during our period against the apparent duality of Antiochene theology was directed against two documents, the Tome of Leo and the Definition of the Council of

[1] Dom. R. Connolly, *Liturgical Homilies of Narsai*, No. 17.

## THE COLLISION AND COLLAPSE OF ORTHODOXY 29

Chalcedon.[1] They were attacked because it was believed that they had given canonical sanction and perpetuity to this view of a double life within Christ's Person, and had therefore shut the door against all intelligible study of the Lord's life as an historic figure and psychological subject until the nineteenth-century liberalism freed men from their bondage to such "outworn" doctrines. It is true that in one famous passage of the Tome, St. Leo contrasts a number of actions of Christ which he alternately ascribes to each of the natures. Thus St. Leo writes: "Unum horum coruscat miraculis, aliud succumbit iniuriis. Et sicut Verbum ab aequalitate Paternae gloriae non recedit, ita caro naturam nostri generis non relinquit. Unum enim idemque est, quod saepe dicendum est, vere Dei filius, et vere hominis filius", and so forth. But the Pope is clearly inveighing against a doctrine according to which Christ's nature is neither properly that of God nor man, and he demonstrates from Our Lord's life the unmistakable evidences for the presence both of true Deity and real humanity. Furthermore, he safeguards himself from any crude Nestorian dualism by a very significant expression in a previous passage: "Agit enim utraque forma cum alterius communione quod proprium est".[2]

To vent their animosity against the Definition of Chalcedon, as many of our writers did, had even less to justify it. That document is of a dialectical character. It states the presence, within the Person of Christ, of the natures of God and man, and in a few brief strokes it marks out the integrity and completeness of each of them. To approach one's Christology from the point of view of two complete natures, rather than one Person, may conceivably not be the ideal plan of investigation, but to describe the definition as "unscientific" as Dr. Temple did in *Foundations* is both erroneous and irrelevant: for theology is the exposition of what God has done for us and what he wishes us to know about himself, and the question "how?", as in the manner of the empirical sciences, is one which does not necessarily constitute an object of theological investigation; from the point of view of the science of theology, the dialectical method is scientific—only so much God will have us know. Nor does the Definition of itself

[1] E.g. H. R. Mackintosh, *The Person of Christ*, p. 13, and part III, ch. X; A. M. Fairburn, *Christ in Modern Theology*, pp. 348, 354; C. Gore, *Diss.* II; J. Caird, *Fundamental Ideas* . . . , vol. II, p. 107; and W. Temple, *Foundations*, p. 230.
[2] *The Tome of Leo*, IV. 4.

advance the notion of the independent control or activity of the two natures regarded in separation.

It is an open question whether even the Alexandrian Christology entirely escapes the dualism of action: sometimes the Logos is envisaged as acting congruously with humanity, and at other times as acting with his full power. Liberal scholars would argue that even here there is no possibility of studying Christ as an intelligible unit of personality.

The subject of the dyothelite controversy may here be referred to: it will engage us more closely in the ninth chapter. Despite the false start given by Honorius, the Church settled upon what might at first sight appear to have been an Antiochene solution. The idea of two wills might appear to add substance to the dual-control mode of regarding Christ's actions, by providing a human will to be the motor of those occurrences in the Gospel narrative attributed to his humanity. But as long as the will was regarded as a mere faculty of Christ's impersonal humanity, such an inference could not be drawn from the dyothelite formula. It was only at the turn of the present century, when the older psychology was abandoned, that men began to regard the formula as destructive of Christ's personal unity.

The first to protest against the Antiochene mode of dividing up the activities of Christ according to his two natures was, it need scarcely be said, St. Cyril of Alexandria. In his Fourth Anathema he writes as follows: "If anyone assigns to two persons or hypostases the words of the evangelic or Apostolic writings, which are spoken either of Christ by the Saints or of himself by himself, and applies some to a man considered apart from the Word who is from God, and others, as God-befitting, solely to the Word from God the Father, be he anathema". This Doctor has been hotly pursued on this point by many, in fact the majority, of thinkers in our period—the same criticism might have been uttered word for word in 1889 or 1900.

It was contended that, if Christ is to be studied, understood, known, worshipped, and loved, he must possess one single and homogeneous personality—one which can be appraised as a whole, and which possesses one single continuity of reference and responsibility, and not one thing now and another thing then. A Christ who knew or did something one moment by one nature, and knew or did something else the next moment by another nature, would be perfectly incomprehensible. Of such a person we should always be under the necessity to ask which particular aspect of him was operating at any given moment. We have already alluded to the way in which Antiochene theology was looked upon as shielding the divine impassibility: this appeared in another context as well. For it was urged by some writers that such a type of Christology was fatal to any genuine soteriology—this does not, of course, apply to the radical liberals who saw nothing further in Christ than a purely human example; but only to the realms of serious Christology. It was argued that the definition of Chalcedon and the separation-method stated quite clearly that only Christ's humanity suffered on the Cross. If the Son of God did not himself bear our griefs, but only an assumed and extraneous nature, where is the Atonement? The classical Protestant doctrine of the Atonement was almost entirely summed up in the idea of substitution, the Son of God himself suffering to fulfil the punishment that man could never bear. Hence it must be the Son of God who himself suffered; his human nature alone would have been of no avail. Such an objection to Antiochene Christology naturally weakened as the older doctrine of the Atonement gave way to one of example. This is not to say that in the Catholic theory of the Atonement the divine nature of Christ is not conceived to have played a decisive part, but those who embrace a doctrine largely constituted by the idea of representative, rather than substitutionary, sacrifice are bound to view the question of theopaschasianism with different eyes from those who believe that God's sufferings were put in place of what man rightly owed.

Much as one cannot help but sympathize with some of the modern criticisms of Antiochene Christology, the significant point for the present purpose is to understand the motives that lay behind those criticisms. The detailed discussion of these will appear in later chapters; they were, briefly, three in number: a curiosity regarding the inner workings of the Lord's personality (ch. VII), a new doctrine of personality requiring unity of consciousness (ch. IX), and presuppositions regarding soteriology, already alluded to and discussed further in ch. IV. The second of these is by far the most important. Dr. Mackintosh writes that dual consciousness and will make historic study of Christ impossible.[1] The admission of two centres of knowledge and action within Christ's Person—which appeared to be the logical

[1] *Person of Christ*, p. 13.

outcome of Antiochene Christology—made him in the eyes of liberal scholars nothing less than two separate persons.

One aspect of Antiochene Christology, therefore, was immensely valued by our theologians, whilst in another respect the system could not but evoke the most intense dissatisfaction.

## The Reaction against Alexandrine Christology

The Cyrilline Christology, on the other hand, had adopted as its point of departure the unity of Christ's Person, or more exactly, the doctrine that the Son of God was Incarnate and made man. The whole personality of Christ as known to men was divine, not God and a man, but simply God as man dwelling, actually and not in any merely metaphorical sense—as certain liberals misleadingly retained the old formula. His Mother was therefore rightly designated "Theotokos" (Anathema I). All his words were the words of God the Son (Anathema IV). His flesh was the flesh of God the Son (Anathemas II, V, VI and XI). God the Son suffered in this flesh (Anathema XII), and by reason of its being the flesh of God it is life-giving (Anathema XI). In the flesh, the Son of God is our high-priest (Anathema X), and to that flesh the son of God is personally united (Anathema II). This was all to the good in the eyes of most moderns. There was one and only one Christ who was both Son of God and Son of David, of whose single personality all the Evangelic record might be predicated.

But there are many serious difficulties to be encountered by those who begin with these presuppositions. Cyril and the ancients who followed him saw the problem in this form: How can the infinite, immutable, and impassible God become the centre of a finite and passible human personality? Being theocentric in outlook, they were naturally approaching the problem of the Incarnation from the point of view of God. The Alexandrines countered the difficulty with a doctrine of *kenosis*, where God the Son is conceived of as permitting the circumscription and the suffering of the humanity thus assumed to prevail even in his own case, in so far as was compatible with the essentials of his divine nature, and furthermore that he so restrained his divine powers so as not to overwhelm his human nature, nor interpose what would have been improper or incongruous for humanity to possess or exercise. It would be improper and unnecessary here to enter more fully into the question of the precise significance of the Cyrilline doctrine of *kenosis*. For in modern times the scene has almost completely changed, and this question, like most others, was approached in our period from the anthropocentric point of view. It became a question, How can a man be truly a man if he possesses divine powers such as omniscience? The enquiry was begun from the point of view of human consciousness rather than from the being of God. Judged by such modern standards as this, the Cyrilline expedient appears to be utterly inadequate, it seeks to make no provision for what we ourselves understand by human thinking—it never envisages such a question. One typical example will serve to illustrate both Cyril's own method and the modern objections to it. Jesus professed ignorance of the exact time of His Parousia (Mk. 13. 32). It was quite sufficient for an Alexandrine theologian to comment on this passage that here, as elsewhere, Christ is speaking "economically", that is to say, although, absolutely speaking, he did know the day and the hour of his coming—as he knew everything—yet it was not a fit thing for men to be told, nor was it congruous with his own human state to know such a thing, hence for the sake of his hearers he assumed ignorance of it. Another variant of the same exegesis is to suppose that Christ is here speaking in the person of his Church, not absolutely as Son of God. In his own day, Theodoret was a voice crying in the wilderness when he rejected this exegesis as blasphemous—to assert that truth could itself tell a lie—but in modern times, Protestant theologians practically without exception support his protest. The Cyrilline theology began with the fact of the Incarnation—an *a priori* method—and the details of the Evangelic record have to be fitted into it as best they may: this is not unscientific, it simply means that these scholars had a totally different conception of what constituted "being truly a man"—they did not restrict the term "humanity" to the possession of a limited consciousness. Cyril's exegesis of Mk. 13. 32 now came to be assumed to be quite out of the question; but, more than this, it proved to be the straw that broke the camel's back, for it indicated to liberal theology the inability of the Alexandrine system as it stood to account adequately for the fact of Christ, his humanity. It was not that its presuppositions were wrong, or its aims at fault; what it said to begin with was absolutely necessary. The system was thought to have given impetus to a tendency in theology which sped on unchallenged by scholars till the nineteenth century—the exclusion of any forthright doctrine of the Lord's humanity. The Fifth and Sixth General Councils witnessed the Cyrilline mode of approach to Christology firmly established as the sole recognized method. The doctrine of the impersonal humanity which became part of the accepted Faith through the labours of Leontius of Byzantium—a doctrine which became so much disliked and misunderstood in our period—also tended in the same direction. The consequences of this movement are matters of history, recognized not solely by Protestant liberal historians but also by so eminent a Catholic theologian as Karl Adam in our own day.[1] In the Eastern Orthodox and Monophysite Churches the humanity of Christ ceased to have any active significance for theology. To all intents and purposes, Christ was no longer regarded as man's brother and high-priest pleading on his behalf before God; he had changed sides, as it were, and was now the awful *Pantokrator*, whose presence even in the Eucharist was that of the unapproachable divine splendour. This is fully borne out in both the art and literature of these Churches. With it went the obliteration of practically all human traits from the life of Christ as it was understood and taught. In the west, Docetism rarely showed its head so boldly as in the east, and the wide and lasting popularity which the cult of Christ's Sacred Humanity enjoyed—whose rise is associated with the name of Bernard of Clairvaux—would make it appear that full justice was being done in western thought to Christ's genuine manhood. Such, it was argued, is far from the case. Latin scholasticism, e.g. Part III of the *Summa Theologica* of St. Thomas, is said to portray a Christ who is scarcely recognizable as the Jesus of Nazareth depicted in the Gospels. His human features are whittled away by the incursion of divine attributes; above all, ignorance and weakness are virtually denied to him. Even the cult of the Sacred Humanity was and still is but the worship of a supernatural manhood: the wounds are "beautiful", the agony is "glorious", and the Sacred Heart, far from aching with real human despair and shrinking from death and suffering, is looked upon as bleeding with conscious love for the souls of all men. Such a devotion appeared to our theologians to be as remote from the Jesus of the Gospels as the idle debates of the schoolmen—such as, for example, whether Christ's body now in heaven is sitting down or standing up.

[1] *Christ Our Brother*, ch. III.

The Reformation, it was thought, did not materially affect the situation. The intellectual content and background of the Reformers' minds being as it was the most decadent form of scholasticism—most of Luther's doctrines can be traced as logical outcomes and exaggerations of the Scotist system in which he was brought up—it was not surprising that no return was then possible to what nineteenth-century folk were pleased to call "The Jesus of history". On the contrary, two new motives introduced themselves which were destined to solidify the existing situation. The Lutheran doctrine of the Atonement, as pointed out already in another connection, required that the Person who hung upon the Cross should be the Son of God, and in addition, consciously offering himself to the Father as a substitute for the human race—no human consciousness, merely, fighting against despair in the anguish of ebbing faith. Secondly, there arose the Eucharistic controversy, to be touched upon in the fifth chapter, which led Luther to his curious doctrine of the communication of properties, whereby the humanity of Christ is regarded as partaking of those powers properly belonging to the divine nature. Hence it had come about that orthodox Protestant theology envisaged a Christ, who, in his life upon earth, was no less a supernatural figure, paying but courteous deference to the laws of nature, than had been his predecessors in mediæval or monophysite theology. He was, it was contended, a mere figment of theological imagination.

Consequently the Alexandrine type of Christology, whether as taught by Cyril, the monophysites, or, in its later forms, was widely regarded as almost fundamentally impossible. "By their fruits ye shall know them"; and the fruits of this system appeared to be always and inevitably a minimization of Christ's humanity—the very source of our knowledge of him and his message. It was said by some, and not without a certain justification, that the Church had never taken the humanity of Christ seriously since the time of the Antiochenes. This was a sore grievance indeed to modern thinkers, first because such a Christology seemed quite out of touch with the facts, that is, inconsistent with the literal and inductive exegesis of the Gospels—understood in their "plain meaning" as they often said. Secondly, such a Christology could not but stand in disfavour at a time when the supernatural was at such a discount. The supernatural Christ, with his divine powers, and only seemingly real human experience—for his human experience was even more eagerly cherished than his human appearance—was completely out of place in the modern humanistic atmosphere. He had to be dissolved.

The Doceti of ancient times had been condemned for disallowing the reality of Christ's bodily human life: traditional orthodoxy was now to be condemned because it had disallowed the reality of Christ's mental and spiritual humanity.

Much of the animosity against the Alexandrine Christology and its successors was vented upon the doctrine of the impersonal manhood of Christ. This doctrine had always gone hand in hand with the Cyrilline Christology, for since Christ was but one personal subject, and that Person was God, then it followed that his humanity of itself was not personal, but was only an individual man insomuch as the Son of God by assuming it gave it individuality. Though the doctrine itself did not become explicit till late in the Patristic period, it is clear that the reasoning that led up to it was at the root of Apollinarius' peculiar teaching.

To the liberal scholars, the doctrine appeared as just one more attempt to eliminate Christ's truly human experience, and as such it was ruled out of court by many even of the most magnanimous writers of our period. It was argued that a Person whose conscious centre was undiluted Godhead could scarcely be a complete subject of all human experiences, nor could he properly be our brother, since faith and moral struggle would be impossible to God the Son, of himself. This doctrine, it should be pointed out, was not specifically attacked by some of the kenoticists—though some of them even attacked it—for they had a doctrine that rendered the Son of God himself capable of such completely human experiences; but in any case, such criticisms of the doctrine spring from a misunderstanding of it, and show how completely different was the psychology of the moderns from that of the ancients. To the moderns, the idea of person included, as has already been said, the will and the consciousness, but to the ancients, it was not so; these things were parts of human nature regarded as a whole, they did not by themselves constitute personality. To the Fathers, the belief that Christ had a human will and human experiences did not mean that the Son of God was united to an individual man—those things belonged to the impersonal nature he assumed; whilst to the moderns, the idea of an impersonal humanity suggested a humanity without will and without moral consciousness—to them a quite inconceivable idea

## THE COLLISION AND COLLAPSE OF ORTHODOXY 37

in view of what was becoming known with regard to the intimate connection between bodily and mental functioning, quite apart from the theological objections. If the doctrine were to be retained, therefore, it would certainly have to take on a totally new dress to suit the new ways of thought.

In view of the unceasing insistence upon true humanity, it is perhaps not unfair to ask what in fact liberal theology conceived to be the essence of genuine manhood. On what grounds, for instance, is it asserted that the possession of unlimited knowledge contradicts the true nature of man? It is most difficult to assign a clear content to their terms. Broadly speaking, they might have said—to be human is to be what we ourselves are. That is to say, of a temporal, limited, and discursive consciousness—limited in knowledge, understanding and judgment; of a free and yet restricted will, and so forth: all these things became freely attributed to Christ. Yet the great difficulty in the definition of true humanity which we have inferred from the principles of liberal theology is this: Our nature also has many other attributes; we are circumscribed not simply in knowledge, but also limited in our sympathy and our love—partly indeed as a result of our limited knowledge and understanding (that is why the omniscient God is alone capable of perfect love, and why also, incidentally, God's attributes may not be separated without harm to the whole, as certain kenoticists attempted to do). But above all, we possess an innate bias towards evil, which is as much a reality to us as anything else in our experience. What then are we to say of Christ's humanity? Are we to say that it was so completely manlike as to be limited in its love and sympathy towards us; and are we to say that he was so much like ourselves that he was not only tempted—as any free will might be tempted—but that he possessed an inherent bias towards evil? The liberal theologians did not ever face these questions. In the first place, the liberal Christologians of our period completely ignore the difference between fallen and unfallen man. As it stands, their Christology would appear to imply a purely Pelagian view of the human will, making no essential distinction between our own fallen state in which the will is not free, and the unfallen state in which the will is free and hence perfectly integrated to the will of God—to say nothing of the many other differences that must pertain to that nature as it was originally fashioned. It is not therefore very helpful to say that Christ assumed *our* nature as we know it, without facing certain further questions that were deliberately scouted in order to avoid the introduction of doctrines such as the fall and original sin, which were causing great embarrassment at the time. "The doctrine of Our Lord's Divinity modifies the truths connected with his humanity in this way, that he who was both God and man, cannot be thought of even as man in exactly the same way as if He were not God", wrote Mozley in his treatise on the Augustinian Doctrine of Predestination, yet the whole purport of liberal Christology would appear to be the denial of such a presupposition.

It has thus been made clear that, although the Alexandrine interest in the unity of Christ's Person was also a cherished axiom of modern theologians, they could not accept the manner in which that unity had been established, and were forced to protest against the Alexandrines and their successors for their mishandling of the Lord's manhood. There thus set in a serious reaction against the standard Christologies of earlier times, in which it was considered that Christ was reduced either to a phantom or a freak. Looking back upon it, the reaction is understandable, but to what extravagant limits it was driven only one who has ploughed his way through the voluminous literature of the period can appreciate. Every single theological writer appeared to feel himself under an obligation impelled by some ineffable power to give a clear demonstration of Christ's humanity. The same proof-texts—Mk. 13. 32: Lk. 2. 52 and scores of others—pointing to Christ's limitation of knowledge, his circumscription in time and space—are catalogued with monotonous regularity. Was there ever witnessed anything so grotesque in the history of Christian doctrine, when the whole energy and ingenuity of scholarship was devoted—not to proving to mankind the Divinity of our Lord and the truth of the Gospel of the Incarnation—but to demonstrating that he was really and truly a man?—a conclusion which every single man in the street would arrive at without fail without its having to be proved to him. Was there ever so sad a misdirection of the Church's apologetic? Docetism was placarded as the most deadly enemy of the truth of the Incarnation at the very time when Docetism was precisely the one heresy which no one was likely to lapse into. Surely Dr. Gore did not seriously anticipate being mobbed by a gang of Nicolaitan undergraduates on leaving St. Mary's church, or assailed by a party of Docetic dons in the senior common room, or harangued by a bevy of Aphtharto-

## THE COLLISION AND COLLAPSE OF ORTHODOXY 39

docetic business men in his London club? To the educated man of modern times, the first and most obvious interpretation to put upon the fact of Christ is that he was a man and nothing more—an outstanding saint and teacher perhaps, but nothing more: this was the problem with which liberal theology should have concerned itself, not with the refutation of heresies already as dead as good Queen Anne.

Apologists there were, and good ones, who began with the plain man's apprehension of Christ's humanity and led up to his Divinity, but they might have been far more numerous had not so much time been lost at so vital a moment by internal questionings that were irrelevant to the external situation.

To sum up, therefore: it has been noted that the liberal theologians of the English-speaking world took as the two foundations of their Christology the basic interests of each of the Patristic schools. Like the Antiochenes they felt bound to insist upon Christ's true and complete humanity; from the Alexandrines came the necessity of his personal unity. For almost the first time in the history of doctrine these two principles were brought into proximity in our period. It was for this reason that neither of the ancient systems that had cherished these principles separately could serve adequately en bloc, since each school in asserting the one had seemingly denied the other. From the Patristic point of view, therefore, our modern Christology was of hybrid stock: in other words, the seeds were present for the cultivation of a plant far richer than either of its parents, for the fundamental principles were now laid side by side upon which might have been erected the most solid building ever yet produced; a Christology might have been developed which by its very breadth of comprehension might have dimmed the one-sided efforts of the ancients. But unfortunately, the dream never came true. The pillars of the old orthodoxy were blasted away one by one as the liberal exegesis and the humanistic presuppositions were applied more and more to the doctrines of the Faith; yet upon such magnificent new foundations as the two ancient principles provided, nothing is now to be found but the rubble of jerry-built Christologies—books, theories, reinterpretations, even authors, which, even at so short a distance as the present, are scarcely ever heard of except in the manner of interesting fossils in a museum.

Far, in fact, from giving birth to a new and all-sufficient system for which Christendom had ever been waiting, the union of the two old requisites, it will be seen, provoked a crisis of great moment. The men of our period were not attempting to substitute a novel Christology where there already existed a more or less satisfactory system in their eyes; they were essaying to formulate a doctrine to meet an entirely new situation, a situation for which no compatible provision had, or could have, been made or foreseen by already existing systems. This is sufficiently obvious from what has been said in the first chapter of the entirely new approach to doctrine, and in the present chapter with regard to the new psychology; but it must constantly be borne in mind, for the fact of the already non-existence of an adequate rationale profoundly affected the method of theology. A writer such as Suarez or Franzelin would believe himself to be expounding and enlarging upon a set of known and assured facts, for which there existed ample and adequate proof. A liberal theologian, on the other hand, is a man with a belief in his heart that Jesus Christ is both human and divine—a belief which he has to justify—with four enigmatic Gospels in one hand and the crumbling weapon of inductive humanistic criticism in the other, to an eclectic and arrogant audience, or else take the collar from off his neck.

It may well be asked at this point whether German theology had nothing to contribute in such a situation; for the year 1889 had been preceded by more than a century of intense theological activity in that country along liberal lines, and all the questions which were now exercising the English world had surely been faced long before over there. Had nothing of value to our own students emerged from that vast melting-pot of opinion, tried by the fire of such a withering criticism as was there the common rule? A very great deal; but just as the chemical elements that feed our bodies have to be first made into vegetable compounds, so for the most part the German systems as they stood were quite unpalatable to the Anglo-Saxon world. The intellectual backgrounds of the two peoples were very different; another factor was the ecclesiastical situation. Continental Protestantism had found it comparatively easy to dispense with the bonds of theological and ecclesiastical orthodoxy; in Britain and America, on the other hand, there was a strong and diehard conservatism. This was due as much as anything to the unique position of the Anglican communion. Claiming as it largely did to be a reformed Catholicism, its accredited representatives felt themselves under an obligation to the consensus of traditional ecclesiastical opinion,

## THE COLLISION AND COLLAPSE OF ORTHODOXY 41

and particularly to that of the Patristic period, as embodied in the Creeds, Councils and Doctors of the Church. The other English Protestant Churches were not, of course, under any such obligation, and hence were more quickly converted to the liberal point of view, but even among those communions there was a vigorous conservatism. Thus an interpretation of the Person of Christ which might gain instant acceptance or at least attention by a body of scholastic opinion in Germany simply on its own merits would be suspect from the first in Britain or America if its conclusions meant parting with some cherished axiom of classical theology. This conservatism was itself responsible for the fact that the period of greatest conflict in these countries did not occur until the post-*Lux Mundi* era instead of half a century earlier as in Germany. This is not to say that German Christology did not play a large part in the shaping of English, particularly in the direction of its research and reinterpretation. It did more than point a warning finger towards paths already tried and found treacherous; it did a great deal of spade-work, particularly in the department of Scriptural criticism, which had not to be repeated and thus prepared the groundwork for the application of the inductive method. The thorough and enthusiastic disciples of particular German schools were few, but to every disciple there were a hundred other scholars who unconsciously adopted their criteria.

Radical liberalism was a later development within our period, and even when it did appear, it was scarcely large or virile enough as a movement to form itself into definite schools of thought.

Thus the German schools and theories as they stood were quite untenable, except in limited circles. The highly intellectualised theory of Hegel, in which Christ gains his importance from being the embodiment of the fundamental idea of the union of God and man, and of the basic principle of the universe; the humanism of Strauss or Renan, in which the Gospel narrative is religious legend and Christ himself little more than an idyllic dreamer; the theology of Schleiermacher, where Jesus is the focus for the religious energies of man through his faculty of feeling; and the system of Ritschl, in which the Divinity of Christ is established by a clinching application of the criterion of value-judgment: all these theories, though they evoked many indistinct echoes, yet left the majority of English thinkers cold, since they did not appear to provide a sufficiently effective definition of Christ's Deity, one which could permanently satisfy the faith of all Christians. One objection to most of these radical systems, which was recognized by many—even of the moderately advanced—English liberals, was that such Christologies carried a sting in their tail. Whether Jesus is thought of as a perfect moral example, or as one who has lit a glowing flame of spiritual life which all men must follow, it would be merely the faith *of* Jesus which we should possess, and not faith *in* Jesus, as the living Son of God, who continues to have personal relations with his believers. A definition of Christ's Person that only amounted to this view would not serve as an adequate intellectual counterpart of the classic Christian experience.

P. T. Forsyth writes: "Christology is the corollary of soteriology; for a Christology vanishes with the reduction of faith to mere religion. It means that the Deity of Christ is at the centre of Christian truth for us because it is the postulate of the redemption which is Christianity, because it alone makes the classic Christian experience possible for thought". And again, a little later: "For Christ was not the epiphany of an idea, nor the epitome of a race, nor the Incarnation, the precipitate, of a metaphysic—whatever metaphysic he may imply".[1] John Caird writes: "Christ is something more for us than a beautiful historic personality; he is an indwelling ever-present spirit, co-operating with us".[2]

This is not to suggest that the argument from "religious experience" is to be regarded as the be-all and end-all of Christology. Owing to the breakdown of certain apologetic arguments for the Deity of Christ—previously regarded as objective—which will be described in the seventh chapter, many Christian thinkers during the liberal era were falling back upon arguments from experience, religious valuation, and the like—language the content of which was generally ill-defined. If the argument from religious experience is intended to convey merely the judgements and feelings of individual believers, then the Faith is reduced to mysticism, and all hope of consensus, let alone of dogma imposed by the consensus of the church, is banished for ever. There is another sense, however, in which the appeal to Christian

---

[1] *Person and Place of Jesus Christ*, pp. 6, 9; also chs. II and IV. Mackintosh, *Person of Christ*, part III, ch. IV.
[2] *Fundamental Ideas*, II, p. 94.

experience is of decisive importance. There is what may be called the total Christian witness, the witness of the whole Church now and from the beginning, and not simply the emotional experiences of its members, but the witness of the Church's existence and life, the witness of the Church's constant intellectual life, as well as the moral and spiritual testimony of its saints and doctors.

We conclude, then, with two remarks. In the first place, the conjunction of the two axioms, unity and humanity, tended to heighten the tension between the divinity and humanity in Christ a thousandfold. It is now not simply the Son of God who offers living waters to the woman of Samaria, and the Son of Man who says "I thirst": he who is weary by the roadside and ignorant of the future is himself God living as man—so inextricably bound together are his two natures into one consciousness. What is divine in him is human, what is human in him is divine. The natures, or two sides of his being, possessed no separate significance for liberal theology—just as the modern biologist or psychiatrist can conceive no effective distinction between body and "soul". This view had a profound effect upon the idea of the mode and content of revelation. Higher critics had drawn attention to the human ignorance of Christ: it was no longer possible, in the Antiochene style, to write this off as merely a characteristic of the human nature alone—it was the ignorance of Christ, the whole and single Christ. The old orthodoxy, it was thought, with its doctrine of two wills and operations on the one hand, and its superhuman Jesus on the other, had tended to soften down that tension between the divine and the human in his Person, in the first case by introducing a duality and in the second place by the assimilation of attributes; but now the tension was shown up in its starkest relief.

Secondly, therefore, the crisis of the time was reached, not simply by the impact of higher criticism upon a stony wall of orthodoxy of one type or another, but because at that moment the theological ship grounded in a place where two seas met. The new knowledge, the results of the inductive study of the New Testament, could probably have been reconciled with either of the ancient types of Christology taken separately, but in the face of the new situation, a conflict and a heart-searching was bound to ensue. The following chapters will attempt to describe the precise manner in which that conflict arose and resolved itself.

# 3

## THE GOSPEL EVIDENCE FOR THE KNOWLEDGE OF OUR LORD

It is now our business to consider the crisis which was inevitably precipitated by the operation of those forces described in the two preceding chapters. The battlefield was not chosen deliberately by either side, it was brought into prominence by the pressure of circumstances. This fact necessarily incurred a certain loss of perspicuity in the delineation of the problem, and, in fact, the two central questions at issue were for the most part left wholly out of sight during the course of the controversy. Briefly stated, the problem was how could the Jesus of the Gospels with his circumscribed knowledge be the omniscient Son of God; or conversely, how could the omniscient Son of God have become or assumed a finite intelligence. Now it is obvious that this was by no means a side issue for Christology, then or at any time. If, let us say for the sake of argument, the issue had taken this form: "How could the all-sufficient Son of God have become the subject of human hunger?" most theologians, we may assume, would have been content to reply that it was merely one specific aspect of the great mystery of the Incarnation itself. But the case of our Lord's knowledge is different, for through his mind and his speech he performed a vital part of his mission among men; hence with this question is also involved his whole authority as an infallible teacher, and his perfect character as Truth and Righteousness. The controversy was therefore fought on all sides with great vigour and animosity, since what was at stake was considered to be the very basis of the Christian belief in the finality of the teaching of Jesus Christ.

From Patristic times it had been consistently maintained in orthodox theological circles that Jesus Christ as man was in possession of almost unlimited knowledge: generally speaking, one might say that he was regarded as having access to the divine omniscience, in so far as that could be assimilated or reproduced by a finite intelligence. Had Christ not accurately predicted the future? Had he not been able to pierce the secrets of men's hearts? Had he not displayed a knowledge as to the whereabouts of absent friends? Scholastic theologians, in fact, discussed at great lengths the types of super-normal knowledge which the Saviour's mind enjoyed—not on the basis of the analysis of New Testament evidence, of course, but as deductions from the premises of the ancient Christological formulæ in conjunction with the Aristotelean metaphysics. The highly systematized Latin theology was largely abandoned by the reformed Churches, but although non-Roman scholars rarely gave voice to such pious reflections as that the Heart of Jesus beat with conscious love for the whole human race whilst he was still within the Virgin's womb, yet the belief in the virtual omniscience of the man Christ Jesus remained as an essential element in Christology, being looked upon as a surety of his infallibility as also of the hypostatic unity of his Person. Such then was the accepted belief on the subject.

The question, however, was not in the first place raised by the innovators, in the sense that liberal theologians began the controversy by setting before the public their new interpretation of the Gospel evidences. On the contrary, the subject was first invoked by conservative scholars in order to establish a defensive wall against another oncoming wave, namely, the sudden intensification of the labours of English higher criticism. This peculiarity of its beginning coloured the whole course of the debate, and furnished throughout one of its strongest motives, since in the case of many writers, it would almost appear that their interest in defending or controverting the traditional view of Christ's knowledge was subordinate to their interest in defending or denying the rights of higher criticism.[1]

As early as 1866, Canon H. P. Liddon, in his celebrated Bampton Lectures, indignantly rejects a view of the Old Testament—especially the Pentateuch—which would see in these Scriptures no more than a gradual evolution of Hebrew religion involving as it did the abandonment of the traditional authorship of these documents. Dr. Liddon's attack was directed against early adventurers in the critical field such as Bishop Colenso. The one argument which Dr. Liddon believed must foreclose all such theorizing was this: our Lord in his utterances constantly assumed the traditional authorship of these writings; and not only so; he also based his claims and his teaching upon that assurance.[2]

[1] This is clearly to be seen in the numerous pamphlets written in opposition to Dr. Gore's contribution to *Lux Mundi*.
[2] Lecture VIII, sec. 2.

Christ's claims to Messiahship were thus being flouted; yet he had spoken, and his human mind being hypostatically united to the divine nature, his words must be regarded as infallible. "We have lived to hear men proclaim the legendary and immoral character of considerable portions of those Old Testament Scriptures upon which our Lord has set the seal of his infallible authority".[1]

This serves to explain the peculiar manner in which the subject is cautiously broached by Dr. Gore towards the close of his essay in *Lux Mundi*.[2] This essay proved to be the signal for battle to commence on this issue. The subject of our Lord's knowledge is introduced in a seemingly incidental manner. Dr. Gore does *not* say—as men were soon to do—that since higher critics have decided that certain books of the Old Testament were not written by those men who were previously regarded as their authors, therefore it follows that Jesus' knowledge must have been inaccurate. Nor does he say: "The problem for orthodox Christology has been rendered acute by the advent of higher criticism"; nor even: "Someone must be wrong, Jesus or the higher critics, and the latter can scarcely be impugned". He confines himself to parrying Dr. Liddon's argument, and with the greatest care avoids committing himself to any assertions regarding the knowledge of Christ which would be calculated to give offence—though in actual fact, the essay caused very great offence in many quarters.

Dr. Gore first describes the general attitude of higher criticism to the Old Testament history: that the Jewish people were a school, designed to teach the world the truth of monotheism; that inspiration is not a miraculous communication of facts other than may be learned through the normal channels of knowledge; that even the Fathers sometimes assume the unhistoricity of certain portions of the Old Testament; and finally, he broaches the topic of our Lord's use of the Old Testament in his teaching, by posing the question, "Whether Our Lord's words foreclose certain critical positions as to the character of Old Testament literature".[3] He limits himself to this single point without advancing any particular views of his own. The implication of his argument may be described thus: Jesus illustrates his teaching with reference to the adventures of Jonah, and the days before the

[1] H. P. Liddon, Bampton Lectures, 2nd ed., p. 454.
[2] *Lux Mundi*, Essay VIII: The Holy Spirit and Inspiration.
[3] *Ibid.*, 10th ed., p. 359.

## GOSPEL EVIDENCE FOR KNOWLEDGE OF OUR LORD  47

flood, as well as from popular belief and speech—as when he alludes to the sun rising. Jesus also asks many questions, many of which are admittedly to test men's principles, others, more apparently, for information. Therefore, quite apart from the final question whether Jesus did or did not actually know what happened to Jonah or that the sun does not rise, the immediate point is that Jesus chose to be a man of his age, to lead men to God not by casting himself from the pinnacle of the temple but by the power of his sinless personality. Therefore, argues Dr. Gore, if we do not find Jesus making a show of superhuman knowledge by explaining that it is the earth which rotates—and not the sun which rises—neither should we expect him to make an exception to this principle in the case of the authorship of the Old Testament Scriptures: he did not explain the one: why should he explain the other? Thus he concludes: "He willed so to restrain the beams of Deity as to observe the limits of the science of his age, and he puts himself in the same relation to its historical knowledge".[1] Such an attitude turned out to be a mediating position in the controversy, a compromise which certain conservative scholars continued to hold for some years, but which was not found to provide any widespread or lasting satisfaction, and in fact Dr. Gore himself never alludes to it again. As will be shown later, it raises more questions than it answers, but it did meet the immediate objection of such writers as Liddon to higher criticism, and that after all was sufficient for *Lux Mundi*, whose purpose was not to suggest new theories but "to succour a distressed faith".[2]

We have thus illustrated the manner in which the controversy arose. A liberal theologian had appealed against the view that the literal word of Christ was sufficient to decide a question that was in fact a subject of historical investigation. A storm of protest was thus evoked on the grounds that such a view overturned Christ's authority, and implied an interpretation of his Person that was radically at variance with orthodox theology. The attention of scholars was thereby at once turned to the examination of the use which Christ had in fact made of the Old Testament in his teaching. But it was at once discovered that this point could not be considered in isolation, for the whole content of our Lord's mind was involved, and hence every portion of the Gospel evidence had to be scrutinized in this quest. From this examination of the same

[1] *Lux Mundi*, 10th ed., p. 360.
[2] *Ibid.*, Preface.

Four Gospels, the two schools of opinion, whom it is most convenient to designate "Liberal" and "Conservative", drew their quite opposite conclusions. Writers of the former school believed themselves to have established beyond doubt that the picture of Jesus in the Gospels is that of a man exhibiting no more knowledge than was possible or proper for a man of his time; whilst the latter school was confident that it could be established beyond question that Jesus had a knowledge that was practically unbounded. This observation is not made in any spirit of cynical criticism; it merely illustrates the extent to which theology as a rational system exercises in men's minds a primacy over the study of history—even when that history is the study of the revealed word of God, regarded by Protestants as the first and final source of dogma.

Within the Anglican communion, the liberal interpretation gradually gained ground. From a slender and unpopular beginning—as is witnessed by the storm produced by *Lux Mundi*—it gradually made its way forward, its course being to a great extent parallel to that of the acceptance of higher criticism, until by the outbreak of the first world war it was predominant.[1] The more progressive sections of Free Church theology were already familiar with these matters by the year 1889. Competent writers such as A. B. Bruce[2] had laid a firm foundation, and the liberal point of view was accepted more rapidly, as in any case the Free Church theologians felt their hands far less tied by traditional orthodoxy than did their Anglican brethren.

The significance of the victory thus gained in so large a measure for the liberal point of view must never be overlooked during the consideration of the controversy. For the belief that Christ's knowledge was human, normal, circumscribed, had behind it the whole weight of the contemporary sympathy for a Christ who was absolutely natural to our race in every respect. Whatever be the view taken of the possible inferences from the Gospel evidence, no one can doubt that if conservative exegesis was coloured by dogmatic predilections, the humanistic and anti-supernaturalistic

[1] In 1915 the sixth volume of F. J. Hall's *Dogmatic Theology* was published, which treated of the Incarnation. Hall was one of the foremost of conservative and traditionalist scholars within the Anglican communion, and twenty years previously he had appeared as one of the bitterest opponents of Dr. Gore's theology; yet in this later work he freely admits the limited character of our Lord's knowledge.

[2] *The Humiliation of Christ*, 1881.

GOSPEL EVIDENCE FOR KNOWLEDGE OF OUR LORD 49

bias of the time coloured even more every liberal judgment of the material. The full consideration of the interests that lay behind the present controversy are to be postponed to the following chapter. There, the various theories relating to the Lord's knowledge which were put forward will be described, and the charges and countercharges regarding his authority and sinlessness will be treated. It has here been simply necessary to recount the steps that led up to the choice of this subject as the battlefield for the Christological crisis.

*A Synopsis of the Gospel Evidence*

In this chapter an attempt will be made to set forth exactly what the Gospels tell us of the knowledge displayed by our Lord, as this was seen by either party to the controversy, and the use which was made of the material. It is a most difficult task, in the case of any of the writers involved, to separate what is in effect their contribution towards the objective study of the Gospel evidence from their argumentation regarding the larger issues involved, but for the sake of clarity it is vital that this attempt should be made. It is often, for instance, virtually impossible to determine whether a writer is citing a certain text in support of the authenticity of the Old Testament, or the infallibility of Christ, or as a proof of his omniscience—it may be all three at once. Nor has it been found possible in this and the succeeding chapter to proceed on the method of allowing the various writers to speak for themselves, or to follow the course of the controversy step by step. For, in the first place, books, pamphlets and articles, were poured out in an uneven stream during the last decade of the nineteenth century, by writers working from many points of view and with varying motives, and with deplorably little attempt to profit by, or to build upon, each other's labours: and in the second place, the confusion of issues already alluded to would render such a method incapable of conveying any clear understanding of the situation. Particularly is this present plan justified when considering the ways in which the Gospel evidence was marshalled, since the same set of proof-texts for either point of view are listed and discussed by every writer on the subject with the most monotonous regularity.

At the present day it is still possible for any honest enquirer to re-examine this Gospel material, and in the light of his other religious beliefs, to arrive at his own conclusion consonant with them. A suspicion remains in the minds of some that this question was fought out and decided in the 'nineties, once and for all, and that it is equally impossible to return to the traditional view of Christ's unlimited knowledge as it would be to return to a literal belief in Adam and Eve. This is not, however, the case. The liberal interpretation of the Gospel evidence, as also all radical liberal Christology that gained a foothold in the Anglo-Saxon world, is motivated not so much by a purely objective exegesis as by a set of rationalistic principles that bias every judgment of fact or opinion in which an element of the supernatural is involved. In the times of which we are writing, many even of the most well-meaning of orthodox theologians felt it incumbent upon them to bow to such principles, which appeared to have behind them the support of the new dictatorship of natural science. To-day, however, as in all past ages of the Church's history, the liberal era excepted, students of Christian theology may reject without any qualm or embarrassment the principles of humanism and rationalism: the universe is a far more mysterious place than nineteenth-century science imagined it to be, and the supernatural in its every manifestation deserves its rightful place in any system of thought which pretends to embrace the whole of reality. The younger generation has been charged with fostering a return to obscurantism; this charge belongs rather to the age which is passing away. In addition to this widespread reaction to liberal theology now under way, Roman Catholic theology—still the largest organized body of Christian opinion—has remained unmoved by the events of the last fifty years, and though much of it is of a character little calculated to impress the rest of Christendom, its witness for the old and wider principles of thought still remains significant.

It is therefore now possible to adopt a far more open-minded attitude towards the question of our Lord's knowledge than would have been tolerable a quarter of a century ago; for the issue is after all simply one aspect of the working of the supernatural in history. Consequently, in order to assist the mind to a fair verdict upon the evidence, certain remarks may be offered in preface to the synopsis hereafter to be presented.

In the first place, the enquirer has to ask himself: Am I prepared to entertain seriously any statements which the Synoptic Gospels—to say nothing of the Fourth Gospel—may make with

## GOSPEL EVIDENCE FOR KNOWLEDGE OF OUR LORD

regard to any supernatural knowledge possessed by Christ, and to accept them at their face value? Unless the evidence for supernatural knowledge is to be taken at exactly the same value as any other evidence, a just inductive conclusion is impossible.

Secondly, whatever supernatural knowledge Jesus may have possessed, it presented no such difficulties to the Evangelists as it did to the scholars of the 'nineties: it did not in the least occasion any embarrassment to their belief in his true manhood—a reality of daily experience to his followers. Consider how such a theme as "The Omniscient Man" would have been treated in a novel by Mr. G. K. Chesterton or Mr. H. G. Wells. Through what embarrassing and tragic escapades would the hero of such a story be drawn in consequence of the possession of so terrifying a faculty! Nothing could possibly be farther removed from this than the narrative of Jesus in the Gospels. Every aspect of his personality appears in perfect harmony. Whenever he exercises abnormal power or displays extraordinary knowledge it never appears to be intruded as an element foreign to his nature. At bottom this would be due to the fact that Jesus never could in the slightest degree utilize the divine prerogatives that he possessed to any irrelevant or selfish end. This would have been to yield to the first of the three satanic temptations. For the present, however, the significant fact is that this perfect harmony in the Gospel life of Jesus results from the fact that men who had known him in his earthly life could relate with unaffected naturalness numerous instances of the Lord's superhuman powers side by side with instances of his human frailty, without feeling that they were compromising his complete humanity. The Evangelists as, opposed to liberal scholars, saw nothing inconsistent in such a method of juxtaposition.

Thirdly, it must be asked, why should it be assumed as a matter of course that the verdict of liberal scholars should be considered final as against the overwhelming mass of traditional theology? It will be replied, that liberal theologians were, practically speaking, the first Christian thinkers to apply the principles of scientific criticism seriously to the Gospel records. This belief, in fact, that the verdict of liberalism on this question is based upon higher critical enquiry has in large measure contributed to the prestige of the decision. Yet what higher critical labours are involved in exalting the question: "Where have ye laid him"? into a final judgment upon Christ's limited knowledge, as opposed

52    CONFLICT IN CHRISTOLOGY

to a text such as "Thy brother shall rise again"? None at all. The Fathers were just as familiar with the Gospel evidences of Christ's human limitations as any liberal scholar: the determinate factor was not a critical one, it was a philosophical one—the humanistic predilection against the miraculous—that was the principle involved.

The following synopsis of the Gospel evidence does not claim to be an exhaustive survey, with every piece of possible evidence enumerated. It contains rather a full selection from the various materials which were employed by either party to the controversy.

*Christ's Knowledge and Use of the Old Testament*

We begin with our Lord's knowledge of the Old Testament because it was the point at which the controversy began. In itself, however, this proved to be neutral ground. The interest was chiefly in relation to higher criticism: whether, as already shown, our Lord's words do or do not foreclose the radical criticism of the Old Testament. Naturally, his words on this subject cannot be used either to prove his omniscience or his limitation of knowledge. Against the latter attempt it could always be argued that he used the traditional terminology in a consciously conventional manner. In actual fact, only the camp-followers of either side did employ this material as proof-texts; though in the case of the liberals, the pressure of justifying higher critical conclusions remained as a constant undercurrent, which presses upon the interpretation of other evidence of a more relevant character. Nevertheless, the Old Testament question, contrary to popular belief, remained on the periphery of the subject.

(a) Authorship of Old Testament books. There are a number of passages in which reference is made explicitly or implicitly by our Lord to the traditional authors of Old Testament scriptures. This is notably the case with the books of the Pentateuch, his language differing in no degree from the accepted beliefs of his generation on the subject.

Mk. 1. 44 (to the leper). " . . . See thou say nothing to any man: but go thy way, show thyself to the priest, and offer for thy cleansing the things which Moses commanded, for a testimony unto them": Mt. 8. 4, Lk. 5. 14, cited from Lev. 14. 2–32.

Mk. 7. 10. "For Moses said, Honour thy father and thy mother;

## GOSPEL EVIDENCE FOR KNOWLEDGE OF OUR LORD

and, He that speaketh evil of father or mother, let him die the death." (Mt. 15. 4 instead reads "For God said . . ."; and the same rendering of "God" in place of "Moses" occurs at Mt. 22. 31, "Spoken unto you by God".) Cited from Exod. 20. 12 (the Decalogue) and Exod. 21. 17.

Mk. 10. 3. ". . . What did Moses command you?" To which they quote Deut. 24. 1–4. The Matthaean form differs but with the same implications—Mt. 19. 8. "Moses for your hardness of heart . . ." cf. Mt. 5. 31; same subject with same implication.

Mk. 12. 19. "Master, Moses wrote unto us, If a man's brother die, and leave a wife behind him . . ." Cf. Mt. 22. 24, "Moses said, If a man die, . . .", Lk. 20. 28, as Mk., cited from Deut. 25. 5.

Mk. 12. 26. "But as touching the dead, that they are raised; have ye not read in the book of Moses, in the place concerning the Bush, . . ." Mt. 22. 31 " . . . Have ye not read that which was spoken unto you by God saying" (as Mk. 7. 10: Mt. 15. 4). Lk. 20. 37 "But that the dead are raised, even Moses shewed, . . ." cited from Exod. 3.

Jn. 7. 22. "For this cause hath Moses given you circumcision"; v. 23 " . . . that the law of Moses may not be broken": Gen. 17. 10.

Jn. 8. 5. "Now in the law Moses commanded us to stone such": referring to Deut. 22. 24.

It will be observed that very considerable proportions of the Pentateuch are covered explicitly, and the whole implicitly, as of Mosaic authorship. To these may be added a number of general allusions.

Lk. 16. 29. "But Abraham saith, They have Moses and the prophets."

Lk. 24. 27. "And beginning from Moses and from all the prophets, he interpreted to them . . ."

Lk. 24. 44. " . . . How that all things must needs be fulfilled, which are written in the law of Moses . . ." Jn. 5. 45, 46 " . . . There is one that accuseth you, even Moses, . . . For if ye believed Moses, ye would believe me; for he wrote of me".

Jn. 7. 19. "Did not Moses give you the law, and yet none of you doeth the law?"

Other traditional ascriptions referred to:

Mk. 7. 6. " . . . Well did Isaiah prophesy of you hypocrites, as it is written, This people honoureth me with their lips", and Mt. 15. 7 from Isa. 29. 13.

Mt. 13. 14. "And unto them is fulfilled the prophesy of Isaiah, which saith, By hearing ye shall hear and shall in no wise understand": Isa., 6. 9–10.

The evidence considered so far cannot be by itself decisive either as a rebuttal of higher criticism or in ascertaining the content of the Lord's mind. For at the outset of the controversy it is admitted by so conservative a scholar as the reviewer of *Lux Mundi* in the *Church Quarterly Review* that Jesus may be here using the names of Moses and Isaiah in a purely conventional manner.[1] Far greater difficulties are believed to arise in regard to the passage in which David is alluded to as the author of Ps. 110.

Mk. 12. 35 ff. "And Jesus answered and said, as he taught in the temple, How say the scribes that the Christ is the son of David? David himself said in the Holy Spirit, The Lord said unto my Lord, sit thou on my right hand till I make thine enemies the footstool of thy feet. David himself calleth him Lord; and whence is he his son?": Mt. 22. 41 ff., Lk. 20. 41.

The value and significance of this passage in support of either view must be carefully assessed. In the first instance, it is argued, e.g. by *Lux Mundi*, that Christ is here employing an *ad hominem* argument against the pharisees, confuting them on their own premises. On this view it does not follow that Jesus necessarily shared their belief in the Davidic authorship of the psalm in question: in other words, the passage is not decisive evidence for Christ's knowledge, any more than the preceding instances. Gore thus avoids any scandal; he does not say, as he was perfectly justified in doing, on his own principles, and as was soon to be done by other writers, that the passage demonstrates the fact that Jesus shared the contemporary beliefs of the time regarding this psalm and therefore was at variance with truth as now apprehended by higher criticism. He asserts simply that Christ bases no positive dogma upon the supposed authorship of the psalm, but is simply debating a point of exegesis, and hence such an error, if it was an error, would not militate against his infallibility as a teacher. Our Lord is giving voice to a current belief, as when he speaks of the sun rising. It was, on the other hand, strenuously contested by conservative scholars that the passage is of crucial importance both for the Biblical and Christo-

[1] *CQR*, April 1890, p. 195.

logical issues. The article on *Lux Mundi* in the *Church Quarterly Review* for April 1890—already referred to—at once takes up the cudgels. It may be well enough for Christ to employ the speech of every-day in general conversation; but it is far different, the writer argues, when what he refers to is made the basis of what he teaches. After alluding to our Lord's use of the stories of Lot's wife, the days of Noe and the men of Nineveh—to be discussed presently—the writer proceeds: The climax is reached in this passage on Ps. 110. David is not here quoted as merely a traditional psalmist; the whole force of what is said rests on the truth of the fact that the special individual who the Pharisees said was forefather of Messiah is the speaker in Ps. 110. *Lux Mundi* had said that the passage was analogous to the passage "Why callest thou me good?" But in that instance, Jesus is simply driving the young man on from one truth to another; in this case it would be driving men from a lie to a truth were Christ aware that the psalm was not Davidic. Neither is it analogous to Jesus' speaking of the sun rising; for Jesus never built any truth upon the idea that the sun rises, as he evidently does in the present instance.

In all fairness it must be pointed out that in this passage Christ's remarks to the Pharisees are addressed in the form of an exegetical conundrum, and hence it is impossible on this point alone to ascertain his own attitude, which has to be seen in relation to his general view of Old Testament prophecy. There seems little doubt that, like the evangelists who wrote of him, he regarded the Scriptures as the divinely uttered sanction for his authority and claims. The events of his life—especially is this clear in regard to the Passion—are looked upon as inevitable: "For thus it is written". Hence it would be in perfect harmony with the rest of Christ's teaching to regard the passage on Ps. 110 as a claim to Messiahship drawn from an exegesis of an Old Testament Scripture on the basis of the belief that David was the author of the psalm—whether we hold that belief to be true or false. The passage, therefore, may be of importance for the question of his authority; it cannot decide the matter of the content of his knowledge.

(b) Christ's use of persons and events in the Old Testament. One of the most characteristic features of our Lord's teaching is his painting of pictures drawn from Old Testament stories to illustrate and enforce his message. In the main these are warnings —of the unexpectedness of the day of the Son of Man, of the treatment which contemporary peoples and cities will receive at the day of judgment. This naturally opens up by inference the question of Christ's knowledge of the future and especially of future cosmical events; but our reference here is simply to his knowledge of the past. The "future" will be treated of shortly.

Mt. 11. 21. "Woe unto thee, Chorazin! Woe unto thee, Bethsaida! for if the mighty works had been done in Tyre and Sidon which were done in you, they would have repented long ago in sackcloth and ashes. Howbeit I say unto you, it shall be more tolerable for Tyre and Sidon in the day of judgment, than for you. And thou, Capernaum, shalt thou be exalted unto heaven? Thou shalt go down unto Hades; for if the mighty works had been done in Sodom which were done in thee, it would have remained unto this day. Howbeit I say unto you, that it shall be more tolerable for the land of Sodom in the day of judgment, than for thee": cf. Lk. 10. 13, 12.

Mt. 10. 15. "Verily I say unto you, it shall be more tolerable for the land of Sodom and Gomorrah in the day of judgment, than for that city."

Here are the direct warnings he gives:

Mt. 24. 37–39. "And as were the days of Noah, so shall be the coming of the Son of Man. For as in those days which were before the flood they were eating and drinking, . . . until the day that Noah entered into the ark, and they knew not until the flood came, and took them all away": cf. Lk. 17. 26, 27.

Lk. 17. 28. "Likewise even as it came to pass in the days of Lot; they ate, they drank, . . . but in the day that Lot went out from Sodom it rained fire and brimstone from heaven, and destroyed them all." 5. 32. "Remember Lot's wife."

In regard to this pericope there are several points which must be borne in mind. In the first place, factual information relating to the past is interwoven with prediction of the future; hence the veracity of the one is probably bound up with the other—this, however, has more to do with the burning question of Christ's authority.

Then again, it would appear that our Lord assumes *sine dubio* the historicity of some of the early stories in the Old Testament. Christ alludes to the cities of the plain in the same manner as that in which he speaks of the renowned city of Tyre, and he treats as accepted fact the story of the flood.

If the verdict of higher criticism be granted—that these stories are legendary in character—it might be argued on the mediating view adopted in *Lux Mundi* that Christ is simply employing arguments calculated to impress his hearers, whilst himself passing no judgment upon the historicity of the material in hand. Against this it would be argued, by liberals, that to make such a pretence would be utterly foreign to the character of Jesus, and by conservatives, that warnings uttered on the basis of past happenings lose all their force if those happenings are merely legendary—this latter argument is primarily directed in support of the authenticity of the Old Testament. It is more probable to suppose therefore that Christ did intend these warnings to be understood as exemplified in actual events of the past—such is the natural meaning of his words. Far, however, from regarding this material as virtually neutral ground in the question of our Lord's knowledge, one writer, Mr. H. C. Powell, employed these passages to demonstrate Christ's omniscience.[1] He points out that since Christ had full knowledge of the spiritual condition of the peoples in the ancient cities—knowing precisely under what conditions they would have repented—his human mind, therefore, must not only have been in possession of all actual facts, but also of all potential ones as well. This view goes even farther than many of the schoolmen would allow. Such deductions are generally regarded as absurd.

Similar arguments are advanced in respect of the two following passages; though here again, the case has little directly to do with the central point as to Christ's knowledge.

Mt. 12. 39. " . . . An evil and adulterous generation seeketh after a sign; and there shall no sign be given to it but the sign of Jonah the prophet: for as Jonah was three days and three nights in the belly of the whale; so shall the Son of Man be three days and three nights in the heart of the earth. The men of Nineveh shall stand up in the judgment with this generation, and shall condemn it; for they repented at the preaching of Jonah; and behold, a greater than Jonah is here."

Jn. 3. 14. "And as Moses lifted up the serpent in the wilderness, even so must the Son of Man be lifted up."

It is held by conservatives—again defending the historicity of the Scripture both New and Old—that the past and the present are inextricably bound together: denial of the one leads to denial of the other. If the story of Jonah's deliverance from the fish is

[1] H. C. Powell, *The Principle of the Incarnation*, part III.

unhistorical and merely figurative, so also is Christ's resurrection unhistorical. If the story of the repentance of Nineveh be figurative, so may the idea of the last judgment be untrue. If the story of Moses' action in the wilderness be a legend, so also may be the notion of Christ's redemption.

A number of miscellaneous passages in which Christ employs the Old Testament in his teaching may be cited in conclusion of the section.

Mk. 2. 25 f. " . . . Did ye never read what David did, when he had need, and was an hungred, he, and they that were with him? How he entered into the House of God when Abiathar was high priest, and did eat the shewbread, which it is not lawful to eat save for the priests, and gave also to them that were with him?" According to the type of reasoning employed by H. C. Powell, it might be inferred from the fact that Jesus alters the name of the high priest and adds the detail that David had companions with him, that Jesus here displays a knowledge of this bygone age superior to the Scriptures themselves. Such an argument, however, will not stand scrutiny.

Mt. 8. 11. " . . . Many shall come from the east and the west, and shall sit down with Abraham, and Isaac, and Jacob, in the kingdom of heaven: but the sons of the kingdom shall be cast forth into the outer darkness."

Lk. 13. 16. "And ought not this woman, being a daughter of Abraham, whom Satan hath bound . . .?"

Lk. 16. 22. "And . . . was carried away by the angels into Abraham's bosom."

Jn. 8. 37 ff. "I know that ye are Abraham's seed . . ." (note *vv.* 39–40). *v.* 56—"Your father Abraham rejoiced to see my day; and he saw it, and was glad." (This verse is of great importance to conservative scholars.) *v.* 58—" . . . Before Abraham was, I am."

Here, quite clearly, even more so than in the passage concerning Ps. 110, the argument rests upon the historical existence of the patriarch Abraham. Not only the patriarch's existence is postulated, but his life and work, the promises made to him, his prophecy of the coming of Christ and his actual "seeing" of the prophecy fulfilled. The passage played so insignificant a part in the discussion owing to the fact that it occurs in the Fourth Gospel, as opposed to the Ps. 110 passage in the synoptic Gospels. Another similar instance is:

GOSPEL EVIDENCE FOR KNOWLEDGE OF OUR LORD 59

Jn. 5. 46. "For if ye believed Moses, ye would believe me; for he wrote of me."

Jn. 6. 32. " . . . It was not Moses that gave you the bread out of heaven; but my Father giveth you the true bread out of heaven."

Lk. 4. 25. " . . . There were many widows in Israel in the days of Elijah, when the heaven was shut up three years and six months, when there came a great famine over all the land; and unto none of them was Elijah sent, but only to Zarephath, in the land of Sidon, unto a woman that was a widow. And there were many lepers in Israel in the time of Elisha the prophet; and none of them was cleansed, but only Naaman the Syrian." This is analogous to Christ's warnings: whole stories from the Old Testament are taken as instances of God's free working among his people.

To sum up, therefore, it was urged by conservative scholars that a warning or a teaching loses all its force if the past event upon which it is based turns out to be no more than a legend; equally absurd would it be to say—refrain from eating apples tendered by strangers: remember the fate of Snow-white. Such writers were already convinced (a) of the authenticity of the Old Testament history, and (b) of the perfect knowledge possessed by Jesus. Their position was now being assailed from both sides. In vain did they try to hold the two together by making them mutually dependent, in a circular argument; at other times they tried to defend each separately. In this fray, the Old Testament references were used as a shuttlecock, being bandied about to defend first one and then the other interest.

To the liberal scholar, on the other hand, there was a burning question to be answered. He came to the Gospel evidence with his mind already made up on certain critical conclusions regarding the Old Testament. He began by attempting to show that Christ's use of the Old Testament did not necessarily imply his acquiescence in the traditional beliefs regarding it. He declared that the Ps. 110 passage was simply an *argumentum ad hominem*; he suggested that the warnings did not at all commit Jesus to a belief in the flood. It was soon discovered that this was scarcely a tenable position. The argument that Christ's allusions to the Old Testament are merely pictorial illustrations, drawn from contemporary belief, most calculated to impress his hearers, and having no necessary connection with the question of their historicity, is a point of view now so familiar to us that it is easy to forget how unsatisfactory it is. Christ's own words lend no substantiation to the belief that he was disinterested in the historical value of the Old Testament scriptures. Hence the camps became more sharply divided as a more frank interpretation of the Gospels prevailed: If Jesus was omniscient, then the higher critics are wrong; if, however, the higher critics are right, then the knowledge of Jesus was limited; the middle course is ruled out of order.

### General Restraint or Limitation of Christ's Knowledge

"He never enlarges our stock of natural knowledge, physical or historical, out of the divine omniscience", writes Dr. Gore.[1] As already alluded to more than once, Jesus employs the popular cosmogony as in Mt. 5. 45. " . . . For he maketh his sun to rise on the evil and the good . . ." With this attitude no one would quarrel, for it was manifestly not the purpose of the Incarnation to bestow upon men a deposit of knowledge of a naturalistic order—which in any case men were able to acquire by their own efforts—it would have been the "oldness of the letter which killeth". Quite clearly then it does not essentially affect the question of the limitation of his knowledge, since we ourselves speak of the sun rising. It might well be argued that in the everyday circumstances of life, there must have arisen many occasions upon which an abnormal knowledge of the physical world, had he possessed it, must necessarily have had startling results, of which there is no trace in the Gospels—with the possible exception of such a domestic miracle as at Cana in Galilee. It was therefore argued that had he been in possession of unlimited knowledge, his earthly and domestic life must have been a perpetual sham, the only way to avoid which would have been for it to be really limited. Such a pretence would have been the height of docetism and would have utterly robbed the Incarnation of its genuine character.

### Specific Evidences of Limitation

We turn next to a more difficult and complex catena of texts. There are, in the first place, numerous instances which, to many

[1] Bampton Lectures, p. 149.

scholars, indicate that Christ possessed a knowledge that was discursive, like our own, as opposed to a permanent state of illumination. In the second place, there are occasions upon which Jesus displayed emotions which liberal thinkers believe to be quite incompatible with omniscience. In the third place, there are numerous examples of questions addressed by Jesus which would appear to be indications that his knowledge of those matters was incomplete. A selection of the most obvious instances of each class will here be given.

### 1. *The Discursive Character of Christ's Knowledge*

In weighing the value of this evidence it should be borne in mind that, even if we possessed definite proof, which by the nature of things we cannot, that Christ's knowledge was present to his human consciousness in a discursive manner, it would not of itself discount the belief that he had at his disposal practically the whole of the divine omniscience. As the anonymous reviewer in *Church Quarterly Review* of H. C. Powell's "Principle of the Incarnation" points out, the human mind which was the medium through which the Divine Logos spoke and acted would, one might expect, be normally capable of cognizing only a very limited range of facts at once; hence although all knowledge might be possible to it, that mind might genuinely be said to come to know or to realize any given matter.

Mk. 2. 8. "And straightway Jesus, perceiving in his spirit that they so reasoned within themselves . . ."

Mk. 6. 48. "And seeing them distressed in rowing . . ."

Mk. 8. 33. "But he turning about, and seeing his disciples, rebuked Peter."

Mk. 12. 34. "And when Jesus saw that he answered discreetly, he said unto him . . ."

Mt. 9. 2. "And Jesus seeing their faith . . ."

Mt. 9. 36. "But when he saw the multitudes, he was moved with compassion for them . . ."

Mt. 12. 15. "And Jesus perceiving it withdrew from thence: and many followed him."

Mt. 22. 18. "But Jesus perceived their wickedness, and said, Why tempt ye me, ye hypocrites?"

Jn. 4. 1. "When therefore the Lord knew how the Pharisees

had heard that Jesus was making and baptizing more disciples than John . . ."

Jn. 6. 15. "Jesus therefore perceiving that they were about to come and take him by force . . ."

Jn. 5. 6. "When Jesus saw him lying, and knew that he had been now a long time in that case . . ."

Jn. 16. 19. "Jesus perceived that they were desirous to ask him."

Jesus receives information:

Mt. 4. 12. "Now when he heard that John was delivered up, he withdrew into Galilee."

Mt. 14. 12. "And his disciples came, and took up the corpse, and buried him; and they went and told Jesus."

Jn. 9. 35. "Jesus heard that they had cast him out."

The obvious weakness of much of this material as a demonstration of the limitation of Christ's human knowledge is that whilst many of them from one aspect appear to suggest that Jesus *came* to know these facts at a given point of time, yet many of them are simultaneously examples of the exercise of supernatural and uncircumscribed cognition—a knowledge which far surpasses the bounds of normal human mental capacity, and they would not have found a place in this digest had they not been put forward as evidence by so eminent a scholar as Dr. A. J. Mason.

## 2. *Emotions Incompatible with Omniscience*

Mk. 3. 5. "And when he had looked round about on them with anger, being grieved at the hardening of their hearts . . ."

Mk. 6. 6. "And he marvelled because of their unbelief . . ."

Mk. 10. 14. "But when Jesus saw it, he was moved with indignation, and said unto them . . ."

Mk. 10. 21. "And Jesus looking upon him loved him."

Mk. 14. 33. "And he taketh with him Peter and James and John, and began to be greatly amazed, and sore troubled."

Mt. 14. 14. "And he came forth, and saw a great multitude, and he had compassion on them, and healed their sick."

Lk. 7. 13. "And when the Lord saw her, he had compassion on her, and said unto her, Weep not."

The argument regarding these quotations is of a subtle character. On certain occasions our Lord is clearly represented as exhibiting the emotion of surprise. In Mk. 11. 12 ff. we read how, when he was entering Jerusalem from Bethany the day after the Palm procession, he came to a fig tree, hoping to find fruit on it, and was surprised to find none. The whole episode of the cursing of the fig tree, and his disappointment, is no doubt a sacramental parable, after Hebrew prophetic type, sealing the fate of Jerusalem, and hence its basic importance in the present argument is doubtful. It serves, however, to illustrate this emotion, characteristic of the Gospel representation of Jesus. In addition to this, the Lord displays certain other emotions, such as anger, amazement, gratification, which in the normal course of things are generally associated with the sudden acquaintance with certain facts. Such passages, therefore, are cited as evidence of the limitation of Christ's knowledge. First, let us deal with the emotions other than surprise. Such emotions may be, let us frankly admit, the symptoms of a limitation of knowledge, and in the case of all other men it is the element of shock—however much expected—that contributes to the degree of the appropriate emotion. On the other hand, it is not legitimate to argue that such emotions are incompatible with omniscience. Many writers stated such a proposition without realising what consequences it holds for the doctrine of God. It is the Christian belief that, whilst God possesses a perfect knowledge of everything which is going to happen or can happen, he nevertheless, being a Personal being, experiences and expresses all righteous emotions. Whilst sustaining a constant attitude of love towards his creatures, God may none the less be moved—to use the Scriptural phrase—with wrath, indignation, appreciation, or compassion. Such emotions will also be looked for in the life of the Incarnate Son, and they are, in fact, there to be found. To maintain, however, that the discovery of such elements in his personality necessarily involves the admission of his limitation is a fallacy that deserves to be exposed. If it be retorted that the ascription of such feelings to God is a relic of primitive anthropomorphic conceptions of the Deity, it can only be replied that the denial of such emotions to God renders him scarcely recognisable to man as a Personal being. Such a denial would be the carrying to excess of the Greek idea of the impassible, unchangeable God—a concept which is redeemed and balanced in Christian theology by the idea of the Incarnation and the Cross.

The case is more complicated in the matter of the emotion of "surprise". In one sense, the omniscient God experiences surprise—at men's conduct—even though he be perfectly aware beforehand of what will be man's choice of action. There is also the human emotion of surprise, evoked by the appearance of the unexpected. If other evidence were present in support of the hypothesis that Christ's knowledge was limited, it would be legitimate to construe his surprise as being of the human type; such an interpretation appears on the face of things to be the more natural explanation in such a passage as the cursing of the fig tree, whilst in the cases where the conduct of men is the subject, our Lord, with his understanding of the people around him, could scarcely have been very surprised—in the normal sense of the word—at the attitude adopted by his enemies or friends on given occasions. The ascription of emotions to Christ, therefore, is no evidence of limitation, with the possible exception of surprise, which is patient of an explanation conformable to other evidence. So much was written on this topic that it was essential to state the issue in a manner free from the confusion of those times.

### 3. *Questions asked by Christ*

Within this section there appear the most striking—and always the most convincing—data advanced on behalf of Christ's limitation.

Many of Christ's questions are manifestly designed to lead men forward by making them use their intelligence, or else are simply rhetorical.

Mk. 2. 25. "Did ye never read what David did?"

Mk. 8. 27. "Who do men say that I am?"

Mk. 11. 30. "The baptism of John, was it from heaven or from men?"

Mk. 12. 10. "Have ye not read even this scripture; the stone which the builders rejected . . .?"

Mk. 12. 16. " . . . Whose is this image and superscription?"

Mk. 12. 35. "How say the scribes that the Christ is the son of David?"

Mk. 14. 37. " . . . Simon, sleepest thou? Could'st thou not watch one hour?"

Mt. 17. 25. " . . . What thinkest thou, Simon, the kings of the earth, from whom do they receive toll or tribute? From their sons, or from strangers?"

Lk. 22. 35. " . . . When I sent you forth without purse, and wallet, and shoes, lacked ye anything?"

Lk. 17. 17. "Were not the ten cleansed, but where are the nine?"

Jn. 3. 10. "Art thou the teacher of Israel, and understandest not these things?"

From these we pass to questions whose explanation appears more and more to be that our Lord was seeking for information. No two scholars agree which questions are merely didactic and which are intended as requests for information. A certain number are generally regarded as coming under the former, and others as coming under the latter head. But since the purpose of the Incarnation was *propter hominem*, it can never be said for certain in any given instance that the question was a request for information and not rather a question spoken for the sake of the hearers. The arguments which suggest a didactic explanation of a question to one scholar may equally be applied to any other question by other scholars; and the divergence on many points amongst liberal exegetes shows their reasonable reluctance to pin down all or even the majority of Christ's questions to the fact of his human ignorance to the exclusion of this other most important consideration. The natural meaning of some of the questions would appear to be that our Lord was in fact seeking for information on matters with which he was not fully acquainted.

Questions such as the following are regarded by most liberal scholars as uttered for the sake of the person addressed—exclusive of the knowledge enjoyed or not enjoyed by our Lord.

Mk. 8. 23. " . . . He asked him, Seest thou ought?"

Mt. 9. 28. " . . . Believe ye that I am able to do this?"

Mt. 13. 51. "Have ye understood all these things?"

The remainder of Christ's questions may now be grouped together unselectively, as all of them are regarded each by some scholars as a direct request for information, though particular doubts may attach to individual examples.

Mk. 5. 9. "And he asked him, What is thy name?"

Mk. 5. 30. "Who touched my garments?"

Mk. 6. 38. "How many loaves have ye?"

Mk. 9. 16. "And he asked them, What question ye with them?"

Mk. 9. 21. "How long time is it since this hath come unto him?"

Mk. 9. 33. "What were ye reasoning in the way?"

Mk. 10. 36. "What would ye that I should do for you?"

Mk. 15. 34. "Eloi, eloi, lama sabachthani?"

Lk. 2. 46. "Both hearing them and asking them questions."
Lk. 2. 49. " . . . How is it that ye sought me? Wist ye not that I must be in my Father's house?"
Jn. 8. 10. " . . . Woman, where are they? Did no man condemn thee?"
Jn. 11. 34. "Where have ye laid him?"
Jn. 1. 38. "What seek ye?"

As remarked above, certain of these questions, without any semblance of special pleading, are open to an explanation other than that Christ was in ignorance of certain facts. Especially is there ground for such a contention when a question—superficially a request for information—is joined to one of an entirely different character. Thus, if one were to admit that, "Who say ye that I am?", is designed to draw out the confession of the disciples, it might reasonably be inferred that the preceding question, "Who do men say that I am?", is also part of the same method of opening the disciples' mouths rather than a desire for news about the popular estimate of his Person. So too it might reasonably be contended that "How many loaves have ye?" was spoken for the sake of the disciples, as was the preceding question, "Whence shall we buy bread . . .?", which, as St. John tells us, "He said to prove him".

If it be considered that too conservative a bias is visible in these pages, my object is to correct the balance. For many conclusions, hastily adopted half a century ago, which have survived with virtually axiomatic authority have now to be subjected to the closest scrutiny, to sift from them the bias of sceptical humanism, in order to leave bare what really constitutes true evidence.

The questions, then, addressed by Christ to those around him undoubtedly constitute the corner stone in the inductive argument for the limitation of his knowledge. Though any may be explained away, the plain meaning of the passages as a whole would appear to be—apart from other considerations—that on these occasions Christ was seeking for certain knowledge which he did not possess.

To the digest must also be added a more doubtful class of passage to which some of the more radical scholars attach great importance.

Christ, it is argued, is represented as sharing in the erroneous beliefs of his time regarding demon-possession and exorcism, and

GOSPEL EVIDENCE FOR KNOWLEDGE OF OUR LORD 67

in primitive animistic beliefs. Thus, Jesus performs exorcisms: Mk. 1. 25–34; Mk. 3. 11–12; Mk. 5. 1–20; Mk. 7. 25–30; Mk. 9. 15–27. His apostles are ordained to exorcise: Mk. 3.15; and, Mk. 6. 7, 13, they are sent out to do so. Mk. 3. 22–30 is the Beelzebub controversy with the Pharisees.

Mk. 4. 39. Christ rebukes a storm, as though it were a person.

The significance of this evidence naturally depends upon the question whether belief in demon-possession is or is not an outworn superstition.

Finally, it is pointed out by T. Adamson that on two occasions Christ allowed his disciples to put to sea when a storm was brewing, Mk. 4. 36, 6. 45. Such rationalizing as this is generally discounted.

*The Loci Classici*

To the present juncture has been postponed the consideration of the three texts which, it is argued, attest more than any other Gospel evidence, the circumscribed character of Christ's knowledge.

Lk. 2. 40 (A.V.). "And the child grew, and waxed strong in spirit, filled with wisdom: and the grace of God was upon him."

Lk. 2. 52 (A.V.). "And Jesus increased in wisdom and stature, and in favour with God and man."

Mk. 13. 32. "But of that day or that hour knoweth no one, not even the angels in heaven, neither the Son, but the Father." (In Mt. 24. 36 many ancient authorities omit the clause "οὐδὲ ὁ υἱός".)

In regard to the Lucan passages, it is argued on the one hand that their plain meaning entails the belief that our Lord's knowledge increased as he grew in the same manner as normal human beings—increase in wisdom being interpreted in the same sense as growth in stature. A moderate liberal, Dr. A. J. Mason, treats the texts in a less rigorous manner. Luke does not say that Jesus advanced in knowledge—wisdom is a larger thing than knowledge, and hence he does not directly imply that Jesus began by knowing nothing.[1] The distinction between wisdom and knowledge was in fact turned to good effect by conservative writers, who contended that it implied the growing appreciation of and application of knowledge already possessed, and does not directly refer to the acquisition of new facts. This is as it may be. They demanded that

[1] *Conditions of Our Lord's Life*, p. 127.

increase in wisdom should be treated as parallel to increase in favour with God and not as parallel to growth in stature—this, however, is scarcely warranted by the construction of the sentence.

Nor is the situation less complicated in regard to Mk. 13. 32: in fact it is more so. The straightforward liberal argument is that any universal generalization requires but one exception to shatter it: only one white cat need be produced to overthrow the thesis that all cats are black; hence the doctrine of Christ's omniscience, they say, needs only one single instance of ignorance on his part to disallow it. Here then is such an instance, where Christ explicitly disclaims knowledge on a particular matter. If he was ignorant on one point, they would continue, it may reasonably be inferred that he was ignorant about many other things; if this were not so it would be difficult to see how he was made in all points like his brethren; so argues W. S. Swayne.[1] This is not, of course, a logical inference, and it might be argued against it that the very form of the passage suggests that it was looked upon by the Evangelists, as by Christ himself, as in some sense a somewhat remarkable and exceptional thing that he should be ignorant on a point such as that. It is more helpful to confine the study to the exact meaning of the text itself rather than to inferences which may be drawn from it such as the above.

The text had been discussed by a very large number of ancient Christian commentators. The Fathers generally adopted the view that Christ did actually know the time of the Parousia, but, since he was speaking in the person of the church or of his human nature, or simply for the sake of men, he refrained from telling his disciples. Such explanations continued to be offered, as by H. E. Clayton.[2] The Incarnation was for the good of mankind, and since it was better for mankind not to know the day or hour, the Lord refrained from disclosing it.

Theodoret's clarion protest against the economic explanations of the passage was noted in the preceding chapter. Yet conservative scholars, for some time, at any rate, clung bitterly to the classical explanations, since the publication of *Lux Mundi* had aroused a cry "Nestorianism": to confess that Christ as man did *not* know was like splitting his personal unity, since as God he must know.

[1] *Our Lord's Knowledge as Man*, p. 39.
[2] In a pamphlet—*The Advancement of Our Lord's Humanity*.

There is yet one other interpretation of this passage that deserves attention. It was advanced by writers among whom was A. J. Mason, already alluded to more than once. He calls attention to the very special use of the word "Son" in this passage. Christ did but seldom refer to himself by this title—as recorded by the Synoptists—though it occurs rather more often in the Fourth Gospel (22 times). It is used of the Lord's special relations to the Father—as in the passage beginning at Mt. 11. 27. The term "Son of Man", on the other hand, refers rather to his relations with mankind and to the events connected with his mission in the world. Mason therefore concludes that it is not simply Christ's human nature that is referred to in Mk. 13. 32, nor even any restrictions imposed upon the divine Son in consequence of the Incarnation, but something which has reference to the eternal relations of Father and Son within the Blessed Trinity. That it is the cosmic Christ here referred to is further borne out, Mason believes, by the use of the words "in heaven". Thus it is an example of that subordination which Holy Scripture reveals to us. That there can be something known by the Father which even the Son does not share is as profound a mystery as when Christ says of the coveted position in the Kingdom desired by the sons of Zebedee, it "is not mine to give". If this explanation had been advanced by a conservative scholar in defence of the authenticity of the Old Testament it might be justly appraised as such; but since it was put forward by a scholar of great eminence who himself was led to a belief in the limitation of the Lord's knowledge, it deserves every attention.

## *Christ's Knowledge of the Future*

Our Lord's predictions for the future may be divided into two parts: his prognostication of the imminent destruction of Jerusalem, and his teaching with regard to the *parousia* and judgment. Neither of these classes of material provides any decisive evidence, one way or the other. In the case of the prophecies regarding Jerusalem, it is a matter known to every schoolboy that they came true in a grim and literal manner not many years after the Lord's Ascension. But, on the other hand, it may be urged that such a calamity could have been foreseen by anyone with eyes to see and to read the signs of the time—as Jesus clearly had, even on the human level; and it is, moreover, open to higher critics, particularly in respect of the Lucan apocalyptic material, to argue that its content has been coloured by the knowledge of the fulfilment of the prophecies which had already taken place when that Gospel was compiled. Even more tangled is the assessment of the remaining predictions. Nineteen hundred years have elapsed, and neither *parousia* nor judgment, nor consummation of the age, has taken place. Radical liberals have urged that our Lord's belief in angels, heavenly judgments, cosmic catastrophes, and the like, is actually a demonstration of the circumscribed character of his knowledge. The impression created by the apocalyptic material in the Gospels is certainly that all these things are close at hand, and, in our own day, serious theologians have come to the conclusion that the explanation of this material must be sought for in the field of "Realized Eschatology". It would be precarious for anyone to attempt to use such material in the study of Christ's knowledge, and, in fact, the subject scarcely figured in the controversy.

## Evidences of Christ's Supernatural Knowledge

The conservative scholars, far from contenting themselves with a defence of their beliefs regarding Christ's knowledge on the basis of *a priori* dogmas—as their opponents unkindly asserted—advanced a formidable array of empirical argumentation from the Gospel text upon which their conclusions were based. It will be our business to subject this evidence to the same criticism as was meted out to the former series of evidences.

Dr. Darwell Stone, one of the most rigorous protagonists of the conservative position, and the author of a number of the articles in the *Church Quarterly Review* dealing with books relating to Christology, drew up in an appended note to a later work a concise list of the Gospel instances of supernatural knowledge displayed by Christ. We could not do better, therefore, than adopt his summary as our own outline.[1]

Section 1. Mk. 2. 8. "And straightway Jesus, perceiving in his spirit that they so reasoned within themselves . . ."

Mk. 12. 15. " . . . But he, knowing their hypocrisy, said unto them, why tempt ye me?"

Mk. 14. 18. " . . . One of you shall betray me."

[1] *Outlines of Christian Doctrine*, appended note No. 23.

Mt. 12. 15. "And Jesus perceiving it withdrew from thence."
Mt. 12. 25. "And knowing their thoughts . . . ."
Lk. 6. 8. "But he knew their thoughts . . ."
Lk. 7. 39, 40. "And Jesus answering said unto him, Simon, I have somewhat to say unto thee . . ."
Jn. 2. 24 f. "But Jesus did not trust himself unto them, for that he knew all men, and because he needed not that anyone should bear witness concerning man; for he himself knew what was in man."
Jn. 6. 70, 71. "Did not I choose you twelve, and one of you is a devil? Now he spake of Judas . . ."
Jn. 13. 21–26. Further prophecy of Judas' betrayal.

Such examples do not of themselves carry a proof of supernatural knowledge. They could naturally be recounted of one who possessed to an extraordinary degree an insight into the minds of his fellow men. Persons endowed with gifts of this order can read infinitely more into the look, gesture, tone of voice of others than is generally possible, as in a grotesquely distorted manner the paranoiac detects the motive—often correctly—behind the unintentional word or deed. If the Freudians are only partially right in declaring that every single motion, however trivial, is not without its significance, the possibilities of reading the minds of others are practically unbounded.

2. Under his second heading, Dr. Stone groups Christ's predictions of his impending passion.

Mk. 8. 31. "And he began to teach them, that the Son of Man must suffer many things, and be rejected by the elders, and the chief priests, and the scribes, and be killed, and after three days rise again." Also Mk. 9. 31 and 10. 33, etc.

Mk. 9. 9. "And as they were coming down the mountain, he charged them that they should tell no man what things they had seen, save when the Son of Man should have risen again from the dead."

Jn. 2. 19–21. " . . . Destroy this temple, and in three days I will raise it up."

Jn. 12. 32, 33. "And I, if I be lifted up from the earth, will draw all men unto myself . . . This he said, signifying by what manner of death he should die."

Jn. 13. 1–3. "Now before the feast of the Passover, Jesus knowing that his hour was come that he should depart out of this world . . ."

Jn. 18. 4. "Jesus, therefore, knowing all things that were coming upon him, went forth . . ."

It must have been obvious to our Lord, practically from the outset of his ministry, that the course of action adopted by him and, the form of his teaching, would in due course bring down upon him the only fate that might be expected at the hands of the Jewish authorities. Furthermore, if his reflections upon his mission were coloured, as many have thought, with the picture of the Suffering Servant of Isaiah, there would be nothing remarkable about the predictions of his own sufferings and death.

Section 3. Mk. 5. 30. " And straightway Jesus, perceiving in himself that the power proceeding from him had gone forth."

4. Jn. 11. 11, 14. "These things spake he: and after this he saith unto them, our friend Lazarus is fallen asleep . . . Then Jesus therefore said unto them plainly, Lazarus is dead."

5. Jn. 1. 48–50. "Nathanael said unto him, Whence knowest thou me? Jesus answered and said unto him, before Philip called thee, when thou wast under the fig tree I saw thee."

6. Jn. 4. 17, 18. " . . . For thou hast had five husbands; and he whom thou now hast is not thy husband."

7. Mt. 17. 27. " . . . Go thou to the sea, and cast a hook, and take up the fish that first cometh up; and when thou hast opened his mouth, thou shalt find a shekel: that take, and give unto them for me and thee."

8. Mk. 11. 2. "Go your way into the village that is over against you: and straightway as ye enter into it, ye shall find a colt tied, whereon no man ever yet sat."

Mk. 14. 13. "And he sendeth two of his disciples, and saith unto them, go into the city, and there shall meet you a man bearing a pitcher of water."

It is only fair to point out that an equally possible explanation of these two passages is that they constitute our Lord's carefully laid plans for the two vital acts in the drama of his last days upon earth, and hence do not in the least carry with them any suggestion of supernatural knowledge.

Mk. 14. 30. " . . . Thou to-day, even this night, before the cock crow twice, shalt deny me thrice."

This evidence taken together provides a goodly array of proof-texts in support of the view that Christ was in possession of a knowledge of a higher order than that enjoyed by other men. It does not demonstrate his omniscience, but the fact that he had at his command when circumstances and the good of others demanded it, an access of springs of knowledge belonging only to God himself, and if this material be taken at its face value, it would be hazardous to declare in the face of it that Jesus was truly ignorant in any given circumstance. Such would be the verdict in the court of law.

# 4

## CONCERNING CHRIST'S KNOWLEDGE AND AUTHORITY

IT has been shown how the advent of higher criticism raised the question of our Lord's knowledge, by establishing certain conclusions which were in opposition to the traditional beliefs accepted by Christ in common with his contemporaries. The admission that our Lord may not have enjoyed that insight into history now at the disposal of modern students, raised difficulties with regard to the veracity and finality of all his teaching, and the verity of his sinlessness, which topics form the subject of the present chapter. Nevertheless, the examination of this controversy, even in these larger aspects, would be lost labour were it not set in relief against the larger background of the Christological crisis as a whole. Our purpose will have failed if it be not seen that this controversy was the given point—dictated by many historical circumstances—at which the tension (to use the hackneyed word) between the two Christological postulates of the age became acute. It was no human nature, related to the Divine Logos in some abstruse metaphysical manner which was ignorant of the day of judgment or the Maccabean date of Ps. 110, but the One Person, the Son of God.

We begin, then, at the point reached in the preceding chapter. Upon the basis of the evidence set out in that chapter were established the two opposing beliefs regarding the content of Christ's mind. Scholars of the liberal type arrived at the view that not only was his knowledge limited in regard to certain facts of a historical nature but that his mind was in general restricted to the measure of a normal human intelligence. In opposition to this, conservative writers deduced the conclusion that, practically speaking, the mind of Christ was unlimited in the knowledge which it did, or could, possess. The fact that the discussion was always complicated by the intrusion of many issues and interests, strictly speaking irrelevant to the objective study of the Gospel evidence, renders it often a most difficult task to discern the wood from the trees. It will be convenient therefore to continue the method already employed in the preceding chapter. The plan adopted here will be to treat first of the various interpretations which were advanced to account for the facts of the Gospel records on the subject, and in later sections of the chapter to treat of the bearing of such interpretations upon the Lord's authority and sinlessness.

*Adjudication of the Gospel Material*

The superficially contradictory nature of the Gospel picture of Jesus—as one who knows the whereabouts of absent friends, and yet asks questions for the most trivial information—makes it possible for a wide variety of interpretations and explanations to be promoted, each with some degree of verisimilitude; and in these times, not a few such explanations were trumpeted abroad as bestowing a rationale of all the known facts.

There are, to begin with, two thoroughgoing views to be found at either end of the scale. They are arrived at, and maintain their self-consistency, by waving aside, rightly or wrongly, all the evidence which would point in the opposite direction to which their verdict points.

On the one hand, to those who accept the presuppositions of, follow the methods of, and embrace the conclusions of radical German criticism—be they disciples of such diverse scholars as Wrede, Bousset, Schweitzer or J. Weiss—there can be but one answer: Jesus was a man, possessing a finite human intelligence and nothing more. For them there is no Christological problem at all; their only problem is an historical one, the necessity of explaining how it happened that the man Jesus came to be looked upon as God the Son and how such divine powers as supernatural knowledge ever came to be attributed to him. Those who hold such a view—and in the 'nineties, they were very few indeed—would argue that several of the most striking instances of Christ's higher knowledge, such as are associated with Nathanael, the woman of Samaria, the death of Lazarus, and the ascription of complete insight into men's minds (Jn. 2. 24–25), are located in the Fourth Gospel, and may therefore be written off at once by all those who are pleased to regard themselves as "sound" critics. Of the rest, some examples of superhuman knowledge are to be explained as misunderstandings of the facts (for instance, Christ's instructions regarding the colt and the man bearing the pitcher of water—which in reality were pre-arranged plans); whilst others are embellishments of a gift, possessed by Christ like other prophets in virtue of the pureness of his mind, of insight into human character and motives. Such a view, let it be remembered, is prompted and executed on the *a priori* assumption that the miraculous—even though absolutely speaking it *can* happen—in actual fact does not occur.

Such an interpretation of the Gospel record would therefore be held irrespective of the array of evidence for supernatural knowledge which might be gathered together. This outlook did not make any general appearance, in its naked form at any rate, in the early years of the controversy, though it did take its place as a recognized point of view in the following decade in liberal theology of a more developed type. In the early controversy the anti-miraculous outlook played the part of a motive, hidden like the true motive in a dream, its true character being disguised, "displaced", from the dreamer's consciousness under the form of other symbols and desires. Defence of the rights of historical criticism, defence of the genuineness of Christ's humanity—as against a docetic scholasticism, defence of the literal interpretation of the Gospels; these were the good and legitimate aims through the exaggeration of which and under the disguise of which, the humanism of the time worked for mastery. The majority of liberals, both Anglican and Free Church, were in those early years eager to prove the limitation of Christ's knowledge, not by hacking out pieces from the Gospel record, but by interpreting the documents as they stood, "in their plain meaning", to quote a phrase which is often met with.

The situation was far different in regard to the point of view at the opposite end of the scale; for to say the least of it, it had on its side all the forces of religious conservatism, human inertia, and the perennial resistance against the necessity to rethink one's whole intellectual position from a new standpoint. Like the view already considered, it was based on an *a priori* assumption, in this case, that the union of the two natures in Christ to constitute one single person must result in the communication of part at any rate of the content of the divine mind to the human: that Jesus Christ had access to the limitless knowledge of God. The misuse of the epithet *a priori* has already been discussed; here it is employed to condemn no one; but a warning must be here given, which will later be fully explained, that the dogma of Christ's human omniscience resulting from the hypostatic union—although it does in fact constitute an element in the old scholastic theology—was at this time grounded upon a particular view of the nature of personality as being equivalent to consciousness, and hence to thinkers of this time, as will appear from many angles, the union of natures would involve communication of knowledge. If men are prepared to accept the record of the miraculous at its face value, as of course conservative scholars were, a far better case can be made out to corroborate the ascription of omniscience to Christ from the Gospels than is generally supposed. Certainly, if its presuppositions be granted, it rivals the former extreme view in the matter of consistency of application. The apparent exception admitted by Christ, Mk. 13. 32, is introduced in such a manner as to suggest that it is somewhat abnormal and surprising in his case. The large number of positive examples of supernatural knowledge is balanced by no explicit statements to the contrary, but only by negative assumptions drawn from his requests for information, which are always susceptible of other interpretations. He who knew the time of the death of Lazarus can scarcely be supposed to have been ignorant of so slight a detail as the location of his sepulchre—at least, in a court of law one would have great difficulty in establishing a presumption of ignorance in the light of such circumstantial evidence.

Such then was the conservative attitude towards the subject, defended at this time with all the vehemence and literary persuasiveness which any religious issue could provoke. Yet even so, its defence was undertaken to a very large extent in pamphlets and articles; for with one or two striking exceptions the period even as a whole produced very few major works on Christology by out-and-out conservative scholars. There was Alfred Mortimer's *Catholic Faith and Practice*, a manual of very dogmatic theology in two volumes, written, from the Anglo-Catholic point of view, in America, and in 1896, and from the same country also came W. G. Shedd's *Dogmatic Theology* (1889), in two even larger volumes, from the traditional Calvinist view. In Britain, the most impressive defence was that made in the current articles on the relevant works in the *Church Quarterly Review*, a full list of which appears in the bibliography.

The conservative position, however, was not presented in a uniform manner by all its protagonists; for certain modifications in it were admitted by some in order to offer a tentative solution to the problem in hand, though it must be pointed out that, strictly speaking, for the thoroughgoing conservative as for the thoroughgoing critic there is no problem. For him, Christ is both omniscient and infallible. Christ has spoken and there is nothing more that man can say to alter or modify it.

Conservative scholars may be divided first in regard to the amount of actual knowledge believed to have been in the possession of the Incarnate Christ. Some, as Darwell Stone, teach with Aquinas that Christ's human mind was possessed of the knowledge of every actual fact but not of every potential fact, whilst others teach that his mind was conscious only of those facts in the divine omniscience which were capable of being understood by a finite intelligence. The majority of traditionalist Christians, let it be remembered, did not speculate upon these matters at all, being content with a declaration of the supernatural character of the Lord's knowledge.

With regard to the manner in which this knowledge was present to Christ's human mind: Some held that the knowledge which he possessed in virtue of the hypostatic union was always fully present to his consciousness, as a complete reality, and hence that his thinking was never discursive in character as ours is, since every relative fact in a given situation was simultaneously present to him. Others, on the other hand—for example, the reviewer of H. C. Powell's "Principle of the Incarnation" in *Church Quarterly Review*, and A. H. Strong, *Systematic Theology*, New York, 1886; *Outlines of Systematic Theology*, New York, 1908—held that this supernatural knowledge was possessed by him after the manner of latent memory, his actual consciousness being limited and discursive, as is ours, and yet at the same time possessing this infinite reservoir upon which he could draw when occasion arose for him to do so. There was also the view of Juxtaposition, namely, that Christ was both omniscient and limited simultaneously, the relation of the two being part of the mystery of the Incarnation which man may not fathom; of this view more will be said later.

An interesting example of the more irregular theories and explanations which were offered to account for the facts of Christ's knowledge is to be found in a slight pamphlet by G. J. A. D'Arcy, *The Human Mind of Our Lord*. The mind of man, he declares, consists of two sections, the objective and the subjective or in the language of modern psychology, the supraliminal and the subliminal consciousness. The range of our subjective mind is very vast: it may gain by a flash of intuition what would otherwise take years to attain: it is in fact our sixth sense—which the writer then proceeds to eulogize in the following manner: "There is no language under the sun with which it is not acquainted: there is no system of philosophy with which it cannot deal, in the accurate terms of that philosophy: to it, the past, the present, and the future are alike open: neither time nor space can bind it down: it can read the thoughts of others easily: it can see even through closed books and sealed letters: and in fact it is hardly too much to say that the memory of the subjective mind is perfect, at all events there is every indication that this is the case.[1] What then of the sixth sense of Christ? "In our Lord's own case, however, we are not dealing with fallen, but unfallen human nature, and therefore one might reasonably expect to find in his Incarnate life a perfect synchronization of both the objective and the subjective mind. That is to say, in his human mind he stands forth different from all other men, and as he willed, able to use either side of his mind, according to what seemed the needful circumstances of the moment."[2] Christ was thus able to call on this limitless power as he willed, and his use of it shows the perfect powers and possibilities of manhood. One can only hope and trust that this is not a fair sample of what happens when theologians dabble in contemporary science. In case anyone should observe a superficial resemblance between this theory and that advanced some years later by Dr. Sanday, it should be pointed out that the two are really quite different in character. D'Arcy's view is concerned solely with the human faculties of Jesus, whilst Sanday is engaged by the relations of divine and human in Christ's Person, and at so late a date was scarcely at all interested in the question of our Lord's knowledge as the earlier writers.

Another modification of the conservative position which was advanced at this time was that the divine and the human manner of knowing are so completely different that they could co-exist within one person without causing any confusion or interference with the latter. Such a view was proposed by a writer already alluded to, H. C. Powell, in his *The Principle of the Incarnation*

---

[1] *The Human Mind of Our Lord*, p. 7.
[2] *Ibid.*, p. 8.

(1896). The upshot of a tedious exposition couched in what Sanday called "rather disreputable philosophy" is as follows: The human consciousness cannot possess knowledge without conscious attention, induction, and comparison; knowledge is proportionate to our faculties (part I, ch. I). The human understanding only functions in a strictly discursive manner, and can only appreciate matters when split up into component parts. He makes much use of the conception of the "fettered mind". Owing to these facts of its nature, then, the human understanding cannot have any positive knowledge of things in the infinite (ch. 2). Nor is our imagination a widening of our field of knowledge into the infinite scale, but simply a deepening of consciousness (ch. 3). As God's knowledge does not come to him through faculties, it must be co-eternal with him, and indivisible from him; there must therefore be a correlation between the divine knowledge and the divine manner of knowing; hence there must be as great a difference between his manner of knowing and our manner of knowing as there is between his knowledge and ours (ch. 4). The two knowledges possessed by Christ—different in kind, not just in degree—could be possessed by a single "Ego" without embarrassment to either.[1]

## Liberal Solutions to the Problem

At this time, the majority of English liberal scholars, whilst all too ready to cast off what was believed to be the heavy yoke of scholastic theology, were nevertheless unwilling to embrace the excesses of Teutonic rationalism. They were for the most part men whose theology and piety were grounded in Patristic or Reformation classics, and in the conviction that Jesus Christ was divine, and no mere human prophet—it was this belief that gave to the problem in hand its vital urgency for them. Their approach to the problem, therefore, took the form of applying the historical method to the Gospel evidence, in a reverent and sympathetic manner, in order to discover precisely what the New Testament did say about Christ's knowledge, and to frame their Christology upon their findings, rather than upon preconceived theories, as the humanists and conservatives appeared to do.

Taking the Gospels, therefore, at their face value, without skimping or trifling with any portion of their witness, the following

[1] Based upon Mansel's theory of human inability to conceive of the infinite.—Bampton Lectures, 1858.

facts emerged. It was first observed that on numerous occasions Christ is represented as displaying a supernormal knowledge. These instances are never the disclosure of information which it would otherwise have been impossible for any other human being to know. Not only are they never revelations of hidden historical or scientific truths; they are generally of a kind of knowledge displayed by others who have been attributed with supernatural powers: in other words, though they transcend the bounds of normal human knowledge, they never in their nature transcend the bounds of normal human intelligence.

It appeared equally plain that on other occasions Christ manifested a human limitation of knowledge. He admitted ignorance even of the day and hour of his own Advent. "Along with this goes the fact that he makes enquiries and manifests surprise; but that in doing so he was acting a part is credible only to the incurably docetic mind". Strong language for so fair-minded a scholar as H. R. Mackintosh.[1]

It was furthermore noticed that not a few of the instances belonging to one category are juxtaposed by the Evangelists, without any apparent embarrassment, to examples belonging to the other category. Thus, for instance, we read in Mk. 5. 30 that Jesus perceives that power has gone out from himself to heal the woman; yet he is apparently obliged to ask, "Who touched my garments"? Again, to quote the best known example, Jesus knows from a distance of the death of his friend Lazarus; yet he must ask his sisters, "Where have ye laid him"?

We consider first a view which, though it was put forward solely by conservative scholars, has been postponed to this point as it is an attempt to give a due place to both sets of evidence. In the second chapter, a method was described in which the elements in the Gospel record relating to Christ's divine powers are placed side by side with the evidences for his human weakness and limitation. Further speculation into the "Hows" and "Whys" is rejected as irreverent intrusion into the mystery of God's saving acts. This has ever been regarded as a laudable approach to the study of Christ's Person, and in a new form has many able exponents in our own day. It had little to commend itself to the prying mood of the nineteenth century; but, to refrain from speculation and rationalization is one thing: it is quite another

[1] *The Person of Jesus Christ*, 1912, p. 13, also p. 397. See also P. T. Forsyth, *Person and Place*, ch. XI.

matter when the juxtapositing is carried into literal conclusions. It was declared that Christ was simultaneously omniscient and limited in knowledge. Such a declaration ostensibly accounts for all the Gospel facts, and in a manner conformable with the principle of the Chalcedonian definition. At bottom, however, it is not different from the normal conservative standpoint in any particular except its pretentions. It is argued by those who support it that whereas Christ understood many things by infused or intuitive knowledge, yet it may none the less be truly said that he "came to know" these things in the normal human manner, by questioning and observation. For similes in justification of this view we are pointed to the fact that lessons, that a man learns theoretically from his teachers, may be as truly said to be learned afresh when the man discovers the truths he has been taught before by experience in the hard school of life. Again, conclusions relating to surveying may first be calculated on paper by the use of mathematics, the results being afterwards tested and proved with the theodolite. It was objected by liberal scholars that here is a distinction without a difference, and that the view is in fact equivalent to saying that Christ was omniscient. To say that Christ possessed an omniscient and a limited knowledge simultaneously, and that he could discover afresh what he knew already was likened, not altogether happily, to the famous story of the Irishman who cut two holes in his door, a large hole for the cat to get through, and a small hole for the kitten to go through. The view was therefore discarded as useless and a scholastic blind alley by those scholars who were anxious to set up a Christology that would be truly based upon the facts of Scripture, and the dictates of a logic uncompromised by the mere playing with words which had little relation to human experience.

If the method thus described were untenable—the simultaneous possession of omniscience and limitation—it followed that one, and only one, of the two was the normal condition of the Lord's conscious mind. The idea was never seriously entertained that a normal state of omniscience in the mind of Christ was subject to numerous lapses of memory or to sporadic interruptions of function. The idea would have been grotesque; and in any case, those who professed belief in his omniscience had other explanations of the seeming evidences of ignorance.

It followed then that the norm of the Lord's conscious mind

was the state of limitation. This seemed the logical explanation of the facts, and had infinite merit apart from that in that it satisfied the needs of the liberal theology of the time, still struggling to free itself from traditional Apollinarianism, as it believed. It did away at one stroke with a miraculous attribute of Christ's Person, thus easing the problem of apologetics in a world long impatient of the supernatural. It also provided a straightforward explanation of how it came about that Jesus embraced erroneous views with regard to the authorship of Old Testament Scriptures: they still had to show how Christ could be wrong about the authorship of Deuteronomy and right of necessity when he made a pronouncement about sin or the day of judgment; but it was so gratifying to have solved the immediate problem, that the implications of the solution could be worked out in their own time. The above therefore became the standard liberal interpretation of the Gospel record, and was argued out by every work dealing in any degree with Christology at this time, with always the same procession of proof-texts *ad nauseam*.

It is now difficult to recapture the spirit of the decade under discussion, and to appreciate with what fervour men fought for the admission of the truly human character of Christ's mind. Every stone laid down and tried by higher criticism was to them a victory for science and enlightenment over superstition and tradition. Higher criticism to-day is almost universally recognized, outside the Roman Church, as an invaluable and necessary instrument in the hands of the Christian exegete; but particular pronouncements of higher critics are not now regarded with that awe bestowed upon them as on *ex cathedra* utterances. It is now widely recognised, in fact, that many such conclusions, although they have not yet been exhaustively criticized, were too readily erected upon the shifting sands of particular views regarding the evolution of religious truth, that in many cases they are braced together by evidence of a type which could never be countenanced in any other branch of scientific research. But in the period, every result established by German higher criticism was, particularly if it referred to the Old Testament, taken in deadly earnest—the time had not yet come when men would be equally impressed by radical theories relating to the New Testament. To all this, the traditional view of Christ's omniscience was a serious embarrassment which had to be faced—and set aside.

To return to the reconstruction, however. Christ could not be simultaneously omniscient and limited in knowledge; nor could the instances of limitation be regarded as interruptions of a state of omniscience; the normal and habitual state of his mind must therefore be limited; that was the point reached above. What then of the evidence of his supernatural knowledge?—if that too is to be taken as literally as the evidence of his limitation. In the first place, no doubt the perfection of Christ's soul rendered his intuition and mental insight—especially into human character and motives—extraordinarily clear and acute. It was, none the less, pointed out with force by these early liberals that such human qualities would not of themselves account for some of the more striking illustrations of higher knowledge furnished by the Gospels, for which a definitely supernatural explanation must be sought.

We have already noted how such instances of higher insight, though they transcended human knowledge, never transcended human intelligence. His supernatural knowledge was never at random, it was always selective in character; and hence it was never of a type which would violate on the one hand the normal psychological processes of his own mind, nor scandalize the onlookers. These two points follow directly from the fact of its being within the range of human intelligence. To become aware of the death of a friend, for example, would, on the one hand, not override the normal mental activities of a man, and would, on the other hand, be a fact intelligible to those with whom it was discussed, whereas, suddenly to become aware of the nature of molecular structure, might not only derange his own mental activities but would also be unintelligible and incongruous to the hearers as well.

Such knowledge, then, even though bestowed upon his human mind in a supernatural manner was such as any man of his age might through other and normal channels have become the possessor, and therefore such higher insight never divested him of his truly human character and state of life, especially as regards his human mind. It was on this guarantee of non-interference with Christ's humanity that this view gained admittance to theological recognition at that time. For such knowledge is never found to differ in kind from that displayed by other miraculously endowed persons—whose true human nature could scarcely be impeached. Gore himself pointed out[1] that this knowledge is always

[1] Bampton Lectures, p. 147.

of the type vouchsafed to prophets and apostles. For example: Jesus perceived the hypocrisy of Scribes and Pharisees—Peter and John perceived the guile of Simon Magus. Jesus foresaw his passion—Agabus prophesied the imprisonment of St. Paul.

The question of "miracles" will be dealt with fully in later chapters. It must here be noticed, however, how the controversy regarding Christ's knowledge is part of the general trend of opinion against the miraculous—for supernatural knowledge is certainly a "miracle". The ways of approach to the present subject did in fact run strictly parallel to the manner in which miracle was dealt with. Rationalists said there were no miracles at all: conservatives said Christ was omnipotent—there are the two extreme views. Moderate liberals said there were miracles, but like Christ's supernatural knowledge in particular, they were selective, limited in character and circumstance, e.g. "He could there do no mighty work".

There are, however, certain questions of a more technical and searching character which must be asked in connexion with the right-wing liberal view already outlined, and to which no clear answers were forthcoming. We are presented with a Christ whose normal mental condition was a state of circumscription and limitation, who, none the less, from time to time manifests a knowledge of a higher character. In the first place "How"? It is not easy to envisage the possibility of a circumscribed human consciousness consciously willing itself to acquire a knowledge of which it already knows nothing. Hence it was generally conceded that this supernatural knowledge was communicated to Christ by God from outside the limited consciousness of the Incarnate. Christ's faith and his prayer are generally regarded as the channels through which such a communication was made possible and effective. But this doctrine can be stated in such a way as to make it appear that the supernatural knowledge is a mere *donum superadditum*, bestowed gratuitously from without—as it might be upon any man—without any essential dependence upon the fact that Christ partook of the divine Nature. Even less satisfactory, in the second place, were the answers given in reply to the query "Why"?—What is the point and significance of this gift which Christ possessed? If the divine Glory was revealed primarily—if not exclusively—through the human nature of Christ (a belief which was rapidly gaining ground at the time), what relevance have the examples of supernatural knowledge? Attempts were made to relate the manifestation of supernatural knowledge to the matter of his infallibility, and it is for this reason that the explanations offered by these liberal scholars for the "How" and "Why" of Christ's supernatural knowledge are postponed to the section dealing specifically with his authority as a teacher. This section will therefore be concluded with two remarks, the full force of which will be appreciated in due course.

Although on the surface the early liberal view here described is the most coincidental with the Gospel evidence, in reality it is fraught with more difficulties than the conservative and radical views put together. The attempts to draw from such a ground-plan a clearly integrated Christology dissolved largely owing to the failure to account adequately for the supernatural element, which was left high and dry without sufficient explanation.

Such a Christology denied Christ's historical and scientific infallibility whilst defending his spiritual infallibility. Later and more radical liberals were to deny both. In this they were more logical than their forerunners; for though denying human ignorance to Christ, liberal principles, once admitted, led yet further, as is amply shown by the arbitrary nature of their mediating theories.

## Three Doctrines at Stake

It has been made clear from the first that the controversy which arose in regard to the knowledge possessed by our Lord was no mere academic parley. The discussion whether Jesus did or did not possess a limited human intelligence was never conducted with that degree of refined good humour with which the savants would debate the merits of Berlioz or the date of the burning of Jericho. It was urged with deep conviction by traditionalist scholars that an admission of limitation in Christ's range of knowledge would deal a shattering blow to three fundamental Christian doctrines: the unity of Christ's Person, the authority of his teaching, and the sinlessness of his character. Nor must it be supposed that liberal theologians were in any way blind to these dangers; they were equally alive to the new problems raised by their postulates. But they had arrived at their conclusions by processes which they believed to be both scientific and rational, and they were prepared to abide by them whatever the cost, and to seek for new ways of apprehending and explaining the old truths relating to Christ's Person and work.

The challenge made in the name of the three above-mentioned doctrines and the liberal replies will be considered in turn. The conservative contention of how the new admission affected the doctrine will first be reviewed, and then the attempted solutions offered in reply to it.

## Of the Unity of Christ's Person

The statement that the recent apprehension of certain facts militates against ancient dogmatic presuppositions was one calculated to evoke a very different degree of sympathy from varying schools of opinion within our period. To the conservative scholar—especially of Catholic leanings—the Church in its primitive days and early centuries, being nearest to the actual events of Christ's life, and being in the full vigour of its purity and youth, must have been in a situation, impossible to be repeated, of knowing and understanding fully all those relevant facts relating to Christ upon which dogmatic statements regarding him must be built. Nor was the world into which the Gospel came one of baneful ignorance and stupidity: it was a world that, though far inferior to our own in regard to the empirical sciences, possessed none the less a rich and vigorous intellectual life; a world far more devoted to, and so far more adept at, the affairs of speculative reason than is our own, and hence peculiarly suited to be the cradle of Christian theology. Therefore it would be argued that the notion that we now possess new data—unearthed by scientific research—which may in any important degree modify the dogmatic conclusions formulated of old is rejected as sheer arrogance. To the liberal, on the other hand, the present was virtually a new Apostolic age. New methods of study and exegesis had arisen; new facts had been brought to light, and the process of dogma-making could not do better than begin all over again. Such a new world did the nineteenth century believe itself to be, that a new heaven in theology was the very least which could be expected to match it. Most liberal scholars, even of the later and more radical variety, were eager to admit that the substance of what the Creed and Councils had said was true, that they had in fact furnished a picture of the nature of Christ that did adequate justice to his position in the religious life of man; but, when it came to a matter of specific dogmas, they were not prepared to surrender one iota of what they believed to be the fruit of historical investigation to appease the demands of Patristic or Scholastic logic.

All this has particular relevance to the first doctrinal—as opposed to exegetical—argument which conservative theologians advanced against the liberal postulate of Christ's limitation of knowledge. For it illustrates how an argument which to one school of thought may be convincing or even decisive may to another appear flimsy or even irrelevant.

It was maintained, then, that the union of God and man in Christ, the Logos being made one with an impersonal manhood, entailed the presence within his Person of one single self-conscious subject. Such a subject could not be furnished by the impersonal humanity but only by the Logos himself, who being divine was of necessity omniscient, however much, and in whatever manner, this omniscience was modified in its expression and application by the circumstances of the life which Christ lived. It was therefore urged that to attribute ignorance on any matter to Christ posits either ignorance on the part of the Divine Logos himself—which they rejected as impossible—or else the existence alongside the omniscient self-consciousness of the Logos of a finite human centre of thought, living its own life and thinking its own thoughts; such a view would appear to cast away every vestige of the hypostatic union, revealing itself as a pure form of Nestorianism. The cry of "Nestorianism" was in fact a useful tool in the early stages of the controversy, as no one desired a divided Christ, and it appears prominently as an argument against the new Christology, particularly in the batch of pamphlets which *Lux Mundi* brought down upon itself. As will be seen in the following chapter, Dr. Gore was accused of Nestorianism even several years later, when it should have been crystal clear to all that that was precisely the last heresy that he was likely to fall into. But the contention itself, that the new admission militated against the hypostatic union, still held good for many scholars at a much later date. For unable to accept the liberal short-cut solution (to be described in the next chapter), the difficulty of positing two separate mental lives still held good. The voice which spoke with unwitting ignorance, and the mind which wrestled in limitation and obscurity, could not be the voice and the mind of God.

The conservative argument from this doctrine is advanced in force in one of the paragraphs of a weighty declaration made by a group of Christian thinkers of the Anglican communion at the height of the controversy. As was frequently the case in such matters, their primary object appears to have been the defence of the historicity of the Bible against the growing threats of higher criticism. But the Christological issue comes plainly into view as an integral part of their standpoint as a whole.

### Declaration on Inspiration of Holy Scripture

Paragraph No. 6 reads as follows:
"Since the human mind of our Lord was inseparably united to the eternal word, and was perfectly illuminated by the Holy Spirit in the discharge of his office as teacher, he could not be deceived, nor be the source of deception, nor intend to teach, even incidentally, for fact what was not fact". There is an immediate reference here to the economic view suggested in *Lux Mundi* that even had he known, he would not have disclosed. But the criticism is meant to hold good equally whether he were consciously or unconsciously giving utterance to erroneous statements on historical matters.

It is interesting to observe the signatories to the declaration:
"G. Body; H. R. Bramley; W. Bright; T. T. Carter; W. M. G. Ducat; C. W. Furse; D. Greig; C. E. Hammond; W. H. Hutchings; J. O. Johnston; E. C. Lowe; P. G. Medd; W. C. E. Newbolt; F. W. Puller; B. W. Randolph; D. Stone; R. J. Wilson; A. J. Worlledge".

A distinguished company, to be sure.[1]

The liberal reply to this argument, an argument whose full force it honestly attempted to meet, took an indirect form which will constitute the subject of the next chapter. It was concerned to show that there need be no cleavage whatsoever between God and man—as is above inferred—and it achieved this by proposing that the Logos himself partook in all those limitations in which a human being exists; this, it was argued, was the price which the Son of God paid in becoming man for our salvation.

Before passing to the next subject, one further conservative argument in support of a belief in Christ's omniscience should be noted. It is of a strictly doctrinal character and hence comes into place here rather than in the evaluation of Gospel evidences. By its form it was calculated to make less impression at the time than any argument could possibly have done.

[1] Quoted from Ven. W. H. Hutchings—*Life and Letters of T. T. Carter*, 1903, pp. 196–197.

It was suggested that, on the one hand, it was incongruous for the Son of God to be ignorant, quite apart from the metaphysical difficulties involved in such a supposition, and on the other hand, it befitted the dignity of Christ's Person that his human mind should have been endowed with divine gifts, up to the limit of its capacity—hence his omniscience. Arguments from "congruity" had played a great part in the debates of the schoolmen. By congruity, they had decided that the planets moved in circular orbits; by congruity it had been taught [1] that the end of the world would take place when the sun is at its zenith! It was poignantly observed by more than one writer [2] that if we had to rely solely upon this argument for our knowledge of Christ's earthly life, we could never accept the fact of his crucifixion, since that is practically the most incongruous thing we could have imagined to have befallen the Only begotten Son of God.

## *Of Christ's Authority as a Teacher*

Whatever we may look upon as the focal point of Christ's saving acts, whether the Cross, the Resurrection, the Incarnation itself, or Christ's example, it is quite clear that his teaching is a factor of major importance. Through his words, not simply in general teaching as the Sermon on the Mount, but in his reaction to every request and situation of life, our Lord delivered his vital message for mankind. Even if it be contended that the all-important factor was the set of acts through which the drama of his life passed, it still remains true that what we know of the meaning of events such as the crucifixion largely depends upon what he himself taught us about them.

Christ's teaching is a part of what he bestowed upon mankind by his Incarnation; hence to the Christologian it is specifically part of the doctrine of the *work* of Christ, in distinction to the doctrine of his Person, and hence in order to appreciate the very dissimilar attitudes which were adopted in regard to Christ's authority, it is necessary to take the subject in hand from the general point of view of soteriology. Speaking broadly, interest in soteriology was at a low ebb at this period. Certainly the subject was never in the foreground of theology: mankind was far too busily engaged in trying to save itself to worry much about the

[1] E.g. by the writer of St. Thomas in the supplement to the *Summa Theol.*
[2] E.g. W. S. Swayne: *Our Lord's Knowledge as Man.*

salvation offered by God. This indifference from without permeated to the very heart of Christian Theology. It might also be said to be the most obvious characteristic of all liberal theology that it not only failed to lay the emphasis upon the initiative taken by God on man's behalf, it positively ignored it. There are, of course, numbers of exceptions to this rule during the period, such as Dale and Forsyth, but these exceptions only show up more clearly what was the general situation at that time. Furthermore, there were few theologians, liberal or conservative, who in any measure realized the full soteriological implications of the Christological crisis—except in the particular question of Christ's authority and sinlessness. Besides this, there was a growing dislike for, and consequent drift away from, the traditional theories of the atonement—both Catholic and Protestant.

Christ had ever been regarded in Christian thought, and was so at this time by conservative thinkers, as one whose word was a final declaration of God's will for men, an unquestionable authority upon religious and moral issues, and whose life was a unique and perfect expression of the Father's will, and man's destiny. The liberal scholars of the early part of the period also paid great homage to these beliefs, and approached the subject with great care and reverence. It might therefore have been imagined that both parties would have striven to place the infallible word of Christ upon as secure a dogmatic basis as could possibly be found. The scales were not, however, balanced in the controversy as might have been supposed. The indifference of liberalism to the doctrine of Christ's verbal infallibility is not only shown by the refusal to accept this consideration as a determinant in the assessment of Christ's knowledge, but also by the half-hearted way in which adequate demonstrations of his authority were sought for. The later abandonment by radical liberalism of any and all formal doctrines of Christ's infallibility (in the verbal sense) was not simply a logical sequence built upon the principles of earlier writers, it was a gesture of honesty, which others had been too terrified to make.

An age, a Church, or a school of thought is naturally prone to construct its Christology in such a way that its Lord and Master is seen to be most suited to fulfil that part of his mission which it considers to be most important. Thus an age in which reason is regarded as paramount and which consequently emphasizes the teaching of truth as Christ's principal function will tend to lay the stress upon the supernatural sources of knowledge possessed by the Lord. A school which is pre-eminently absorbed in Christ's redemptive mission will take as his prime attributes his unity with God, the inclusiveness of his humanity, and the purity of the oblation which he offered. A group which interests itself primarily in morality and the uplifting of human life will tend to extol the example of Christ, his virtues, sinless character, and the completeness of his moral victory. Whilst an individual whose chief need and interest is inspiration towards a fuller communion with God will concentrate upon Christ's consciousness of unique sonship, and the realities of his spiritual experience.

It would be generally conceded that our period exhibited a steady movement away from the first two of these interests towards the second pair. This transition had already been under way for many years. *Essays and Reviews*, Seeley's *Ecce Homo*, and the writings of Matthew Arnold were a few of the earlier milestones in the transition. In fact, as will appear, the conservative stand which was made on the question of Christ's authority was virtually the manning of a last strong-point in the protracted struggle: that strong-point was never assaulted; it was passed by in the onrush, and its significance reduced through indifference. Attention and interest, and in consequence that lack of due proportion in theology which is always the high-road to heresy, was moving away from what had hitherto been regarded as the principal positive works of Christ. Allusion has already been made to the neglect of the fundamental principle of grace—the initiative taken by God for man's salvation, an offer made freely and undeservedly. In considerable sections even of the Evangelical Churches the redemptive work of Christ could only be made palatable when it was served up in the form of a mild mysticism—which had a certain vogue at the turn of the century.[1] But equally striking was the impatience of the period of any form of authority or coercion from without. When treating, a short while back, of the supposed jeopardy to the hypostatic union, it was urged that liberals regarded themselves as competent judges of what was Christian truth and what was not. In the same manner, their insistence that the mind of man must be free to think, without any shackles from the past—and now, by the aid of his science, he was thinking as never before—made it inevitable that the conservative argument regarding the infallibility of Christ (presently

[1] E.g. Dr. Inge's Bampton Lectures, and the writings of von Hügel.

to be dealt with) for the most part fell on deaf ears. It was not that men were at that moment consciously prepared to reject Christ's authority as a divinely inspired teacher, as they would be prepared peremptorily to cast off the authoritative dictates of any other voice from the pre-scientific era (be it literally inspired Bible or infallible Pope), but the concept of Christ as a revealer of otherwise unknowable truths made little appeal to them. This at first may appear a strange fact; a paradox, indeed, that in an age in which objective or factual truths were demanded as the matter and the conclusion of every topic, there should have been so little enthusiasm for a Christ who was set forth as the bestower upon men of exact and objective facts in the subject-matter of religion. To those thinkers to whom Christ is a revealer of truths—not simply truth, in some broad sense—the evaluation of the basis of his infallibility is of the highest moment. To those, on the other hand, who do not look upon Christ as a super-oracle the question is not altogether relevant; hence the somewhat lame and arbitrary character of the liberal replies to the conservative plea.

At bottom, the point of difference hinges upon a fundamental divergence in the conception of the Incarnation itself. The one side conceives it not simply as a revelation of the nature and character of God in and through a human life—all the terms being translated into those of personal experience—the human personality is not merely in itself the transmuted divine revelation, it is a vehicle that bears a revelation of God's glory, wisdom, and love, that appears in addition to the glory which shines through the humanity itself. Thus, Christ's supernatural knowledge and wisdom, his power over disease, demons, and the forces of nature, and his control over matter and space demonstrated after his resurrection, are the manifestations of God's glory vouchsafed in addition to that glory exhibited in his purely human life: in these instances, his manhood is acting as the passive agent through which the heavenly majesty of God is in some measure displayed.

According to the other view, which gained increasing popularity among liberal thinkers, there is no revelation of glory except that which is given in the exclusively human life of Christ. The perfect human life is looked upon as the counterpart in terms intelligible to us of what God is in his own nature. God himself we cannot see, the metaphysical attributes are virtually unintelligible to us, we can only know God when he is presented to us in exclusively human form. This view, cradled in the Kantian critique of metaphysics, provides the ultimate reason for the disinterest in Christ as a bringer of truths relevant to the sphere outside our human ken. It also accounts for the growing desire to exclude from Christology all considerations relating to the structure of his Person that were of a metaphysical character: this is particularly apparent in the matter of the theory to be discussed in the following chapter.

*The Necessity of Infallible Authority*

It has been shown how conservatives argued that the admission of Christ's limited knowledge militated against the hypostatic union. Their second argument, that such an admission offered a challenge to his doctrinal authority, made a far wider appeal at first, since superficially, at any rate, it was less concerned with abstract speculation. In brief their contention amounted to this: to admit that Christ's knowledge was circumscribed, implying as that did imperfection in the data that were at his disposal for the formulation of any complete particular judgment in a given instance, or of a universally valid judgment—to say nothing of looking into the mysteries of heaven—is tantamount to saying that he could err or make mistakes in his teaching.

If it be here objected that the logic does not follow of necessity, it may be pointed out that as a matter of fact the liberal view was actually formulated in order to account for the apparent fact that Christ had erred in regard to certain matters. If then it be admitted that Christ did err on certain matters—so the liberals would contend—what possible guarantee can we have that he did not equally err upon other subjects? It is a similar logic to the liberal deduction from Mk. 13. 32—the single contradiction which overthrows the universal rule. Admit one single error on the part of Christ, and the doctrine of his infallibility falls to the ground. Such an argument has become a classic rebuttal of the doctrine of Papal infallibility—instances such as Liberius and Honorius being chosen as the instances of contradiction. A use far more akin to the present conservative argument, however, is St. Augustine's contention in defence of the infallibility of the Scriptures. St. Jerome in certain Commentaries had apparently admitted the possibility of minor inaccuracies in the Scriptures. St. Augustine thunders out that if one even well-intentioned falsehood be granted, then it is open to anyone's caprice to deny the truth of any single statement which the Bible contains.[1] Christ, they argued, is a teacher of factual religious truths: of the nature and will of God, of his own nature, and the relation of himself and the Paraclete to the Father. It would be gratuitous to assume that in all such matters he has perfect knowledge, if in earthly affairs he possessed no more understanding than an average Jew of the first century. The accurate and perfect teaching of morality and the things pertaining to the destiny of man, moreover, requires more than a pure heart and a grasp of abstract principles: it necessitates a perfect knowledge of contingencies, on the one hand, and vision into the future and the mind of God, on the other. If Christ be admitted to have erred in certain of his statements, then the truth or validity of any one of his utterances is left open to be questioned by the first scholar who can present a sufficiently plausible argument, and, as will appear in the seventh chapter, such indeed happened. If the possibility of error be admitted, on what grounds can we demonstrate that "I and My Father are one" is necessarily truer than "Moses wrote of me"?, asks R. C. Oulton in his pamphlet on Gore's essay in *Lux Mundi*.

In dealing with a subject of such complexity, a certain amount of apparent repetition is unavoidable; and it is now necessary to return to the question of Christ's use of the Scriptures. As evidence in the inductive assessment of Christ's knowledge, we have seen that this material cannot by any stretch of imagination be regarded as decisive, one way or the other. In relation to our Lord's authority, however, the topic is of far greater moment and of no little embarrassment to many of the clearest thinkers of that time. To the out-and-out conservative scholar, Jesus Christ was omniscient and hence infallible, and hence also the views of the higher critics must be wrong on those matters where they conflict with the explicit or implicit utterances of our Lord. To admit that the critics are right, and Jesus wrong, they would continue, is to deny his omniscience, to deny his infallibility and reliability, and to cast a haze of doubt over his Gospel and his claims. For it is not simply a question of Jesus having erred in regard to the authorship of some scripture or the historicity of some event: the vital point is that Christ's whole teaching with regard to himself and his mission is represented by him as logically and necessarily following and fulfilling a certain well-marked-out scheme in the

[1] St. Augustine: *Ep.* 28.

relations of God and man. In other words, his teaching presupposes at least the general historicity of the story of the relations of Jehovah with Israel, as set out in the Old Testament: a personal revelation to the patriarchs with promises for the future, a miraculous deliverance from Egypt of the chosen people, culminating in a solemn covenant between the nation and God; the bestowing by God of a law, followed by subsequent apostasies and regressions from its standards; finally, the line of canonical prophets who filled in the picture of the promises made of old, and who called the people back to the standards of Mosaic religion. It is therefore urged that the views of Graff and Wellhausen—which became the standard critical theory—in which Hebrew religion underwent a long evolution from a welter of animism, and only became distinguishable from neighbouring Semitic cults centuries after the time of Moses, owing to the influence of the prophets, would make nonsense of much of the thought and message of Jesus, who believed himself to stand in a particular relation to that sequence of Old Testament events, not only that he accepted the whole of that history as true, but that he was the one foretold from the first, whose new covenant with men was typified and prophesied in the old covenant made between him and the Israelites.

Let us suppose, for the sake of argument, that the critics are right, suggested the traditionalists; what is the situation which then faces us? Christ then has erroneously referred many scriptures to wrong authors; he has based his claims to Messiahship upon the assumption that certain writings are written by their traditional authors, when in fact they are not; he has issued warnings on the basis of events which never happened; and he has assumed an interpretation of the Hebrew history and made it the basis for his teaching which is now rejected.

One might in the first place attempt to take refuge in the mediating position, referred to already more than once. One might assert that the conclusions of higher criticism do not affect the doctrine of Christ's omniscience, since he might well have possessed that attribute and still have made use of the Old Testament in the way in which he did. Being possessed of all knowledge, he nevertheless had to adapt himself to the conditions of his time and only give utterance to facts and truths such as his hearers could comprehend them. To have employed the Old Testament in an economic manner, therefore, would have been fully in accord with his restraint in the use of the divine omniscience as a whole. He would thus be merely accommodating himself to the intellectual background and standards of his hearers; thus he named the Scriptures by their traditional authors; he taught his lessons of the nature of God and of man's perils with the help of stories which were a vital part of the mental background of those who heard him—a method best calculated to take full effect. He even demonstrated his own claims to Messiahship upon premises and interpretations of the Scriptures which could not fail to convince; which in no way proves that he himself regarded such feats of exegesis as the real basis for his identity with the expected Messiah.

This view met with a storm of protest which did not simply come from one quarter, but from many differing shades of theological opinion. It was contended in the first instance that, as was seen in the preceding chapter when the Ps. 110 passage was under review, his use of the Scriptures in this manner would *not* be a parallel to an economic use of knowledge in any other sphere. In the case of the Scriptures, he is actually basing his teaching and his claims upon these foundations; it was thought utterly incompatible with the loftiness of his ethical principles that he should have based his claims upon foundations which he knew to be false and non-existent. The argument is even pushed one stage further by some writers: Had Christ known that his contemporaries embraced false and misleading ideas with regard to the Old Testament, it is impossible to believe that he would not have corrected them. Thus, John Seaver[1] asks whether it was even consistent with the loftiness of Christ's ethic consciously to give way to erroneous interpretations of the Old Testament. For, Seaver points out, Christ opposed certain scribal interpretations, and modified the law as he wished in the Sermon on the Mount; why not have done more had there been more to say? (Seaver is here attacking higher criticism.) H. E. Clayton[2] also urges that it is impossible that he would not have corrected people's errors, had he known better. In a word then, the economic view proved untenable; such an attitude on the part of Christ would not, it is thought, have been simply docetic but downright dishonest.

It will be remembered that we are following out the by-ways of the conservative contention that Christ's omniscience and the

[1] *The Authority of Christ in the Criticism of the Old Testament*, 1891.
[2] *The Advancement of Our Lord's Humanity.*

veracity of the Scriptures are the inseparable bulwarks of his authority. With these scholars we have supposed for the sake of argument that the higher critics are substantially right in their conclusions. We have seen that, if this be so, then Christ can scarcely have been omniscient—the economic view being untenable. We are therefore led to suppose in addition that Christ's knowledge was limited—the two cannot escape one another. What is the position then? We are presented with a Christ who bases his claims to Messiahship not only upon erroneous authorship of Old Testament Scriptures but upon a mechanical view of prophecy which is itself rejected by all liberal scholars. The whole method of interpreting the Old Testament as a series of consciously uttered factual predictions regarding the Person and life of the Messiah which was in vogue in the rabbinic schools, and is illustrated for us in the Gospels, the Acts and the Epistles and in the teaching of Jesus himself, is admittedly quite out of keeping with the conclusions of higher criticism. If then Christ's exegesis be at fault, and his historical knowledge inaccurate, his claims are based upon false foundations; and the question may seriously be asked whether such a false construction may not have bolstered up in him what had in the first place been a subjective delusion regarding his life work. If the house be built on sand, great may be the fall thereof. Such was the problem which liberalism had to answer, for it accepted both the critical conclusions and the limitation of Christ's knowledge. In fact, it was never brought into a satisfactory synthesis at all, and the relation of Christ to the Old Testament has ever since remained a loose strand in the thought of the age. To sum up then, conservatives urged that error was no more possible to Christ than sin. Christ's omniscience and his authority are inseparable; so also are the veracity of his claims and the historicity of the Old Testament Scriptures related.

## *Liberal Defences of Christ's Authority*

The reply to the contention that the admission of limitation in knowledge undermined Christ's infallibility and authority was in the main advanced along two lines of argument.

### 1. *Inspiration*

In the first place, it was maintained that in virtue of Christ's possessing a divine nature, and the belief that his humanity rested in perfect submission to the will of God and maintained a perpetual communion in spirit with the Father, his human mind was necessarily protected from contracting or expressing any falsehood in all matters connected with his Person, his office, his saving work, and in all questions relating to spiritual or moral truths upon which he was called upon to make a pronouncement. It is fallacious to imagine that limitation and infallibility are incompatible: they are not; and it is conceived that Christ was in fact both circumscribed in his knowledge yet by his nature none the less protected from error on vital matters. The divine infallibility only influenced his mind on matters strictly relevant to the above-named subjects; its purpose was not to furnish information or illumination upon other fields of knowledge. Christ did not come to teach men natural science or history, and hence his knowledge on those subjects might as well correspond to the popular beliefs of his time. He came to bestow knowledge of God and of God's will for men, and of men's ultimate destiny in response to that will.

The liberal reply to the conservative argument based upon Christ's use of the Old Testament follows the same line. His ignorance on matters only now discovered by modern historical research is quite natural and in keeping with his knowledge as a whole. It is protested that Christ did not employ the Old Testament as a battery of proof-texts, but as a mirror in which he saw the foretelling and expression of the things which he himself felt to be true in the depths of his consciousness. That consciousness of his is alone the touchstone of divine origin and authority, not the adding together of factual prophecies, like the searching for the outward marks on the child who is believed to be the reincarnation of the Lama of Thibet. On this theory also, Christ's human intelligence was left free to grow and expand by the forces of its own natural organic development from within, and by the assimilation of knowledge and experience from without—thus doing full justice to Lk. 2. 52. Such in brief were the lines of argument adopted by Dr. Gore and many other writers of the time. Two such contributions may be noted.

Such a view is advanced by T. Adamson,[1] though in a somewhat exaggerated form. He can discover but eleven indisputable instances of supernatural knowledge displayed by our Lord and concludes that such a gift was sporadic and incidental to his real

[1] *Studies of the Mind in Christ*, 1898.

functions. It was in fact a special aid bestowed upon his humanity at given moments—"At first when he was untried and inexperienced, it confirmed his actions; and at the end, when staggering under the load of responsibility borne by his frail humanity, it upheld him." [1] This modification of the usual view has the merit that it does seek to account for what the writer conceives to be the Gospel evidence—that the instances of supernatural knowledge occur chiefly at the beginning and end of Christ's ministry—without any attempt being made to unite such evidences with a belief in his infallibility. For the impression generally conveyed by the writers of this type is that the special inspiration bestowed upon Christ's humanity relates solely to his religious teaching and is therefore somehow linked with what the Gospels tell of his supernatural knowledge. According to Adamson, then, Christ's supernatural knowledge is a mere *donum superadditum*. His infallible authority sprang not from a permanent faculty of omniscience but through the inspiration bestowed upon him in like manner from without. This cut-and-dried view is unfortunately marred by some quite wild speculations later in the book. For instance: "Now we know that Thou knowest all things". This he declares to be a case of the wish being parent to the thought. [2] His disciples wanted their master to be omniscient, but in their heart of hearts they knew he was not.

"Omniscience was a thing to which Christ attached no value in the matter of salvation. In fact, he looked on it, not only as unnecessary, but even as hurtful and crippling. For his purpose the knowledge he had was far superior. It was for him flexible, apt, natural, easily adapted to, and not needing to be revealed for, special occasions". [3] This passage has been quoted because it well illustrates the licence, the irresponsible licence, which certain liberal theologians allowed themselves. The Christian theologian holds in trust what is a grave responsibility, not only for explaining the facts of revelation to his own satisfaction but also for the intelligible presentation of those facts to others. Yet these were like young people when first given a latch-key. They had protested against the far-fetched deductions of scholasticism, yet they themselves speculated at random from their own premises in far more dangerous and arbitrary ways than ever had those whom

---

[1] *Studies of the Mind in Christ*, p. 48.
[2] *ibid.*, p. 73.   [3] *ibid.*, p. 75.

they set themselves to judge. The Christ of the above passage is a figment of theological speculation, with little connexion to the Gospel evidences. Further, how can anyone in his senses speak of a knowledge which is superior to omniscience? But enough of this.

A more typical view is that of W. S. Swayne.[1] He argues that Christ's limitation of knowledge does not imply his fallibility for the simple reason that it was self-imposed. "If we hold that our Lord as man normally possessed a merely creaturely knowledge, save when for the sake of those he taught his Deity willed to communicate, and his sacred humanity to receive, a higher and infallible knowledge, his manifestation of knowledge becomes strictly parallel to his manifestation of power, his word becomes parallel to his work".[2] "Love therefore impelled him to communicate to and through his humanity a divine and infallible knowledge. It becomes at once possible to understand how our Lord could know and not know with regard to nearly the same set of circumstances".

It is not easy to see how a self-imposed ignorance is any less fallible than one which is not, unless it be imagined that a small door was still left open into the regions which had been renounced; but Mr. Swayne does not tell us. His doctrine is clearly one of inspiration from without—"For love of us" a higher knowledge was from time to time bestowed upon Christ's human mind.

Roughly the same view is adopted by C. F. Nolloth, *The Person of Our Lord*, 1908.

It was not recognized by those who formulated it, as is actually the case, that this theory bears all the marks of traditional orthodox dogmatizing, just as much as the "out-worn" theories which it was intended to supplant. Like them, it is constructed upon a set of *a priori* dogmatic assumptions, and, I submit, is not in itself a hypothesis formulated by a process of strict induction from the historical evidence: it is a makeshift and a stop-gap. These theologians protested violently that metaphysical considerations should not be introduced to weigh down the scales in the adjudication of the mind of Christ. When considering the question of the knowledge possessed by our Lord they resolutely refused to take into account the most significant element—namely, that he was himself God the Son—saying that an *a priori* belief such as that should not be introduced to interfere with an objective

---

[1] *Our Lord's Knowledge as Man*, 1891, p. 55.
[2] ibid., p. 41.

investigation. Yet when they come to the question of his authority, they at once invoke the dogma of his Deity upon which to construct their belief in his infallibility, as though it were the most natural thing to do! The Jesus of the Gospels, furthermore, appears to know nothing of this arbitrary distinction between infallibility on certain subjects and fallibility on others. He appears to speak with the same untrammelled confidence throughout, whether it be of the fowls of the air, the people of Sodom, or the angels in heaven.

It must also follow on such a hypothesis that unless Christ's human mind were providentially constructed and prepared by God in such a way that it arrived of itself at certain truths and conclusions—a species of determinism which itself savours of *deus ex machina*—then the infallibility must of necessity have impinged at some moments upon, and restrained the movements of, Christ's human intelligence, even if it did not actually insert novel material into its understanding.

More serious is the fact that although this theory is designed to safeguard Christ's authority as a teacher, and may in fact do so, it takes little account of, and has virtually no place in it for, the actual evidence in the Gospels of his supernatural knowledge. The whole point of the theory is that it postulates an infallibility solely upon moral and religious questions, the human mind of our Lord being left free to err upon matters of history and present fact: it is vaguely hinted that the evidence for his supernatural knowledge lends substantiation to the doctrine that he was inspired in a special way by God. But, in reality, most of the plain instances in the Gospels of Jesus' exhibition of extraordinary knowledge refer not to the bestowal of dogmatic or moral precepts but to practical affairs in the day-to-day business of his ministry, such as those connected with Nathanael, the stater, the man bearing the pitcher. This evangelic material fits into the theory most clumsily, if at all, which may therefore be challenged by taking a leaf out of the liberal book. The theory of selective infallibility was clearly devised on an *a priori* basis to meet a certain situation, and is clearly not designed in the first instance to take account of all the available Gospel evidence.

The liberal reply to the conservative plea regarding the Old Testament is quite unsatisfactory. The argument that Christ used the Old Testament merely as a collection of pious meditations is untrue to a frank interpretation of the Gospels. The pill cannot be made sweeter by trying to pretend that there is no problem connected with the Lord's use of the Old Testament. The higher critics may or may not be right; Jesus may or may not have been omniscient; what is certain is that he did appeal to the Scriptures as a foundation for his claims, and as an indisputable authority regarding the action of God in both past and present. This use made by Christ of the Old Testament, in perfect harmony with current methods in his time, cannot be smoothed away with rhetorical phrases such as "the reflexions of the inner motions of his soul". It is no light matter that the founder and central figure of a strictly historical religion, such as Christianity claims to be, should have invoked as the necessary background and interpretation of his mission a series of actions believed to have been performed by God in the world before his coming.

## 2. *The Separateness of Religious Truth*

The second line of argument, which at first was introduced merely to supplement the other, but which later was to assume an altogether independent existence, held that authority in spiritual matters is in no way dependent upon empirical knowledge or authority in earthly matters. The spiritual and the material are two fields as wide apart as the poles; knowledge of each is derived in a totally different manner, and even preserved in separate vessels. One may therefore be a genius in the one sphere whilst remaining an ignoramus in the other—as many of the saints have actually been. Therefore, to argue that because Jesus did not know where Lazarus was buried or how many loaves the disciples had brought, he must therefore be held unreliable when he pronounces upon religious truths is an utterly false approach to the subject.

It is curious that men whose whole theological outlook was becoming increasingly coloured by an emphasis on the divine Immanence should have adopted this absolute dualism as their starting-point. The idea thus embodied, of a spiritual authority and infallibility in a higher order than that of natural knowledge, represents so much that we know to be true in the relation, or rather the distinction, of natural and spiritual, that it is not easy to detect the trends of thought that lie behind it. It is only when the fruit had ripened from the seed that its colour could be seen. The ideas involved in this distinction between Christ's spiritual ascendency and his human ignorance were later to issue in beliefs such as these: that Christ's subjective consciousness of union with God was the very essence of his message; that this in fact was the only genuine proof of his Deity—since outward signs belonged to the material world which was irrelevant to the spiritual truth of the dogma; that there is in fact a cleavage between the spiritual truths he brought and the material vessel which contains them; that a rigorous criticism must be applied to the teaching of Christ to sort out what is his real Gospel and what belongs simply to his material and historical environment. These concepts, which will be discussed in the sixth and seventh chapters, are seen in embryo in this attempt to shield our Lord's infallibility under the dualism between the spiritual and the material.

Such a clean line of cleavage between the spiritual and the natural as postulated in this explanation is far more difficult to draw in regard to the actual subject-matter than would at first appear. Christ's religious teaching appears to contain not merely an outpouring of spiritual ideals, moral principles, or mystical impressions—if it does so at all—but a large number also of factual statements, explicit or implicit. Christ embraces a well-developed belief in the existence and activities of demons and angels. Accurate knowledge of such things does not solely belong to a spiritual intuition completely divorced from the intellect. Are we then to say that these things do not belong to the sphere of pure religion in which Christ's knowledge was perfect, but belong rather to the material realm, and hence may be discarded at our discretion? The later liberals who developed the dualism would reply, certainly yes, they are not an essential part of religion, but belong to the environment in which Jesus lived. To a traditionalist Christian, however, they are a part of revealed truth, and the question remains whether knowledge of such things does belong solely to a genus of knowing entirely different from the intelligence upon ordinary facts of life. Again, Christ devotes much of his teaching to predictions of the future; are we then for consistency's sake to assert that such teaching lies outside the realm of the spiritual knowledge, since it deals with actual events which are to overtake peoples upon the earth? It is possible to dismiss all of Christ's references to the future in ways described before. Thus the view which would draw a hard-and-fast line between the spiritual and the factual, whilst it may in the first instance appear to be a reasonable division of categories, and allow for the apparent facts of Christ's human limitations, in the long run makes it impossible to accept the word of Christ, or to deduce from his words, as a final authority upon any objective fact whatsoever. Doctrines connected with the nature of the Godhead, the Persons of the Trinity, the peoples inhabiting celestial realms, the origin and destiny of man, the judgment: on nothing may reliance be based save when Christ pronounces—if he ever does—upon the realms of subjective religious experience. In the words of the veteran scholar, James Orr:

"Naturally, the treatment of those who proceed on purely humanitarian assumptions tends to conclusions which would, if adopted, destroy reliance on Christ's consciousness on any matters involving objective knowledge. Those, on the other hand, who accept the postulate of the Incarnation, while acknowledging the difficulty on many points of arriving at an exact settlement, can take much more positive ground, and will attribute to Christ's consciousness, not only an absolute self-certainty on all that relates to himself and his mission to the world, but a uniqueness of vision and depth of insight into things both spiritual and natural, arising not simply from purer intuition, but from the unveiled intercourse he sustained with the Father, and the elevation above ordinary conditions of knowledge resulting therefrom".[1]

The liberalism which flourished in Britain and America was very far removed from what is normally understood by "liberal Protestantism"—as exemplified, for instance, by Harnack or Ritschl. For the writers of this time, the authority of Christ was in any case guaranteed by the doctrine of his essential Deity, which, however, it was conceived to operate, prevented of necessity the human mind of Christ from committing error where error would have led to false religious beliefs. Some of the methods, however, which were employed to defend that belief, such as the concept described above, far from closing the door against the inroad of a relativising doctrine of Christ's Person, actually set forth on the broad highway to such conclusions as were later to follow when the shackles of traditional dogma were fully shaken off.

In conclusion then it must be pointed out that even the liberals of this controversy could not find an adequate basis for the doctrine of Christ's factual infallibility without invoking the metaphysical dogma of his Deity. This means that all were

[1] *The Progress of Dogma*, p. 338.

in agreement that infallibility and authority depend—not merely upon a humanity attuned to the spiritual world—but upon the wisdom of God applied directly through his Person. This holds good whether it be conceived that the Son himself partakes in some sense of the human ignorance, or the ignorance be confined to the human consciousness alone: his authority and infallibility are consequences of divine omniscience, whether that knowledge be consciously possessed by the mind which utters it or not; in this, the conservatives had proved their point.

## *Of the Sinlessness of Christ*

To a considerable extent, the arguments relating to Christ's authority reproduced themselves in the discussion of his sinlessness. The question was certain to have come under review at some time during the period owing to the new insistence upon the Lord's humanity (e.g. whether impeccability is compatible with true manhood), but it was precipitated in the knowledge controversy for the same reason as the question of his authority—namely, because it was evoked by conservative scholars as a third scarecrow against new speculations.

From Patristic times, traditional theology had maintained that Christ not only lived a life free from sin, but that he was impeccable, that is to say, sin was not only never an actuality for him, it was not even a possibility for him. This was maintained (a) because if Christ as man could sin (as God he obviously could not), it would imply that the Person of Christ could be dissolved by a contingent force, and his mission overthrown by Satan; (b) since Christ in any case possessed no human individuality, his manhood was impersonal and wholly subordinate to the will of the Logos; (c) for although he does in fact possess a human will as well as a divine will, the former cannot operate as a rebel within his Person—in fallen man, the emotions, instincts, and faculties war against each other, each for its own particular ends, whereas in Christ as in Adam before the fall all the various elements lay in their proper order, each subject to the higher, and all informed by grace; thus by his very constitution it was impossible for the human will to take any inordinate actions as an individual organism independent from the whole Person. Even so, Christ's sinlessness was only guaranteed by his possession of the divine omniscience, which was one of its necessary prerequisites.

Therefore to admit the limitation of his knowledge was tantamount to allowing that he could, and perhaps actually did, commit sin. This argument from the first never attracted quite so much sympathy as the contention regarding his authority. To describe the events of the day of judgment may require supernatural knowledge, but to walk perfectly before God may be the result of absolute submission to unconsciously operating grace. But to the conservatives of the time it appeared that conduct which was to be perfect in every detail requires perfect knowledge, not only of the nature of God and the principles of morality, but of every contingent circumstance which could play a part in our decisions of the moment. One must certainly have the power to do the will of God, but also a perfect knowledge to decide in particular events what is the will of God. Sin and ignorance are so closely bound together that they cannot be separated except in thought.[1]

It will be observed that this outlook is concerned with acts rather than dispositions. It is concerned with the commission of sins rather than with the state of sinfulness. For it is not denied by writers such as Stone, Hall, Mortimer, and Powell, that a man may enjoy a state of justification before God be he the most ignorant of men; what is asserted, however, is that it is impossible to avoid the commission of sins; since even the most obviously universal commandments of the moral law are open to modification under the acute stress of conflicting loyalties. It was necessary to make this observation, since liberal scholars persisted in ignoring it.

The conservative argument had been formulated to serve as an attack upon the belief in the limitation of Christ's knowledge. To blunt the force of this argument, it was not necessary to admit that Christ was peccable, but simply upon the traditionalists' own premises one could say that Christ's limitation of knowledge does not militate against his impeccability, since that is assured by the fact of the hypostatic union. This seems to have been the attitude adopted by Dr. Gore; though in addition, he does make a strong attempt to give reality to Christ's temptations. Such was, however, a mediating position and it met with as much criticism as the older view. The criticism of it from the scholastic point of view is that impeccability effected in this way, without the omniscient co-operation of the subject, would entail a certain pressure or determinism upon the thoughts and actions of Christ's humanity.

[1] W. F. Hobson, pamphlet on *Lux Mundi*

More typical, however, is the following approach to the subject by liberal theologians. The conservative plea for omniscience as a necessary prerequisite for sinlessness is not valid, since righteousness is of a higher order than knowledge, and may be present without it—the peasant may be a truer saint than the professor: this, of course, is the second liberal argument for Christ's authority appearing again, though here it has more apparent relevance. But far from being contented with a refutation of the conservative plea, the liberal theologians were already entering into the problem much more deeply. To them, the doctrine of Christ's impeccability appeared to be a vitiation of his truly human nature even more destructive than the doctrine of his omniscience. We have already considered their postulate, "It is human to be ignorant"; the counterpart to which is apparently not, "It is human to sin"—though certain writers of the "New Theology" group may have been ready to subscribe to such an article—but, "It is human to be tempted". And temptation, they said, necessarily presupposes the possibility of yielding to that temptation. Free will, with its accompanying liability at all times to sin, is a permanent and universal attribute of human nature. Christ can, therefore, scarcely be said to have possessed such a nature if sin was from the first an impossibility to him. In the Scriptures we are taught that Christ was tempted by the Devil: the traditional view that he was tempted yet remaining all the while impeccable is rejected as ludicrous. One of the supreme values of Christ's life to us is its example, yet the significance of this example lies in Christ's thorough and consistent conquest of temptation. This would be utterly lost if his temptations were unreal. Yet Christ possessed a free human will, and evil was a possibility to him and a constant menace; the glory of his life was his constancy throughout to the will of the Father. "His will was free, and evil was a possibility to him as well as good". "While he was without sin his moral perfection was no physical necessity, but a personal victory over all temptation".[1] Naturally, it is maintained by all the writers of this time that Jesus *did not* sin. Such a belief did not rest upon the doctrine of the hypostatic union or of his omniscience but upon an assessment of his character as seen in the Gospels; his pureness of heart and his perfect love for the Father left no doubts regarding the perfection of his nature.

Nevertheless, that human nature and personality which he

[1] Garvie, *Studies* . . ., p. 469.

## CHRIST'S KNOWLEDGE AND AUTHORITY

possessed was conceived of as undergoing a development as it grew—parallel to the growth in knowledge. Jesus grew in "favour with God and man" as well as "increased in knowledge". Christ's mind and intelligence grew with age; what is even more startling to learn is that he also underwent a similar moral development—but this is just as plainly taught in the Scriptures, writes A. C. A. Hall.[1] Just as he had to learn all he knew as he advanced from childhood, so did his perfection and flawless character develop by trial, and repeated and constant success over new temptations. Temptation does not spring from sin, the holiest of men are tempted.

Dr. Mason also writes: "All the phenomena of Christ's inward experience during his life on earth which are recorded for us combine to suggest that his moral growth as he increased in favour with God and with the men of God—was of the same kind as ours, at its best, only so immeasurably better".[2]

In general criticism the following may be offered. The question which we will call "theological" must first be faced. Can it be conceived that God the Son could sin? That in the end is the crucial question. Yet in the Gospels Christ is represented as being tempted, in the wilderness, in Gethsemane, and the Epistle to the Hebrews teaches that he was tempted in all respects as we are. Temptation, therefore, was a real experience through which he passed. P. T. Forsyth makes the significant suggestion that perhaps Christ, in his human and Incarnate consciousness, was not aware of the absolute impossibility of sin, hence temptation was a real experience to him.[3] Any explanation, therefore, must take cognizance of the two facts—God's impeccability and the temptations as taught in the New Testament.

The debate primarily arose in connection with the knowledge controversy and to the bearing of that factor we must return. If a barrier is conceived to exist within Christ's Person shutting out the divine omniscience from his human mind, or else the Logos himself is believed to have been exinanited to the finite level, then—apart from inspired knowledge or coercive grace—an error of judgment on a moral issue would be just as possible to Christ as an error about the authorship of Ps. 110. On the other side it is argued, if knowledge is necessary for righteousness, then

[1] *Christ's Temptation and Ours*, p. 18.
[2] *Conditions of Our Lord's Life*, p. 80.
[3] *Person and Place*, p. 302.

no mortal with finite knowledge can become perfect. If God's moral laws are of absolute, eternal, and universal validity, like the laws of mathematics, then the pure soul by God's help can apply them in every circumstance of life.

This sounds well enough in theory but unfortunately is found to be difficult in practice to apply. When, for instance, we come to apply St. Augustine's judgment that an untruth is never justifiable, we feel that we are administering a code which bears little relation to the best interests of life. Casuistry is not a black art invented by Rabbis and Jesuits, it is a moral necessity, and a method which every one of us practises in daily life. Choice between good and evil, therefore, does require knowledge, knowledge of circumstances, and knowledge of possible consequences. We have to do the best we can; Christ must have had all knowledge or been peccable. This view, as we said, deals with sins rather than with the state of mind of the subject. Hence the most helpful aid to the solution of the dilemma is the scholastic distinction between formal and material sin; it is surprising that this distinction was never invoked during the controversy. Christ, we may assume with liberal scholars, was never guilty of formal sin, since the essence of that is consent of the will. This is the kind of sin liberals meant when they talked of righteousness being a state of heart not a condition of knowledge. Material sin may be committed through inadvertence or ignorance. To avoid purchasing an article acquired unknown to us in the black-market, or to avoid committing stealing in childhood not knowing it to be wrong, all such instances require knowledge. Hence Christ, if limited in knowledge, may, *must* in fact, have committed material sin—if only in some slight manner such as purchasing a pair of sandals from a caravan not knowing that they were stolen property or produced with sweated-labour in Baghdad. This is the crux of the argument: do we mean that Christ's sinlessness consisted in freedom from both kinds of evil? Presumably traditional orthodox theology requires freedom from both. Christ entered, and identified himself with, the sinful world without himself becoming stained by it. How he was able to do this, and how he, who was God and could not sin, became our brother, tempted as we are, is but one aspect of the mystery of the Incarnation which positively defies rationalization.

# 5

## THE KENOTIC THEORY

THE thoroughgoing and not always reasonable application of the historical method to the Gospel narratives, issuing in a rehabilitation of Christ's humanity—and in particular the establishment of the limited character of his knowledge—erupted a group of theological problems of the first magnitude. "Every essential element of true human life was observable in him, and has been recorded for us in the New Testament".[1]

Yet it was not as though this fully emphasized humanity of the Saviour, with all its limitations, lay on the periphery of his personality, as something incidental or detachable or even as something simulated: it was part of his very consciousness and constitution. "Although it is in virtue of his human nature, not his divine nature, that the Lord is the subject of growth and progress, yet it is he that advances and that is conscious of the advances—not some outlying group of faculties remotely connected with his real self. It is the very personal Word of God Incarnate who thus passes from such a state of sensation, perception, knowledge, as belongs to the embryo, the babe, the child, relatively perfect in each stage, to that of the full-grown man".[2]

It has already been seen how the admission that Christ possessed not only a human body but a mind of the like measure was the occasion of many heart-searchings in respect of his doctrinal authority and sinlessness. Of far deeper consequence and of more enduring interest, however, was the final question—"How could the Son of God have become the subject of such a limitation in knowledge"?

In the preceding chapter it was observed that this matter, like so many other of the consequent issues, was first raised by conservative writers—as in the declaration of the twenty churchmen on higher criticism—in the form that, if Christ's human mind be limited, then there is a rift in his personality between that mind and his omniscient divine mentality. The most eminent

[1] C. F. Nolloth, *The Person of Our Lord*, p. 277.
[2] A. J. Mason, *Conditions of Our Lord's Life on Earth*, p. 130.

liberals of that day saw just as clearly that here indeed was the chief problem raised by the new exegesis. We must therefore look more closely into the causes that led up to this dilemma—that Christ's person is divided, or else the Son of God is ignorant. For it is not quite so obvious as would appear why at this particular juncture in the long history of theology so acute a problem should have arisen.

It was urged in the second chapter that the two predominant interests of Christology, the unity and the true humanity of Christ, which were, practically for the first time, demanded by the same school of thought, were bound sooner or later to come into collision with one another; the demand for rationalization had reached such a pitch that the Incarnation could no longer be left as a mystery whose solution was indefinitely postponed. But why, it may be asked, did this one particular symptom of Christ's humanity — his limited knowledge — itself provoke the crisis? The fact, granted by all, that Christ's body, whilst on earth, was not omnipresent had caused no embarrassment to the theologian. Why then should the possession by Christ of a finite mind cause such difficulties? No urgent problems were occasioned, at least in modern times, by positing the belief that every human individual consists of an eternal soul and a corporeal body—the two are so different as to cause no infringement of the proper functioning of the one by the other: they are each necessary partners in the whole. Anyone who held to the contrary would have been laughed out of court as a hopeless monophysite. In the case of the union of the divine and a human mind, however, the case appeared to be radically different. For human psychological processes are at least in some sense analogous to the eternal omniscience of God. "My thoughts are not your thoughts" is true enough, but to confess that man is made in the image of God at least implies this much: that to say, "God knows such-and-such" is employing the word *know* in a similar way as when we say "A man knows such-and-such", the difference between the two being that in the case of the former the word implies eternal comprehension, and in the latter case, a transient and only partial appreciation of the thing. Thus it was not impossible to imagine how an almighty spirit could inhabit a weakly body, but incredible that an omniscient mind could be united to a finite mind, without the former swallowing up the latter completely. As described in the preceding chapter, the possibility of Christ's

## THE KENOTIC THEORY

possession at once of two such minds was rejected as being akin to the hole for the kitten besides the hole for the cat: this particularly applied to the scholastic distinction between knowledge possessed intuitively, and knowledge acquired through experience.

Of far greater significance, however, than the supposed analogy between divine and human thinking was the particular definition of Personality accepted by all at the time, which restricted the connotation of the term to consciousness and memory: a narrow view indeed, and the most important factor at the root of the Christological dilemma of the age.

Eutyches had been condemned for teaching that the divine and the human in Christ were so mingled together that the properties of the one—i.e. the human—nature were almost wholly swallowed up by those of the divine, like a drop of vinegar in the ocean. The liberal theologians, who seem to imply that they understood this to be precisely what orthodox Christology stood for—much though they reacted against it—yet themselves embraced much the same presuppositions as Eutyches had done. They assumed that if one person possesses two natures, each with its own set of attributes, then the person resulting therefrom must in some sense exhibit the resultant of those attributes together. To change the metaphor from one of physics to one from mathematics; the person would exhibit the lowest common multiple of those attributes. Thus, such a human attribute as limitation of knowledge in the Person of Christ would cancel out into the divine omniscience. This appeared horse sense even to those who were not particularly prone to a Eutychian or Lutheran view of the fusion of the natures in Christ. Such was the case because to them the word person connoted not some abstract substance or Ego, but a rational, knowing, self-consciousness, whose most obvious characteristic is a continuous memory. This was the almost universally accepted unit of spiritual individuality at that time. For the writers to be considered in this chapter, the definition was assumed rather than formulated or discussed—which accounts for their amazing failure to comprehend the Christology of past ages, which was built upon a quite different definition. Hence the fuller treatment of the topic is postponed until the ninth chapter, to a time when the full bearing of the matter came fully into view. Here we are concerned simply to draw attention to this general assumption made by all writers of the time—including most conservatives—that the essence of a person consists in this realm of conscious memory, from which was drawn the conclusion that everything which Christ knew, experienced, or willed, he knew, experienced, or willed within one single self-consciousness. Anything which might have suggested that Christ possessed two spheres of thinking or knowing within his own self would have been utterly foreign to the ideas of the time, and would have rendered him unintelligible to them as an individual person. This was to be the hall-mark, and in one respect the weakness, of the Christology of the whole period, that instead of beginning its enquiry from the standpoint of two whole and perfect natures, it took its stand upon what was believed to be a more realistic—though actually "idealistic"—category. Christology became shackled to a narrowing and restricting form in which everything had to be explained in terms of human consciousness, which at most is only a fraction, and a small one too, of the human personality. This fact fully accounts for the difficulty under discussion, where the problem was to relate limitation of knowledge and divine omniscience in a single human-like consciousness. It also accounts for many other subsequent failures to arrive at a satisfactory rationale of the manner of God's Incarnation: not that we suggest that such a rationale is to be found, but that it was certainly impossible with the tools then employed.

Quite apart, however, from this definition, which has its roots in the current psychology and in the still-popular idealistic philosophy, the quasi-monophysitism of the time has a direct theological ancestry, which gave definite and relevant Christological content to what was otherwise a matter of mere philosophical speculation.

It is now generally recognized by the most able theologians, both catholic and protestant (e.g. F. J. Hall and A. B. Bruce), that through the exigencies of the Eucharistic controversy Martin Luther was led to introduce into Christian theology a novel and wholly unsatisfactory element: the communication of the properties belonging to the two natures of Christ. Since the consecrated bread of the Eucharist, present upon innumerable altars at the same moment, contained along with the substance of bread the real presence of the natural body of Christ, that body, he held, must be endowed with the property of ubiquity for this to be possible. Luther therefore postulated the doctrine that through the hypostatic union of God and man in Christ the properties or attributes of God are communicated to the humanity.

## THE KENOTIC THEORY

This rendered his humanity omnipresent, potentially at any rate. Obviously this is a totally different idea from the Patristic doctrine of the *communicatio idiomatum*, which simply states that forasmuch as two distinct and complete natures are possessed simultaneously by one Person, it is legitimate to predicate of that one single person—who may be designated by titles proper to either nature—the actions or experiences belonging to either of the natures. The Lutheran doctrine, on the other hand, teaches that the human nature of Christ is actually enriched by, and possesses, the qualities properly belonging to the divine nature. This doctrine occasioned endless strife and speculation amongst Lutheran theologians. For, it was asked, if Christ's humanity was so deified by the reception of divine attributes, how, during the period of the Incarnation, did his human nature contrive to appear human at all? How, for example, being endowed with ubiquity, did Christ keep himself in one place at a time? Upon this topic raged the bitter controversy of the seventeenth century between the schools of Tübingen and Giessen; the former teaching that during the period of the Incarnation the divine properties possessed by Christ's humanity underwent a process of veiling—*krypsis*, whilst the latter school held that they were temporarily abandoned by him—*kenosis*. This controversy is alluded to here to illustrate the workings of the Lutheran Christology, and also to register a point that has apparently caused a little confusion: the doctrine of *kenosis* as taught by these early Lutheran divines has nothing whatever to do with the theory of the same name which appeared two centuries later; for in the seventeenth century, the only abandonment which was envisaged related to the divine properties communicated to the humanity, and not to an exinanition of the divine nature itself.

The tangled mass of bitter controversies and scholastic subtleties which went to make up this Lutheran theology, "wears the aspect", to quote A. B. Bruce, "of a vast pyramid resting in a state of most unstable equilibrium on its apex, Christ's bodily presence in the supper; which again rests upon a water-worn pebble—the word of institution . . ."[1] But the doctrine which underlay all this theologizing, the communication of properties, had left an indelible mark upon all protestant Christologies, and led to the envisaging of a Christ surpassing in docetic artificiality

[1] *The Humiliation of Christ*, p. 84. This work is by far the clearest English history of continental protestant Christology.

anything which the medieval scholastics had ever produced. He was, in fact, a monophysite Christ, whose humanity at practically every point was subsumed or dissolved in the divine essence. It was precisely this conception of a Christ which the liberal theologians were in revolt against, and in time swept away, but unbeknown to them, the monophysite ghost still walked, and the trace of the Lutheran doctrine lived on as a *hereditas damnosa*, well into the twentieth century, until it was frankly recognized for what it was.

That this is no idle speculation may be shown by a single quotation from an American scholar of some repute, who actually voices the Lutheran doctrine in no uncertain terms. He writes: "The union of the divine and the human nature makes the latter possessed of the powers belonging to the former; in other words, the attributes of the divine nature are imparted to the human without passing over into its essence, so that the human Christ even on earth had power to be, to know, and to do, as God".[1] The same writer continues that this power was latent during the period of the Incarnation, by reason of the humiliation, but when it was required, it was mediated to him to his humanity, by the Holy Spirit; hence Christ only knew and taught what the Holy Spirit permitted, but when he did so, he was not acting like the prophets, inspired from without, but by reason of his own inner energy.

This is a plain statement of the old Lutheran theology in modern terms, and designed to meet the modern problem for Christology. It is sufficiently interesting in itself as an unusual attempt to solve the Christological problem along the lines of an old-fashioned theology; though by its nature it was incapable of general acceptance. For the majority of men, the influence of the Lutheran doctrine was subterranean: it was simply assumed as a matter of course that Christ's knowing, thinking, and willing, must be one; that there could not possibly be within one person two sets of psychological processes held in watertight compartments. If Christ knew a thing by virtue of his divinely omniscient consciousness, then in his human mind he could not conceivably be said to be ignorant of it. It was accepted, virtually as an axiom, that two natures so united as in the Person of Christ must integrate themselves into one single conscious unit if they are to form one person and not some divided self. What in fact it amounts to,

[1] A. H. Strong, *Outlines of Systematic Theology*, p. 187.

## THE KENOTIC THEORY

expressed in yet another form, is that we have an admission that the old term "Nature" has for all practical purposes vanished—it has coalesced with the term "Person". Owing to the change in the definition of the term person, the older term, nature, human nature, contained elements which could not be present without the possession of individual personality. This fact explains, among other things, the failure to comprehend the conciliar doctrines of the impersonal manhood, and the Two Wills in Christ. A being who possessed two sets of psychological functions, two wills, for example, would to these thinkers have been not simply one person, but two. Person was no longer a principle of individualization, an ego, but a set of psychological functions, in particular the self-consciousness, which was commonly believed to be that element which furnished continuity of personal existence and hence moral responsibility. One person cannot possess two sets of memories, two personal continuities, two separate self-realizations, but one: nothing but a monophysitism in modern dress was intelligible; for the two natures even if separated in but the slightest degree as regards psychical operation would have dissipated the unity of Christ's person.

Here then was the problem as it faced the liberal theologians: A commonly accepted psychology, which pointed to self-consciousness as the focus or summit of personality, human or divine; an inherited theological bias towards a doctrine of mutual sharing of the properties between Christ's natures—if these were granted principles, Jesus of Nazareth could not but be possessed of the riches of divine omniscience. Such a conclusion, however, could not be admitted, since the historical evidence pointed against it, and theology, it was not altogether unjustly maintained, must bow to historical and literary criticism.

By a strange irony of fate, however, Dr. Gore and his friends were at first accused by some of their opponents of Nestorianism! This initial misunderstanding of the basic principle of the new Christology was largely occasioned by the somewhat piecemeal manner in which their investigations and conclusions were presented to the world. In essay No. VIII of *Lux Mundi*, Dr. Gore had merely posited the possibility of the general limitation of our Lord's knowledge, suggesting that the recorded instances of his possession of miraculous knowledge were in fact revelations to him upon those several occasions for specific purposes. The Bampton Lectures and the Dissertations were as yet far away from the press, and hence the core of the new system of Christology remained obscure. The immediate implications, on the other hand, of what had already been disclosed, were somewhat misleading. As the matter stood in 1890, the following might roughly be inferred from what was already delivered: Christ's divine and human natures are to such an extent separated that it is possible for the human nature to be ignorant of all supernatural or supernormal matters except in so far as these are specifically communicated to it by the divine nature; and the apparent infrequency with which this communication is believed to operate is itself a measure of the unity, or rather of the disunity, between the natures, which would appear to be little more than that which may pertain between the believer and our Lord, and the prophet and the God who inspires him. Naturally, this savoured of Nestorianism to the men of that time, who were only too ready to use the name as a cry of protest against a theology which was not only dividing Christ, but seemingly also shattering the foundations of religion by its denial of the literal accuracy of the Scriptures. So argued the pamphleteers—R. C. Oulton, *On Gore's Essay in Lux Mundi*, for example, and W. F. Hobson, *Some Aspects of the Incarnation; chiefly in reference to Lux Mundi*, who writes—"There is solid ground for fearing that Nestorianism is at the heels of all theories of our Lord's ignorance: they tend on their last analysis to the dividing of Christ". Certainly the early language of Gore and others, when they were simply engaged in demonstrating Christ's limitation of knowledge, might well have created such an impression as the above; though nothing could have been farther from their minds than a Nestorian solution. The really significant point with regard to these conservative protests and their argument, for our present purpose, is that they too shared with the liberals precisely the same presuppositions. For they too imagined that any separation of psychological functions within the being of Christ would divide his person. They too, as Dr. Gore and his friends, had long abandoned and forgotten the old psychology upon which the conciliar Christology with its doctrine of two wills had been based; they too looked upon conscious mental functioning as the essence of individuality, and hence believed that if two minds—however dissimilar—were to be united in one, and one person was to subsist, those minds must of necessity coalesce to constitute one psychical unit of cognition and conation.

## THE KENOTIC THEORY

Liberal theologians were therefore placed in a deadlock. The Jesus of the Gospels was demonstrably ignorant of many things—that was the verdict of modern exegesis which could not be gainsaid. On the other hand, this same Jesus was held to be divine; yet on their principles, whatever knowledge the Son of God Incarnate possessed must also be shared to the full, they believed, by the human mind and soul with which it was united.

The Gordian knot was seemingly cut by the introduction into English theology of a now familiar expedient known as the Kenotic Theory. This theory had flourished like a green bay tree in Germany during the middle quarters of the nineteenth century, had been adopted by certain scholars of other countries—such as Godet in France and Martensen in Denmark—and by 1889 was well on its way to a natural death, at least so far as the continent was concerned. The main tenet of the theory, which takes its name from the ἐκένωσεν of Phil. 2. 7, is that the Son of God, in order to become man, voluntarily subjected himself to a process of "emptying"—a certain modification of his nature, in order for it to enter into a congruous union with the nature of man.

Kenotic Christology took its rise as a proposed mediation in connexion with the attempts to unite the Lutheran and Reformed churches: its adherents were numbered from both confessions, and, in its essence, the theory partakes of ideas belonging to both systems of theology. From the Calvinistic side came the emphasis on Christ's exinanition and humiliation in becoming man, whilst from the Lutheran theology came the doctrine of communication of properties—now being envisaged in reverse, that is, as human properties communicated to the divine Son. As originally taught, the adherents of the theory may, broadly speaking, be divided into two groups, corresponding to two forms of the theory.

In the first place, there is the form of the theory as represented for us by Thomasius, a Lutheran Divine. He divided up the attributes of God into two classes: the moral, such as love, holiness, and justice; and the physical, omnipotence, omniscience and omnipresence. The former he declared to be essential to the nature and character of God, the latter, incidental, and it was this latter group of attributes which God the Son abandoned in order to become and dwell as man. Thomasius admits that he is applying the Lutheran principle of communication of attributes in the opposite direction, and claims that his theory fulfils Luther's dictum of *Nec Verbum extra carnem, nec caro extra Verbum*: his view of the Incarnation being clearly of that type, considered in a section of the previous chapter, in which the revelation takes place entirely within the compass of the normal human activities of the life of Christ. On this view, the Son of God retains his full consciousness of Godhead and of his relations to the Persons of the Blessed Trinity, merely being divested of those powers of God of a relative character which could not possibly be present to him when dwelling *sub hominis conditionibus*.

With the other type of Kenotic theory, represented in its extreme form by the Calvinist Gess, it is far different. According to this writer, the Son of God in becoming man underwent a transformation, in which his Person was converted into a being such as a human soul. The words of St. John, "Et Verbum caro factum est" are to be taken quite literally: he underwent a metamorphosis which not only had the effect of stripping off his "physical" attributes, but also of changing the whole manner of his consciousness. He ceased to be conscious of his life and fellowship within the Blessed Trinity—some kenoticists, in fact, held that during the Incarnation he actually ceased for the time to uphold the world and to be a source of the Spirit's procession. The Logos, furthermore, ceased to be conscious of the fact that he had descended from heaven, and even lost the consciousness of his own identity, which he had to win back during his Incarnate life through prayer, reading the Scriptures, and other exercises of his humanized spirit. To Gess, the consciousness of being God would have been just as inconsistent with a true life on earth as the possession of omniscience. Such then in very brief were the forms in which the kenotic theory had made its appearance.

It will be seen at once that this was the very solution to the Christological problem for which English liberal scholars were searching. It appeared to provide an exact and satisfactory solution of the difficulty in hand. It yielded a Son of God who could be united in the most intimate manner to a human mind without overriding or displacing it in any degree. Thus, Christ could still be regarded as a psychological unity, without any stresses or strains between an omniscient Deity and a finite manhood. There need be no artificially-constructed theories distinguishing between intuitive and acquired knowledge; there need be no fears of separation or schism within the Lord's Person: a simple explanation had been brought forward—the Son of God in becoming man had emptied himself of the divine omniscience,

# THE KENOTIC THEORY

and thus partook in the limitation of knowledge displayed by the Jesus of the Gospels. According to their standards and presuppositions, therefore, a Christ could be envisaged who was truly human and truly one. He was the actual subject of all the experiences common to man, and at the same time he was an intelligible psychological unit. The two requisites of the age in regard to Christology were therefore satisfied in full by the theory.

It is, of course, uncertain at what date the kenotic theory began to be taken up seriously in Britain and America as a possible solution of the problems of the time; certainly a good many years before 1889, in some circles. It was undoubtedly brought to the notice of a wide section of the theological world by the work of Dr. A. B. Bruce.[1] The theory, even in some of its extreme forms, made a deep appeal to many notable free-church thinkers.

Within the Anglican communion Dr. Gore had generally been looked upon as the introducer and father of kenotic Christology; and he does, in fact, make no allusions or acknowledgments in his major works to any predecessor in the field: on account of which, the celebrated Prof. T. K. Cheyne of Oriel raps his knuckles: "The principle of the *kenosis* (or, as it has been lately paraphrased, the self-limitation) of the divine Son, and that of the continual guidance both of the church and of each faithful Christian by the Holy Spirit, seemed to me in 1883 and 1888 (as they still seem to me in 1890) the only possible foundation for a reform of apologetic suited to our English orthodoxy". Dr. Cheyne was delighted to find his own point of view expressed in *Lux Mundi*; and he continues: "Now I will not accuse Mr. Gore, who is a right theological thinker, of borrowing from me without acknowledgment. But fairness and brotherly feeling must impel him to recognize that the movement which he advocates for the reform of the Old Testament section of apologetic theology was initiated in the Anglican church on almost the same lines by another."[2]

One final remark will be made in conclusion to this prolegomenon. The men who developed the kenotic theory in English Christology were neither sceptics nor humanists. They did not seek to overthrow the traditional orthodox Christology of

---

[1] *The Humiliation of Christ*, 1881.
[2] *The Origin and Religious Content of the Psalter*, Bampton Lectures for 1889. Introduction, p. 25.

Christendom: on the contrary, they sought to establish it, by removing it from where it was in danger of being attacked by modern critical methods. Neither were they men who denied or even doubted the dogma of the Deity of Christ, in the fullest sense: if they had been, the kenotic theory would have been pointless. Kenoticism, in Britain and America, as well as in Germany, was a movement within orthodoxy. This is shown conclusively by the manner in which it was presented. Many of its adherents were those who criticized the older systems as docetic and the fabrications of *a priori* deductions; but if they criticized in this way, it was not because they themselves were to offer a totally different method of study. On the contrary, their method was substantially the same. True enough they laid stress upon the frank exegesis of the Gospels; but their solution of the problem was itself based and built upon the dogmatic foundation of the Deity of Christ, his two complete natures and the centrality in his personality of the Incarnate Word of God. Heresy, novelty, restatement even, were the last things for which they sought.

## *The Philippian Exegesis*

Before proceeding to consider the forms in which the kenotic theory actually made its appearance in English theology, it will be as well to deal with the question of Scriptural exegesis—the basis which was sought for the theory in the teaching of the New Testament. Owing to the fact that the kenotic solution was often confused with the question of Christ's limited knowledge, many Scriptural texts that lent colour to the belief in the limitation of his knowledge were frequently cited as though they supported the kenotic theory. Thus Mk. 13. 32 is often quoted as though it were a proof-text for the *kenosis*, when in reality it is nothing of the kind. The *kenosis* is one way of explaining Christ's apparent limitation of knowledge, but by no means the only possible way, and hence the confusion was most unfortunate; for it was a trap of logic into which many even of the ablest writers fell headlong.

Nevertheless, one, and possibly two, passages of Scripture have a very clear bearing upon the subject, and appear constantly in the argument as the corner-stones of the kenoticists' position, though the particular interpretation which they put upon them with such confidence is far from being as clear as the noon-day.

The celebrated passage, Phil. 2. 5 ff., in which St. Paul exhorts his converts to emulate the selflessness and humility of Christ, became the *locus classicus* for the kenotic theory—since its very name is taken from this text—and hence it became a focal point in the controversy: for conservative scholars did not accept the kenotic solution lying down: they controverted its rationality and verity even more hotly than they had dealt with the questions of Christ's knowledge and authority. Of such importance was the passage believed to be, that no work touching upon Christological affairs was considered complete without some exposition of it. Indeed, at all times the passage must be of prime importance for the interpretation of the Christology of St. Paul and of the New Testament as a whole—its importance was no new discovery of the nineteenth century.

Not a few writers adopted a curiously superior attitude towards the controversy regarding the interpretation of this passage. Some went so far as to assume that these sentences were merely a string of *obiter dicta* of St. Paul, whilst others were without doubt that, even though the passage contained "great depth of meaning and significance", yet that meaning was by no means assured, and it was impossible to press from its language any exact theological statements. Yet, astoundingly enough, it was frequently the case that those writers who winced at the grip of philological exactitude were just those who most eagerly enlisted the passage in support of their own theories.

But clearly, in the Epistle to the Philippians we are not at grips with a liberal theologian with a compromising air, but with a theological genius who paints the image of worlds of reality with a few strokes of his pen. Therefore, even though we may not always discover the whole content of what is said, it ought at least to be possible, by close scrutiny of the language, to exclude what are in fact erroneous or even merely unsubstantiated deductions from it.

No attempt is here made to provide a complete philological analysis of the passage. The main points in the argument regarding it will simply be set down in the way in which they appeared to the parties to the discussion. Here again, if undue proportion is bestowed upon negative and conservative exegesis it is not due to any bias, but simply that the passage was so dear to those liberal scholars who expounded it to support their theory that they gave little if any heed to the real difficulties involved in the interpretation which they demanded from it—convincing though their own case may be. And it is, further, the case that the liberal interpretation and its ramifications are so familiar to the present generation that it is now more worth while paying attention to the less familiar aspects of the enquiry.

Phil. 2. 5 ff. τοῦτο φρονεῖτε ἐν ὑμῖν ὃ καὶ ἐν Χριστῷ Ἰησοῦ, ὃς ἐν μορφῇ θεοῦ ὑπάρχων οὐχ ἁρπαγμὸν ἡγήσατο τὸ εἶναι ἶσα θεῷ, ἀλλ' ἑαυτὸν ἐκένωσεν, μορφὴν δούλου λαβών, ἐν ὁμοιώματι ἀνθρώπων γενόμενος. καὶ σχήματι εὑρεθεὶς ὡς ἄνθρωπος ἐταπείνωσεν ἑαυτόν, γενόμενος ὑπήκοος μέχρι θανάτου, θανάτου δὲ σταυροῦ.

## *The Epexegetical Argument*

Appeal has often been made to the bearing which the context has upon the passage in order to support more than one point of view. It is often the case with St. Paul, that utterances of the profoundest moment for theology are produced not in the manner of a consciously framed dogmatic code but almost by accident in the course of some exhortation or treatment of a subject of a quite secondary character: so it is in the present instance. Love, accord, lowliness, first thought for the welfare of others, are the virtues for which the Apostle is pleading: and the action of Christ in becoming man for our salvation and suffering on the Cross is cited as a crowning example for men to follow.

It is argued, on the one hand, that there is no real example of self-sacrifice for the Philippians to imitate if Christ, in becoming man, merely added to his heavenly glory an additional sphere of operation. There can only be a genuine pattern for men to follow if he did actually abandon powers which he possessed, and had a right to possess, as God. On the other hand, it is argued that people are not being bidden to imitate an actual stripping of their own natures, but a renunciation of self-glory and their own rights and privileges; hence, if a radical *kenosis* of the nature of Christ is intended by St. Paul, the parallel between it and what the Philippians are intended to do in response to it is not so apt—indeed, it is difficult to imagine how such an act could be imitated by them at all. Even his active submission to the death on the Cross is robbed of its full weight if he was not at that time in full possession of his divine powers, and hence perfectly free to have avoided it.

It can only be pointed out that, of the act of the Incarnation itself, it constitutes an act of perfect, selfless love, whether Christ accepted it in addition to his already-enjoyed glory within the heavenly state, or whether he did not retain the exercise of all his divine powers but submitted his nature to some form of temporary modification. At most, therefore, the epexegetical argument is not conclusive by itself, and at least it cannot be introduced in support of any novel argumentation.

## The Critical Analysis of the Text Itself

The word ὅς in v. 6 is unversally taken, in our period, to refer to the Son of God in his pre-Incarnate state. This appears to be quite legitimate, since the passage is concerned with what Christ underwent in becoming, or in order to become, man, and not what happened to him after he had assumed human nature. It is interesting to note, however, that most orthodox Lutheran Divines have understood the word to refer to the Logos ensarkos, upon the basis of which they had constructed their own particular kenotic theory relating to the divine attributes communicated to Christ's humanity, already described.

Postponing for a few moments the consideration of the expression μορφῇ θεοῦ, the next matter which detains us is the interpretation of the participle ὑπάρχων. Broadly speaking, it signifies "being", R. V. Marg, "being originally": hence, an additional point against the old Lutheran view, it refers to Christ's eternal status, not to something which he possessed as incarnate and afterwards gave up. Yet, having established this result, accepted by all those partaking in the controversy, the matter is not at an end, for there is an element of doubt regarding the precise interpretation of the time-factor in the form of the word. It is claimed by kenotic writers that this term refers to a state of existence which pertained to Christ *prior* to what is afterwards described as occurring, and hence a state which was terminated when what is described took place. The second state described is envisaged as displacing the former. The contrast between the imperfect tense of this participle and the aorists which follow is attributed to the distinction between what had been the state o Christ's nature from all eternity as opposed to the temporal state for which it was exchanged. There can be little doubt that the term may be intended as referring to something which existed before contrasted with something which took its place when abandoned.

It cannot be doubted, however, that the term is patient of another interpretation. It is contended as against the above view that the term relates to a state of continued existence, not simply as from eternity in the past but as continuing into the future, that is to say, during the events afterwards described. It is argued that this view is a logical deduction from the arrangement of the participles in the sentence, the imperfect—referring to indefinite continuance of time—being contrasted with the following aorists which allude to definite points in time.

In support of this view that the word ὑπάρχων signifies continued existence, writers such as E. H. Gifford in his invaluable study on the passage,[1] quote many instances in which the word is used in this sense in Greek classical literature. Of more interest are the alleged parallels in the New Testament, and in St. Paul's writings in particular.

For general use of the expression, we are referred to Lk. 23. 50 where Joseph of Arimathea is spoken of as βουλευτὴς ὑπάρχων, and to Acts 2. 30, where David is spoken of as προφήτης οὖν ὑπάρχων. In the writings of St. Paul, the expression is found in a parallel construction in the following passages: 2. Cor. 8. 17, σπουδαιότερος δὲ ὑπάρχων ; 2 Cor. 12. 16, ὑπάρχων πανοῦργος. For its use in the same sense but in a rather different construction we are referred to the following passages: Rom. 4. 19, ἑκατονταέτης που ὑπάρχων ; 1 Cor. 11. 7, εἰκὼν καὶ δόξα Θεοῦ ὑπάρχων; Gal. 1. 14, περισσοτέρως ζηλωτὴς ὑπάρχων ; Gal. 2. 14, Εἰ σὺ Ἰουδαῖος ὑπάρχων.

It is clear that in all these cases the participle has a reference to indefinite continuance; from which it is argued that in the Philippian passage it is illegitimate to maintain that the one form is regarded as ceasing to exist at the time when the events described took place.

And yet there is a certain weakness in these comparisons; for in all of them, the participle has no reference to anything that could be modified by what is to be described. The fact that David wrote a certain Psalm could not conceivably be interpreted as modifying the fact that he was a prophet—and the same applies to all the instances: in this sense, therefore, they are not strictly parallel to the Philippian passage in which the matter which follows bears directly upon the state designated by the participle. The transition from the imperfect to the aorist still, however, remains a significant point.

[1] *The Incarnation*, 1897.

Widely differing interpretations are put upon the expression ἐν μορφῇ Θεοῦ. Here, however, the opposite interpretations are not exclusively confined to kenoticists on the one hand and their opponents on the other. For example, there are opponents of the kenotic theory who take the phrase to mean no more than the "appearance" or "manifest glory" of God, associating the verb ἐκένωσεν to it. Others, such as E. H. Gifford, take the phrase to refer to the attributes of God's nature, interpret the participle ὑπάρχων to continued existence, and dissociate the verb ἐκένωσεν from this phrase as its indirect object. Kenoticists generally assumed that the Form of God referred to whatever in their particular theory the Son renounced in becoming man. Thus to one who followed the theory of Gess it would connote the very consciousness of Deity and life within the Blessed Trinity, whilst to one who followed Thomasius, the phrase would describe the relative attributes of Deity. All such writers agreed in relating the phrase Form of God to the verb ἐκένωσεν as its indirect object.

The general Christological position of Dr. Gore will be discussed more fully later in the chapter. It is, however, worth while noting his observations on these words, since he was an interpreter whose influence upon his age was of immense importance. R. L. Ottley, whose *Doctrine of the Incarnation*[1] became the standard history of Christology at that time, follows Gore very closely.

Despite the fact that Dr. Gore holds that St. Paul was employing his terms in a loose untechnical sense, he is able to write: "The word 'Form' transferred from physical shape to spiritual type, describes—as St. Paul uses it, alone or in composition with uniform accuracy—the permanent characteristics of a thing". In this sense it would imply the permanent characteristics or attributes of God; but Dr. Gore continues—a little farther on— to modify this to "the permanent characteristics of the life of God"—a subtle difference; and yet a little further on this definition appears to be equated to "the prerogatives of equality with God"—thus making ἐν μορφῇ Θεοῦ equal to τὸ εἶναι ἴσα Θεῷ. This, then, is even more confusing than the original language of St. Paul by itself. But it would appear that Dr. Gore is quite serious at first when he speaks of μορφή as the permanent characteristics of a thing, and in this sense most scholars have understood the Dissertation: for those things which he envisages

[1] 1896.

the Son of God as having "abandoned"—omniscience and omnipotence, are indeed within such a category.

Other interpretations of the phrase were, however, equally common at the time—generally put forward by opponents of the kenotic theory. The *Guardian*, for example, of Jan. 1st, 1896, commenting on the Dissertation, argues that the taking of the word Form in each or either case in the technical sense of essence or specific character is one which no Greek philosopher, except perhaps the materialists, would use. Moreover, continues the *Guardian*, since servitude is a relationship, to talk about the essence of a slave is meaningless: and the article concludes that St. Paul must have been using the word in a loose sense. An equally popular impression was that μορφή Θεοῦ stood for divine appearance, and was therefore a complementary or synonymous expression to τὸ εἶναι ἴσα Θεῷ. On this view, the μορφή Θεοῦ is something separable from God's unchangeable nature, hence the two Forms may be regarded as set in opposition to one another, the one appearance—of a slave—being substituted for the other. Μορφή, they hold, has nothing whatever to do with *ousia* or even *physis*.

One further example of such an interpretation may be offered, namely, H. C. G. Moule in his *Philippian Studies*.[1] He paraphrases the passage thus: " Who in God's manifested being subsisting, seeming divine, because he was divine, in the full sense of Deity, in that eternal world, reckoned it no plunderer's prize to be on an equality with God; no, he viewed his possession of the fullness of the eternal nature as securely and inalienably his own, and so he dealt with it for our sakes with a sublime and restful remembrance of others; far from thinking of it as for himself alone, as one who claimed it unlawfully would have done, he rather made himself void by his own act, void of the manifestation and exercise of Deity as it was his on the throne, taking a bondservant's manifested being, that is to say, the veritable human nature which, as a creaturely nature, is essentially bound to the service of the Creator, the bond-service of the Father; coming to be, becoming, in men's similitude, so truly human as not only to be but to seem man, accepting all the conditions involved in a truly human exterior".[2]

Dr. Moule continues that the Incarnation rendered Christ liable to growth and suffering "but never for one moment did it,

[1] 1897.   [2] *ibid*., p. 92.

## THE KENOTIC THEORY

could it, make him other than the absolute and infallible master and guide of his redeemed".[1] The *kenosis*, he argues, does not mean making himself ignorant about the authorship of Old Testament books: the emphasis is on his becoming the absolute bondservant of the Father; in which service he conveys perfectly of the Father's mind, in the delivery of his message. Hence the *kenosis* as taught by Paul is the guarantee not the denial of Christ's infallibility.

It will be observed that writers such as Dr. Moule agree with Dr. Gore and the kenoticists in regarding the μορφὴ Θεοῦ as the indirect object of the verb κενόω differing merely in regard to the content which they give to the term μορφή. A quite different view on this matter is advanced by E. H. Gifford. He argues with great force and erudition that μορφή is inseparable from οὐσία, and that without it there can be no φύσις with ἐνέργεια, but only φύσις δύναμις—potential nature. He therefore defines μορφή as the one unchangeable form proper to a thing. He urges that in Aristotle it means that which must be added to the substance to give it definite character. Therefore it is the nature or essence, not in the abstract, but as actually subsisting in the individual and retained as long as it exists. If this definition be true, he argues, it would be quite impossible and even ridiculous to conceive of Christ's emptying himself of it: it would be equivalent to saying that the general can exist without the particular, which is impossible. But as we shall presently see, Gifford delivers himself from the jaws of the kenotic theory by contending that the expression ἐν μορφῇ Θεοῦ has no relation whatever to the verb κενόω.

Τὸ εἶναι ἴσα Θεῷ next attracts our attention. As already observed, many scholars have believed it to be synonymous with μορφὴ Θεοῦ—either in the minimum or maximum sense of that term. The Latin form of the expression, "esse se aequalem Deo", lent some colour to the view that it was equivalent to μορφή Θεοῦ in its maximum sense. According to Gifford—who being anxious to show that this expression is the indirect object of ἐκένωσεν is most eager to define the present expression in a minimizing form— it does *not* mean "of the same nature as God", but equal to God in the various forms in which that nature can manifest itself. The neuter-plural form of ἴσος he holds implies this; it is therefore adverbial as in the passage 2 Cor. 8. 9, where man is still man whether rich or poor: εἶναι is a substantive verb with ὅς as its

[1] 1897, p. 99.

subject: some have argued, he continues, that the phrase does not mean "the being equal to God", which would have been they think τὸ εἶναι ἴσος Θεῷ, but "The God-equal existence", thus making ἴσα Θεῷ an attributive to τὸ εἶναι. Gifford argues that such a view would violate a known rule of Greek grammar which requires the attributive to be between the article and its substantive, and not after the latter.

The expression, then, might be defined as the things which pertain to the equal status with God: probably a subordinate term to μορφὴ Θεοῦ, but one which can perhaps mean almost anything such as "State of existence", circumstances of state, but relative attributes or suchlike only by stretching its connotation somewhat. It would therefore intend the glory which Christ enjoyed in the heavenly life before the Incarnation.

Ἐκένωσεν: to what then does this verb refer, and what is its precise significance?—this is surely the heart and key to the passage as a whole. As already seen, most kenoticists assume that this verb refers specifically to the μορφὴ Θεοῦ of which they believe Christ divested himself when he became man. It is argued that the μορφὴ δούλου which resulted from the emptying is placed by St. Paul in antithesis to the μορφὴ Θεοῦ—his pre-Incarnate state. On the other hand, it may be urged that the construction of the sentence does not bear out this assumption. The phrases open out from the centre, as it were, fanwise. Taking the balance of the phrases, the μορφὴ Θεοῦ is certainly contrasted with the μορφὴ δούλου: but the verb ἐκένωσεν is almost certainly contrasted with the phrase οὐχ ἁρπαγμὸν ἡγήσατο: and this assumption is more than borne out by the use of the well-known construction οὐχ . . . ἀλλά employed to point out definite phrases in opposition to one another. Thus here: "He did not grab . . . he emptied himself". Since the two are contrasted, it would naturally follow that Christ emptied himself of that which he did not regard as ἁρπαγμὸν to possess: so argue Gifford, Bruce and Westcott.

On the basis of this reasoning it is urged by opponents of the kenotic theory that Christ in becoming man did not divest himself of the Form of God but only of those things pertaining to the equal glory with the Father. In reply to this, however, it is possible to argue that these two phrases are to some extent modified by the two phrases which lie next to them along the converging arms of the fan. There may be a relationship, even if not an actual equivalence, between τὸ εἶναι ἴσα Θεῷ and its pre-

## THE KENOTIC THEORY

decessor ἐν μορφῇ Θεοῦ: and there certainly is a clear relation between the verb ἐκένωσεν and the phrase μορφὴν δούλου λαβών which follows. For it is generally admitted that the A.V. rendering of the following phrases is open to objection. v. 7 in the A.V. reads as follows: "But made himself of no reputation, and took upon him the form of a servant, and was made in the likeness of men": Such a separation of the clauses divides off the two participles as though they referred to a sequence of separate events: whereas in actual fact λαβών and γενόμενος qualify the verb ἐκένωσεν. Christ emptied himself *by* taking the form of a servant, thus *being* found in the likeness of men. (This, incidentally, is a strong argument against the old Lutheran doctrine of the *kenosis* as an event subsequent to the Incarnation.) Thus the R.V. is much to be preferred: v. 7, "But emptied himself, taking the form of a servant, being made in the likeness of men": In view of this clarification it is possible to argue that the peripheral phrases, the two Forms, are in fact regarded by St. Paul as alternatives, the one being substituted for the other, though this is by no means obvious.

Another argument frequently advanced by the opponents of the kenotic interpretation of this passage is that St. Paul never uses the verb κενόω in anything but a metaphorical sense. It is not altogether easy to appreciate the force of this contention. All human language, without exception, when employed to describe the things pertaining to God is used in a metaphorical sense. Whether then the verb in this passage is used to describe some physical transformation in the nature of God, or merely some change in the outward relationship of Father and Son, or some alteration in the moral status of the Son or of his outward glory, the meaning is metaphorical; in any case the depth of the metaphor can only at most be a question of degree.

Κενόω is sometimes used with a genitive of the thing emptied of; here it is used intransitively, which accounts for many of the difficulties in regard to it. Obvious difficulties arise in regard to the expression μορφὴ δούλου. In the passage it is defined as ὁμοιώματι ἀνθρώπων. Gore defines it as that nature common to all men. According to Gifford, μορφή and ὁμοίωμα refer to his human nature in itself, whilst σχῆμα means that nature as it appeared from without. The participle γενόμενος (γίγνεσθαι) naturally designates a temporal entrance upon a given state. Gifford attempts to make capital out of this by pointing out how careful and accurate is St. Paul's choice of verbs in the passage: ὑπάρχων comes first, referring to the eternal substance or form of God which remains constant throughout; εἶναι to states or conditions at particular times, presently to be laid aside; and finally γενόμενον to the entrance upon a new existence "In the likeness of men".

In the preceding pages an attempt has been made to sketch out some of the main lines of argument which were adduced for and against the kenotic interpretation of the Philippian passage. We are not here concerned to press any of them to their utmost limit nor are we concerned to arrive at any final judgment, if that be ever possible, of the Apostle's meaning. Fortunately, the question which faces us in this essay is a more simple one. The words of St. Paul in Phil. 2. 5 ff. were appealed to as Scriptural proof of a doctrine that God the Son in becoming man divested himself of certain attributes—typical of which is omniscience—in order fully and genuinely to enter upon a human life. Is such a doctrine a necessary inference from the above-named passage? To this question the answer must be given, unequivocally, No. Even if the linguistic arguments against the hypothesis do not amount to probabilities—as some at least of them appear to do— but only to possibilities, then it is scarcely in the interests of strict honesty for this passage to be placarded as though it were a *locus classicus*, bestowing final authority upon a speculation which is only at most one possible exegesis of the Scripture in question.

The participle ὑπάρχων *may* refer to the indefinite continuance of the Form of God; τὸ εἶναι ἴσα Θεῷ *may* be the indirect object indicated by the verb κενόω. With such evidence before us, it is impossible to assign to the passage that decisive place which it obviously holds in the construction of kenotic Christology.

On the second passage alluded to little need here be said. It is the celebrated passage in 2 Cor. 8. 9 (A.V.): "For ye know the grace of Our Lord Jesus Christ, that, though he was rich, yet for your sakes he became poor, that ye through his poverty might be rich". It is interesting to note that the participle employed in this verse is ὤν and not ὑπάρχων, for in this verse there is no question of a Form which might continue to exist, but only of those riches which Christ surrendered for our sake. For the passage is metaphorical in the highest degree, and no precise dogmatic statements could possibly be refined from it; it simply implies that the Incarnation was an act which did in very truth cost the Son of God a great price.

For when all is said and done; when the linguist and the literary critic have had their say, it must be clearly admitted as a plain teaching of Holy Scripture—in this case of St. Paul—that Christ's becoming man, just as his death on the Cross, was no mere side-show or play-acting carried on in addition to an otherwise untrammelled existence, but something which entailed a sacrifice or a temporary giving-up on his part, something which involved a renunciation of things which it was his right to possess: this much is clear, however much we may dislike the particular rationalizations of this doctrine which were offered. The kenotic writers do in fact deserve more credit than is sometimes bestowed upon them by our own generation; for they rescued from the fire something that had wellnigh been reduced to a cinder in the history of Christian theology. It is therefore most fitting and in all fairness, in view of the criticisms which are to follow in this chapter, to conclude this introductory material with a quotation from Fr. Tyrrell that should be borne in mind throughout the discussion of the subject here and elsewhere, at a time when both liberals and the new orthodox have exhibited a tendency to sneer at this bold attempt at the reconstruction of Christology. Fr. Tyrrell writes:

"The whole doctrine of Christ's *kenosis* or self-emptying can be explained in a minimizing way almost fatal to devotion, and calculated to rob the Incarnation of all its helpfulness by leaving the ordinary mind with something perilously near the fantasmal Christ of the Docetans. When the theologian has finished his treatise, *De Scientia Christi*; when he has impressed upon us that Christ was exempt from the two internal sources of all our temptations, sc. the darkness of our mind and the rebellion of our body; that in his case temptations from without met with no more response from within than when we offer food to a corpse; we cannot help feeling that under whatever abstraction this may be true, yet it cannot be the whole truth, unless all who have turned to Christ in their temptations and sorrows have been woefully deluded—unless the *lex orandi* and the *lex credendi* are strangely at strife".[1]

## *Types of English Kenotic Christology*

There would appear to be no evidence worth recording of the acceptance by British or American writers of the extreme meta-

[1] Quoted from Tyrrell by A. R. Vidler, *The Modernist Movement in the Roman Church*, 1934, p. 156.

morphic doctrine of *kenosis* as taught originally by Gess, in which God the Son is not only envisaged as having abandoned certain relative attributes but also his whole consciousness of Deity. Even William Newton Clarke,[1] who was looked upon by his contemporaries as one of the extreme brethren in the field of kenotic Christology; even he does not deny the continuance of Christ's life within the Blessed Trinity or his cosmical activities.[2] Far more typical in Anglo-Saxon theology were the representatives of the theories advanced originally by Thomasius and Bishop Martensen and the advocates of a theory which restricted itself to the use of expressions denoting the restraint of divine powers, rather than their absolute abandonment. Just as English theologians have never taken kindly to the radical systems of German higher criticism, so too they were ever reluctant to commit themselves wholeheartedly to the equally radical theories of German orthodox protestant theology. The idea of the Heavenly Father taking over the reins of the universe during the temporary absence of the Son whilst on earth appeared to English minds strange and mythological, just as the Lutheran doctrine of the angry Father punishing his Son for the sins of the human race had always seemed crude and alien from the spirit of the Gospel. Hence we shall expect to find the kenotic theory free from all excesses and crudities when presented by the English writers of our period.

## *Abandonment of Physical Attributes*

Of the type of kenotic theory which A. B. Bruce designates by the term "Dualistic" there were not a few exponents in Britain and America during the period. In this system, as already pointed out, the properties of Deity are divided into two parts: those which constitute the moral character of God and are hence inseparable from his Personality, and those which are manifested in his relation to the finite creation and hence described as "relative", which properties, in fact, the Son of God is held to have given up when he entered that finite sphere with which they would have been incompatible. Two representative exponents of this system will be considered in turn, J. Macpherson and A. M. Fairbairn.

[1] *An Outline of Christian Theology*, N.Y., 1899. Clarke was professor in Colgate University, Hamilton.
[2] *ibid.*, p. 294.

*James Macpherson*, Christian Dogmatics, 1898.

Macpherson writes from the point of view of a modern Calvinism, which is interesting in view of the origin of the kenotic theory abroad. His Christology takes its rise from his soteriology being located in the third part of the book entitled *The Doctrine of Redemption*. Christ, he holds, passed through a process of physical and moral development during his life on earth in no way different in kind from our own. This normal humanity of his was not vitiated in the least degree by the intrusion of the supernatural: thus his knowledge was human and limited; such abnormal insight into the minds of others as he seems to have possessed was due entirely to his moral perfection and insight: "It was a purely human gift".[1]

That God the Son could so live as man is explained thus: "When the Son of God, the Divine Logos, became flesh, he submitted himself to the limitations of time and space, and surrendered the eternal mode of existence in assuming the temporal mode of existence. This of necessity meant that the limitations of his mode of manifestations gave no room for the exercise of those attributes of God which do not recognize the restrictions of time and space. It is quite distinctly implied in the Gospel story, and throughout all the New Testament, that Jesus Christ in his Incarnate life was absolutely without the divine attributes of omnipotence, omniscience, and omnipresence".[2]

If this may appear to be a somewhat exaggerated humanization of Christ's Person, scarcely doing justice to all the Gospel evidence, it should be borne in mind that in this type of kenotic theory it is required that Christ should be completely disengaged from these attributes, since even their partial or sporadic retention would overthrow the whole conception of the Incarnation thus envisaged.

For it is contended by these writers that only through the disappearance of these properties could the Incarnation take place at all. Only so could an infinite being enter the sphere of finitude; only so could an omnipresent being enter the domain of space; only so could an omniscient being enter the time process. The question—Can God undergo such a process?—is answered simply by the statement—the Incarnation has actually taken place.

[1] *An Outline of Christian Theology*, N.Y., 1899, p. 300.
[2] *ibid.*, p. 300.

It is contended, then, that God in his nature possesses two distinct sets of attributes; one set being inseparable from his Person, and the other set separable. The former, which consist of love, justice, righteousness, are generally designated "essential" or "moral" attributes; without these, the character of God would cease to exist. The latter set of attributes, those dealing with God's presence, knowledge, and power, are generally styled "relative" or "physical"; and it is contended by the kenotic writers at present being considered that these properties could be, and were, abandoned by the Son of God without affecting his essential nature of Divine Personality, they could safely be shed without God ceasing to be God.

In Macpherson, the theory takes the form of a full and real abandonment of these attributes, no mere restriction or veiling of their operation. The Christ so constituted is absolutely without supernatural powers or knowledge: power is given to him as he needs it to work specific miracles as a gift from God, and not of himself; and such power when it does come is only such as can be exercised within the conditions of space and time. Likewise also his supernatural knowledge, Macpherson argues, is sporadic, as is shown by Mk. 13. 32, and the fact that the exact nature of his death is only gradually revealed to him. On the other hand, that he still possessed all the ethical attributes of God in full is amply shown by the Gospel picture of Christ's self-consciousness of sinlessness and the like.[1]

Macpherson has also a doctrine of the fully personal humanity of Christ, which though not germane to the present subject helps to illustrate his kenotic theory. Since the exinanited Divine Logos possesses no irreconcilable attributes, in the Incarnation there is no need for either of the natures to be impaired.[2] The doctrine of the impersonal humanity is therefore unnecessary and even harmful; for "It is characteristic of human nature, as created after the image of God, that its personality, without any impairing of its essence, can be made to embrace the divine consciousness of the Logos; and it is characteristic of the Logos' consciousness, that without the destruction of its essence, it can enter into the mould of human personality".[3]

Such a doctrine as this was a curious by-product of the time. It was made possible by a view which became increasingly popular

[1] *An Outline of Christian Theology*, N.Y., 1899, p. 301.
[2] *ibid.*, p. 319.   [3] *ibid.*, p. 319.

during the age of the interpenetration of personalities. Its dangers are that it sometimes leads to a view of the Logos as sub-personal—as will be seen in the eleventh chapter—or to a conception of Christ as a unique being, neither properly God nor properly man—as will be shown in the ninth chapter. For the moment it must suffice to point out that it thus implies that the Logos—as far as the Incarnation is concerned—is reduced, from the physical point of view, to the measure of a being compatible with a complete communion with a human spirit, differing from It not physically, and morally only in degree, owing to the spiritual affinity between God and man. General criticism will be reserved until the next writer is dealt with.

*A. M. Fairbairn*, Christ in Modern Theology, 1894.

The most celebrated English exponent of the Thomasian dualistic kenotic theory was none other than the Principal of Mansfield College, Dr. Fairbairn. His *magnum opus* ranks as one of the major theological writings of the time, and like another equally great book, Moberly's *Atonement and Personality*, it is not primarily concerned with any specific details or difficulties of the moment, nor is it even concerned to expound any one single dogma of faith: it is rather a complete setting and viewpoint in a total appraisement of the central doctrines of the Christian religion.

The book has already been cited in the first chapter as an example of the contemporary emphasis upon divine immanence. Dr. Fairbairn writes that "In speculation there is now a clearer insight into the affinities of the divine and human natures . . . The affinities of the natures may be said to be the common principle of our higher philosophies".[1] He arrays Descartes, Spinoza, Malebranche, Berkeley, Kant, Schelling, and Hegel on his side. Nor is his doctrine of the moral affinity unconnected with his doctrine of divine *kenosis*; far from it: it constitutes in reality its background and possibility. For the fact that God and man share a nature which is spiritually and ethically akin not only renders the Incarnation a practical possibility: it means that what is most important, most enduring, most significant, for God and man, is this inward nature which they share in common: what divides them is merely outward appearance, incidental attributes which refer only to time—not to eternity—

[1] *An Outline of Christian Theology*, N.Y., 1899, p. 472.

to space and the circumstantial relationships between God and the world as it now is. These lesser and circumstantial attributes, then, may be modified by God's will in accordance with the needs and principles of the truer nature which lies beneath them. In this way, therefore, "God is, as it were, the eternal possibility of being Incarnated, man the permanent capacity of Incarnation".[1] He thus envisages the *kenosis* as a logical outcome of that affinity which must in the end actualize itself in the union of God and man in Christ.

In Fairbairn's thought, moreover, the *kenosis* is made to fit into his doctrine of the Trinity. Here again he is in advance of many of his fellows by making the kenotic theory an integral part of a larger whole, instead of leaving it merely to fulfil its function as a stop-gap in the immediate crisis of Christology. Thus he argues that only the Son, and not the Father or the whole Trinity could be Incarnated, for two reasons: first because "he was the ideal of the actual world; it existed in him before it was; he was, as dependent and reflexive and receptive, the symbol of the created within the uncreated; as the object of eternal love and subject of eternal thought, he was the basis of objectivity within the Godhead. And so it was but fit that he should manifest his ideal in the forms of actual being, exhibit under the conditions of space and time those relations of the eternal nature which the created natures were intended to realise".[2] Secondly because, as will appear, whilst physical attributes are indispensable to God as a whole, the ethical attributes are alone essential to the relation of the Persons within the Godhead.

The Incarnation, therefore, demanded by God's ethical nature, and made possible by the affinity with mankind, necessitated a supreme act of renunciation on the part of the Son of God, an exinanition of the physical attributes of Deity: "There could be no real assumption of the nature, the form, and the status of the created Son, if those of the uncreated were in all their integrity retained. These two things, the surrender and the assumption, are equal and coincident; but it is through the former that the latter must be understood".[3] Internally, the two natures are akin and differ only in degree; externally, they are quite incompatible without renunciation and modification. Fairbairn thus is led to his most characteristic utterance: "Physical attributes are

---

[1] *An Outline of Christian Theology*, N.Y., 1899, p. 473.
[2] *ibid.*, p. 476.   [3] *ibid.*, p. 476.

essential to God, but ethical terms and relations to the Godhead. In other words, the external attributes of God are omnipotence, omniscience, and omnipresence; but the internal are truth and love. But the external are under the command of the internal; God acts as the Godhead is. The external alone might constitute a creator, but not a Deity; the internal would make out of a Deity the Creator. Whatever, then, could be surrendered, the ethical attributes and qualities could not; but God may only seem the more Godlike if, in obedience to the ethical, he limit or restrain or veil the physical".[1] The act of the Incarnation was in fact demanded by God's love and justice towards mankind. "We may say, then, that what marks the whole life of Deity is the regulation of his physical by his ethical attributes, or the limitation of God by the Godhead".[2] "And this surrender the Son made when he emptied himself and assumed the form of a servant".[3] This is quite the clearest and most unequivocal exposition of the kenotic theory in English theological literature. It is singularly unclouded by qualifications and reservations, or by side issues relating to controversies of the moment.

The general criticisms which pertain equally to all forms of the kenotic theory are postponed until the final section of the chapter. Certain specific criticisms belong particularly to this version of the theory, and will be treated of here in addition to a mention of them in the general summary at the end.

Allusion has already been made to the difficulty of accepting a view which necessitates the assumption that God the Son in becoming Incarnate was obliged temporarily to surrender his functions as upholder of the universe. It is a matter for surprise and regret that a writer of such ability and candour as Fairbairn should have omitted to deal frankly with this matter. It may perhaps be inferred that he would have dealt with it along the lines of his distinction between what is proper to God and what is proper to the Godhead, thus de-restricting the cosmical functions from the specific Person of the Son: this would itself, however, be a break with traditional Trinitology and an admission of the irregularity of his theory. Divested of those attributes which constitute him sovereign Lord and Creator, the Son is obliged for the duration of his Incarnate life to transfer to the Father's governance that place which he occupied in relation to the

[1] *An Outline of Christian Theology*, N.Y., 1899, p. 476.
[2] *ibid.*, p. 477.   [3] *ibid.*, p. 477.

created universe. By many, this theory has been rejected owing to its mythological savour: that is not a sufficient criticism of it. It is not legitimate for the Christian theologian to erect doctrine upon the basis of mere speculation—unless it be explicitly confessed that such is a mere pious opinion. Doctrine may only be presented as such when it is based upon legitimate deduction from the data of revelation. Now a theory of the Incarnation, such as the Thomasian kenotic theory, which has as its corollary—and perhaps even its presupposition—a doctrine such as the cosmical absenteeism of the Son, cannot reasonably be countenanced unless that doctrine be seen to rest upon the sure foundations of revealed truth. In the New Testament, the three passages in which Christ's cosmic activities are specifically dealt with—the first chapter of the Fourth Gospel, the Epistle to the Colossians, and the Epistle to the Hebrews—have nothing to say of such an abnegation of powers; in fact the plain exegesis of the latter two of the passages is against such a view. Nor have the countless doctors and scholars of the church, before the nineteenth century, ever found it even possible to deduce such a view. This is the real force of the oft-repeated conservative plea against the kenotic theory, that it is *new*: as presented, for example, by F. J. Hall.[1] It is not argued by such a writer that the church cannot henceforth define new truths—as they may be deduced from the known facts—nor that the light of modern criticism should be ignored—for higher criticism can scarcely be expected to shed much light upon the cosmic activities of the Logos: but simply that when the speculations of one age are found to contradict the whole reasoning of all past ages, those new theories cannot conceivably be entertained without overwhelming proof in Scripture and logic of their legitimacy: and in the present instance, it can scarcely be pretended that such demonstration is possible.

Such a criticism has here been solely applied to the supposed relinquishment of cosmical functions: it may apply equally to the major tenets of the theory.

Serious objections are also advanced in regard to the distinction between the moral and the physical attributes of God, and the relegation of the latter to an unessential rôle in the constitution of the Personality of God. It is regarded as gratuitous to assume that God may dispense with certain of his attributes, and not others, and still remain God. It is argued that God is a simple, indivisible

[1] *The Kenotic Theory*, N.Y., 1898.

unity; and being such, the various attributes which we ascribe to his nature are separable from one another only in thought, not in actuality. God's form, nature, and essence are of a piece—they too can be separated only in thought; and to suppose that the form or nature of God can be modified or changed is as ridiculous as to suggest that his essence can be mutilated.

It is claimed by these kenoticists that in the normal workings of the universe we see the supremacy of God's moral over his physical attributes; that his power is restrained by his love: that a bully, for example, who beats his wife is not more powerful but less so than one who with the same physical strength forbears to do so. This argument, however, simply begs the whole question: for the fact that God's every power is exercised in common with and conformity with every other is no argument whatsoever that he may dispense with certain attributes and still remain God—on the contrary, it simply attests the complete harmony and simplicity of the divine nature. The fact that God's omnipotence is in every respect conditioned by his love does not therefore imply that he can be divested of it: for whatever God chooses to do, whether to avenge or forbear, whether to create a world or redeem it, his every action requires his omniscient mind to conceive it, and his omnipotent will to carry it into effect; these are indispensable elements in his personality, without which God is not God. And, pray, in what category of properties does the divine attribute of "eternity" fall: is it a physical or a moral attribute? If it is a physical one, surely it ought to have been abandoned by Christ as truly inconsistent with the human limitations of time into which he entered; but if so it would imply that God the Son made himself capable of extinction! This should afford a headache for the supporters of the dualistic *kenosis*.

Nor is Fairbairn's excursion into Trinitarian doctrine of much assistance. His distinction, in fact, between what is possible for God and what is possible for the Godhead, or the individual Persons of the Trinity, is itself a most startling innovation. To assert that the Son can submit to a distortion of his nature without affecting the "Deity" or the other Persons of the Trinity is virtually a denial of the dogma that all three Persons share the same essence and nature, which therefore cannot be divided, or modified in the case of one member of the Trinity.

A less substantial criticism is that Christ, divested of his physical attributes, could not be recognized by men as God, nor would he merit even the divine title. The answer to the first part of the objection will be discussed in the following chapter, in which an attempt to construct an apologetic not dependent upon the supernatural powers of Christ will be reviewed.

With regard to the second part, it is argued, e.g. by R. A. Knox,[1] that a celebrated archæologist who lost his memory after a fall off a horse could scarcely be designated or regarded by men as that same reliable expert: he might be termed a man who was once a great archæologist, but scarcely one who was still a great archæologist; his designation must be changed just as his whole usefulness is vanished. This argument naturally has particular reference to Christ's teaching authority. Macpherson appears to have envisaged the difficulty of so designating the depotentiated Christ as God: he is criticising the theory of the eternal manhood: "If only for the years of his temporal existence he was self-emptied of the divine omnipotence, omnipresence and omniscience, we may still call him God in the fullest sense; but if, from all eternity, he never had these attributes, then he never was, and of course never could be truly God".[2] Here the contradiction to this writer's previous statements is manifest. If the fact of never possessing the physical attributes make it impossible for him to be called God—in other words admitting that the physical attributes are essential to the being of God, a fact which he had previously denied—then how can it be possible to call Christ God whilst Incarnate simply in virtue of the fact that *once* he possessed the essentials of Deity? If they are essential to Godhead, then one who does not possess them here and now can scarcely be termed God. A strange contradiction is thus involved; but in his following sentence, Macpherson gives utterance to a still more singular statement, which interest compels us to include: "The self-modifying of the divine consciousness which this implies cannot be regarded as peculiar to the state of humiliation, since it continues with the exalted Christ. The union is thus effected without any essential impairing of the divine consciousness".[3] On the kenotic view, the most obvious modification required of the divine consciousness in order for it to live a human life was the abandonment of omniscience; does this mean, then,

[1] *Some Loose Stones.*
[2] Macpherson, *op. cit.*, p. 312.
[3] *ibid.*, p. 319.

that such a state of relative ignorance continues to be the lot of Christ in his exalted state, that in relation to his glorified humanity, at any rate, his physical attributes are still in a partial state of exinanition?

It was noted in the previous section how that E. H. Gifford defined the term μορφή as the nature or essence of a thing, not in the abstract, but as actually subsisting in the individual, and retained as long as it exists. On this definition, Gifford argues, it would be ridiculous to conceive of Christ emptying himself of the Form of God, for it would be like admitting that the general can exist without the particular. Now the relative attributes, as defined by the dualistic kenoticists, are in fact part of the Form of God as thus defined by Gifford: to put it in another way, they may not be the whole Form, but they are certain at least of the accidents belonging to the substance of Deity: that the essence of God can subsist without them is to the conservative a denial of the simplicity and unity of God, but to the kenoticist it is a saving necessity. Curiously enough, there does exist a precedent for such a view, or rather a converse of it, in the history of Christian theology, namely, the Thomistic doctrine of Transubstantiation. According to that doctrine, the substance of the material elements of the Eucharist is withdrawn, the accidents still remaining intact —the substance of the flesh and blood of Christ taking its place. In the Thomasian kenotic theory, something akin to the reverse of this process is envisaged: certain of the attributes of God (and those attributes which, like the dimensive qualities of matter in the case of the Eucharist, are the most noticeable characteristics of Deity), are removed, leaving the divine essence intact and apt for its act of Incarnation. Hence if there were sufficient Scriptural basis for, and preponderating logic in support of, the kenotic theory as put forward in this form—which there is apparently not—objection could scarcely be raised to it by those conservative brethren who loyally embrace the Aristotelian philosophy as presented to Christian thought by the schoolmen.

## *Charles Gore*

The following theory was largely propounded in its precise form to meet one of the most glaring objections to the Thomasian theory—the difficulty of Christ's cosmical absenteeism.

Charles Gore, if not the first to introduce kenotic Christology into Britain, was at least its most characteristic Anglo-Saxon exponent and champion. Around his name the controversy raged for many years: he was the man who, in the name of all who shared his views, bore the brunt of the invective of his fellow churchmen, and he above all others was the most determined and sincere protagonist of what he believed to be the only true and honest interpretation of the New Testament doctrine of the Person of Christ. On the other side of the picture, Gore's wide influence and leadership, and his great reputation as a scholar, largely account for the undeniable vogue which the kenotic theory enjoyed, despite the violent opposition which it sustained from conservatives at that time, and later from the more radical of liberal scholars.

As already shown on more than one occasion, the general direction of Dr. Gore's thought is to be seen in his essay in *Lux Mundi*, which proved to be the inception of the open controversy over the limitation of our Lord's knowledge. At that time, then, the question is simply whether our Lord is or is not to be regarded as normally in possession of knowledge regarding certain historical events recorded in the Old Testament, and the like.

The Bampton Lectures for 1891—No. 6 in particular—make a considerable advance on this position. In the Sixth lecture, the Gospel evidence for the true human ignorance of Christ is set forth at great length and with much force of argument. The next step is to assign this limited consciousness to its proper subject. To avoid any scandal of Nestorianism or Docetism, this human ignorance is then attributed—largely by inference at first—to the Son of God himself, and a demonstrative hand is pointed towards the Christological passage in the Epistle to the Philippians as the key to the problem thus created.

The full exposition of the theory, however, was not given to the world until 1895 in the promised volume of Dissertations On Subjects Connected With The Incarnation; and it will conduce to clarity as to brevity if our enquiry be limited to the relevant passages in this latter volume.

It must be borne in mind that, outwardly at any rate, the Second Dissertation is still largely concerned with the establishment of the thesis that our Lord possessed the limited intelligence of a man of his age: and that the kenotic theory is then proposed, and made to confront the reader, as the only consistent explanation of that established fact. This method of introducing the theory is somewhat reminiscent of the old parliamentary device of "tacking", in which the Commons would attach a small piece of irksome legislation on to the bottom of a necessary piece of legislation, such as a finance bill, which the Lords were bound to accept. As an example of Dr. Gore's method in this respect: he contrasts his own view—of Christ's limited knowledge, plus the kenotic theory—with other views: "It is opposed, then, on the one side, to the view, which I must call the *a priori*, dogmatical and unhistorical view that Christ's human mind was from the first moment of the Incarnation and continuously flooded with complete knowledge and with the glory of the Beatific vision. . . . It is opposed, on the other hand, to the *a priori* humanitarian and also unhistorical view that the Son in becoming man ceased to be conscious of his own eternal Sonship, and became, not merely a human, but a fallible and peccable teacher".[1] In other words: the thesis regarding Christ's ignorance, which is certainly based on a good deal of concrete evidence, is contrasted with other views which do not seem to possess the same foundation in fact; whilst it is made to appear that it is the kenotic theory—the only possible explanation of those facts, according to Gore—itself which is being contrasted with these views; since he is unable to offer any alternative explanation of the facts which he has adduced.

Here, however, we are concerned exclusively with Dr. Gore's particular interpretation of the kenotic theory itself. His exposition of this theory properly begins when he turns from considering the Gospel picture of the human Jesus to the interpretation of that picture as given by St. Paul. Here, as far as possible, Dr. Gore must be allowed to speak for himself, for his language is of set purpose cautious, and he is most anxious not to be wise above what is written, and to take his stand, in true loyalty as he believes to Anglicanism, upon the teaching of Scripture. On Phil. 2. 5 ff. he writes as follows: "The word 'Form' transferred from physical shape to spiritual type, describes—as St. Paul uses it, alone or in composition, with uniform accuracy—the permanent characteristics of a thing. Jesus Christ then, in his preexistent state, was living in the permanent characteristics of the life of God. In such a life it was his right to remain. It belonged to him. But he regarded not his prerogatives, as a man regards a prize he must clutch at. For love of us he abjured the prerogatives

[1] Diss, p. 94.

of equality with God. By an act of deliberate self-abnegation, he so emptied himself as to assume the permanent characteristics of the human or servile life: he took the form of a servant. Not only so, but he was made in outward appearance like other men and was found in fashion as a man, that is, in the transitory quality of our mortality. The 'Form', the 'likeness', the 'Fashion' of manhood, he took them all. Thus, remaining in unchanged personality, he is exhibited as (to use Dr. Westcott's words) 'Laying aside the mode of divine existence' in order to assume the human".[1]

Thus Dr. Gore has established his first point, namely, that, in becoming man, Christ was "emptied", his divine mode of life giving place to the human. The passage would almost seem to be deliberately obscure. In the earlier section in which his references to the Philippian passage were reviewed it was noted how the exact turn of the phrases is modified as he proceeds, but it would seem on the whole as though his first definition of the term μορφή Θεου is seriously intended, i.e. the permanent characteristics of God—in other words, God's attributes. But it is not specifically stated here that Christ emptied himself of these or any of these attributes, the characteristics of God, but that "he so emptied himself as to assume". That Christ did actually cease to possess these attributes might well be inferred from the passage, but the very least that it can mean is that Christ so modified these characteristics as to make them compatible with a human consciousness. There may exist reasonable doubt whether μορφή Θεοῦ does in fact refer to the sum of the properties of God, and even more so may it be open to doubt whether St. Paul's language is patient of the interpretation that the μορφή Θεοῦ was in fact emptied out; the point at present, however, is that Dr. Gore would deal in such merchandise as "permanent characteristics of" Deity, and hence there is far more involved in his language than the abnegation of the appearance or outward glory of Godhead. This has been, and will be, pressed further again, in view of the fact that certain writers have attempted to enlist Dr. Gore as the protagonist of a very much modified form of the kenotic theory: such a watering-down is not borne out by the plain meaning of his utterances.

The discussion of the second so-called kenotic passage in St. Paul, 2 Cor. 8. 9, takes Gore a stage further in his argument. "This is how St. Paul interprets our Lord's coming down from

[1] Diss, p. 88.

heaven, and it is manifest that it expresses something very much more than a mere addition of a manhood to his Godhead. In a certain aspect indeed the Incarnation is the folding round the Godhead of the veil of the humanity, to hide its glory, but it is much more than this. It is a ceasing to exercise, at least in a certain sphere, and *so far as human thought can attain*, some natural prerogatives of the divine existence; it is a coming to exist for love of us under conditions of being not natural to Godhead".[1] In the case of the attribute of omniscience, it would appear as though the expression "ceasing to exercise" means ceasing to know.

With this passage may be compared the first of his preliminary conclusions.

"The Incarnation of the Son of God was no mere addition of a manhood to his Godhead: it was no mere wrapping around the divine glory of a human nature to veil it and make it tolerable to mortal eyes. It was more than this. The Son of God, without ceasing to be God, the Son of the Father, and without ceasing to be conscious of his divine relation as Son to the Father, yet, in assuming human nature, so truly entered into it as really to grow and live as Son of Man under properly human conditions, that is to say also under properly human limitations. Thus, if we are to express this in human language, we are forced to assert that within the *sphere* and *period* of his Incarnate and mortal life, he did and as it would appear did habitually—doubtless by the voluntary action of his own self-limiting and self-restraining love—cease from the exercise of those divine functions and powers, including the divine omniscience, which would have been incompatible with a truly human experience".[2]

These passages provoke the following comments: In theology, as in other topics of life, much depends upon the precise shade of colour or insinuation of the actual words and expressions we use. Just as "A hotted lump of a dead animal" and "A delicious slice of roast beef" can quite well refer to the same article; so also, to describe the Real Presence as "God in a bit of bread" was a scrap of polemic which did protestant writers no credit: it all depends upon the name we give to a thing. But when Dr. Gore deprecates an interpretation of the Person of Christ that makes the Incarnation appear as a "mere addition of a manhood", or a "mere wrapping around the divine glory",

[1] Diss, p. 90.
[2] *ibid.*, p. 94.

it is not so obvious at first sight that by this innocent turn of phrase he is flying in the face of one of the most celebrated principles of Patristic Christology. This principle is constantly repeated in variations of the phrase—μένων ὃ ἦν ἔλαβεν ὃ οὐκ ἦν.[1] Remaining what he was, he assumed what he was not (before). It was considered essential alike for the maintainance of the doctrine of the Trinity and of Christ's two whole and perfect natures to assert that, in the Incarnation, Christ lost nothing of his divine essence or nature. His Person, and his divine nature, which was inseparable from it, must obviously remain intact if he is to be regarded as truly God as well as truly man. This is not to say that Christ did not enter fully into human experience; by his almighty power he added to his Person a new sphere of experience, action and relationships—a human nature. But this is clearly *not* what Dr. Gore means. In his view it is impossible for God the Son to undergo human experience in addition to his divine life; he declares as clearly as he could that the Son of God cannot assume a human existence and nature without first doing something to that divine nature, to make that nature itself commensurate with human experience: it is the divine nature itself that, in Dr. Gore's view, becomes to him the vehicle of human experience, not a new nature which is added to it. Chalcedonian theology, in its plain meaning, he simply cannot accept.

So far, then, Dr. Gore has indicated that it is the permanent characteristics of Godhead that are affected by the Incarnation; and that such an exinanition is the essence of that act rather than the addition of a new nature to his Godhead. The next step is to attempt to estimate what, in Gore's opinion, actually happened to those properties which Christ surrendered. The following are some of the phrases with which he describes the act of *kenosis*. "Abjured the prerogatives of equality with God"; "By an act of deliberate self-abnegation, he so emptied himself";[2] "A ceasing to exercise";[3] "Cease from the exercise of those divine functions".[4]

An argument often adduced against the Thomasian kenotic theory has been postponed to this point in order to compare it with the slightly different though cognate argument in the present instance. It is contended that the theory contains a logical

---

[1] Tert. *De Carne Christi* 103 and Origen *De Principiis*, i. 4.
[2] Both *ibid.*, p. 88.
[3] *ibid.*, p. 90.  [4] *ibid.*, p. 94.

contradiction which renders it beyond the pale of reasonableness. Assuming that the *kenosis* is a voluntary act, it is in the first place impossible for omnipotence to will itself to be limited. If the *kenosis* be looked upon as a continuous restraint, as Gore appears to do, the contradiction is even worse, for it would require an omnipotent will constantly in operation to restrain omnipotence. Similarly omniscience cannot will itself to unknow or forget; and assuming that such an act of *kenosis were* possible, then it would require an omnipotent will and an omniscient mind to perform the transformation back again, which, *ex hypothesi*, the kenoted Christ did not possess. Dr. Gore's doctrine, then, is different from the Thomasian view, namely, the doctrine of abstention from use of the divine properties. Christ abstained from exercising his omnipotence, he ceased to use his omniscience, he restrained his omnipresence, and so forth. This, incidentally, became the most usual and popular form of the kenotic theory in Britain. It apparently secures the religious advantages of the kenotic theory—the genuine self-sacrifice on the part of Christ and his true humanity without the necessity of dividing up the attributes, or the mythological strain of the metamorphic theory. On closer examination, however, it would seem to be open to the same, if not a more severe, logical objection as the Thomasian theory, and in point of fact to amount to much the same meaning. If it is regarded as impossible for God the Son absolutely speaking to part with any portion of his essence or nature—a proposition to which Gore would unquestionably assent; it is surely equally impossible to speak of Christ's not possessing certain attributes, simply because he refrains from exercising them—a mere quibble of words, in fact. A boy who attains to years of discretion abandons, restrains, ceases to exercise, his power to smash windows, surrendering it in order that he may live under the conditions proper to a civilized society; yet no one would suggest that the boy is thereby incapable of smashing windows—he still possesses that power. So when we are informed by Dr. Gore that Christ in becoming man abandoned, or ceased to exercise, his divine omnipotence, if it does not mean that he absolutely ceased to possess that property, it can only mean that he *did* possess it, but normally refrained from employing it. If the theory implies so very little in the case of omnipotence, whatever significance can it possess in regard to omniscience? If Christ as God the Son knew a thing in virtue of the divine omniscience, he cannot cease to know it without parting with that attribute of Deity; that may be the case, but to speak of restraining one's knowledge, if it does not mean such a complete parting with the attribute can mean nothing more than that Christ acted in life as though he did not know. The language of "restraint" is therefore misleading, for it is clear that Dr. Gore intended to teach that Christ's self-consciousness, as divine as well as human, is reduced and limited on some topics of knowledge to that of a man of his age. This criticism may seem a trifle rationalistic in tone, and, in fact, Gore seems alive to the apparent contradictions of the situation and seeks refuge in the mystery of God's nature—why not have done this in the first place, one may well ask. "May not then the sympathetic entrance of God into human life have carried with it—not because it was weak but because it was powerful—something which can only be imagined or expressed by us as a real 'forgetting' or abandoning within the human sphere of his own divine point of view and mode of consciousness"?[1] And again: "May it not be that because God is perfect and his attributes inseparable from his Person, therefore his knowledge is, far more than can be the case with us, under the control of his personal, essential will of love".[2]

It is most difficult for rational man to appreciate, let alone accept, this *a priori* speculation as to the control of the divine attributes by the divine will. Far from revealing the affinity of the divine and human natures, such a theology presents a Deity whose modes and actions flatly contradict all we know of personality and the laws of reason implanted in us by his hand. A Deity who can so modify his consciousness as to forget what he knew, and the possibilities of his powers, and then regain them again by an act of his depotentiated will and limited mind, may appeal to some school of abstruse scholars steeped in dialectic and speculation: it could scarcely be expected to appeal to the harsh rationality of the nineteenth century.

It is a singular fact that Dr. Gore should have attempted to safeguard his whole position by presenting a categorical assertion that God's attributes are inseparable from him: one can only quit this portion of his work, therefore, with a seeming contradiction and uncertainty before one: "The attributes of God on account of the perfection of his personal unity, are not so to

[1] Diss, p. 219.
[2] *ibid.*, p. 220.

speak separable from one another or from his Personality but are identically one".[1]

Far more interesting and important, however, the thing, in fact, which gives this particular theory its distinctive character, is the account which Dr. Gore gives of the relation of Christ's Incarnate life to his cosmic life. Holy Scripture, he believes, teaches quite clearly that God the Son is the permanent upholder of the natural creation; and he therefore rejects any view which would imply that Christ ceased to exercise his functions in the natural order as creator and sustainer, or that in becoming man he virtually relinquished his seat within the Blessed Trinity—though on this latter point he is not so explicit.

For example, he believes that the Epistle to the Hebrews teaches that the Logos was still the sustaining power of the universe— "This writer also must have believed the self-emptying in the one sphere to have been compatible with the cosmic function in another sphere".[2] We may point out that it is not at all obvious that the writer to the Hebrews envisages any such self-emptying, as Gore understands it, on the part of the divine Son in becoming man; but it is true that this writer stresses the continuance of Christ's cosmic functions as does the passage Col. 1. 15 ff.

"Nor can we dissociate the fulfilment of the cosmic functions from the exercise of omniscience. We must suppose, then, that in some manner the humiliation and the self-limitation of the Incarnate state was compatible with the continued exercise of divine and cosmic functions in another sphere. But although we cannot but suppose and believe this, we must remember that the language of the New Testament is much more full and clear on the fact of the human limitations than on the permanence of the cosmic functions . . ."[3] So much for Gore's own words.

In most of the passage preceding as quoted from Dr. Gore, we have become familiar with such expressions as "within a certain sphere", "within the sphere of the Incarnation", and so forth. Or again—"The view expressed above involves no limitation of the divine activity of the Word absolutely in himself or in the world, but only within a certain area".[4] And yet again—"Withdrawing these (divine attributes) from operation within the sphere of the humanity he yet himself lived under human conditions"

[1] Diss, p. 219.  [2] ibid., p. 92.  [3] ibid., p. 93.
[4] ibid., p. 210.

Hence Dr. Gore would appear to teach a duality in the operation of the Divine Logos. Christ is not envisaged as abandoning or veiling his divine attributes from his whole being or consciousness as such and living simply and solely as a man on earth. He lives a perfect human life, and yet at the same time he possesses all divine properties and functions as before, which he continues to exercise in every corner of the universe. He thus possesses at one and the same time the blissful ignorance of a child on Mary's knee, and the omniscience of the heavenly Creator. This sounds orthodox Christology enough; for it would appear to afford place within Christ's Person for the operation of the two whole and perfect natures. But owing, I am much disposed to fear, to Dr. Gore's own psychological presuppositions, the upshot of the doctrine is far from being so felicitous. It has been maintained all along that Dr. Gore's doctrine of personality, like that of the majority of his contemporaries, was stated in terms of self-consciousness—or quite simply, consciousness. To him, the older doctrine of a substantial soul, or an ego, an individuating principle, or central point of reference, possessing two quite distinct natures was meaningless. This explains his failure to accept Chalcedonian Christology as it stood. Hence to him, this human sphere in which the Logos for a time subsists, was not simply a nature assumed by him and operated by him; for it was itself a self-conscious existence, and such consciousness was to Dr. Gore and his contemporaries not simply a part or faculty of abstract human nature, it was itself almost the essence of personality. Hence the possession of these two modes of existence by the Logos, practically amounts to his having lived his life from two life centres. This is how Dr. Gore's doctrine differs so radically from the scholastic doctrine of the Incarnation—though superficially the two are akin. When an older traditionalist theologian speaks of Christ at one and the same time being a feeble babe in Mary's arms and disposing the stars in their courses, he means that one and the same Person possesses two complete organs of function and expression—two natures. By the same expression, however, Gore would mean that the Logos himself is divided into two compartments, the Logos himself, and not an impersonal manhood personalised by him, being the subject of the human experience of Christ.

Dr. Gore gives final shape to his doctrine thus—"This seems to postulate that the personal life of the Word should have been

## THE KENOTIC THEORY

lived as it were from more than one centre—that he who knows and does all things in the Father and in the universe should (reverently be it said) have begun to live from a new centre when he assumed manhood, and under new and restricted conditions of power and knowledge".[1]

This theory of the dual life-centre of the Logos, which, as Dr. Gore admits, was originally invented by Bishop Martensen, has the very clear advantage over other kenotic theories that it avoids all those difficulties involved in the assumption that Christ for a time relinquished his cosmic functions. Yet it too has many defects. It is, to begin with, a novelty in the Christian tradition; and being a metaphysical theory of such startling complexity, could scarcely be accepted without some clear indication being furnished in the Scriptures or traditional thought of the church that such is indeed a possibility.

Perhaps the chief intrinsic objection to the theory is the fact that on the given psychological presupposition of the age, it is difficult to see how one can avoid speaking of the Logos having become by the Incarnation two persons. Consciousness, in the thought of the day, had steadily become divorced from the idea of nature and had become attached to that of personality. On Gore's own showing, the Logos assumes another consciousness, and a consciousness, moreover, which is to all intents and purposes maintained in a watertight compartment, since the Divine Omniscience is excluded from it. What then in Gore's opinion unites these two centres of conscious life? Presumably the divine nature: which itself would be an admission, generally denied at the time, that nature, the divine nature, can subsist in the abstract not being specifically related to one consciousness; if they had only admitted the converse, that two natures can be held simultaneously by one Person, their most pressing difficulties would have been solved. Furthermore, Gore would reply that the duality was but a temporary phase—"Now in his glory we must conceive that the manhood subsists under conditions of Godhead, 'The glory of God'; but formerly during his mortal life, and within its sphere, the Godhead was energizing under conditions and limitations of manhood". But to Dr. Gore the essence of true manhood consists in being limited in knowledge and power—and more radical liberals would add, peccability. The manhood, then, as it now exists in heaven, glorified and apparently without

[1] Diss, p. 215

these restrictions, is simply not manhood in any sense intelligible to the nineteenth century, and the Incarnation therefore was something quite transitory, a mode of appearance, or a state of experience, engendered by the Logos within his own consciousness, to meet the needs of the moment.

We may, in fact, press this criticism yet one stage further. According to Gore, it is the Logos himself who constitutes Christ's human consciousness; it is his will which is restricted, it is his mind which is limited. Surely this is nothing less than a modern Apollinarianism; for all that is left is a truly human body; the portions of the Lord's psychic make-up which in olden times were regarded as elements in human nature are now regarded as constituents of individual personality, and hence in Christ's case belong to the Deity.

But there are three criticisms of a different character that must needs be alluded to. First, there are grave objections to the employment of spatial language in connexion with entities which by their nature are not subject to space. Naturally such language is merely metaphorical; but the use of such terminology even in a semi-physical science such as psychology has led to many blunders; in connexion, for example, with zones, levels, or thresholds of consciousness. Much more cautious then should the application of such language be to spiritual categories. What intelligible meaning can be attached to the statement that the Son of God is omniscient in one sphere and limited in another? Can he who contains all things, and is in his fullness in all things, be anything but completely himself in any part of them?

But secondly, assuming the spatial language, for the sake of argument, here is practically the most glaring contradiction contained in this type of kenotic theory: if God the Son remains during the period of the Incarnation in the full and complete exercise of his functions "in the Father" and in the universe, and is only limited within the sphere of the Incarnation, a sphere which for him did not previously exist, then wherein lies the self-emptying? As Lord of the universe and second Person of the Trinity he remains inviolate: he is only emptied within the sphere of the Incarnation, they say; but that sphere of activity and consciousness did not previously exist; he did not empty himself in regard to any sphere of activity which already existed, but only in one which up till then did not. Hence on this theory the most that can be said of the Son is that in becoming man he assumed a new sphere in which his activities were very limited and his mode of operation circumscribed. But to call this a self-emptying on the part of God the Son is a stretch of language scarcely admissible.

Thirdly, at the end of a long and tortuous path, Dr. Gore has arrived at the following statement of Christology: The Son of God in becoming man entered upon a new sphere of operation in which he possessed what is practically a new consciousness—that of a finite, human, intelligence. Hence for thirty-three years he lived a double life at one and the same time, the omniscient Logos and the finite Jesus.

How, it may be asked, can this theory possibly be proffered to the world as more Scriptural, logical, simple, more acceptable to the modern mind, more easy to grasp, than the ancient scholastic Christology which it is intended to replace?

In the ancient system there is a duality of a sort: two natures are believed to be possessed by a single substantial Person; what has here happened is that the duality has been pushed back a stage—instead of a duality of natures we have a duality of Logos consciousness: and pray, how is it to be thought more intelligible that the Logos should live a double life in himself with a dual consciousness, than that the Son of God should be the subject of two whole and complete natures, human and divine? Surely it is no easier to conceive of the Logos being in his own nature simultaneously omniscient and limited than it is to suppose that he possessed a human nature endowed with such limitations: and the new view-point has many additional difficulties which the traditional doctrine did not possess.

No mention has purposely been made of the extensive investigations which Gore and Ottley engaged in with the object of securing Patristic support for their views. On their own admission, their findings are scanty—a few inconclusive references from Irenaeus, Origen, and Hilary of Poitiers. Here it will suffice to observe that in the brilliant dawn of Christian theology, when the facts of divine revelation were for the first time coming under the examination and interpretation of the human intellect, it is scarcely to be wondered at that men of the originality and genius of these Fathers should have given utterance from time to time to inferences and speculations which the wisdom and more mature consideration of later ages either dismissed or found it impossible to follow up. Therefore to seek support for any new theory in

156     CONFLICT IN CHRISTOLOGY

isolated utterances of these writers, on the plea that such remarks—if carried to their logical conclusion by those writers—would have led inevitably to the theory thus seeking support, can scarcely be entertained as a legitimate occupation for the expositor of the Christian Faith.

The doctrine of a dual life of the Logos was followed by many writers of the time, who, however, have little to add in substance or explanation.

For instance, T. C. Edwards[1] holds that if the Logos had not shared the human ignorance and fear of death etc. he would only have assumed man in a superficial manner.[2] The Logos thus filled two distinct spheres of action,[3] and there is a true *communicatio idiomatum* within the Logos between his two states, for each is experienced by one and the same Person though in different conditions. Even in his Incarnate state Christ possessed moral omnipotence, which ensured his sinlessness.[4] This latter statement is a good example of the quite arbitrary way in which such metaphysical speculations were manipulated in order to fit in with immediate theological necessity.

William Newton Clarke, already referred to, writes that the *kenosis* does not imply that the Logos was withdrawn from the universe and localized in Jesus, nor that he was withdrawn from God and occupied solely in the Incarnation; for the Logos is capable of more than one activity at a time. The Logos is still as ever, therefore, the medium of God's revelation with the universe.[5]

P. T. *Forsyth*, The Person and Place of Jesus Christ, 1909.

Some of the later kenotic writers had far deeper interests than the mere solving of the dilemma regarding the limitation of our Lord's knowledge; the consideration of perhaps the best known of them is, in fact, postponed until the tenth chapter for this very reason. But for completeness' sake, a brief reference should here be made to another of them, for though his thought goes far beyond anything that was envisaged in this direction in the 'nineties, he is none the less a true kenoticist, prepared to accept the full consequences and implications of that doctrine.

The quotations which were made from his work in the course

[1] *The God-man*, 1895.     [2] *op. cit.*, p. 118.
[3] *ibid.*, p. 108.     [4] *ibid.*, p. 130.
[5] *An Outline of Christian Theology*, N.Y., 1889, p. 294.

# THE KENOTIC THEORY

of the first chapter would serve to show the true starting-point of Forsyth's thought. For him, soteriology, the initiative and the grace of God, the free gift of salvation, and the experience of forgiveness in Christ, these are the true source of everything else. Metaphysics, Christology even, only arise from the first group of facts and therefore must be subordinated to them. Hence to him, even more than to most kenoticists, logical and metaphysical objections to the theory are met with stern dismissal, since his theory would appear to him the only reasonable interpretation of the facts of revelation and redemption. We turn then to the eleventh chapter of his work.

"If there was a personal pre-existence in the case of Christ it does not seem possible to adjust it to the historical Jesus without some doctrine of kenosis. We face in Christ a Godhead self-reduced but real, whose infinite power took effect in self-humiliation, whose strength was perfected in weakness, who consented not to know with an ignorance divinely wise, and who emptied himself in virtue of his divine fullness".[1] Forsyth is not blind to the inherent difficulties in such a doctrine; they are, however, scientific and not religious. But what is of such importance is that he recognised that those difficulties do not simply apply to the kenotic theory, they equally refer in other forms to the Incarnation itself: he sees clearly that the basic problem for theology is not, how did the Son become ignorant of the authorship of Ps. 110? but how can the eternal and infinite God enter into the processes of time and space?

"We cannot form any scientific conception of the precise process by which a complete and eternal being could enter on a process of becoming, how Godhead could accept growth, how a divine consciousness could reduce its own consciousness by volition".[2] Forsyth does, it is true, speak of omnipotence and omniscience as "less ethical attributes", but he does not press any clear distinction between the properties. Rather, he emphasizes the supremacy within the divine unity of the properties of love and the necessities which such a property entails. He cites the example of men who sacrifice the exercise of genius for their ideals; and adduces the picture of a son who relinquishes a brilliant philosophical career to carry on the business at home after the death of his father: "Is not this a case where a moral and

[1] *Person and Place of Jesus Christ*, p. 293–4.
[2] *ibid.*, p. 294.

sympathetic volition leads to a certain contraction of consciousness"?[1] Christ too then "lives out a moral plerosis by the very completeness of his *kenosis*".[2] Here then is the principle enunciated in another way—moral power gives great power for self-renunciation. In Christ's own case, "his divine energy and mobility would have a power even to pass into a successive and developing state of being, wherein consciousness of perfect fullness and changelessness should retire, and become but subliminal or rare".[3] It is at this point that Forsyth introduces his suggestion that Christ may have been unaware even of his own impeccability.

Now it is obvious that something more, or at any rate something different, is here envisaged than the mere abnegation of certain purely physical attributes; there is a real alteration in the mode, not simply in the extent of the Logos' consciousness. Forsyth in fact frankly admits this fact when he works out his own system in criticising the work of Thomasius. He contends that the relative attributes cannot simply be cut off, they must always be latent: but "Let us cease speaking of a nature as if it were an entity; of two natures as two independent entities; and let us think and speak of two modes of being, like quantitative and qualitative, or physical and moral. Instead of speaking of certain attributes as renounced may we not speak of a new mode of their being? The Son, by an act of love's omnipotence, set aside the style of a God, and took the style of a servant, the mental manner of a man, and the mode of moral action that marks human nature".[4] "Take the attribute of omniscience, for instance. In its eternal form, it is an intuitive and simultaneous knowledge of all things; but when the eternal enters time it becomes a discursive and successive knowledge, and the power to know all things only potential, and enlarging to become actual under the moral conditions that govern human growth and the extension of human knowledge. Here we have not so much the renunciation of attributes, nor their conscious possession and concealment, as the retraction of their mode of being from actual to potential".[5] It thus becomes possible to see how even Christ's consciousness of being Divine gradually developed in him as it emerged, so to speak, from the potential to the actual. This is indeed a unique, and in one sense a radical, doctrine of *kenosis*, but there are elements of more

---

[1] *Person and Place of Jesus Christ*, p. 289.
[2] *ibid*, p. 300.  [3] *ibid.*, p. 300.
[4] *ibid.*, p. 307.  [5] *ibid.*, p. 308.

permanent value in it than in those doctrines and theories evolved in the heat of controversy in the 'nineties; especially is this value seen in the emphasis upon the omnipotence of God's love being seen in the limitations of Christ; it is the Lord's own doctrine of life through death, and the Pauline conception of the "weakness" and "foolishness" of God revivified for us; says Forsyth again, "There was more omnipotence concentrated in the Person of Christ than was spread in all creation".[1]

*The Theory of Continuous Self-Restraint*

Allusion should finally be made to a not-inconsiderable group of writers who never embraced the idea of a real abandonment on the part of the Son of God of any of his attributes but preferred to speak rather of a self-restraint in the exercise of them. They maintain that throughout the Incarnate life Christ, absolutely speaking, had the full possession and use of all his powers at his disposal, but he so willed by his sovereign power not to use them, that they did virtually cease to be present in relation to his human circumstances, and he was thus enabled to live a truly human life. That he only did allow his divine power and knowledge to break through the veil in cases when it would befit and benefit his hearers, and would not impair the integrity of his humanity, is the true measure of his power and restraint, and accounts, in fact, for the sporadic character of his miracles and supernatural knowledge. The most celebrated exponent of this view was Frank Weston, *The One Christ*, but as his whole book belongs rather to a later stage in the development of English Christology, it has been relegated to a later chapter. The theory of continuous self-restraint was also embraced by a number of lesser lights, among whom one from either side of the Atlantic may be mentioned. The Donnellan lectures for 1911-12 were given by E. Digges La Touche, who took as his title *The Person of Christ in Modern Thought*. They form a weighty and thoughtful survey of modern Christologies, especially German. His constructive effort, however, is confined to a following-out of some of Weston's ideas. Another work, published in the early years of the kenotic controversy, contains tendencies which, if developed, might have led to a similar version of the theory; this was L. F. Stearns' *Present-Day Theology*.[2] We are told in the preface that

[1] *Person and Place of Jesus Christ*, p. 315.
[2] N.Y., 1893.

Mr. Stearns sprang from a fine old New England Presbyterian family, that his aunt in fact was responsible for a volume entitled *Stepping Heavenwards*. Stearns, holding that Christ abandoned the τὸ εἶναι ἴσα Θεῷ, maintains that he underwent the normal physical, intellectual, and spiritual restrictions proper to manhood.[1] He protests against the tendency of moderns who wish to maintain the one Person of Christ, as against two consciousnesses, even at the expense of his two natures: a striking point.[2] It is interesting that one who was converted to kenotic Christology at so early a date should have been able to avoid some of its worst pitfalls, as Stearns undoubtedly does.

*General Summary*

It is not proposed here to set out in detail every aspect of the argument for or against kenotic Christology. Many of the contentions of either side have already been discussed, and their full repetition would be unnecessary since many of them relate to specific types of kenotic theory. Some broader considerations will therefore be described which hitherto have at most been alluded to in passing: they are not intended to constitute a formal defence or condemnation of these theories.

The inherent strength of the kenotic theory, apart from the fact of its timely intervention in the Knowledge controversy, lies in its religious appeal. Not only does it secure a Christ whose humanity is franchised from the disembodying influence of divine attributes: it renders that humanity and that Incarnation infinitely more adorable by presenting it as an act of real and costly self-sacrifice on the part of God's Son. It projects, as it were, that wondering devotion to the sacrificing love of God, which had previously been focussed alone upon the Cross outwards on to the whole drama of the Incarnation itself.

Again, whatever logical or scientific arguments may be brought against the kenotic theory, its exponents do, in one sense at any rate, stand upon fact; they begin with something that has actually taken place, they place upon that fact a straightforward interpretation, and the onus of disproving it lies with their opponents. The Incarnation had actually taken place: the almighty and eternal God had in fact lived a finite life on earth, with all the

[1] *Op. cit.*, 1889, p. 144.
[2] *ibid.*, p. 160.

outward appearances of true manhood. The impossible had become passible, the eternal subject to change; and the obvious meaning of this fact was that the Son had undergone a mysterious process of self-limitation—even Cyril of Alexandria saw this. A thousand and one objections might be advanced against the particular forms of expression which the kenotic theory took, but the basic difficulty in refuting the kenotic theory—or rather theories—was and still is that it or they do at bottom represent a truth and a fact which cannot be gainsaid by any save a pure Nestorian.

The kenoticist, moreover, has one further matter of actual fact to which he can and did point in explication of his theories: that was the existence of the natural creation. It is urged by these writers that a helpful and significant analogy to the self-emptying of the Incarnation is afforded by God's self-limitation of his powers in creation. Two specimens of this type of approach may be offered.

The American professor, Newton Clarke, writes: "All God's active relations with his creation probably take place through some kind of self-limitation and no reason appears why he should not so limit himself as to enter into that humanity which he created in his own likeness".[1]

And the English Dr. Garvie—whose great service to theology has always been that he expresses everyone's view better than they could ever do for themselves—writes in the present connexion: "The conception of the divine immanence affects not only our view of the world but also our idea of God. If God is expressed and exercised in the processes of the world which is subject to limitation, then creation is a self-limitation of God. The infinite in creating, as it were, reduces himself to the measure of the finite. Creation itself is *kenosis*, self-emptying. Infinite power expresses and exercises itself in finite forces. Infinite wisdom is displayed and present in finite laws. Infinite truth communicates itself in the process of finite knowledge. The infinite righteousness realises itself in the development of finite character. Infinite grace humbles itself in the uplifting of the finite soul to God".[2]

An artist who paints a picture can scarcely be said to express anything like his full meaning on a canvas of two dimensions, however delicate the colouring: he is in fact limited by the

[1] *An Outline of Christian Theology*, p. 293.
[2] Studies, p. 524.

media through which he expresses himself; so it is with God in creation. It should be borne in mind, however, that such a species of *kenosis*, limitation in the manner of action and expression, is a matter far different from the abandonment by God of part of his eternal nature according to one or other of the speculative theories.

A very clear and sympathetic statement of the religious and theological premises of kenotic Christology is to be found in H. R. Mackintosh, especially valuable since that writer refrains from committing himself to any particular speculative interpretation of those premises.[1]

"People who live in glass-houses should not throw stones" is probably the most obvious charge which can be levelled against the kenoticists by both conservatives and radical liberals. No group of writers harped so monotonously upon the theme that *a priori* dogmatic theology is artificial, unhistorical and harmful, than did these writers. Gore's Bampton Lectures and Dissertations, Fairbairn's volume on Christology, and the writings of Ottley, Swayne, T. B. Strong, and many others, abound with such criticism. We are told that in place of *a priori* dogmas must come historical and scriptural induction; that in place of metaphysical contortions must come the ethical approach. Yet what could be more speculative or more metaphysical than the kenotic theory? Conjectures regarding the possibility of the dividing up of God's attributes, or the supposition that divine attributes can be controlled, dispensed with, and regained, by the divine volition: such things can scarcely be termed inductions from the testimony of Scripture. The same Garvie writes that "The idea of a Logos depotentiating himself with a view to Incarnation is not only a speculative curiosity, but has even a mythological aspect".[2] A metaphysical theory, and yet its exponents constantly attempt to protect it from a frank examination as such by protesting that since it is the revelation of a God who is primarily an ethical being, such logical considerations would be irrelevant.

It is also argued by many that emphasis upon the *kenosis* results in a grievous distortion of the whole purpose of the Incarnation, which was to reveal God to man, not to hide him behind an impassable veil, or in a nature through which nothing specifically

---

[1] *Doctrine of the Person of Jesus Christ*, 1912. On Phil. 2. 5, p. 67. On Irenaeus, p. 145. On German theories, p. 265, and his own reconstruction, part III, ch. X.   [2] *Studies*, p. 517.

divine could percolate; for indeed God is most clearly distinguished from us by his physical attributes, his moral nature being akin to ours, according to modern immanentist writers. That God is omnipotent, omniscient and omnipresent is a fact which alone gives reality to every fact in the world; on it rests every atom of faith and hope in this existence and the next; without it, God could not be worshipped as God—for he would not be God at all.

From the theories themselves, we return to the actual situation of the age which produced them, in order to regain the true perspective of events. These kenotic theories were in the main propounded with three aims in view: aims, as distinguished from the long-term motives and factors which produced the situation itself. These aims naturally vary in very different proportions in the various writers.

1. There was in the first place the pressing need to secure an immediate reconciliation between the new exegesis of the Gospels, depicting as it did a Jesus of a limited knowledge, and the ecclesiastical orthodoxy of past ages, still regarded as the unquestioned norm for theology by all right-wing liberals of this time.

2. But even more serious as time went on was the urgent need for *holding* the Christological situation from falling headlong into chaos. There was the danger of the English schools rushing into a headlong and unconditional acceptance of the findings and theories of the continental higher critics: for in Germany, higher critics and their theories were rapidly taking the place in that country of formal theology—even many of the most celebrated exponents of Ritschlianism were higher critics.

3. One can see a desire, after the heat of the controversy had died down, to employ such a system as kenotic Christology provided as a category through which there might be established some permanent and intelligible means of understanding the relations of the Incarnate Christ to the life of the eternal Trinity, not merely in respect of the single human attribute of limited knowledge, but of what the Incarnation as a whole involved.

Most of those writers who have been considered in this chapter were indeed primarily at grips with the first of the three aims. That situation has already been amply described; and in the minds of great numbers of thinking Christians down to our own day, the kenotic theory has remained the sufficient answer to that problem.

In regard to the second aim, the most far-seeing at that time realised that the Anglo-Saxon world could not for ever be a theological island. More advanced conclusions were to be accepted with regard to the historic person of Jesus which would create so wide a breach between traditional orthodoxy and liberalistic conclusions as no kenotic theory could bridge. How this came about will be traced in the three following chapters.

Of the third aim, there was as yet but little to show. The theological horizon in the 'nineties was far too restricted to allow of a larger view of the subject being taken, but in the ninth and tenth chapters the subject will be reopened, with the larger purposes before us: for kenotic Christology, at least in a modified form, had become a permanent feature of the Christology of Britain and America.

# 6

## THE CONSCIOUSNESS OF JESUS

WHEN once the discussion of Christ's mind and what it contained had been opened up; when once men had dared to draw aside the veil of reverent agnosticism and calculate the contents of the Master's human brain, it was not to be expected that the matter would be allowed to rest merely with a debate upon the limitation of his knowledge or the manner of his sinlessness. Such an investigation, in fact, once begun, enlarged itself a thousandfold, until no single element or aspect of Christ's spiritual or mental life remained undiscussed, or more accurately, unconjectured about.

*Studies of the Mind in Christ* and *Studies in the Inner Life of Jesus* are titles of books which testify to the new approach. It was a manner of examining the Person and life of Christ and of constructing Christology quite unique in the history of Christian thought. The examination and appraisement of the Lord's knowledge had to many appeared as a dangerous intrusion into those regions where man may not pry. To the modern man, however, it is almost an axiom that there are *no* regions into which he may not pry. Here then was something far more scandalizing to the sentiment of an earlier day than the "Knowledge" controversy—though it must be regarded as a logical development from it—namely, that the very spiritual growth of Christ's soul, his most intimate relations with the Father, should become the subject of a searching scrutiny, and further, that the results established by this enquiry should be made the pivot upon which belief in his Divinity should rest. Much of the paraphernalia of this study of the interior life of Christ has become as nauseating to the orthodox Christian of to-day as it would have been to any generation prior to the liberal era, but at the time it seemed the only road to a secure basis for faith, and must receive sympathetic treatment if on that count alone.

This new study of the growth and content of Christ's consciousness had the ground of its possibility in the prevailing trend of psychology, which was becoming increasingly engaged in the examination of subjective consciousness. Nor was this interest unparalleled in the world of thought at large, since the Romantic movement had given an impetus and a rich colouring to the appreciation of the value of subjective feeling, whilst the still ascendant philosophy of the idealists, in part at any rate, focussed attention upon experience within rather than occurrence without. But more than all, the study had its immediate motive power in the urgent need for a new apologetic for Christ's Deity.

It appeared, moreover, to many students to be a stepping-stone towards a richer understanding of divine and human personality, and towards a permanent rationale of the doctrine of the Incarnation; and it consequently enjoyed a wide vogue not only among the genuine truth-seekers but among those who desired to be considered liberal, modern, scientific, progressive, and the like. But it must be borne in mind that its first English exponents, like the exponents of the kenotic theory, were not men who desired to part company with the traditional faith of the church, but men who desired to put that same faith on newly-adjusted and unshakable foundations; they were quite distinct from the more radical liberals whose work will be discussed in the two following chapters.

To begin then with the apologetic motive. The apologists and theologians of earlier times had appealed for their evidence of the Divinity of Christ to what we may conveniently describe as the External Proofs. Christ had indeed lived a human life, but not exactly as other men live their lives. He had done certain outstanding things in his life which other men do not and cannot do in their lives, under normal human circumstances; notably, he had entered the world and left it again in a manner in which it is not given to other men to enter or leave it. It was therefore in these unique and supernatural occurrences that men sought for the demonstration of the Lord's divine nature. The virgin-conception, for instance, demonstrated his supernatural origin; the celestial voices heard at such times as his baptism and transfiguration testified to his unique relationship to the Father; his numerous miracles bore witness to his Lordship over the natural creation; his supernatural knowledge attested his all-knowing wisdom; above all, his resurrection and ascension, with all that those events included—the empty tomb, the bodily appearances, and the words of command and commission therein given—these all

## THE CONSCIOUSNESS OF JESUS

were regarded as indisputable evidences from the Gospel history that Jesus was the Christ, the Son of God.

In this connexion, Dr. Garvie recalls that Dr. Denney cites as the features that give objectivity to Christ's Godhead: 1. His supernatural birth; 2. His pre-existence as taught by St. Paul; 3. The doctrine of the Incarnation of the Logos, at least as taught by St. John.[1] Garvie comments that the older apologetics usually added: 4. The physical resurrection from the dead; 5. The fulfilment of prophecy, and 6. The performance of miracles.[2] It may be observed that two of these items, the teaching of SS. Paul and John, stand in a somewhat different category from the rest of the external proofs. At this period it was all too easy for these witnesses to be discounted as "Hellenistic speculations", "Corruptions of Jesus' simple Gospel" and so forth, and their value was therefore but slight. It is only in our own day that the witness of the Apostolic age to the truth of Christian doctrines has come into its rightful place. The case of prophecy-fulfilment was different. It was an external proof, a miraculous set of coincident circumstances, which all could see and read. This too, however, had already lost all its significance through the new attitude to the Old Testament engendered by higher criticism. But what of the external proofs alluded to in the first instance? These had ever been regarded as concrete and unshakeable evidence: they were historical and objective in character—things which had actually occurred, not simply the fruits of someone's pious reflections. In an age in which the historical method had assumed so predominant a position in all manner of thinking, it might have been imagined that the external and historical proofs of Christ's Godhead would have sprung to new life and importance as the outstanding touchstone of the verity of the Gospel. But in actual fact the very opposite proved to be the case. For whilst higher criticism, on its more conservative side at any rate, had attested the substantial veracity of the Gospel picture of Jesus, it nevertheless cast a haze of doubt upon many specific episodes in the Gospel narrative, notably those of a miraculous character. In Chapter I. B. it was observed how strong the tide was ebbing from the miraculous, and in the chapter which follows we are to see how the idea of the Incarnation itself as a miraculous intervention in history was to be

[1] Cited by Garvie from J. Denney, *Studies in Theology*, p. 14.
[2] A. E. Garvie, *Studies in the Inner Life of Jesus*, p. 400.

challenged. For the moment we are dealing with one short-term result of this movement in thought. A student of the Scriptures in such a frame of mind as we thus envisage was naturally disposed to give ear to any higher critic who could advance sufficiently plausible reasons for regarding as untrustworthy any narrative in the Gospels that contained an element of the miraculous.

An excellent example of this type of thinking is afforded by the ready way in which the supposed untrustworthiness of the opening chapters of SS. Matthew and Luke was accepted, on seemingly all too slender grounds from the purely literary point of view. These chapters contain the thorny miracle of the Virgin Conception of Christ. Virgin conception is a slightly more accurate term than the customary "Virgin Birth", since the fuller doctrine of Virgin *Birth* does not appear until later in the Fathers; e.g. Leo's Tome—*Virgo concepit, virgo pepperit.* Quite apart from the supposed unreliability of the chapters as a whole, a certain ancient reading of the Lucan narrative of the Annunciation, which omits all reference to the Virgin Conception, was gladly seized upon by many as a purer source—even against vastly superior MS. evidence—simply because it provided a way of escape from a difficult miracle.

The doctrine of the Virgin Conception was in fact at this time taken out of its context in the scheme of Christian dogmatics and isolated for special attack, and for many years a controversy in magnitude out of all proportion to the place of the dogma was carried on relentlessly between liberal and conservative scholars. It practically became a touchstone in theological circles—"Does he believe in the virgin birth"? To the liberal, the dogma appeared as a cumbersome miracle, easily dispensed with, difficult to set before a sceptical world, and at worst a slight on human nature that Christ should not have been born as other men. To the conservative, on the other hand, the dogma was vital to the doctrine of the Incarnation, assuring as it did that the Godhead was the centre of the Incarnate personality. After saying this, it is not proposed to treat of the controversy any further since nothing novel was engendered by it. Nor would it be helpful to repeat the mistake then made of isolating this one dogma for sustained treatment; since it is far better to regard the attack made upon it as just one instance of the generally bewildered and embarrassed attitude of Christian thinkers towards miracles.

As more radical criticism came to the fore in Britain and

America, the narratives of Christ's resurrection also bore the weight of a sustained attack. In this instance, however, the majority even of quite advanced liberal scholars outside Germany were prepared to admit that some historical happening did underlie the story, but the various apparent inconsistencies in the different narratives were constantly harped upon.

Perhaps the most voluble criticism was reserved for those miracles wrought by Christ during his ministry: his healings, exorcisms, and the nature miracles.

Mr. J. M. Thompson of Magdalen, in his two books, *Miracles in the New Testament* (1911), and *Through Facts to Faith*, the St. Margaret Lectures for 1912, is probably most representative of the negative view. His thesis that the Gospel miracles either did not happen or are capable of some other explanation is developed as meaning that Christ possessed a unique insight into human character and worked some faith-cures, and that the rest of the miracle material is legendary. Mr. Thompson and those with him were careful to avoid the grossness of early German rationalism; they did not insult our Lord by any such suggestion—popular a century before—as that he walked on a raft to gull his disciples into thinking he was walking upon the sea.

Mr. Thompson's central argument, however, is on the question of congruity. It is not that miracles *cannot* happen, absolutely speaking; it is simply a thing inconceivable that Almighty God should tinker with the wonderful order of his creation, and violate the laws which he has made for the whole in a haphazard way. The order in the creation, the laws which govern it, are designed to secure the ultimate perfection of the whole, and it would be a retrograde step to violate those laws for some lesser end. Sporadic miracles wrought by Christ, moreover, would simply be immoral. What justice could there be in the Lord curing just those few persons with whom his human life came in contact? This is human arrogance with a vengeance, but it is certainly a question worth taking the trouble to answer. However, the question will have to be dealt with in a larger context in the following chapter, and has been alluded to here as an instance of what was being said by not a few in the latter half of our period.

This is not to suggest that any considerable body of those theologians who respected traditional Christian doctrine had abandoned their belief in the Virgin Conception, the Resurrection, or in miracles in general. But a situation was created in which these factual occurrences were rendered quite impotent for apologetic purposes. The burden of Christ's Godhead could not be laid upon a catena of proofs any one of which might have doubt cast upon it by the next phase in the then-swiftly-moving development of higher criticism. Even the stoutest hearts were beginning to quake, and it could never be expected that the masses of mankind would accept as proofs things which were the object of doubt and criticism to the learned. In fact, by a strange irony miracle itself became the subject of apologetic rather than its bulwark! For instance, A. T. Lyttelton, *The Place of Miracles in Religion*, C. G. Lang, *The Miracles of Jesus*, Dr. Gore's Dissertation on the Virgin Birth, and Dr. Armitage Robinson's little book on the same subject, are in reality defences of the authenticity of the Bible and of the place which miracles hold in traditional Christian doctrine—J. M. Thompson makes this very observation, and he is perfectly correct. Thus it came about that in an age of historicity, history became virtually useless. That men were at all prepared to sacrifice any part of the historical basis of their religion has its roots no doubt in the Hegelian philosophy, in which it is the ideas, the motives, the ideals, in fact, the metaphysic that matters and alone gives final reality and significance to history: the historical events, therefore, whether they be what we ourselves should describe as actual or fictitious, are but the pictorial and hence the temporary (since they are within time) embodiments of eternal truths. This shows the direction in which matters were drifting. In this chapter we are engaged with the transitional effect of the eclipse of history. In the following chapter it will come into fuller view. For the moment it is sufficient to repeat that the external proofs, convincing though they may have been to the ages of faith, were now not so much exploded as rendered powerless and hence were discredited. No set of miracles, however well attested, could be made the basis of Faith, not simply because higher criticism might at any moment declare them one and all unreliable, but also for the deeper reason that such miracles did not bear the same close relation as heretofore to what was to be proved. In earlier times the wonderful, the uncanny, the miraculous, spoke directly of God, the Almighty one, who can alone do such things at will. But to the modern mind it was felt that they do not speak directly of God, who is conceived as the God of nature and order, and not simply of arbitrary power. The miracles of Christ spoke directly of his Divinity then, but now such things of themselves did not do so.

A new and sustaining basis for faith had thus to be found. A new defence line must be secured which would be such as could never be assailed by historical criticism. It was under these circumstances that a totally new apologetic was evolved. More radical students were to give up the struggle altogether, and look for the basis of religion quite outside the historic beginnings of Christianity, but with those now being considered it was different. These apologists took their stand upon the Gospel evidences for the interior and spiritual life of Jesus. The witness of Christ's own pure soul and consciousness to his Divinity, to his Messianic mission, to his own sinlessness; here was believed to be a rock which no storm could ever remove. It will appear that the position was not quite so impregnable as was at first supposed, but for the moment we must pause to say something of the other influences which shaped the path of the new apologetic and Christology.

Psychology, in the hands of the many, was a new toy. On its theoretical and speculative side psychology had always formed an integral part of the philosopher's curriculum, and on its practical side it had for some time been the object of research by various schools within the medical profession. But at the turn of the century it suddenly became the plaything for all men with half the curiosity of the Elephant's Child. This was in no small measure brought about by the publication of William James's brilliant Gifford Lectures.[1] Henceforward, education, history, ethics, politics, and not least theology, no study of these or any other subject touching the life of man was complete without "The Psychological Approach". Like many other new discoveries in modern times, it was thought by its first exponents to be the key to all problems.

The psychology thus popularized, moreover, was of a particular type.

Hitherto, the subject had been studied almost exclusively along the lines of an objective method. Mental functions had been divided up into faculties, and the mechanical processes and relations of the mind were thus treated like the faculties and limbs of the human body. The mind was thus treated from the functional point of view and, as it were from without. Now, however, the gaze was turned inwards. The centre of study became the

[1] *Varieties of Religious Experience*, 1901.

human consciousness, and those states of so-called consciousness which were believed to underlie it. Light was expected to be shed upon men's motives, thoughts, and actions, sudden changes in temperament and belief, with reference to states of consciousness. Normal waking consciousness and its sensations were realized to be inadequate to explain more than a small fraction of man's mental processes: hence it arose that the conception of the subliminal consciousness came into being and prominence—or, as it was sometimes spoken of, differing layers of consciousness. William James's interpretation of religious conversion is an excellent example of the application of this method. By its aid it became possible to envisage the conscious and unconscious growth of ideas and aspirations within the human mind of the Saviour.

It is interesting to observe, though this is somewhat irrelevant, how the whole method and interest of psychology have again altered. During the course of this century, the centre of attention has moved away from consciousness, and its whole tone in largely behaviouristic in character. The systems of Freud, Jung, and Adler, which still largely dominate the field, are concerned with mental functions and their determination of thought, speech, and behaviour, though they are naturally far removed from the faculty psychology of earlier times. Whereas in the times with which we are dealing, it is the feeling, the self-realization, and inner development of the subject which is the matter for enquiry.

In a less theoretical but equally effective manner the romantic movement also directed attention towards subjectivity. The poet who contemplates what it must feel like to be a primrose is only first cousin to the theologian who wants to know what it must have felt like to be Messiah. There could be nothing attractive to such an outlook in a figure whose human features, conflicts, and passions were subsumed in the almost mechanical operation of divine attributes within his Person. The things which he said and did were important, but it was the inner springs of his life, which he lived and transmitted so abundantly, that made him what he was and were alone of supreme interest.

Such then were the causes that led up to and fostered the study of Christ's interior life: the need of a new apologetic, the introspective psychology, and the introversion and idealism of the Romantic movement. It thus came about that the religious significance of Jesus was looked for almost exclusively in the

THE CONSCIOUSNESS OF JESUS 173

realm of his inner consciousness as reflected in his personal relations to God and to men. His Godhead, his sinlessness, and the genuineness of his mission, were attested, not by a series of hair-raising miracles, but by the witness which his own consciousness bore to himself. Allusions were made in the preceding chapter to the re-orientation of the doctrine of the Atonement; this too came into line with the new study, for the efficacy and power of Christ's work was sought for not so much in the outward event of the Crucifixion, as in the example of his God-directed soul and the spiritual energy which proceeded from it. The new apologetic evolved along these lines, whilst it was the child of necessity, was also calculated to make the only appeal on behalf of Christ that stood any chance of being listened to at the time. The act of studying the development of Christ's mental and spiritual life not only presupposes his genuinely human nature: it adopts his humanity as its starting-point. From a study of the inner religious life of this human subject, the apologist could work upwards and outwards by a process of induction to a final conclusion that he can be none other than the Son of God. The appeal was directed to, and the method conditioned by, the humanism of the time. Dogma and the miraculous might reasonably be inferred at a later stage in the argument, but to satisfy their own consciences and the needs of their hearers our theologians had first to lead off up their own garden path. It was in this method of apologetics that English theology made its closest approach to the theology of the Ritschlian school. It is the method of von Harnack,[1] as also of Ritschl himself. Not that the German school won many followers in other respects, for the English Apologists were otherwise of widely differing traditions. The method was adopted and expounded with great effectiveness by such widely differing scholars as, for instance, Dr. Garvie, who is, or was then, generally regarded as a right-wing Ritschlian, and Dr. DuBose, who ranks with Dr. Gore as one of the most able and thorough exponents of traditional Christian theology in his age. The method affords perhaps the clearest example of the positive reaction against scholastic theology. We have seen ample evidence of the negative criticism levelled against the construction of dogma by deduction from given principles: here then is a type of theology designed to take its place.

Let us first contemplate the ground-plan upon which the

[1] *Das Wesen Des Christenthums*, 1899.

edifice was to be built. Let us delineate the picture of Jesus from which the apologist and Christologian is to take his start—the bare minimum, the mere skin and bone, which the humanist needs to grasp in order to follow the enquiry. We may permit Dr. Garvie himself to paint this picture for us.

"Jesus though divine did not possess any of the attributes of the transcendent God displayed in his immanent relation to the world, omnipresence, omnipotence, or omniscience. He dwelt in a body subject to the condition of space. He was absent from his disciples, and only promised a continuous presence in the future. His miracles were acts wrought in dependence on God by power entrusted by God, and were conditioned by human faith. He expressly disclaimed knowledge of all things. His perfect knowledge of the Father did not involve knowledge of the day or the hour of his second coming. The limitation of his knowledge is proved by his disappointments and surprises, his enquiries, his increase of knowledge by experience, his looking to God for guidance in the course of his ministry, his exposure to temptation. His liability to temptation not only shows the limitation of his knowledge, but also the subjection of his moral character to development".[1] Here then is the English liberal version of the "Historical Jesus", a man in every attribute and circumstance like ourselves, differing solely in the quality of his soul. It is from here that we begin.

In the spiritual life, then, which the soul and mind of Jesus lived, it was believed that two topics of thought stood out pre-eminently before him: his consciousness of his vocation as Messiah, and his consciousness of his unique relationship to the Father. These two dominating themes are naturally in the last analysis not two but one. It is pointed out that in the thought of Jesus the one always suggests or includes the other. Hence it is legitimately concluded that he was never conscious of either in separation from the other. Nor had either an independent growth or origin in his mind; on the contrary, the growing appreciation and understanding of the one always brought with it a richer appreciation of the other. The two stand side by side enhancing one another as they grow.

It is impossible to exaggerate the importance for liberal theology of this view of Christ's inner life centring, as was supposed, on these two foci. For these two supposed elements were made the

[1] Garvie, *Studies in the Inner Life of Jesus*, p. 468.

## THE CONSCIOUSNESS OF JESUS

twin bulwarks of all Christology. Upon the certainty that Christ's soul was not deceiving him in these matters everything was made to hang: the Gospel he brought of the possible relations between God and man was attested by his own spiritual experience; the Atonement he taught was guaranteed by his own sense of the Father's love and his indisputable consciousness of being sinless; his own Divinity was proved by the uniqueness of the relations he sustained with God the Father—all these and a thousand and one other truths, such as the infinite significance and worth of human personality, could be deduced directly from what was believed to be known of the content of Christ's soul and mind. It was optimistically believed that Christian theologians had at last seized upon the element in the Gospels which was of the most penetrating significance and alone of permanent value. Here, indeed, was the treasure so long hidden in earthen vessels. The vessels were now being cracked by higher criticism and the treasure was thence being virtually forced upon men by this remarkable occurrence!

We treat first of Christ's sense of vocation. This is generally described as his "Messianic consciousness", a phrase which became almost a watchword. No treatise great or small dealing with the fundamentals of Christianity produced in the first two decades of this century was complete without a section dealing with the "Messianic Consciousness" of Jesus. Not that any orthodox theologian had ever suggested that Jesus did not claim to be Messiah—know himself as such, in fact, and much more besides; but now that Christ was reduced to a being whose whole spiritual and mental processes could be analysed and understood in terms of human experience, it was necessary to demonstrate how it came about that the human Jesus arrived at this unshakable conviction that he was the Messiah. To begin with, the presupposition itself must be observed as something new in Christian thought, namely, that the interior life of Jesus—God dwelling as man—is capable of being explained and understood exclusively in terms of human thought and human mental processes. This, they would have said (if the question had ever been placed flatly before them), was precisely the upshot of the Incarnation, that the transcendent and unknowable God did actually become as one of his creatures who was capable of being analysed just as one of us, be it in respect of heredity, environment, thought, or conduct. That, in fact, it is just as legitimate to enquire how Jesus arrived at such and such a judgment or conclusion as it would be to investigate the same of one of us. On these grounds, then, their quest was perfectly justifiable. To the question, how Jesus came to think of himself as Messiah, it was now not sufficient to respond that since his person was divine it was natural for him to possess full knowledge of himself as God's Son and man's Saviour. For it was supposed on the evidence of the Gospels that his mind was limited in respect of external facts in the world, as also of eternal truths which it would have been incongruous for him as human to have possessed. All his conscious experience was therefore mediated to him through normal human channels. To such writers, the older conception of the automatic bestowal of illumination and power through the hypostatic union savoured of the *deus ex machina* Christ whom all liberals were determined to banish: yet another instance of the struggle between the supernatural and the humanistic—miracle versus nature. A Christ who descended from Heaven already endowed with perfect knowledge of God, complete understanding of his mission and his teaching, and with his plans for life already cut and dried, may well, they said, have sufficed for an uncritical and unscientific age, but was utterly inadequate in present circumstances. It had therefore to be shown how the human Jesus, not only through the inner springs of his spiritual nature but through the external events and influences of his life on earth, was led to contemplate himself as the anointed one of God, and what is even more shocking still to the traditionalist, how he realized that he was God's only Son. It has been tedious to labour these points, but until recently sufficient attention has not been paid to the truly revolutionary character of the principles that underlay this new study.

The importance which the study of Christ's realization of his vocation assumed in our period is admirably summed up in the following quotation:

"The Messianic consciousness of Jesus is the most important contribution that we have, or can have, to the Christian doctrine of the Incarnation".[1]

It is the belief of those who expounded this subject that the outstanding formative influence upon Jesus in the matter of his realization of vocation was, as might be expected, the Jewish hope and the national picture—in some of its forms at any rate—

---

[1] J. Macpherson, *Christian Dogmatics*, p. 290.

of the Messiah. This would have its immediate stimulus in the rapid tempo of expectation that existed at that particular moment in Jewish history. From the days of the Maccabees the conviction had been steadily ripening that God's intervention in the affairs of the Jews was at hand. With this catastrophic intervention was generally associated the person of the Messiah, in the inception of the cosmical drama at any rate. All this is amply attested by the voluminous "Apocalyptic Literature" as also by the constant political unrest of the time. The Roman had succeeded the Greek as overlord, but the hope and the fervour were still growing. To be born into such an atmosphere must necessarily have had a profound emotional effect upon anyone whose soul was stirred with such faith in God and longing for the well-being of his fellows as was that of Jesus.

But of far greater moment than the outward excitement of the times, they say, was the formative influence of the national hope as portrayed in the scriptures. In the scriptures Jesus is thought to have seen the reflections, the concrete embodiments, of those longings which stirred his inmost soul. In the Scriptures he must have seen persons and types in whom he recognized those purposes and ideals which animated his own thoughts. Especially must this have been the case with his contemplation of the lives and writings of the prophets, from Moses who led his people from captivity and bestowed upon them the Law, to Jeremias who suffered weariness and imprisonment that the truth might prevail. These historic persons, with the types and ideals which he found in the Old Testament, gave definite content and direction to his own impulses, which were thence transferred back again to himself and his own life, remodelled, no doubt, by the genius of his own personality. Jesus would meditate upon the prophecies of the perfect representative of the Davidic house who was to be the ideal King and shepherd of his people—the anointed one who was to save and conquer—especially would this be significant to him if there actually was some tradition in his family that pointed to a Davidic ancestry. He would also meditate upon the prophecy in Dan. 7 of "One like the son of man" who comes with the clouds of heaven and receives an everlasting dominion. Whatever the original meaning of this prophecy may have been, the figure thus portrayed had assumed great significance in apocalyptic circles—cf. e.g. the Book of Enoch—as a picture of the coming Messiah, and did in fact determine the title which

Jesus commonly adopted in reference to his mission. This piece of construction became so important a link in the Messianic-consciousness case that it is not surprising that the thesis of Hans Lietzmann that the expression "son of man" is no more than an Aramaic periphrasis for "man", met with such a cold reception outside Germany. Old Testament characters would also play their part in moulding Jesus' conception of his office. Ideal priests such as Melchizedech and Aaron, ideal fathers and leaders of the people such as Abraham, Isaac, Jacob, and Moses already referred to; ideal kings such as David; and ideal prophets, Samuel, Elijah, and the canonical prophets—all these would play their part.

But above all, it is held, Jesus might have contemplated the character and fate of the "Suffering servant of Jehovah", as portrayed in the four poems in the latter half of the Book of Isaiah. The influence of these poems upon the mind of Jesus is thought to have been paramount.

"There seems to be very little doubt that meditation on the prophecy of the Servant of Jahveh, who saves as sufferer, gave definite content to his sense of his own vocation".[1] It was this that gave to Jesus' conception of the Messianic office its most striking and unique characteristic as applied to himself. If popular Judaism had painted a one-sided picture of Messiah, emphasizing simply his kingship, and the rôle of conquering deliverer, here was the corrective which in the thought of Jesus was to give an altogether different emphasis. He was to save as sufferer, the only way, as he believed, and the way appointed for him by his Heavenly Father. It is thus that the full meaning in the study of Jesus' thought of such passages as Mk. 19. 45 " . . . to give his life a ransom for many", and the Passion predictions, Mk. 8. 31, 9. 31, 10. 33, is seen in a living context.

A note of explanation must here be introduced. There was in the early years of this century practically no appreciation in English liberal theology of the importance attached by certain recent continental scholars to Eschatology. The work of Johannes Weiss and his followers, though known to widely-read scholars such as Sanday, passed almost unrecognized by the majority of writers. The liberal conception of Messiahship, therefore, and hence of Messianic consciousness, is rather different from the way in which those terms would be understood by one conversant

[1] Garvie, *Studies*, p. 528.

## THE CONSCIOUSNESS OF JESUS

with Schweitzer or Weiss, or for that matter by one accustomed to the traditional Christian attitude to the subject. Messiahship was conceived by the liberals in terms of ideals rather than in terms of participation in transcendental events. To the Eschatologist, the Messiah is a figure who comes to play a part in the drama of certain cosmical happenings of a cataclysmic nature. Similarly, to the orthodox Christian the Messiah is one who, by the events of his life, death, and resurrection, effects a definite and decisive incident in the relations of God and man. To the liberal theologian, as we observed, Messiahship is the fulfilment or embodiment of an ideal. As ideal prophet, priest, king, and servant of God, in his own person, his own life and death, he is the means by which the true ideal of service to God and fellow men is to be inculcated. To say more than this would be to tread upon dangerous ground, for many of the writers concerned embraced a view of Messiahship which is not nearly covered by this description; but this is the main trend of pre-eschatological thought on the subject. They not only interpreted Messiahship along such non-eschatological lines themselves but assume that such was also the mind of Christ.

The development of the concept of Messianic consciousness in the mind of Jesus is generally traced with great ingenuity and imagination through the story of his life.[1] In his education at Mary's knee and in the local rabbi's school a picture would be built up before his mind of one who was to be his people's great hero, the deliverer and king sent by God, whom all were presently expecting. As he pondered himself over the Scriptures in later years the conviction would grow upon him that he himself was that chosen servant of the Lord destined to free his people from their sins. Christ's baptism in Jordan is generally signalized as the point at which his sense of vocation attained its ripeness.[2] The maturity of his consciousness of Messiahship at this juncture is demonstrated by the fact that it was now that he embarked upon a public career which implied that he had a definite message to impart which had some relation to his own person. Much development was nevertheless still to come.

The opposition which was evoked from the Jewish authorities by his teaching and "Law-breaking" and the repeated threats against his life would all conduce to crystallize in his mind the

[1] Also W. Sanday, *Christologies Ancient and Modern*, Chapters 6, 7, 8.
[2] E.g. D. W. Forrest, *The Christ of History and Experience*, p. 98.

conviction that his mission would have to be accomplished through his own suffering and death. (In this connexion, be it observed, the Peirasmos, or fiery trial, brought to our notice by the eschatologists, is not made use of; the only background influences that are recognized are the fate of the Servant of the Lord, and the persecution of the canonical prophets.) Hence it is particularly after the death of John Baptist and the withdrawal to the north that Jesus begins frankly to predict not only his coming sufferings in general but even the precise manner of his decease.

By the time that Jesus made his triumphal entry into Jerusalem and proclaimed himself Son of Man before the High Priest his whole being was flooded with the unshakable conviction of his Messiahship. Even in Gethsemane he only parried with the manner of his mission with no real doubt about his own identity with Messiah, and he went to the Cross certain both of his Messiahship and task. Comment on this sketch will be reserved until later.

As already observed, it is more startling to learn that Jesus had to become aware of his filial relations to God the Father through a process similar to that already described in respect of his sense of vocation. Yet this too follows from the liberal premises. It is almost the epitome of the humiliation involved in the Incarnation that Jesus had as a human person to learn even this, the inmost secret of his nature and being, through the channels and processes common to all men. All men may learn through the experiences of life, by the longings of soul, the sense of dependence engendered by danger, the restful subjection produced by prayer, that they are the children of a Heavenly Father. Jesus learned the true nature of his own being in precisely the same manner.

The growing sense of his unique relationship to God as Son is traced out through his life in a similar manner to the growth of his Messianic consciousness. The gentle influence of his home, the love of parents and friends, his sense of unity with nature, and his reading of the Scriptures, all these things taught him to live his life in utter dependence upon the Heavenly Father who clothes the grass and feeds the wild birds. At the age of twelve years he was fully aware of an allegiance to a Divine Father which was to take prior place over every earthly loyalty and interest. This sense of Sonship was both fostered and realized in those nights of prayer spent alone upon the mountains; yet even this certitude was surpassed in those experiences associated with his baptism and transfiguration. For whatever objectivity there may or may not have been in those heavenly voices, proclaiming "This is my beloved Son", there was brought about in the soul of Jesus a decisive and unparalleled experience of perfect unity with God his Father. This experience, then, was not something bestowed upon him intuitively or arbitrarily but was learned by him in his human life by walking before God in perfect faith:

"How fully he walked with God by faith and not by sight is shown on the one hand by his uncertainty in Gethsemane regarding the necessity of his death and on the other by the obscurity on Calvary of his consciousness of his Father's presence with him".[1]

The question of Jesus' human *faith* assumed a great importance. Just as it was argued that the older doctrines of Christ's impeccability and virtual omniscience had emptied his temptations of any real meaning, so it was also contended that the older theology had also obscured beyond all recognition what was really a shining attribute of his person, namely, his Faith. Had he been in perpetual enjoyment of the Beatific Vision, he would have walked by sight and not by faith. As it was, his whole life is one continuous exhibition of this crowning virtue, exercised even in the blackest crises of life by a perfectly human soul in a human manner. It is the Faith that makes his prayer to the Father so real a thing, the straining of the soul's eye by Faith into the unknown beyond, and so forth.

The *locus classicus* for Jesus' sense of Sonship is Mt. 11. 25 ff. "I thank Thee, Father . . ." especially v. 27 (A.V.), "All things are delivered unto me of my Father: and no man knoweth the Son, but the Father; neither knoweth any man the Father, save the Son, and he to whomsoever the Son will reveal him". Here without doubt Jesus is claiming to stand in a relation to God, not only unlike any other, but also impossible for any other; and himself as the sole mediator of this "Knowledge", which be it observed is immediately followed by the invitation to all seekers after God's peace with himself as the bestower of refreshment— "Come unto me . . ."

Thus the spiritual growth of Jesus is consummated by the absolute saturation of his personality with the love of the Father: and his human consciousness is touched at every point of its life and activity by the Father's will. His moral powers are developed

[1] Garvie, *Studies*, p. 469.

by experience and temptation to a perfect accord with the divine will;[1] his mind and soul are progressively enlightened through prayer and the Scriptures to a perfect understanding of his mission in the world; his heart is taught by suffering and endurance both physical and mental to embrace and show forth to the world the reality of God's Fatherhood and the truth of his own unique Sonship.

No attempt has here been made to set out this material strictly in the manner in which it is generally presented by the new apologists. Attention has simply been called to the main points which were as a rule included in the study, and these have been rendered for the most part in the tone and language of theology at that time.

Upon the basis of this evidence, then, it is argued that such a one as the facts portray, discovering his inmost soul so to correspond with the hopes of his people, and to be able so to respond to the love of God, could in reality be none other than God's Son and Christ. We are primarily concerned with its bearing on Christology proper rather than on the strength or weakness of the case from the point of view of apologetics.

Such then in brief is the psychological picture, painted by many hands, of the life of Jesus upon which our hopes for time and for eternity are to be grounded. But unfortunately, a very considerable part of the story is pure fiction. It is a fine and moving story indeed, this romance of the wistful Galilean pondering over the prophecies of "Deutero-Isaiah", but this Jesus of the Romanticists and psychologists is the most figmentary illusion that *a priori* reasoning ever produced. It claims to be a candid interpretation of the content of the Gospels; it is not. Such a figure, as far as we are aware, never inhabited the land of Canaan, but only the fertile imaginations of liberal Protestant theologians and their followers. A radical change in the outlook of higher criticism, a newer and more objective psychology, a more thorough-going interpretation of the New Testament, have all lent their aid to the discrediting in our own day of this method and its findings. It is strange how an edifice that promised to be so permanent should in one generation have become not only outmoded but almost utterly useless. Several specific points of criticism may here be advanced, though the swing of the pendulum needs far more to explain it than these.

[1] A. C. A. Hall, *Christ's Temptation and Ours*.

## THE CONSCIOUSNESS OF JESUS

(*a*) In the first place, Christ being what he was, it is quite out of the question beyond a certain point to speculate about his inner mental and spiritual processes hoping thereby to arrive at a complete understanding of them. The presupposition that the Son of God in becoming Incarnate rendered his being completely human—and therefore intelligible at all points to us—would only hold good if a theory of total metamorphosis, such as that of Gess, be adopted: which would have been quite out of the question for many an English liberal scholar. In the Catholic doctrine of the Incarnation, the Son of God assumed humanity whilst still remaining God, in the obvious meaning of that word; and therein lies the decisive factor in regard to his person. It may be possible with considerable success to reconstruct the psychological development of some human individual, though even here, especially in the case of genius, there would seem to be elements that defy analysis and the normal laws of development. Even on this plane there may be decisive differences between Christ's humanity and our own. If the doctrine be accepted, even in some diluted form palatable to the liberals, that Christ unlike us was born without the guilt of and bias towards evil, surely it would be of some consequence to the matter in hand. As G. J. A. D'Arcy points out:

"After all it does seem the height of absurdity to try and trace the religious experiences of the one unfallen man by the religious experience of my own fallen life".[1]

But even if this be left out of account, there is in the case of Christ a factor that totally cancels out any such possibility of final analysis in terms of purely human experience. The presence of his Godhead, not merely at the periphery but at the very centre of his personality, introduces an element which is beyond analysis. "My thoughts are not your thoughts, neither are my ways your ways, saith the Lord". In treating of the Godhead, any discussion of psychological processes is out of the question and meaningless. For God does not "psychologize"—to employ F. J. Hall's apt expression. Thinking, knowing, understanding, willing, experiencing, believing; all these terms which have been predicated of Christ's human mind are relative terms. When applied to a purely human mind they possess a certain intelligible content, but when applied to God they must be figurative and nothing more. In him, such things are not processes as with us, but

[1] *The Human Mind of Our Lord*, p. 5.

aspects of the simultaneous yet eternal fact of being God. The fact that the Son partakes of the divine essence must mean that he also in his nature does not psychologize either. Christ's Deity is therefore something to which ideas such as growth of a sense of vocation are meaningless. For to be Messiah and Son is part of his eternal nature. These facts remain true, however the expression of them or even the appreciation of them is conditioned by his human nature—that is to say, in that part of him which comes into contact with his fellow men. He is, in his being, God's Son and God's Christ, and must always be aware of this absolutely. And though it may be conjectured that for a time his human mind was not directly aware of this fact it is impossible to say how or when or in what measure that knowledge was ultimately bestowed upon the human mind. In any case, his Godhead is actually present as part—the most important part—of his being, and hence cannot but take its place in the functioning of his personality. Therefore, even those who do not go the whole way with the metamorphosists and declare that by the Incarnation the Son of God abandoned his normal manner of consciousness to enter upon a state in which human psychological processes became part of his nature, but confine themselves to the assertion that in the Incarnation he submerged his divine consciousness beneath his humanity, allowing himself to win back the full measure of it through the channels proper to earthly life—even these must admit that the divine element in his personality remains present as an indeterminate factor; or, to change the metaphor slightly, it is the factor "Infinity" in the compound fraction which cancels out every other constituent. In view of this, it cannot be a matter of inductive reasoning, or of the correlation of data, but the wildest of speculations to attempt to determine the relations and the proportions of the divine and human modes of thinking and feeling within the person of Christ. The study therefore is not according to its subject-matter a legitimate department of historical criticism or theology since it is attempting to criticize something which contains an element which stands outside the historical sequence. The attempt to ascertain the precise nature of the mental experiences through which Jesus passed in the course of his life is not merely one which must depend for its conclusions upon "scientific guesses" (a phrase which Streeter coined in another connexion); it is simply outside the range of our intellectual capacity altogether. Nor is any help in this particular to be derived from the conception of the moral affinity between God and man. This doctrine was being trumpeted loudly at the time as a solution to the intrinsic difficulties in the way of belief in the Incarnation, almost as if it were some new discovery of the nineteenth century. God indeed is pre-eminently a moral being—Amos was the first to teach this truth, not Ritschl—but as pointed out in the preceding chapter, that must not be allowed to blind us to the real and infinite differences between the creature and his creator. A metaphysic which is not swallowed up in ethical refinements will delineate not obscure the gulf between them. God's infinite wisdom and perfect self-knowledge is something which, even in combination with infinitesimal humanity, exhibits a defiant uniqueness.

(*b*) The picture which has been drawn by liberal theologians of the psychological development of Jesus was described above as fictitious—as fictitious as those early German rationalistic lives of Jesus in which the Lord plays the part of a political agent for an Essene secret society. This is not the case simply on account of the intrinsic impossibility of probing into the mind of one who was God as well as man, but also because it is necessary, in order to construct a life of Jesus such as has been undertaken by these writers, that certain indispensable historical materials should be present. Supposing a psychiatrist be called in to examine a patient. In addition to an outline of the external events of the patient's life, he will require detailed information concerning the patient's character, temperament, his parents and companions; but above all it would be indispensable for him to have access to the actual thoughts of the patient: his memories, his reactions to certain circumstances, his feelings, his motives—perhaps even his dreams—and a thousand and one other màtters which make such an investigation worth while. Yet should he attempt to make such a study of the person of Christ, none of this vital information would be at his disposal. The Four Gospels, the only full-length portraits of Christ which we possess, do not yield to such a treatment. From beginning to end they are behaviouristic in character. They record outward actions of Christ, and numerous events of his life: though even here the instances which they select for posterity are not chosen with a view to throwing any light upon Christ's interior life but simply in exposition of the work he wrought or of how he fulfilled Old Testament prophecy. They provide no information at all as to the character and functioning of his inner life. Even among the recorded utterances of Jesus there are very few which could provide any scientific data about the workings of his mind. It cannot be pretended honestly that Mt. 11. 27 appears as a "Sublime confession or consummation of human faith". It is a clear-cut dogmatic utterance, spoken with the authority and boldness which could only be employed by one who was himself God the Son, and who knew this as a fact and not as a longing or dream. Those passages even in which he does speak of his own person are strictly objective. "The Son . . ." "The son of man . . .", they invariably relate to the functions of his office and never disclose his interior feelings. The tendency of the Gospels to objectify is never far absent; for even in moments when we appear to be reading a description of a mental state passed through by the Lord, the semblance vanishes almost immediately, as in the story of Gethsemane where even there the impression is objectified by the Bloody Sweat. There is no single hint in the Gospels that the theophanies at the Baptism and Transfiguration had any subjective significance for Jesus. They are either explained as "Witnesses", after prophetic type, or else came for the sake of his associates. It is purely arbitrary and unwarranted, except in the light of other good evidence—which there is not—to regard them as moments in his spiritual attainment. Our Lord makes free and copious use of Old Testament prophecy, as God's testimony through the mouths of these ancient writers to his own Person and authority. But there is not the slightest suggestion that he derived his sense of vocation from the Scriptures in the first instance. P. T. Forsyth strenuously deals with this question of the inadequacy of the material. The inside-story of the Lord's life was never told. "It was the secret of Jesus alone. And he kept it".[1]

(c) If the method were valid and the materials to hand, there is yet one further objection. It may be possible to apprehend how the use of the Scriptures enabled Christ to develop and characterize his sense of vocation and Sonship; but this gives no answer to the burning question—how in the first place did Jesus' human mind come to hold such beliefs about himself? This may well be a touchstone of the liberal apologetics.

The Christian of orthodox outlook would point out that the question is vital to the whole veracity of the Christian faith which depends upon the fact that Jesus of Nazareth is personally God

[1] *Person and Place of Jesus Christ*, p. 37.

the Son. He would observe that the idea of a sense of vocation thus developing is not the same as a childish dream which came true. A child may dream of one day becoming Prime Minister of England, and if he is gifted with sufficient ability and determination, he may quite possibly attain to that office one day. But a child who dreams that he will one day be heir to the British Crown is in a far different position; for he must soon realize that that honour is already prepared for another known successor. The second and not the first is the parallel to the question of Messianic vocation. Hence our conservative would conclude that Christ actually was what he claimed to be or else that he was a worthless impostor. The liberal may reply to this by saying that in the first place it was made possible for Christ's human mind to catch a glimpse of his true nature through the veil as a starting-point, as it were, from which his human mind and soul could build up its life. Apart from a somewhat artificial semblance here, the admission that he knew he was God the Son to begin with by virtue of his divine nature begs the whole question for the liberals and renders all their subsequent psychologizing quite superfluous. Another reply which was to be given by many of the more extreme brethren was that the situation is parallel rather to the Prime Minister day-dream than to the Crown day-dream. If Messiahship be conceived in a non-eschatological setting, as already indicated, the embodiment simply of a set of ideals, then it would be possible to say that Jesus by the supreme genius of his soul turned his aspirations and powers to such effect that he did, in fact, fulfil the expectations of his people in the highest degree. The Sonship which he enjoyed would similarly not be interpreted in the metaphysical sense of the Creeds. Many mediating explanations were in fact advanced, such as that the chords of Jesus' soul answered so exactly to the character and work of Messiah and Only Son that he cannot reasonably be regarded as anything short of this—let alone an impostor.

This discussion of the veracity of Christ's claims is of immense importance in the evaluation of liberal Christologies, but it provides a specific object lesson in the present connection. It demonstrates beyond any doubt that the psychological approach to Christ's life, whilst it might under given circumstances shed light upon isolated incidents, is of itself powerless to respond to the fundamental issue raised by the Lord's person: "What think ye of Christ, whose Son is he"?

It would be well to consider the present chapter as a preliminary to the following. For although it has treated of a specific method, the principles underlying that method do not fully come into view except in their more radical garbs now to be considered.

# 7

## THE DIVORCE OF THEOLOGY
## FROM HISTORY

AT the close of the fifth chapter it was suggested that one of the purposes which the Kenotic theory was expected to serve was to hold the theological situation in face of the rapid incursion of German liberal scholarship. In its original context in the English theology of the 'nineties, the Kenotic theory had in fact served as a bridge between traditional orthodoxy and the new learning; or like some great dam, holding back the floods, yet permitting so much to pass through as would irrigate the country beyond. Particularly was this object realized in high Anglicanism, in such circles, for instance, as were later to produce the "New Commentary on Holy Scripture"; where a real sense of unity in thought and purpose with the church of bygone ages was combined with a genuine appreciation of modern historical methods. By the aid of the Kenotic theory it was possible to predicate all those limitations ascribed to Christ's Person by liberal critics of the Christ of the Œcumenical Councils. For many minds the theory continues adequately to fulfil this rôle.

Such a reconciliation, however, only remains possible and complete so long as the critical picture of Jesus remains within bounds compatible with the traditional theology—even broadly understood. But in any case, the settlement thus arrived at was a mid-way position and a compromise, and possessed all the weaknesses of such a location. Traditionalist scholasticism on the one hand and some of the radical modern systems of theology on the other, though each may be open to a total criticism of itself, each comprises a compact unity whose components are mutually dependent upon one another. The reconciliation arrived at on the basis of the Kenotic theory, on the other hand, was a ready makeshift, compounded of elements from two totally different worlds of thought—ancient reason and modern rationalism. To say that it resembled new wine being put into old wineskins, as some have done, though it exemplifies the divergence, tends to beg the question which is in reality the less desirable element. For the moment it will be more impartial to say that demerara sugar and sand may present a seeming homogeneity if mixed together, but the addition of water instantly separates them. So it came about that many thinkers found themselves quite unable to rest in this haven, but were driven by the storm ever farther from the land of their departure. Critical conclusions were forced upon them which it was impossible to reconcile with traditional orthodoxy even with the aid of Kenoticism.

Under the auspices of the Kenotic theory it was possible for a confessedly traditionalist theologian to speculate at random upon many subjects. He could conjecture upon the extent of the Lord's human ignorance and impotence, and, in fact, the type of speculation described in the preceding chapter was in large measure open to him. Yet such a scholar had at his back the Creeds and Definitions of the ancient church, which did two things for him. They gave to him a sense of security that he never could err in any essential particular from the traditional faith of the church, and also acted as a profound inhibitive against the over-ready acceptance of critical theories of a radical nature. The influence of this restraint is to be seen in practically all English criticism, its most characteristic distinction from German criticism.

The decisive fact, however, was that the principles of rationalism and humanism had been introduced into English theology, and their effect could not permanently be inhibited by traditionalism. They had got their foot inside the doorway and would force an entrance. By the aid of Kenotic Christology it had appeared possible to prevent the door being pushed wider; but for many thinkers it was inevitable that the resistance should be only temporary. It is our business in this chapter to examine the situation consequent upon the removal of the above-mentioned restraints. It is only in the light of the struggle to exclude the intruding forces, the pressure upon and the resistance behind the door, that much of the controversy of the time can be understood. It is only thus that one can understand the reason for many of the apparent inconsistencies of moderate liberal scholars. We discover a theologian who is prepared to discount any or all of the miracles in the Old Testament, but will not hear of one single New Testament miracle being doubted. Another will be found expressing doubts regarding the doctrine of Christ's Virgin Conception, and yet looking upon a denial of his physical resurrection as treason

## THE DIVORCE OF THEOLOGY FROM HISTORY 191

against the Faith. It was simply their resistance against the throwing open of the door to a type of speculation that had its grounds in rationalism rather than in the historic Faith of Christendom. They fought a long and bitter defensive action. They fought back inch by inch: every point was contested, every miracle was fought for, every utterance or claim of Christ was defended, every jot of the traditional theology was grimly contested. But for many it was a losing cause.

In consequence there grew up by slow degrees within the Anglican and Free Churches a class, it can scarcely be called a school, of thoroughgoing liberal scholars. Their aim was to eradicate from religion everything that savoured of the pre-scientific era, that men might embrace its essential message without the embarrassment of beliefs emanating from the childhood of the human race. In this pursuit they succeeded better than they could have dreamed; the world at large assumes that they alone represent enlightened Christian opinion, and cannot believe that any thinking Christians to-day take seriously the supernatural beliefs and demands for which they nominally stand. It is our business here, however, to consider the way in which certain representatives of this more radical liberalism handled the central question of the person of Christ. It must be seen with what results their thoroughgoing principles were applied. Yet they brought nothing essentially new into their work. The principles which they applied were simply those of the more moderate liberals who preceded them, now however employed without the old restraints. It will in fact appear that the subjects under which the radical Christology will be discussed are in direct dependence upon the situation presupposed by, and the method described in, the preceding chapter.

Thus: 1. The exclusion from apologetic, and the subsequent rejection as intrusions, of certain miraculous events in the Gospel narrative led inevitably to a distinction between the human element—now greatly emphasised, and the divine message resulting from the teaching of Jesus—a thoroughgoing discrimination between the "kernel" and the "husk". 2. The rejection of miracles which in the first instance so largely accounted for the appearance of the new apologetic grew into a refusal to accept the miracle of the Incarnation itself, and to a totally new account being given of that doctrine. 3. The attempt to revivify the "Messianic consciousness" apologetic as a foundation for an objective doctrine of Christ's Deity was met by: 4. A completely negative reply based upon the same principles. 5. Finally, some account will be given of the attitude of the English disciple of the "Eschatologists". The succeeding chapter is occupied with the description of a school of radical thinkers who constructed a synthesis on the liberal principles of so outstanding a character as to merit special treatment.

Throughout the sections thus outlined there run two constant themes. First, the complete humanizing of the Person of our Lord. The eradication from the Christian account of his life upon earth, not only of the miraculous, viewed externally, but also of every possibility of an objective and intelligible doctrine of his Personal Deity, was in reality a destruction of what had from the earliest times been the foundation of the Christian religion. Hence, secondly, it is not surprising to discover that hand in hand with the humanizing of Christ's Person, that is to say, with the denial of the Incarnation as a specific and unique intervention of God upon the historical plane, there should go a shifting of the centre of theological interest away from the work and the Person of Christ towards present religious experience. It is perhaps the most signal manifestation of that movement alluded to in the first chapter of thought away from theocentricity to anthropocentricity. Thus our two key-notes are the humanizing of Christ, and the consequent divorce of religion from its historical basis.

1. *The Concept of the Kernel and the Husk*

If the Gospel miracles, the old external proofs of Christ's Deity—with the exception of a few faith-cures—are to be regarded as untrustworthy records of fact, merely didactic legends, or dogmatic fantasies, they are plainly later accretions to the true account of Jesus' life. Furthermore, if our Lord possessed the intelligence and outlook of an average Jew of the first century, accepting without question the scientific and religious beliefs of his contemporaries, it would follow that, in order to discover and appreciate his pure message for mankind, the account of his life and teaching must be distilled in order to remove all those impurities and imperfections which would inevitably be present owing to the immature state of human development into which Jesus was born. In other words, to arrive at what is best and permanent in the contribution of Jesus Christ to mankind, one is

## THE DIVORCE OF THEOLOGY FROM HISTORY

obliged to strip off a series of layers which envelop the Gospel as it is presented to us in the New Testament. A selfish miracle, an animistic superstition, an inadequate social consciousness—all of which would have been perfectly natural in the account of a teacher of Jesus' time and background—must be thoroughly cleansed away, it is said. The pure kernel must be separated from the husk. There obviously must be a kernel of infinite and eternal value somewhere to be found, since the message of Christianity has brought new life and hope to millions for nigh on two thousand years. But as in the parable, the treasure itself is buried in a field, and must be delved for in order to be found, in its purest form at any rate. We thus meet again with that strange paradox already alluded to, that in the age of history and historical study, the historical element in religion becomes eclipsed or rejected altogether. Traditional Christian dogmatics had been attacked as a set of *a priori* fabrications, which robbed Christ of his genuinely human nature. Now the criticism was being carried further. The idea of miracle was steadily coming under the ban, as being opposed to what was thought to be the sole principle in the world, the universal laws of nature and the rule of organic growth. In addition, the critical exegesis of the New Testament had wellnigh established the limited character of the Lord's human mind. Such a discrimination against the elements in Christ's teaching and personality that belonged specifically to his historic existence and situation was bound to arise.

That this discrimination between what is of eternal value in Christ and its circumstantial limitations is a logical outgrowth from the new exegesis and the humanistic apologetic of the time is recognized even in the early days of the "Knowledge" controversy, in an incidental allusion in Dr. Gore's essay in *Lux Mundi*. He writes: "He used human nature, its relation to God, its conditions of experience, its growth in knowledge, its limitations of knowledge. He feels as we men ought to feel; he sees as we ought to see. We can thus distinguish more or less between the divine truth which he reveals, and the human nature which he uses".[1] As it will evidently appear, the chief difficulty is to decide how much *more* or how much *less*. It is a frank admission in good time of something which was to play a large part in theology.

In other connections much of the process of stripping off the husks has already been described in previous chapters. There was

[1] *Lux Mundi*, 10th ed., p. 360.

## CONFLICT IN CHRISTOLOGY

in the first place the attack made upon the edifice of scholastic Christology, with its systematization of the relations of the two natures in Christ and of the supernatural powers exercised by Christ in virtue of the plenitude of his Godhead in hypostatic union with manhood. This may be termed husk No. 1 and the struggle to remove it was typified by the liberal campaign to secure recognition of Christ's limited knowledge. At the same time, more advanced brethren were in process of stripping off husk No. 2, namely, the miraculous elements in the Gospel narrative. This entailed a more protracted struggle, but it maintained steady progress. The conviction underlying the liberal attitude towards both of these controversies was the same, that beneath the husks of scholastic dogmatisms and legendary accretions, there stood the "Historic Jesus", his sure and infinitely majestic person with his eternal message for mankind.

A wide freedom was afforded by this distinction to discriminate between what they considered to be kernel and what they believed to be husk, and the wide divergence in which the freedom was exercised bears record to the fact that other than objective study of Christ's Person were the determining factors. The immediate and most striking use or abuse of this freedom was made by the English disciples of pre-eschatological German liberalism. It was now possible for them to have their way with the New Testament records, and with the Person of Christ himself. They could point to him as a teacher of pure ethics and unbridled individualism, and anything in his recorded teaching which savoured of harsh judgment or objective dogma could be dismissed by labelling it "husk". This was clearly stepping far beyond the sanction which criticism had granted. It is one thing to insinuate that Christ shared an animistic superstition when he rebuked a storm, and quite another matter to suggest that when he declares the wrath of God against evil he is voicing a primitive and untenable conception of the Deity. The one, even if the insinuation be substantiated, belongs to the incidental occurrences of his life and dealings with the men of a particular age; the other has to do with the very core of his teaching. It is no matter for surprise that the recognition of the principle of the kernel and the husk should have first opened the door to a liberalism of this type, since all the influences at work tended in that direction. It was seen how even the concept of Messiahship was conceived of in terms of ideals by those who dwelt upon our Lord's inner consciousness. It will therefore be with some surprise that we shall presently see the same principle being employed in quite a different cause. For the moment, it will be necessary to exemplify the use made of the kernel and husk principle by liberals of the earlier type, for which purpose no better than James Martineau could be chosen.

*James Martineau*, The Seat of Authority in Religion, 1890.

A Unitarian by profession, Dr. Martineau is yet a typical representative of that liberalism which flourished in Germany during the middle of the nineteenth century and which during our period was finding its way into Anglo-Saxon theological circles of all Protestant denominations. Since he was no eschatologist but an older liberal true to type, all the trapping of Messiahship, and those other portions of Christ's teaching which were coloured by Jewish apocalyptic were to him simply husk. He also embraces the thoroughgoing humanism as regards the nature of the Lord's Person. If Messiahship is husk, even more so are the metaphysical dogmas of the church relating to his Godhead, as will appear in the quotations.

"The Gospel of Jesus Christ, revealed to him, and constituting his personal religion, was delivered to a very varied world over which its message spread in successive stages through families of men preoccupied with modes of thought dissimilar to it and to each other. Taken up by these and mingling with their speech, its voice was inevitably changed, and like a border dialect, passed into patois pure to neither heaven nor earth".[1] It had already passed through at least three of these stages by the time that the New Testament was written, popular Judaism at home, Hellenistic Judaism abroad, and various types of gentile gnostic speculation. Dr. Martineau proceeds to furnish his rationale of how the husks attached themselves. He is immediately concerned with the first of the media through which our Lord's teaching passed, the Judaism of Palestine. He writes:

"The whole mind of the Palestinian Jews had become saturated with the high colouring of a rude apocalyptic literature . . . from these sources we know for certain that it was not he who filled with its meaning their question, 'Art thou he that should come . . .?' Who drew in their fancy their picture of the Son of David? Who introduced them to the expectation of his

[1] *Seat of Authority*, p. 326.

advent . . .? The whole drama had already been written, and photographed in thought . . . But if Jesus spake of it, it was as of something given, and not of what he brought. For though the pre-existence of the Messianic idea relieves Jesus of the responsibility for its contents, it leaves the question open how far he shared it with his contemporaries, and carried its influence into his mind . . . It is one thing, however, to admit his belief in a reign of truth and righteousness as a promise made 'To the Fathers' and now approaching its fulfilment; it is quite another to affirm that in his own Person he claimed to realize it as its prince and head. That this also is universally assumed is not surprising, seeing that the synoptists assure us that it was so, and tell it as if it were an attested fact and not a later inference. Yet they add (what surely is not without significance) 'He strictly charged his disciples and commanded them to tell no man that he was the Christ'. If the disciples had only kept that injunction instead of spending their lives in reversing it, Christendom, I am tempted to think, might have possessed a purer record of genuine revelation, instead of a mixed text of divine truth and false apocalypse. For, the first deforming mask, the first robe of hopeless disguise, under which the real personality of Jesus of Nazareth disappeared from sight, was placed upon him by this very doctrine, which was not to go forth, that he was the Messiah".[1] He repeats this same idea—"That the Messianic theory of the Person of Jesus was made for him, and palmed upon him by his followers, and was not his own, appears to me a reasonable inference . . ."[2] He then examines the Gospel material critically along these lines. His final verdict is as follows—"The identification then of Jesus with the Messianic figure is the first act of Christian mythology, withdrawing man from his own religion to a religion about him . . ."[3] He admits, however, that the wrapping of the husk may have been necessary in order to convey such spiritual lessons to the people of the first century, but now that the covering is seen to be false, even this consideration falls to the ground. The touch of nineteenth-century self-confidence is here not difficult to detect. What place then does such a Christ, purged of all dogma and Messianic claim, hold for faith? "When once our relation to him has become simply spiritual—a relation of personal reverence and historic recogni-

[1] *Seat of Authority*, p. 329.
[2] *ibid.*, p. 331.
[3] *ibid.*, p. 355.

tion—a looking up to him as the supreme type of moral communion between man and God—must we not own that these terms not only cease to represent any reality but become either empty or misleading as imagery".[1]

Here then is a clearly-defined statement of the liberal conception of the historical Jesus with his ethico-religious Gospel of goodwill and individual mysticism. Like Wrede he has dismissed the Messiahship as a strange garb of later invention. For illustrating the first use made of the kernel and husk concept Dr. Martineau is worth studying, but attention may be called to two points which emerge in reference to his study of Jesus. In the first place he has this in common with all other liberal scholars—even in common with the next writer to be considered, who employs the kernel and husk principle towards a diametrically-opposed conclusion—that he treats our Lord as a human entity, who may be completely understood as such, without a prime reference to a belief in his Godhead—the method of traditional Christology. Secondly, we may note that having thus denuded the Christ of his metaphysical and eschatological attire, Dr. Martineau can only assign to Christ a place in our own religious life of example, or prototype; that he should be worshipped as Lord or apprehended as the living, present, saviour is now excluded.

We turn now from Dr. Martineau to consider another application of the same principle. At a later stage in the development of English liberal theology, the newly incised cleavage between the kernel and the husk resulted in a most curious transformation in the emphasis of theology, but which in the long run produces the same effects as its forerunner. As we have already seen, to a liberal scholar of the type of Dr. Martineau, it would have appeared that first the massive theorising upon the Person of Christ built up by scholastic theology must be removed. Secondly, the miraculous accretions to the Gospel story together with misleading ideas introduced by Jesus' immediate followers had to be excised. These we have called husks 1 and 2. Beneath these was believed to lie the "simple" Jesus with his Gospel of morality, valid for all mankind. But it appeared later that there was yet one further husk to be removed, and it was here that the most serious problems for liberal theology were encountered. The limitation of our Lord's human knowledge had been long recognized; but the application of this critical result to the kernel and

[1] *ibid.*, p. 356.

husk concept had so far been confined to the indication that he shared in some of the less obnoxious religious beliefs of his age. Growing appreciation of the work of the eschatologists, however, gave English liberal scholars for the first time a real glimpse of what was actually involved in their postulate that Jesus was a human being whose mind and outlook were entirely conditioned by the environment in which he lived. It was a startling revelation. Hitherto it had been imagined that even if the mind of Christ could be referred totally to human heredity and environment, he was nevertheless unimpugned as a sublime teacher of ethics, possessing virtually moral omniscience. The elements in his teaching of a circumscribed character were of a temporary and insignificant nature. It became increasingly obvious that the postulate did not simply involve the admission that Jesus believed the sun rose, that David was the author of Ps. 110, and that men may be inhabited by demons. It meant that his whole outlook upon life and upon himself was dominated by the grotesque tangle of contemporary apocalyptic. Such beliefs had been shown to be as much part of his human mind as the geography of his native land. Thus the "Historical Jesus", the supposed kernel of infinite value beneath the husks, when he had been fully disclosed, was not quite so attractive after all. If one attempted to remove even this portion of our Lord's teaching in which the dominance of eschatology was apparent, which we may now term husk No. 3, there would appear to be nothing left at all! Eschatology was far from being accepted by the majority even of advanced liberals outside Germany as the be-all and end-all of Jesus' life and teaching, and for many, a kernel was still to be apprehended within the teaching and example of our Lord. But in the eyes of the more radical thinkers, even to some of those who were no wholehearted supporters of the eschatological position, the historical Person of Jesus was to undergo an eclipse in evaluation unprecedented in the history of Christian thought. Where then was the pearl of great price, if it were not to be sought for in the life of the Galilean? The answer which was given is truly an amazing one. Surely the thing of infinite value for mankind which Christendom bestows is not the figure of a strange prophet of first-century apocalyptic but the Christ-ideal which has been developed and nourished within the Christian church. This heavenly figure, who has been the centre for devotion and endeavour to countless souls, embodies all that is highest and noblest in human aspirations

—this accounts for the universality and permanence of the ideal. This Christ-ideal embodies our longings towards perfection, and our aspirations for complete unanimity with God and fellow creatures; here is the real and vital contribution of Christianity to the life of mankind.

Here then is a revolution, even within liberal theology. The kernel and the husk have virtually changed places! The "Jesus of history", regarded by earlier scholars as the kernel to be apprehended at all costs, is now regarded as yet another husk; whilst the Christ (or at least the Christ-ideal) of the catholic church, who was previously attacked with such vigour as an *a priori* figment, is now to be looked upon as the kernel of eternal truth at the basis of our religion. It is not denied on the newer view that in some sense at any rate—as regards temporal origin— the Christ-ideal is a descendant from the Jesus of history, though the relation of the two is not always clear and will be discussed at a later stage. For the moment it is our purpose to illustrate the lengths to which the humanizing of the historic Person of our Lord proceeded as a result of this changed aspect of belief about him. We therefore select the attitude of one writer who accepted the radical reflex position as above outlined. His sketch of the Person of our Lord illustrates at one stroke the two strands or subjects forming the basis of this chapter, the extreme humanizing of Jesus, and the consequent separation of religion from him, who had before been its rational basis and anchorage.

In the year 1909 a collection of essays relating to Christology by various writers was published as a supplement to *The Hibbert Journal* under the general title "Jesus or Christ". Such a title by itself suggests the concept of the kernel and husk, though by no means all of the contributors enlarge upon this idea directly. The twenty contributors are in fact as diverse as they could be, including such writers as Henry Scott Holland, George Tyrrell, Sir Oliver Lodge, with two German and one American contributions. At the end of the volume an article is reprinted from a previous number of the journal by the Rev. R. Roberts, which bears the same title as the whole volume. It is written in ill-humour, and often with bad taste and careless exegesis, and in itself did not merit one-tenth of the attention which it received. Yet it serves as the best possible illustration of the humanizing of the Lord's Person carried to its possible limits.

It is quite illegitimate, Roberts argues, to take statements belonging to the ideal Christ and use them as if they applied to the historical Jesus; the two must be kept separate. "Are the claims . . . made on behalf of a spiritual ideal to which we may provisionally apply the word 'Christ' or are they predicated of Jesus. The apologists do not frankly face these questions".[1] He admits quite honestly that critical research presents a Jesus who has little in common with the later Christ-ideal—"It may easily turn out that insistence on limitations of knowledge, restrictions of outlook, evasions of issues, and disillusionments of experience true enough of an historic Jesus may not be wholly relevant to a spiritual 'Christ ideal' expanding and enriching through the ages into 'The Christ that is to be . . .'"[2] Between the two conceptions, Jesus and Christ, there is an irreconcilable difference. If, as he says, it is illegitimate to predicate dogmatic utterances of the historic Jesus, a gulf has appeared which no Kenotic theory could bridge—for even more ludicrous would it be to attribute all the human failings of the man Jesus to the eternal Son of God: "To one who was the 'Fullness of Godhead' bodily expressed, 'Very God of very God', they could not be attributed at all, without such a strain as would crack the sinews of language, reducing the sequences of speech to incoherences of thought".[3] So sharp is the distinction here drawn that one is left wondering how such a figure as Jesus is depicted as being could ever become the prototype for the Christ-ideal at all. Roberts proceeds to some specific illustrations: The Gospels afford a very scanty picture of Jesus. (A point used to deadly effect by G. K. Chesterton in his reply to Roberts's article published subsequently in the Hibbert Journal.) The miracles he rejects as "Rubbish from a bygone age". It is also embarrassing to the modern mind that Jesus should have believed in exorcism.[4] It was an absurd belief shared by Jesus with his contemporaries that the world was shortly to come to an end; so too were the ideas that woman was created from man, that suffering and sin entered the world suddenly; these are fairy-tales, but the New Testament still takes them seriously, though it pretends to speak the last word on religion.[5] It is impossible to imagine that Jesus could have understood modern science or Greek culture. The importance of these admissions is this: "If Jesus was man only, these questions are

[1] *Jesus or Christ*, p. 270.
[2] ibid., p. 270.
[3] ibid., p. 270.
[4] ibid., p. 275.
[5] ibid., p. 275.

irrelevant. But if he was God, they raise, for me, an insoluble difficulty".[1]

Most characteristic of this article is its direct attack upon the teaching both ethical and religious of Jesus. His instructions with regard to almsgiving imply his acquiescence in a failure of social justice. He quite inconsistently prohibits the taking of rewards from men, whilst praising the idea of thousandfold rewards from God. He passes no condemnation upon the harsh contemporary law regarding debtor and creditor. He forbids resistance to violence, and the taking of oaths—upon which topics Christians have always disobeyed him as a matter of course. On the matter of divorce, he recognizes the husband's right to throw out his wife—thus admitting the iniquitous principle of sex inequality. His teaching against provident regard for the future has done great harm; whilst even more mischievous has been his acquiescence in the belief in demon-possession. Roberts concludes by again inveighing against those who take elements belonging to the expanding Christ-ideal and attempt to give them a seeming objectivity by predicating them of Jesus of Nazareth, and sums up his argument thus:

"They habitually quote as divinely decisive words and actions attributed to Jesus of Nazareth. This conveys to me the impression that they believe Jesus was God. Yet almost every chapter of the Gospels bears testimony to the limitations within which Jesus lived and wrought. And though the physical limitations are by now freely admitted even by conservative scholars, the political, economic, social, intellectual, and ethical limitations are no less apparent".

It is not worth while answering such an attack upon the value of the historical Jesus point by point. Many of the most obvious shortcomings of the article were pointed out by subsequent contributors to the Hibbert Journal. It is, however, necessary to show the principles which underly such a study—the same principles, with the same results, which form the background of all radical Christologies.

Here, then, presented by Mr. Roberts, is the human Jesus stripped of every husk. In the previous chapter it was observed that the apologetic drawn from the study of our Lord's growing consciousness of Sonship and vocation carried with it the postulate that his mental growth and activity could be understood almost

[1] *Jesus or Christ*, p. 276.

exclusively in terms of human psychology. By many of the writers who followed that method of apologetic the full import and revolutionary character of this postulate was scarcely realized—and for many of them it did not have such far-reaching consequences, since their minds were rooted in the Church's ancient system of belief. We have now, however, come face to face with that postulate carried one stage further—possibly a logical stage further. We have before us a group of writers who seek to understand the Person of Christ in its entirety in the light of the material and human context of his life. It is not denied, by some at any rate, that metaphysical speculations in regard to his relation to the life-spring of the universe, may be legitimate at a later stage in the appreciation of Jesus' work; but primarily he is a man to be criticized and studied as other men are. Therefore, we may seek for the kernel, the significance and power of his name, in the inner springs of his spiritual life—as Martineau does—or in the religious experience and ideal which has grown out of his memory —as Roberts does—but the root principle is the same: Jesus is now a human figure, who must be studied and appraised exclusively in terms of human nature and history, and this study must be unmolested or modified by the intrusion of any metaphysical dogma relating to his person such as the hypostatic union. To appreciate this point of view more fully it will be well to compare it with what has gone before. In the controversy regarding the limitation of our Lord's knowledge, opposite positions were championed by Dr. Gore and Dr. Stone. There were many differences of opinion between these two great churchmen, and in the controversy they appeared to stand for positions that were poles apart. Yet they were both of them men whose thought and devotion were rooted in the theology of the Fathers. In consequence of this, both of them began their examination of the historical Person of Christ from the given doctrines of the Trinity and Incarnation. The fact that Jesus was God the Son was their starting-point and the background of all their exegesis, and to them it was the key that alone unlocked the door to the understanding of his Person and his work. Christ's miracles, sinlessness, authority, teaching, his sacrificial death, his commission to the Church—all these things to such thinkers had their origin and significance in the fact that Jesus was personally the Son of God.

The newer liberals, on the other hand, set themselves to study the life of our Lord and the effects of his life upon the world without these first principles; "nature", to them, human nature, was the beginning and the end of all things, in the context of which alone all reality must be understood. If this appears to be a narrow point of view, an outlook in which the only teleology is the perfection of *this* world, and the only reality is matter and psycho-physical experience, and the only arena of happenings and criteria is the temporal history of man, let it be remembered that physical science had appeared as a fairy with a magic wand which bade fair to reveal every secret of existence.

To conclude this section two points may be advanced in regard to the concept of the kernel and husk. If it be once admitted that such a process of enveloping the historic Person of Christ has taken place; that is to say, if it be admitted that the doctrines of the church and the writings of the New Testament do not in fact furnish an authentic or legitimate account of Jesus' life and meaning, it would remain a function of individual taste and ingenuity to determine what was kernel and what was husk. We have above noted two such applications of the principle which differ from one another in almost every particular apart from the common complaint that husks have in fact been formed. The prevailing trend of higher criticism, the particular type of philosophy in vogue, the immediate shade of Protestant apologetics, these and many other influences, all of which sway like the eddying tide, are the influences that would always condition the distinction between the kernel and the husk.

In particular reference to the development of the concept as developed by such writers as R. Roberts, there is a more serious difficulty. The Christ ideal, it may fairly be said, has produced its striking effects upon mankind largely as a result of a belief in certain events believed to have occurred in connexion with the historic Person of Jesus. The experience of atonement is owed to the sacrificial death of Christ, the sense of power and victory over death depends upon Christ having actually risen the third day, and so through all the varied Christian experiences. If then the historic Person is shown to be something quite different from what the "Ideal" necessarily presupposes, the ideal can scarcely be expected to survive such a disillusionment, in any recognizable form, at any rate. It is quite idle to pretend, as some liberals have done, that a beautiful yet unhistorical legend can have, when recognized as such, the same power over mankind, as had the belief in a unique act of God believed to have occurred before the eyes of men.

## 2. *The Rejection of a Miraculous Incarnation*

Up to the present, we have left undiscussed the principal and most significant attack which the new naturalism made upon the traditional faith of Christendom. Hitherto, the new movement had confined itself to nibbling around the periphery of Christian doctrine; discrediting a miracle here, overthrowing a legendary accretion there. Now at length it was to show itself in its true colours, and one is enabled to see exactly what was being sought for. The new humanism was opposed to the central conception of the Incarnation itself—God becoming man—and not merely to certain miraculous items in the Gospel narrative. The doctrine which lay at the centre of the traditional Christian Gospel was itself the stumbling-block upon which liberal theology sooner or later had to fall. The belief in Christ's omniscience had been attacked because it appeared to produce a figure who was "unnatural": that was precisely the point, for it was the idea itself of a Person entering the world from outside, an unnatural Person, which appeared so foreign to the liberal way of thinking. This was even truer of the attacks made upon the miracles, and especially upon the Virgin conception and the Resurrection which, more than any, point to the fact of Christ's life upon earth as an incident in a life which he lives outside the time-process.

The opposition to the traditional doctrine of the Incarnation may be studied in its clearest light in a series of lectures by Percy Gardner, *A Historic View of the New Testament* (1901). It is not proposed to follow the course of Dr. Gardner's argument but merely to take him as a starting-point for the ensuing discussion. He begins from the assumption that, throughout every department of the universe, there predominates the law of evolution. This excludes, in his opinion, the possibility, or at any rate the congruity or probability, of a sudden interference with nature.

"There are not in history, as there are not in the physical progress of the world, veritable cataclysms, when the regular wheels of the world are suspended and the laws of change turned backwards. Belief in evolution runs as a red thread through almost all modern works on history".[1] He admits that the biological principle must be applied to history with some caution,

[1] *Historic View of the N.T.*, p. 12.

as human personality appears to be so indeterminate a quantity; but here is none the less the point from which the most thoroughgoing attack upon the doctrine of the Incarnation is launched. Dr. Gardner, like many of his contemporaries, accepts the theory of evolution in a very simple and often naïve form. Since his time, the theory has been greatly modified by biologists, for even within the realm with which such scientists deal there are innumerable facts which do not fit into the theory as it became popularized at the end of the nineteenth century—a steady and sustained upward development of life in and through every form and species. If then the processes of organic life exhibit erratic movements with sudden leaps and bounds, how much more precarious is the application of the theory to history, where the genius and the individual play such vital rôles in man's story. As traditionally conceived, and as taught by the New Testament, the Incarnation is a sudden and cataclysmic eruption into the time series from without. It is a miracle, in the most thorough and despised meaning of that word. Whilst being *ipso facto* part of history, the Incarnation has ever been regarded by the Church as not itself produced by history, or evolved through history, except in so far as the sin of man may be said to have caused it—on the Thomist view. It was caused proximately by God, who "sent forth his Son". Though there was preparation in the world— the Roman road, the Greek tongue, the Hebrew religion—yet the act, the initiative and the Person came from God, from without the world. The Incarnation therefore is the miracle of miracles; and hence, whilst liberal scholars may appear merely to be casting doubts upon the story of Christ walking upon the water or the raising of Lazarus, their basic difficulty was the Incarnation which presupposed all other miracles. In a fairy-land world such as was possible in the prescientific era, where demons tore down houses and donkeys spoke as men, the idea of a miraculous Incarnation of God breaking into the world through all natural barriers and processes would not have been so out of place, it is urged by such writers as Gardner. In a world, however, governed by unchanging laws of species and growth, whose God is seen and known as a God of order and not of confusion, the Incarnation stands out as something utterly different, foreign, and in contradiction to its environment. According, then, to those who paid unconditional homage to the theory of evolution, one would require evidence of an altogether thorough and unquestionable character in order to be persuaded that in history one such event, different in kind from all else within the universe, had taken place. If such evidence were forthcoming, it would no doubt redound to the greater glory and significance of the Incarnation since its truly unique character would be silhouetted against an altogether distinct background. The evolutionary character of the universe, however, with its consequent predilection against the Incarnation, was being insisted upon precisely at the time when a purely negative type of higher criticism was being progressively unleashed. In the face of this criticism it was wellnigh impossible to argue that the historical evidence for the truth of the Incarnation was of an unshakable character. Hence the doctrine was left, a stranger in a world of a different order and possessing little of the type of evidential proof calculated to impress the scientific era.

Thus Gardner, after stating his principle that miracle or cataclysm does not occur in human history as in the realm of biology, and hence that the old miraculous doctrine of the Incarnation can scarcely be expected to be believed in the light of such knowledge, lays great stress upon this argument, which was calculated to make a great impression at the time, namely, that our faith must be based upon something sounder than a set of historical events—whose veracity is at most a matter of probability—events which at any moment the higher critics may disallow. A further import of this argument will appear later.

Attempts were therefore made to reorientate the central Christian concept of Christ's Person to bring it into relation with the evolutionary outlook upon the rest of the universe then in vogue, and out of this attempt a type of Christology was born which bears exceedingly slight resemblance to the ancient faith of Christendom. The Person and work of Christ had to be explained exclusively in terms of the processes of nature, and this in its turn entailed the seeking of a new basis for faith. In regard to the first point, the most striking and best-known attempt to reconstruct and revivify Christology on lines compatible with the evolutionary principles of nature whilst preserving the traditional terminology—and a touch of the supernatural as well—was made by the immanentists, whose work forms so compact a unit as to merit consideration in the following chapter by itself. In all such reconstructions, however, if they be logically carried out, Christ can never be more than a man. He may be the first in a galaxy of saints, teachers, religious geniuses, and is on that count of prime importance for the religious life of all men. More than that he cannot be. It is beside him that we must kneel, not before him at his feet as our Lord and our God. If he does not enter the world as a Personal God intervening in a miraculous manner from without, he must be part of and a product of the world of nature, a human being, a man.

Moreover, if evolution be the dominating principle at work in the world, then Christ, if he belongs exclusively to the world, must be a point in that process. It might well be argued that as such it is possible for him to be surpassed in every respect in the future as the race continues to evolve—in fact upon the evolutionary theory as it is naïvely stated by liberal theologians I see no escape from this conclusion. Even stated at its least presumptive measure, namely, that Christ was as it were the crest of a wave in that development of mankind, hitherto unequalled, it must follow from the principle that it is possible for humanity to attain to his level—especially if it be imagined that the goal of evolution is self-perfection. The consequences for Christology of the introduction of the evolutionary idea were seen by none so clearly as by P. T. Forsyth, who writes:

"The evolutionary idea is certainly compatible with Christianity; but not so long as it claims to be the supreme idea, to which Christianity must be shaped. Evolution is within Christianity, but Christianity is not within evolution. For evolution means the rule of a levelling relativism, which takes from Christ his absolute value and final place, reduces him to be but a stage of God's revelation, or a phase of it that can be outgrown, and makes him the less of a creator as it ranges him vividly in the scale of the creature".[1]

The placing of Christ entirely within the framework of an evolutionary view of the universe necessarily reduced him from being God the Son, uncreated and coming from outside, to being the man Jesus, created in the process of the world's growth and hence belonging exclusively to it. Thus the exclusion of the unique and cataclysmic character of the Incarnation produces precisely the same result as the concept of the kernel and the husk: it deposes Christ from his position as not simply the source but the object of religion.

Having thus denied the possibility of God breaking through the

[1] *Person and Place of Jesus Christ*, p. 10.

laws which he has framed for the world's growth by entering upon human life in a miraculous manner, and having thus taken from Christ the place which he held as the matter and the proof of man's essential religious beliefs, the liberal scholar is obliged to seek for some other ground of certainty on which the faith of man may rest. Religion has been forcibly divorced from its old historical allegiance—faith cannot be based upon historical "probabilities" or upon an event that appears grotesque to the modern mind. Gardner's own elucidation of the difficulty is worth studying as an excellent example of the type of substitute that was offered instead of the old faith. Let higher criticism do its worst, he argues: let it tear to pieces the historical records of the life of Christ as it pleases, for the essential basis and facts of religion it cannot touch: "Upon the actual facts of the religious life they have no direct bearing. Religion is at bottom a condition of heart and will—a constantly maintained relation towards a higher spiritual power. And this religion—the religion of experience and conduct—is not immediately dependent upon our historic outlook. It is a matter, not of inference, not of learned research, but of daily life and habit of soul. We need have but little fear that any views as to historic methods can invalidate our religious, our Christian experience".[1] Matters of ancient history, he argues, can never be proved or disproved—at most they are matters of probability; whereas religious experience is a certainty which cannot be moved. Gardner then proceeds to an elaborate inductive apologetic for theism drawn from the recently appreciated fact in psychology at that time that "Will" is the centre of human personality, leading to the conclusion that conscious will is the ruling principle behind the universe, from which he thus argues that "To attain to some communion with this power in exalted feeling and passionate adoration is the highest object of religious passion and enthusiasm. To become a fellow-worker with this power in the visible world is the practical power of religious organisation and ethics".[2] One may well ask, what has all this to do with Christology? The plain answer is, nothing whatever. In the system which Gardner proposes, the faith of the believer has nothing more to do with Christ than a man has connexion with his neolithic forbears. This is seen from the quite arbitrary way in which the work of Christ is fitted on to systems whose real basis is either in mysticism, as in the present case, or in

[1] *Historic View of the N.T.*, p. 16.  [2] *ibid.*, p. 40.

some other speculative synthesis. Symptomatic of his attitude towards the work and person of Christ is a remark of his concerning the synoptic writers: "The two thoughts in relation to the Person of the founder, as apart from his teaching, which especially possess the synoptic writers are his place in the great historic plan of God, and his great spiritual ascendency over men",[1] adding that these aims to us are merely incidental in value. He thus displays complete indifference to the evangelic message, the initiative taken by God on man's behalf, the saving acts of Christ. To designate Gardner's psycho-mysticism a Gospel would be a gross misuse of language. In such a system the Person of Christ can never be more than human like ourselves, and his work for us that of teacher and example. Gardner, it is interesting to note, has his own theory regarding the kernel and the husks. This must always be a major problem for the liberal theologian. To the catholic who believes that the main elements of the Faith were present in essence at any rate from the first, the history of dogma presents no fundamental problems. The liberal scholar, on the other hand, must always be under the necessity of explaining how the Jesus of history was transformed into the Christ of Dogma. Doctrines, he says, are formed like crystals when liquid enthusiasm cools. Miracles and eschatology he rejects as dross. The first veil which was drawn over Christ's spirituality by the evangelists was their misunderstanding of the function of prophecy, degrading it into mere mechanical foretelling of the future and seeking to interpret details of the Lord's life solely in that connexion. The general principle, however, is this: "The history of a religion ... is the history of the gradual translation of divine impulses or ideas into human forms. First into ways of life and behaviour; then, on the intellectual side, into history and prophecy and doctrine; then into organization and ceremony and art. It is in every case an evolution".[2] One might have thought that on his own principles this was evolution in reverse, a decline from the spiritual rather than an ascent to it!

### 3. *The Attempt to Return to Christology*

From the radical modes of approach to the significance of Christ and his Gospel, described above, we return for a brief spell to a system which bears a more obvious resemblance to what the world has hitherto known as Christian theology. It is in fact a new

[1] *Historic View of the N.T.*, p. 109.   [2] *ibid.*, p. 70.

attempt to reinstate evangelical Christianity to its rightful place. It seeks to accomplish this, moreover, from the evangelical starting-point, the experience of salvation—and it calls to its aid the new apologetic, the moral appreciation and evaluation of the Person of Christ. The attempt is also of importance as being an English version of the thought of one of the foremost German theologians of the nineteenth century, Ritschl. The application of this system bade fair to become a promising reconstruction of Christology, and it is with regret that in the fourth section we shall see how in the long-run it has little more to offer than previous writers considered above. We return then to the works of Dr. A. E. Garvie, *Studies in the Inner Life of Jesus*, and *The Ritschlian Theology*, especially the former.[1]

At the beginning of the preceding chapter we had occasion to note Garvie's enumeration of the external proofs of Christ's Deity; after enumerating them, he criticizes them thus: "It is not because the present writer has abandoned in doubt or denial any of these features of the Divinity of Christ that he declines with Dr. Denney to regard any of them as primarily or pre-eminently giving Christ's Godhead an objective character. But in presenting evidence we must consider not only what is true, but also what will most effectively persuade and convince. The present age is suspicious of the supernatural, and miracle is an offence to it: but on the contrary, it is receptive of and responsive to evidence, moral and religious in character; . . ."[2]

As already stated, then, Dr. Garvie begins from the evangelical standpoint. The fundamental fact for the evangelical, be he liberal or traditionalist in character, is the experience of salvation undergone by the subject; it is the characteristic Christian experience, and the fact which makes a man a Christian believer—dogma, to him—is a consequence, an expression in set words of what he has already undergone. Hence, when we say that Christ is God and Saviour, what we are in fact saying is that for us he has acted and been experienced as such.

"Whether doctrine is consciously regarded as value judgement or not, it is quite certain that the controlling consideration in defining the truth about the Person of Christ will be the worth experienced in his work. What he as Saviour has done for us that

---

[1] Ritschlianism (derived from Kant) is perhaps the only form of Modernism which is not Immanentist.
[2] *Studies*, p. 471.

he will be to us; and it is futile to strive for an objectivity of doctrine distinct from and independent of the subjectivity of experience; although on the other hand the common Christian experience should be the standard".[1]

Although Dr. Garvie's general meaning is fairly clear, his use of the words "subjectivity" and "objectivity"—as was common at the time, is far from being well defined. On the previous page he denied that the external proofs give the Deity of Christ an objective character, and here he denies the possibility of an objective doctrine of Christ's Deity apart from the evangelical experience. The plain meaning of these remarks is that, not only is Christian experience the only valid apologetic, but that Christ's Deity without the experience has no reality as a fact. Dr. Garvie's thought is no doubt coloured by idealistic philosophy and on that count it is not altogether easy to see his point of view, but one can at least demand logical consistency. In other words, his statements amount to this: if in history no human souls had as a matter of fact turned to Christ as Saviour and undergone the Christian experience, then Christ would not have been *in se* God the Son. From numerous indications it is obvious that this is *not* Dr. Garvie's meaning. It will appear, however, that it is precisely this to which the method in the long-run conduces. If then Dr. Garvie does imply more than this, he has set out an altogether false antithesis between objectivity and subjectivity. If dogma has no reality except in experience, it is bound to be regarded in the end as personal pietism unconnected to persons or events outside. If, however, dogma—however much it be grounded upon faith—proposes facts which are true without our believing in them, then it is quite absurd to imagine that they stand in any opposition to one another. Dr. Garvie then proceeds to apply Ritschl's principle to the new apologetic to show how Christ's fulfilment of his vocation is a clear demonstration of his Divinity:

"The personal vocation of Jesus was the establishment of the kingdom of God among men, the introduction of men into the same filial relation to God and fraternal relation to one another as was his own . . . He who perfectly reveals God to man and perfectly redeems man to God must have for man the value of God. This religious valuation which is consequent on the ethical estimate of the perfect fulfilment by Jesus of his vocation is expressed in the predicate of his Divinity".[2] This he gives as a summary of Ritschl's position, which he warmly accepts.

[1] *Studies*, p. 472.   [2] *ibid.*, pp. 472, 473.

In the previous chapter it was seen how the perfect correspondence of Christ's mind and soul with the Messianic ideal was pointed to as a proof of the truth of his claims. It might be imagined therefore that in the present instance we are being directed to Christ's perfect fulfilment of his vocation in the same way, as an objective, concrete proof of his Deity, one which may be appreciated by anyone through an inductive study of the Gospel evidence. The appearance, moreover, of quotations from Dr. Garvie in illustration of that other chapter may also lend colour to this supposition. This is, however, far from being the case. For according to the principles of Garvie, as of Ritschl himself, Jesus is seen to fulfil his vocation and thus to be God not by every passing eye but solely by the believer to whom he has the value of Lord and Redeemer. There is no objective historic proof then in itself to be derived from the study of Christ's ethical functioning but only a proof in relation to and dependent upon the faith of him to whom Christ has the worth of God. Even this portion of the argument, therefore, in which there appeared to be a semblance of objectivity is dissolved in the running stream of value judgment.

Dr. Garvie does, however, make the attempt to redeem his position by restating the main proposition with the order of causation the right way round. For, taken baldly, the Ritschlian thesis can mean—Jesus is divine because we feel ourselves saved by him. Garvie therefore directly asserts that what Jesus was in himself constituted what he did for mankind. It is perhaps the most sinister feature of Ritschlianism that it does in fact deliberately obscure the correct sequence of causation. Jesus is God, therefore he can and does save us—that is the Christian belief set in the order in which it appears to common sense; yet Ritschlian theology by constantly speaking of experience and value judgment obscures this fact and *never* states the proposition unequivocally in its true order. Here is the nearest that Garvie comes to it:

"The Person conceived not statically as product of an eternal act but dynamically as process of a temporal development is identical with the work. Jesus is for us what he is in himself".[1]

This pre-eminence given to Christ's work as opposed to a doctrine of his person—if the one *can* be conceived of without the other—is by no means the copyright of thinkers such as Garvie;

[1] *Studies*, p. 474.

it is insisted upon with great vigour by Forsyth. This "active principle" as opposed to static dogma is made the basis of much of Garvie's reconstruction, some of which is of no little interest.

"To get at all that the Person as manifested in the work of Christ means and is worth, we must apply the religious-historical method with a larger purpose and a wider scope than is usual among its advocates. The correlation of phenomena, which is the second principle of the method, is normally dealt with by the use of the category Causality; quite as legitimate an application is possible with the category Teleology. The immediate *how* is not a complete account without the ultimate *why*. It is the dominance of physical science that so narrows the vision even of scholars; the philosophy which answers the question that not only the mind asks but the heart needs answered should come within the range of sight of the student of such a theme as the Person and the work of Christ. Already in the Apostolic age was Christ placed in this larger context. For the Fourth Evangelist . . . Jesus is the Incarnate Word . . . For the Apostle Paul, all things were summed up in Christ . . . This is the value Judgement of these first believers".[1] "What is so plain that he that runneth may read is that Christ had done for, and, therefore, had been to these men, strict Jewish monotheists both, of such unutterable significance and immeasurable value that they snatched up whatever came to hand in the thought and speech of their age and environment which seemed in any way adapted to set before others the glory which they had themselves beheld".[2]

Here then under the form of Ritschlian theology is the final attempt of liberalism to anchor down its religious beliefs to the historic Person of Christ, and amid the ruins of ancient dogmas and venerable apotheosising, to seek afresh for a substantial faith in the Deity of our Lord.

## 4. *The Anchor is Torn Away Once More*

Allusion was earlier made to Percy Gardner's argument against the rationality of resting the essential principles of the religious life upon any given array of historical occurrences. "When doctrine is based on historic record, and when for proof of it we are referred to writings of doubtful authorship, coming down to us

---

[1] *Studies*, p. 489.
[2] *ibid.*, p. 490.

out of the mists of ages, and bearing obvious signs of human weakness and ignorance, we cannot help shrinking in doubt and terror. Is it on such evidence as this that we are to risk the well-being of our souls? . . . It seems impossible . . . We must have some safer anchorage for our souls . . . For this reason there seem to me grave objections to the view of the historic origins of Christianity often taken by English churchmen".[1] Here in fact was the intrinsic doubt ready to be cast in the teeth of any who attempted to pin back the Christian faith to the events of Christ's earthly life. Nor was an appeal such as that made to "Christ's perfect fulfilment of his vocation"—along the lines of the new apologetic—likely to meet with more success. Like all other apologetics, it too rested upon the historic records from "The mists of ages". But there was yet a far more serious objection than the mere unsatisfactory nature of the historical records. For it was to be shown that the apparent objectivity arrived at in Garvie's system is in reality no more than a part of that subjective appreciation upon which it depends: the doctrines themselves have no separate existence of their own.

One of the most forthright exponents of the Ritschlian system, and yet one who more than any other was aware of its true nature and implications, was Mr. J. M. Thompson.[2] Jesus to him possesses the value, the significance of God. But he recognizes that the grounds for this belief lie exclusively within his own soul, his faith and the faith of other believers. Christ by his work and his worth is apprehended by our faith as everything which the creeds predicate of him; but apart from our faith and experience the dogma of his Deity is not only meaningless, it is untenable. Of any objective proof of the Lord's Deity there is none, and can be none, he argues. Mr. Thompson's critique of New Testament theology is radical and searching in the extreme. It is a compact argument which deserves far wider study and more careful refutation than it has up to the present received. First, Mr. Thompson deals with the question of miracle—along the lines alluded to in the previous chapter. He criticizes the dangerous antithesis between mirabilia—works of nature—and miracula—works of God. Miracles in any case are immoral and do not happen, for God's nature is seen in the order and law of the world. Therefore, no set of miracles, however well attested, could conceivably attest for us

[1] *Historic View of the N.T.*, p. 22.
[2] *Through Facts to Faith.*

the Divinity of Christ. Such a series of acts would suggest the activity of the devil rather than God (Mr. Thompson does not actually employ this apt expression). Even so, the fact that a man rose from the dead and could pass through locked doors would not prove he was God; for God is in his essence a moral being, and hence proof of his presence must be likewise of that order to which his nature belongs, and not a series of abnormal physical phenomena which would be quite irrelevant to the question. Likewise Christ's claims—if they were actually made—do not constitute a proof of their authenticity—Mr. Thompson ridicules the apologetic drawn from the Messianic-consciousness, for by his very nature there can be no external—hence outward, proof of Christ's Godhead. Historical proof of the fact that God once walked with men is not only absent, it is impossible. This we may take it is the final verdict of liberal theology, the logical end to which all roads have led—there is *no* historic demonstration of the Deity of Jesus Christ; any attempt to temporize with this result is futile. It might have appeared as though the introduction of Ritschlian theology could produce a measure of objectivity for the dogma and thus anchor down our faith to his Person: its final result was neither of these ends. Its very presence is an admission that the historic tradition within the Church had become untenable, and once that admission has been made, the cord is broken, for the basis of religion cannot be religious experience and Christ's historic Person at the same time; the importance of his Person sinks away as his nature is depotentiated from being the Incarnate Son of God to being an infinitely valuable human being. For the humanized Christ cannot occupy in the soul and mind of man the same position as did the Christ of traditional Christianity, however faith may seek to embellish the former with Olympian honours.

One further criticism of the Ritschlian type of theology may be developed. It was observed that Dr. Garvie denounced the idea of a formulated dogma of the Incarnation existing apart from the religious experience of believers; and in the work of such writers, among whom we must regretfully number P. T. Forsyth, we are constantly presented with this misleading antithesis between an intellectual belief impotent to save of itself, and the belief graven upon the heart and mind through faith and experience. It is a subtle fallacy. In such a contrast the latter is naturally to be preferred, and the insinuation is that the former represents the dry attitude of traditional orthodoxy—the letter which killeth—as opposed to a dynamic view of Christ's work. This is naturally a gross misrepresentation of the catholic attitude towards dogma; it displays a complete ignorance with regard to the catholic connotation of the word "Faith"—which is always "*credo in*" and never "*credo esse*"—for the beliefs themselves are always conceived as not a set of truths to be apprehended *in vacuo*, but the living presuppositions of a life which is lived within the believing fellowship. The antithesis exists only in the mind of liberal scholars, for, in any case, an "Experience" which was undefined by the Christian dogma would be as empty as a faith which was merely intellectual—if such a thing be possible. Such an experience *in vacuo* unrelated to dogma might be anything from a nightmare to inebriotic hallucination. The disastrous consequences for Christology of the forcing of this antithesis, together with the primacy of "Experience", may be shown from the writings of another English Ritschlian, R. F. Horton. He writes: "We must distinguish between the doctrine of the Divinity of Christ, stated in the Creeds as the result of the long controversy of the Œcumenical councils, and the Divinity of Christ discovered in the New Testament, and verified by the experience of faith. The one is metaphysical, the other is practical. The one is established by a process of reasoning, the other by a process of living. The one is usually accepted simply on authority as a dogma, the other is known by the exertion of conscience, feeling, and will, in the pursuit of goodness and Godliness".[1]

This, then, is his statement of the misleading antithesis discussed above: the matter of real importance to which we would draw attention is the conclusion which the writer draws from this setting of experience in opposition to dogma.

"Nothing is more barren than to say that we are saved by believing in the Divinity of Christ. Such a belief does not and cannot save. We are saved by believing in Christ; the Divinity is an inference from the faith; we find him Divine because he has brought us to God. We begin with the man Jesus, that Person who is presented to us in the Gospel narrative . . . We believe in him in his life, in his death, in his words, his teachings, his promises".[2]

Here indeed is the supreme fallacy of Ritschlian theology. It is the insistence on putting the cart before the horse. In dealing

[1] *My Belief*, 1908, p. 94.
[2] *ibid.*, p. 96.

## THE DIVORCE OF THEOLOGY FROM HISTORY 217

with Dr. Garvie we had occasion to note his obscuration of the order of causation—making it appear as though the faith caused the dogma, even though that particular writer saves himself from any gross error on the point. Here is precisely the same reversal of cause and effect with no saving graces to modify it. In treating of the article by R. Roberts, too, it was urged that the Christ-ideal takes its effect upon mankind in virtue of the belief in the veracity of certain historical events and dogmatic beliefs regarding the Person of Christ.

Horton assumes that it is possible to apprehend Christ as Lord, God and Saviour, and then afterwards to arrive at a belief in his Divinity. This as a description and rationale of the Christian experience of salvation is simply *not true*. In the classic evangelical experience, a man makes an act of faith in Christ as his saviour, his God and Lord, by which he obtains the certainty of reconciliation with God. It is quite out of the question to pretend that men can or do make an act of faith in a purely human figure for the forgiveness of their sin, and afterwards discover that the purely human figure turns out to be God the Son. To make such an act of faith in a human figure would be in any case an act of blasphemy! What actually happens is that a man receives in some way a *prima facie* demonstration that Jesus is divine: he then by God's grace makes an act of faith in Jesus as God's Son—taking his words and claims to mean what they say. This is not to say that intellectual certainty precedes faith; what it does, however, preclude beyond all question is the notion that the belief *in toto* is the result of the act of faith. It is impossible to make an act of faith in nothing. The view expressed by Horton can at the most mean that by following the teaching and example of Jesus one realizes through experience that the divine must have dwelt in him to a pre-eminent degree, since his message gives the key to the understanding of life; but to what Christian believers have always understood by faith in Christ it can have no intelligible reference whatsoever. Horton's view, therefore, implies that either the belief in Christ's Deity is a subjective evaluation, which takes from the dogma its objectivity—Christ being one thing to one and another thing to another; or it means that in following his steps we realize that God must have indwelt him. In either case the absolute dependence upon the work of Christ as God upon earth—not only during the period of the Incarnation but also in his living personal presence in his mystical body—is at least obscured, at most denied altogether. Thus the Ritschlian theology, which bids so fair at first sight to provide a basis for faith that will have a direct reference to the historic Person of Jesus, in the long run can admit of no objective and historical proof of the Lord's Deity. Like all other systems of liberal theology it tends in the long run to separate the religious life and experience of the believer from the Christian basis in history.

## 5. *Eschatology and Modernism*

Nor should this chapter close without some reference being made to the influence of the "eschatologists". In the Anglican and Free Churches the new interpretation of Christ's Person occasioned no crisis. As time went on, numbers of the more advanced liberals were gradually won over to the new allegiance, especially when Schweitzer's *Von Reimarus zu Wrede* became accessible to English readers in 1910 under the title *Quest of the Historical Jesus*. But to the majority, eschatology was frowned upon, on the one hand as one more Teutonic excess, and on the other (as Loisy had employed it in his earlier days) as a stick to beat the earlier liberals withal: but in any case, the wide tolerance of modern theological opinion now enjoyed within these communions made it possible for the latest of these theories to enter silently and without embarrassment. Within the Roman communion, however, it was different. Nothing has hitherto been said with regard to Roman theologians, since even their most liberal thinkers played virtually no part in the Christological crisis until this very juncture. But the sudden eruption of the Modernist movement demonstrates clearly that events outside were not unaccompanied by sympathies within that church. Roman Catholics had from time to time been won over to Protestant liberalism, as, for instance, Renan, but the acceptance by some Roman thinkers of the findings of the eschatologists produced a crisis of the first magnitude. The reasons for this it is not our business to discuss here; what is of interest is that so frankly did the modernists embrace the new theory that the most celebrated representative of Catholic Modernism in England may himself be taken as our paradigm for eschatological Christology.

*George Tyrrell, S.J.*, Christianity at the Cross-roads (1909).
The book was written with the object of seeking for a synthesis

## THE DIVORCE OF THEOLOGY FROM HISTORY 219

between the fundamental tenets of criticism and traditional Christianity; the hope of true modernism. Tyrrell was a true disciple of the eschatologists—"Whatever Jesus was, he was in no sense a liberal Protestant. All that makes Catholicism most repugnant to Protestant modes of thought derives from him. The difficulty is, not Catholicism, but Christ and Christianity".[1]

It is of course true, as Tyrrell urges, that he and the Catholic modernists differed vastly from older liberal Protestantism, and his criticism of *Pascendi Gregis* may in this sense be justified; but it is not so easy to see how Catholic modernism differs essentially from Protestant eschatological systems; Tyrrell's article in "Jesus or Christ" shows as little interest in the connexion between religion and the historic Jesus as does that of R. Roberts.

The eighth chapter of *Christianity at the Cross-roads* entitled "The Christ of Eschatology" may well be adopted—with some interpolations—as a convenient summary of the findings of the eschatological school. The primary reference of all Jesus' actions, words, and thinking, was to the imminent world cataclysm in which he himself was to play a decisive rôle—it was the coming of the Kingdom of God. Hence, "his Messianic consciousness was the main determinant of his action and utterance".[2] Messiahship is here employed with a thoroughly eschatological meaning, and there is no suggestion of psychological reconstruction: "Of anything like a development of his Christ-consciousness there is no evidence that will stand criticism".[3] Jesus embraced the whole contemporary Jewish apocalyptic outlook, with the sole difference that he himself was the Son of Man who was to be glorified by God, through whose sufferings the inception of the Kingdom would take place. He did not conceive himself even as the Messiah of the prophets, destined to rule on earth as a king, but as a supernatural figure whose coming would be a prelude to the transcendental Messianic kingdom, which he believed imminent. Jesus continued to expect this divine intervention at various junctures in his life, as when he sent forth his Apostles with the promise that their mission to the cities of Israel would not be completed until the "Son of Man should come": and also at Mk. 9. 1—He again looked for the Kingdom appearing at his triumphal entry into Jerusalem, and whilst he hung on the Cross. As long as he lived upon earth he was still in a sense only Son of Man by destiny. He was not to preach his own glory; God would in his time reveal

[1] *Christianity at the Crossroads*, p. 21.   [2] ibid., p. 46.   [3] ibid., p. 47.

that. The kingdom thus envisaged was to be precipitated and entered into through repentance, and through fire and wrath. This fiery trial—the *Peirasmos*—plays a prominent part in Jesus' thought. Of a coming reign of morality upon earth there is no hint. Even his apparently ethical teaching is not designed for a settled society which would endure, but for a brief period before the final judgment, hence its reckless character. His kingdom was therefore not earthly or moral but transcendental. To take some specific applications of this view in the Gospels: The Sacraments, it is argued, were effectual sealings, pledges of things to come in the kingdom. Thus the Eucharist was a guarantee of participation in the Messianic banquet. The Our Father even is eschatological in content: "Lead us not into temptation" refers to the *Peirasmos*, as does the prayer "Pray that ye enter not into temptation". The Twelve Apostles—representing in apocalyptic thought the twelve patriarchs—were appointed to take part in the eschatological banquet and great assize. The concept of the Ecclesia was the company of the elect who will pass through the fire into the Kingdom; hence also the Power of the Keys has an eschatological significance.

This, then, in very brief, is the Gospel picture of Jesus, according to the eschatologists. He is a figure whose whole interest was centred in the belief in an imminent cosmical crisis. Within the Gospels, says Tyrrell, he alone is to be found; of the advocate of the moral and inward kingdom there is not a shred. The Christ of the eschatologists is by no means an attractive figure. He is a zealous and harsh fanatic, whose life from beginning to end was ground into shape by the relentless pressure of a wild and terrifying idea; his life was a series of bitter disillusionments at every step, and he died with the avowed intention of invoking the power of God through his sufferings, but with the final and heart-breaking disappointment: "My God, My God, why hast Thou forsaken me"?

It should be borne in mind that this picture is a reaction, painted in opposition, not so much to traditional orthodox Christology as to the liberal Protestant interpretation of Jesus' life and work. The liberal picture was itself a one-sided misrepresentation of the facts—a Christ who was depicted in the interests of an ethical humanism, by men with little interest in the supernatural or the hard demands of God. If therefore the eschatological picture of Jesus is a misrepresentation of him, it is

## THE DIVORCE OF THEOLOGY FROM HISTORY

so largely because of and in so far as it sets itself against the older liberal view; in many of its aspects it is a far more genuinely Christian portrait of Jesus than that of Martineau or Renan. To the orthodox mind, whilst its humanistic presuppositions and conclusions are unacceptable, it confirms, as against liberal theories, much that has always been cherished by the church. To the liberal of the older schools, on the other hand, the new eschatology appeared to shatter almost all that was left to him in the Christian religion. He had dispensed with the ancient dogmas and the supernatural context of New Testament occurrences and had built his house upon the sands of an ethical ideal, a teaching of permanent value, and the like. Now, however, his Christ turned out to be something utterly incompatible with such an ethical faith. C. W. Emmet tells us how regretfully he was drawn away from the older liberalism to the new point of view—how its coldness and harshness contrasted with the warmth and reverence of the older writers.[1] Thus, although at first sight it would appear as though the eschatological question belonged rather to the sphere of New Testament criticism than to Christology proper, yet towards the close of our period it was raising in the minds of some exactly those questions which have formed the background of this chapter. If Jesus were a fanatic steeped in a world of ideas utterly foreign to the mind of to-day, what possible relevance can his historic person have for religion at the present day? What can be the significance and value of such a person to us? How can he in any intelligible sense be said to possess for us the religious value of God—let alone be the subject of the church's creeds? Much of Tyrrell's subsequent argument that Catholic doctrine and practice is a logical development of Jesus' thought is to us illuminating and interesting, but affords no solution to his own problems, which, in his own words, is not Catholicism but Christ. On the presuppositions and conclusions of the eschatologists there can be no Christology; no Christian religion with its worship, its rationale and its hope centred in Jesus of Nazareth.

It has thus been shown by examples of liberal theology of very varied types how the humanizing of Christ's Person, be it into a teacher of ethics or an eschatological fanatic, leads inevitably to a severance between the religion of to-day and the Lord's own life and work. With such a divorce between the faith of the believer

[1] *The Eschatological Question in the Gospels*, 1911, an able English exposition of Schweitzer and Loisy.

and the historic Person of Jesus the Christian religion virtually ceases to exist; for it is thereby emptied of those elements which gave to it its power and character, and, pre-eminently, of an objective dogma of the Deity of Jesus Christ, which on the rationalistic principles is impossible. For this dogma, a shadowy pragmatist belief is no substitute. Percy Gardner advances such a view in his article in *Jesus or Christ*: "The crude formula of the unintellectual Christian, 'Jesus is God', however it may offend the philosopher and jar upon the learned theologian, may be for many the direct expression of spiritual experience".[1] The Gospel has always been and always will be foolishness and a scandal; and the fact that at last liberal theology has admitted the scandal is the clearest evidence of its inadequacy to understand the nature of the New Testament message. Such a pragmatist admission that it may be tolerable for the οἱ πολλοι to continue to call Jesus God is the clearest admission of the bankruptcy of liberalism, its utter failure to explain in terms acceptable to human intelligence the facts of divine revelation and the experience of them.

[1] *Jesus or Christ*, p. 57.

# 8

## IMMANENTISM, IDEALISM, AND "THE NEW THEOLOGY"

ALLUSION was made in the preceding chapter to a school of thought in Christology, belonging to the radical liberal type, which constituted the most outstanding attempt to restate the Christian faith in terms compatible with modern thought. It was regarded by many as the only way in which religion could be related, anchored, to history—the historic origins of Christianity. For it sought, by giving a new interpretation of the doctrine of Christ's Divinity, to re-establish that supremacy in the religious consciousness of which modern criticism seemed to be divesting him. It thus possessed all the freshness and vigour of rediscovery; it appealed not simply to the deepest theological predilections of the time, but also to the prevailing philosophical modes of thought in the widest sense; and, by its clarity and simplicity, bade fair to eliminate the majority of those difficulties and paradoxes which had hitherto made the Christian faith so unattractive to modern man.

The system thus to be described was in its day of singularly transitory interest and importance; as an integral system it faded from view before it had even time to become well known—even some of its most renowned exponents either modified their standpoint or quickly disappeared from view. Yet its significance here lies in the fact of its position in the development of English liberalism. Its arrival marks the point of maximum influence and application of those principles described in the second portion of the first chapter, and it came at the precise moment when other attempts to save the situation by the rebuilding upon old foundations were proving unsafe and inadequate.

It must not be supposed, however, that the admitted method of William James is being employed in this essay, namely, that of studying the normal by examples of the abnormal. The writers to be considered in this, as in the preceding, chapter formed in their day but a minority of the believing, thinking Christians of the time, and yet they do in real measure exemplify the implications of tenets and ideas which were becoming tacitly accepted in far wider circles. These wider currents, therefore, can only be seen for what they were when solidified into the radical systems which they could and did produce when applied in a thoroughgoing and consistent manner.

The group of writers, then, herein comprehended form, as no other group during that age, a distinct and unique body of thinkers whose outlook is equally radical, and equally comprehensive, and complementary to the work of each other.

For the "New Theology", as the system was often called, was not simply a new Christology. It was an attempt to restate the whole of the Christian religion in terms of certain clearly-marked philosophical principles. Just as the classical Catholic theology is a unity, each dogma of which depended upon every other, so this reinterpretation was carried through with scrupulous thoroughness: it had a new doctrine of God, of man, a new conception of sin, of the Incarnation and of the atonement: and all these parts were made to be mutually dependent so that it was itself a complete theology, a new theology, and, as will be shown, a new religion—despite its frantic entreaties to be understood merely as the re-embodiment of all that had ever been best in Christian (and for that matter, pagan) religious thought.

For the purposes of exposition, three of the most celebrated exponents of this type of thought will be described and criticised. Dr. J. Warschauer had been educated for the Unitarian ministry, but his brilliant scholarship and wide sympathies—as one of his admirers describes his talents—were not realized until he became the renowned Congregationalist preacher of Bradford. The Rev. R. J. Campbell was at that time as minister of the City Temple attracting great audiences by the apparent originality of his thought and the magnetic influence of his personality. With a different background and in a very different sphere, Dr. Edward Caird at a somewhat earlier date enjoyed an equal place of honour as the Master of Balliol College, Oxford. Dr. Rashdall's work too in the same university did much to advance the new point of view. Naturally, the two last-mentioned writers did not belong to the coterie which later developed the New Theology, but Dr. Caird's work in many ways so strikingly resembles their own conclusions—trumpeted later as something "new"—that he is included here as throwing further light upon one important principle which underlay this type of theology.

## IMMANENTISM AND "THE NEW THEOLOGY"

As already remarked, the New Theology was a complete intellectual system, a Weltanschauung, and consequently its peculiar Christology is quite unintelligible without first obtaining a clear understanding of certain other reinterpreted doctrines—in particular, the doctrines of God, man, and creation.

In the second section of the first chapter, already referred to, we have considered some of the reasons which led to the magnification of the doctrine of divine immanence. The scientific spirit that stimulated belief in the intimate and constant contact of God with nature as a force energizing a living and growing organism; and at the same time, how this militated against miracle, intervention from without, and even against interest in the merely supernatural as such; the influence of the naturalism of German philosophy, especially Hegelianism, with its almost depersonalized God, working through the *cosmos* and in history; together with Schleiermacher's theology of "feeling", and Ritschl's theory of "value judgements";—all of which taught man to look for God, for Divinity rather, for religion, within his own being, rather than towards a separate God on his throne in heaven, manifested through erratic acts of supernal power.

Now in the thought of these writers, this old idea of divine immanence is pressed to the fullest possible extent of its meaning, with two results: First, immanence ceases to be thought of as merely one aspect of God's nature or activity; it becomes for us all that we can intelligibly know of God, and mean by the term, God. God's immanence becomes virtually all that matters to us of him. He may be granted in theory a separate "Personality", but as far as we are concerned, practically the whole of his essence is contained for us in nature, which we can see and know. What in God's being is transcendent is, so to speak, best left alone, or to the technical skill of the metaphysician; since as transcendent, God is unknown and unknowable to man—an infinite being at an infinite distance from human comprehension. The influence of Kant is here quite unmistakable: the conception of a fettered human mind which can only think and reason in terms of the finite, of the empirical, which cannot know anything other than that which is presented to it through the medium of the natural creation, in which it lives. As already pointed out more than once, there is nothing particularly new or startling about the view that God suffuses the world of nature, except to a dusty Deist, but when, as in the present instance, this doctrine is taught to the conscious exclusion of every other relevant consideration regarding God's nature and mode of operation, the matter is quite different. God is in fact brought down from heaven to earth, not by any catastrophic theophany or single act of exinanition, but as an ever-present reality around us: God *is* himself the colour of the sunset; he *is* the song of the birds; but most of all he is to be seen and known in the human character, his highest creation. He ceases to be a far-off and terrible king or judge as he appears as an everyday experience for us all to see, understand, and feel within ourselves.

But secondly, if this exaggeration of God's immanence brought down the Deity to earth, to within man's ken, it equally exalted man himself to the level of the divine. The doctrine cast a halo over the whole of nature—since it embodied and expressed God—and especially over man, its highest form of existence, making him not merely a creature of God or an image of God, but a manifestation of the divine nature: not so much in the sense of a divine likeness but of a self-realization by God, an outward expression by God of himself, related to him in the same relation as, say, the body is to the soul. Hence, man becomes all of a piece with God: what there is knowable of God resides within him, is a part of him and he of it. God truly differs from man in that he possesses an independent personality, but so too does one man differ from another man in exactly the same way, without destroying the fact that they both express the same God-indwelt nature. This manner of regarding God and man has a profound influence upon every other department of the theology of these writers; and this doctrine of God and man will itself be further coloured as it is seen in the various writers being directly applied as the main presupposition behind their exposition of the Incarnation.

## *Warschauer's Doctrine of the Incarnation*

In the thought of Warschauer, the *raison d'être* of the Incarnation—more even than its ground or possibility—is seen to spring directly from the conception of the immanent God, as alone knowable by man through the creation, his manifestation. Since the net result of this doctrine is that God and man are seen as parts of a whole, the constituent elements of a cosmos, in which God is the inner or invisible, and man is the outer or materialized:

## IMMANENTISM AND "THE NEW THEOLOGY"

it follows, first that God and man may never be envisaged as mutually exclusive terms—God here, man there—with a gulf of eternity between them; least of all may they be seen as set in opposition to one another, as they have generally been envisaged by traditional Christian theology. But even more so does it follow in the second place that God's highest revelation of himself may and must and did take place through nature, through a single man, Jesus of Nazareth.

"There can only be one kind of Divinity throughout the universe; but different manifestations of that Divinity. All beings show it forth in the measure in which they are able to do so, and incomparably highest of all stands Jesus Christ".[1] That such a view is now possible is due to the striking resuscitation of the immanence doctrine, he holds: "The doctrine of divine immanence is in a very special and unmistakable manner the rediscovery of the nineteenth century".[2] It is distinct from pantheism, which destroys the personality of God and of man; and is in his opinion the only adequate reply to the agnosticism of the day. If God only is transcendent, then he is unknowable, as the agnostics say. Immanence leaves real room for the distinction of personality; "Man, that is to say, is not identical with God, any more than a son is identical with his father; but man is consubstantial, homogeneous, with God, lit by a divine spark within him, a partaker of the divine substance . . ."[3]

Such language is so different from that of traditional Christian thought that it has to be read and re-read before its full meaning can be fully seen in its true order before the mind's eye.

Warschauer's rationale of the Incarnation is continued for us in the fifth chapter of his *New Evangel*. The one creative energy shown in all creation, in evolution, stimulated the doctrine of immanence. Transcendent God becomes known as immanent through all forms of life, but he is more immanent in man than in any other form. Man's troubled mind and aspirations, his sense of belonging to a higher order, bear witness to this fact. Hence any further knowledge of God must come through a human person, the highest we know of God and his character. Here, on the face of it, is an account of the Incarnation and its possibility which would appear to be in full conformity with traditional

[1] *Jesus: Seven Questions*, p. 100.
[2] *Problems of Immanence*, p. 2.
[3] *ibid.*, p. 19.

belief. For it has always been a bulwark of Christian apologetic and theology to assert that God's highest revelation of himself can best, and only, be made through human personality, created in his own image and likeness. Along these lines, too, Warschauer points to the necessity of the Incarnation: We do not need any special revelation of God's nature as transcendent, of his omnipotence or his omniscience, for these can be inferred by the use of reason a rather curious contradiction to what the writer had already said about the unknowability of the transcendent God, but what we do need, he argues, is a fuller disclosure of the character of God: his character of love, his character as Father. Jesus Christ, then, in this respect, is God's supreme manifestation of himself. In him, the character of God, what we most wanted to know about, is revealed. Possessing, as he did, a unique consciousness of his relation to God, he was able to disclose to us the divine character of love and the true relations which are to exist between God and man—a relationship which exists already in the attitude of God towards man, and which must also be fulfilled by the reciprocal attitude of man to God: he refers the reader to E. F. Scott on the Fourth Gospel, p. 181. Christ comes, then, to reveal the divine character and to open our eyes to our sonship:

"That capacity which we share with him, and which, slumbering in us, it is his function to awaken, is simply the capacity for sonship".[1] Christ's character was unique, but he was not thereby automatically sinless: the miraculously sinless Christ of a Virgin Birth is necessary for the old orthodoxy with its doctrine of original sin and a fall, and substantial atonement. Such a dogma, however, does not fit into the new system. His character, none the less, is quite unique. Theodore Parker and others like him had asserted that it did not matter who taught eternal truths so long as they were true. This, Dr. Warschauer holds to be false both to fact and experience: he quotes Burkitt with approval—Christianity stands or falls, lives or dies, with the personality of Christ,[2] and in another place the same thought leads him to a characteristic utterance—"He taught a religion by being a religion".[3]

Finally, rebutting those who declare that the teaching of Christ contained nothing new, he says: "The reason was this, and the

[1] *Jesus: Seven Questions*, p. 105.
[2] *Jesus or Christ*, Warschauer, ch. I.
[3] *Jesus, Seven Questions*, ch. II.

quality of novelty lay in this, that the one who now proclaimed the Father was no other than the Son—the Jesus who brought this message himself attested it, because he was the Christ of God".[1]

This language gives the impression of plain orthodox platitudes until we remember that the writer has already stated elsewhere his antipathy for the doctrines of the fall, original sin, and the traditional view of the atonement, and hinted that Christ is not other than we ourselves may become; it is then made plain that traditional language is being loosely employed with a totally different meaning from that customary to us. Moreover, in ch. V of "Seven Questions", where Dr. Warschauer discusses whether belief in Christ is necessary to salvation, he writes that the doctrine of salvation only through baptism may be rejected without hesitation; for Jesus saves us by setting up a more attractive rival to sin; his precepts, his holiness, and his personality give a new impetus to the good in us which outgrows the power of sin.

Continuing to describe the work of Christ, Warschauer points out that the new view, in which the Incarnation follows from divine immanence, is better than the old because by it God's nature is not conceived as distinct from human nature, with the one single bridge in history, but as akin to it and always present. The coming of Christ, therefore, is the realization of something that already exists, and it awakens and strengthens our sense of the presence of God within ourselves.

"Christ has by his own existence explained the relation of man to God. It is that of union not of separation".[2] "Christ means to us the discovery of God and of ourselves".[3] He assures the race of its fundamental oneness with God, and so forth.

We may sum up Dr. Warschauer's Christology thus: Jesus Christ is the supreme manifestation of the divine immanence in the world. That is to say, he is the highest possible exhibition of that indwelling of the whole of nature by the divine essence. By thus demonstrating the divine character of human nature he shows us that we are one with God, and that God's character is one of benevolence towards us.

One important presupposition of the "New Theology" may be extracted from this definition. If Christ is a manifestation of divine

[1] *Jesus or Christ*, p. 118.
[2] *New Evangel*, p. 104, quoted from J. M. Wilson.
[3] *ibid.*, p. 104.

immanence, through whose perfection we see our own relationships and possibilities, then it follows, we may justly argue, that his nature must be essentially of the same stuff as our own, however relatively greater than us he may have been in life and character. Here, in fact, we reach one of the crucial points which must be counted in relation to this system: Is Christ's divinity different in kind from our divinely indwelt nature, or at any rate from what it is meant to be; or is he divine Son of God in a sense in which we never can ourselves be, and with a nature different in kind from that which is our lot to possess? Dr. Warschauer himself considers this point, posing the question, was Jesus first among many brethren, or was he from everlasting different from any other human soul?[1] Many writers, such as Dr. Adeney, had held that the Divinity of Christ was of a different kind from that indwelling of God in us men, since with God Christ had a unity of personality and being and essence. Though, says Warschauer, these moderate immanentist writers would not, like Gore, assume that there was something miraculous about his humanity, yet they think it was different in kind, not just in degree. But, declares Warschauer, "Here we can only say that such a difference in kind, such an impassable gulf between Jesus Christ and every other human soul, if it were established, would in our opinion destroy all the value Christ possesses for us as an example in whose steps we were to follow".[2] He presses this point still further with a syllogism, as follows:

"If Jesus were essentially unlike us, he could not be an object of imitation; but he is, as experience attests, an object of imitation; therefore he cannot be essentially unlike us".[3] It follows, then, that in the thought of this writer the word "unique" is not employed in the same manner as in traditional theology—either of Christ's humanity, as something different from all other men in virtue of its unfallen state, or of his Deity in the sense of "*unicum*" or "*unigenitum*" in the Creeds. This will appear clearly later.

The theory thus propounded also embraces a new manner of subordinationism. From the fact that Jesus Christ is placed on man's side of the cosmos rather than on God's, a radical subordination of his person to the being and Person of God himself follows of necessity. The words "I and my Father are one" cannot

[1] *Seven Questions*, p. 69.  [2] *ibid.*, p. 96.
[3] *ibid.*, p. 97.

IMMANENTISM AND "THE NEW THEOLOGY" 231

refer to a fusion or union of persons; according to this writer they state a unique claim to entire and unbroken harmony with God—a claim to have realized the ideal life of Sonship by a continual doing of the Father's will.[1] Thus he would eliminate the doctrine of the Virgin birth, on the ground that by making the immanence in Christ different from that in us, it sets him apart from men, on God's side, as it were. Similarly, the ascription to Christ of supernatural gifts, such as omniscience, would set him apart from us: for all the "touching reality" of his passion would disappear had we to think that he foresaw the end precisely from the beginning—had he foreknown, even as he chose Judas to be his disciple, that the same Judas would betray him.[2] As a final indication of this subordinationism, we may note a passage in which Warschauer urges that we need not be scandalized at expressions like "God died"; for, he says, the Father was greater than the Son; God was not exhausted in the Son; "It is not to be suggested that he who prayed to the Father, was—to use again what we know to be very inadequate terminology—all of God; . . ."[3] Christ was light of light, yet not all the light. In him we get as much of God as we can bear.

In Warschauer, then, we have been introduced to some of the principles of this veritable "New Theology". It will remain for the next writer to carry these principles to their logical conclusions.

### R. J. Campbell

For simplicity's sake, the contents of one single work of this author will be examined—*The New Theology*, 1907.[4] The most remarkable feature of this volume is the distressingly naïve and crude form in which the writer's whole argument is presented. The greatest of reformers, it is true, never believe themselves to be innovators, but merely to be drawing out what was always implicitly believed beforehand—this is indeed to be expected: but to conduct an argument on the oft-repeated assumption that one's predecessors and opponents are hypocrites, or at best, fools, is a baneful species of the *argumentum ad hominem* fit only for the market-place, certainly not for the school of Divinity. Yet this is precisely what Mr. Campbell, the most thorough-going

[1] *Seven Questions*, p. 98.    [2] *New Evangel*, p. 96.
[3] *Jesus or Christ*, p. 126.
[4] At an early date Canon Campbell repudiated this book and withdrew it from circulation. The description refers only to his position in 1907.
16

advocate of immanentist theology, persisted in doing. He practically refused to believe that intelligent Christians of past ages have ever taken their religion seriously! He described the old theology, which regarded the plan of the universe as having gone wrong, as "pitiful"; whilst writing on the articles of the Creeds in the fifth chapter of his book he said: "The first in order of thought is the Godhead of Jesus. As regards this tenet, I think it should be easily possible to show that the most convinced adherent of the traditional theology does not believe, and never has believed, what he professes to hold". On the doctrine of the Virgin Birth, he also wrote: "The most reputable theologians have now given it up". The whole book, in fact, simply teems with this type of statement: abuse and incredulity towards orthodox Christian teaching, and a continual and utterly false distinction between what is called "popular theology" and "the best theology". It is not to be wondered at, therefore, that one with such prejudices and predilections should utterly fail to grasp the meaning of the Catholic creeds and theology.

Campbell's thought is very similar in outline to that of Warschauer; in fact the two men were for some time close collaborators in disseminating the New Theology, but Campbell's ideas are set forth in a much bolder manner, and the method is applied with more rigorous consistency to other branches of dependent theology, such as the doctrines of sin and atonement, which in their turn illustrate to no small extent the revolutionary nature of the proposed Christology.

Campbell begins his exposition by defining the three terms with which we have to deal: these three terms are, Deity, Divinity and humanity. It followed from the first principle of the New Theology that all the three are fundamentally and essentially one, but in scope and extent they are different. By the Deity we mean the all-controlling consciousness of the universe as well as the infinite, unfathomable, and unknowable abyss of being beyond. By Divinity, we mean the essence of the nature of the immanent God, the innermost and all-determining quality of that nature; Divinity equals love which if shown to us we have the divinest thing in the universe. Humanity is a lesser term. It is, in fact, the lesser experience of the divine nature. Campbell then proceeds to illustrate the difference and the unity of these terms:

"Strictly speaking the human and the divine are two categories which shade into and imply each other; humanity is Divinity

# IMMANENTISM AND "THE NEW THEOLOGY"

viewed from below, Divinity is humanity viewed from above".[1]

Applying, then, these principles to Christology, Campbell is able quite naturally to say:

"Granted that the devotion of Christians has been right in recognizing in him (Jesus) the one perfect human life, that is, the one life which consistently and from first to last was lived in terms of the whole, what are we to call it except divine"?[2] He continues that, in a sense, everything that exists is divine.

To an exponent of the New Theology, the term divine is a relative one; hence the above verdict upon Christ's life, though here again it has the sound and aspect of a platitude from the old well-worn apologetics, is meant quite seriously as a truism, not a leap of Faith, but a conclusion which follows as naturally from the premises as "twice two make four". Campbell nevertheless makes some attempt to restrict the use of his term: for although the divine nature is to some extent at any rate embodied and displayed in all creation, "It is wise and right . . . to restrict the word 'divine' to the kind of consciousness which knows itself to be, and rejoices to be, the expression of a love which is a consistent self-giving to the universal life". He then compares various types of the manifestation of Divinity, declaring that General Booth was more divine than a crocodile. It follows from this that the old doctrine of two natures in Christ is meaningless, since he did in fact possess one nature, which from one aspect was human, and from another aspect was divine. His Person, nevertheless, he declares to be unique, and we too must all attain to his standard in order to fulfil our destiny. Yet, "Jesus was obviously not conscious of his Deity". The classical Christology was also at fault in another way: by making Jesus pre-existent, and we ourselves only beginning our lives at birth, it put an impassable gulf between Jesus and all other men. This Jesus of the old Christology is quite a foreign figure to us: "The Jesus of Michael Angelo's 'Last Judgement' is a terrifying figure, without a trace of the lowly Nazarene about him, and yet this was the Jesus of the conventional Christianity of the time". Campbell would appear at this time to have been wholly unacquainted with the work of the eschatologists.

Campbell is at pains to defend himself against the charge of producing a purely unitarian Christ. The unitarians, he argues,

[1] *The New Theology*, pp. 74, 5.   [2] *ibid.*, p. 75.

had previously been just as much at fault as the old Trinitarians. They, equally, had held God and man apart, like the Deists. It was now necessary to get rid of this old dualism, which put Deity and humanity into two separate and exclusive compartments.[1]

Later in the section he develops his Christology still further: "We deny nothing about him (Jesus) that Christian devotion has ever affirmed; but we affirm the same things of humanity as a whole in a differing degree".[2] Again: "Jesus was God, but so are we. He was God because his life was the expression of divine love; we, too, are one with God in so far as our lives express the same thing".[3]

But Campbell does not quite leave the matter there. He would retain a doctrine of the Trinity, a Trinity in which the aspect best known to us is that which may be best described as "archetypal manhood", which may be called the eternal Christ. Therefore, we have to do with that side or aspect of the Trinity which is eternally man. Thus, St. Paul does not say "For me to live is Jesus", but "For me to live is Christ". St. Paul was evidently, therefore, not so much interested in the earthly life of the man Jesus as in the eternal Christ. Now Jesus is for us, Campbell contends, the perfect human representation of this side of God's nature; being the means by which this aspect of God's being is known to us: "Jesus seems to sum up and focus the religious ideal of mankind".[4] And again: "Jesus expressed fully and completely, in so far as a finite consciousness ever could, that aspect of the nature of God which we have called the eternal Son, or Christ, or ideal man, who is the soul of the universe . . . We are expressions of the same primordial being. Fundamentally we are all one in this eternal Christ. This is the most difficult statement of all to make clear . . ."[5]

Before quitting this book, it will be well to complete our picture of the New Theology by glancing at Campbell's doctrine of sin and atonement; it will illustrate the unity of the system as a whole.

On sin, Campbell declares that evil is a negative not a positive term. It denotes the absence rather than the presence of something. It is like the shadow opposed to sunlight, which is only

---

[1] *The New Theology*, p. 81.  [2] ibid., p. 94.
[3] ibid., p. 94.  [4] ibid., p. 70.
[5] ibid., p. 95.

## IMMANENTISM AND "THE NEW THEOLOGY"

seen in virtue of the fact that the sun is actually shining. Evil is not an intruder into an otherwise perfect universe; finitude presupposes it. A thing can only be seen to be evil when the capacity for good is present and unsatisfied. Infinity alone can know nothing of evil. Evil and good are not like armies in deadly conflict with each other: when one is, the other is not. The very word "good" implies the word "evil". Good emerges in our experience only in contrast to evil, and the ideal existence must be that in which good and evil are both transcended in life eternal, when struggle and conflict are no more.

On the atonement he writes that Christ's life was a perfect example for us of endurance unto death. His life would have been incomplete without his death. "The life and death together were a perfect self-offering of the unit to the whole, the individual to the race, the Son to the Father, and therefore the greatest manifestation of the innermost of God".[1] It is our part to cooperate with God's self-manifestation of himself in the universe.

Before concluding this section we would add a quotation from another writer, W. L. Walker. This writer tells us that at first he was driven to Unitarianism, but discovering the weaknesses of a purely humanitarian gospel, he was led after a re-examination of the facts to a "richer faith". He tells of the impossibility for him of accepting the orthodox Christologies with their doctrine of two natures in one person, and continues:

"The view we have been led to take of the Incarnation, however, as the result of a divine process of self-realization in the world, is free from these difficulties, and gives us in Christ one who is at once truly divine and truly human—God and man in one Person; and we venture to think that it is only by a process of self-realization we can ever see God truly becoming man in this world—belonging to our humanity, and yet coming from above it. It is God as Son, the principle and ideal of the world's life, realizing his life 'In the fullness of the times' in that human form he was ever seeking, and as the result of all the working of God as Word and Spirit in nature and in man. It is involved in the very idea of the Logos or Son as distinguished from the Father and in the thought of God's immanence in the world, if there is any real meaning in that thought at all. It implies not a temporal, but an eternal *kenosis* in God, and his self-realization in the world, not as the result of physical processes merely, but of an ethical

[1] *The New Theology*, p. 123.

development 'through the spirit'; and it is not merely a vague 'universal' Incarnation of God in man we thus reach, but the special, unique, Incarnation of God as Son in Christ. It is only by this conception of the Incarnation as a process of self-realization on the part of God as Son in human form that those difficulties felt to be so formidable can be met, and Christ seen to be at once God and man".[1]

## Critique of the New Theology

It is important to realize, in the first place, how this system is related to those movements in thought described in the two preceding chapters. The Jesus thus envisaged is a thoroughly humanized figure. The miracles worked by him are simply ignored, and doctrines such as the Virgin Birth are cited only to be rejected as dogmatic fables. None the less, these writers attach a supreme value to the moral character expressed in the words and life of Jesus. Thus they march in step with the humanism of their day, but not with the radical criticism of their day—as will be shown presently. Thus, whilst sharing the antipathy for the miraculous, they still lean rather to the type of writers who extol the Messianic consciousness than to those who see in Jesus no more than a deluded fanatic. In the terms of the preceding chapter—they shared the humanism of Roberts, but espoused the ethical evaluations of Martineau. This leads us straight to the question, how these writers treat the kernel and the husk and the idea of the Christ-ideal. The kernel and the husk principle is undoubtedly accepted tacitly. The structure of orthodox dogma is rejected en bloc, the miraculous element in the Gospels has vanished; these were the first and second of the old husks. These writers did not, however, go any further and accept the radical reflex position of Roberts—they still apprehended a kernel of infinite value in the historic person himself. Hence it comes about that the Christ-ideal which, in writers like Roberts, is left as a loose cloud floating in the air, is by these New Theologians expanded in two directions, to link it with other expressions of theological belief. In the first place, it is linked up with the historic Jesus. In Roberts, it is extremely difficult to envisage how such a Person as he conceives Jesus to have been could ever have been the source of such a beautiful ideal as later was to bear his name. In Warschauer and

[1] *The Spirit and the Incarnation*, p. 260.

Campbell, however, there is not constructed simply a historic connexion—a demonstration of how the life of a man once lived on earth was transformed into an ideal which later proved of such helpfulness to men in their religious life: a theological connexion is established between the two. For Jesus is declared to be a manifestation, a physical embodiment of that ideal, and the highest embodiment of it that has ever, or could ever, take place. What this amounts to is that in this system the gulf between the historical and the dogmatic Christ, which from the days of the "knowledge" controversy down to the present had been steadily widening, was being bridged by this reassertion of the place of pre-eminence belonging to Jesus in the religious life of mankind.

n the second place, this rehabilitation of the historic foundations of Christianity was strengthened by the expansion of the Christ-ideal in the other direction. Stated at its lowest, the idea of a Christ-ideal could simply mean a conglomeration of pious and romantic thoughts associated with a legendary character. According to the New Theology, however, the Christ-ideal is given a specific metaphysical content—it becomes the "Eternal Christ". The "Ideal" is in fact integrated into a doctrine of the Holy Trinity, which not only gives a definite content to the ideal, but also in its turn tends to strengthen the stress laid upon the historic Person of Jesus, as the embodiment of it. With such drastic attempts to redeem the bankruptcy of radical liberal theology—that is to say, with an attempt to rescue from the humanism a specifically Christian corpus of ideas, it might have been supposed that the New Theology had good prospects of acceptance. But such hopes proved false, not only on account of any inherent weaknesses in the system—many though there were—but because the system thus proposed was itself so largely at variance with the Bible and with traditional theology, that it could scarcely have the effect of endowing humanism with any specifically Christian character.

For the first characteristic of the system which strikes the observer is that it lives up to its name, to the very letter: it is a radically *new* interpretation of Christian facts; despite the insinuations about the insincerity of orthodox thinkers, and chatter about what the "best theology" has always said: the whole system is *new*. The Fathers, the schoolmen, and modern divines, both Catholic and traditionalist Protestant, would maintain consistent loyalty to the following propositions: 1. God in his essence and nature is complete; man is a freely willed creation, separate from him; and therefore man is not divine, but stands in relation to God as creature to Creator, which excludes any necessary partaking of the divine nature, and does in fact preclude it. 2. Sin is open rebellion on the part of man and the angels to the will of God, and deserves damnation since it robs God of his rightful honour and kindles his wrath. 3. Jesus Christ is Personally God, being God made man, and therefore partaking of the divine essence, he alone is God and divine in a sense in which no other man can conceivably be. It will be clear from the lengthy descriptions of the New Theology that it is set in direct opposition to such theses.

Nor is it possible to regard the New Theology as simply a flight from orthodoxy to the pure teaching of the New Testament. The New Testament, consistent with the Old, rightly or wrongly, teaches a doctrine of God, a doctrine of man and of sin which is utterly at variance with the tenets of the New Theology; the whole Bible does, in truth, expose a view of God and man and their relations substantially in accordance with the two propositions noted above; of the quasi-Divinity of men and the complementary character of evil, it says not a word.

Nor is the picture of a "lowly Nazarene"—upon whom, it is imagined, there has been superimposed a mumbo-jumbo of Jewish eschatology and unwarranted divine honours, any more satisfactory than what is evidently meant to be the purest doctrine of God. Such a description of Jesus is one which to-day scarcely requires comment. Angelo's picture can hardly be more terrifying than that which Jesus actually draws of himself as the stern and final arbitrator, dividing the sheep from the goats. Far from the New Testament, then, regarding God and man as partakers of the same nature and the same aims, it virtually regards them as at war one with the other—this is true of the teaching of both Jesus and St. Paul about evil. Into this conflict Jesus steps as a mediator, not arising as a crown of human development, but coming down from heaven, κατελθών καταβαίνων, coming from God's side of the gulf, not from man's: hence he comes with a distinctive nature. Quite apart, then, from the question of its truth or falsehood, this system is a radically "New Theology".

Vigorous attempts are made by these writers to safeguard the pre-eminence and distinctiveness of Christ as a revelation of God, but it must be admitted that this is achieved by a somewhat deceptive use of the term "unique". This word in common speech can have two meanings. First, it can mean a thing which is unlike anything else in nature or kind; and secondly, a thing which is unlike anything else within its own kind or nature. The first implies a distinction in kind, species, or nature; the second definitely implies sameness in kind or nature, with difference in degree, value or quality. It is without any doubt that in the second meaning of the word Christ is described as unique by these writers. It is made plain that God is not regarded as dwelling in him in any manner different from that in which he is envisaged as dwelling in all men. Therefore Christ is a man precisely as other men are, and in nature no more unique and perfect than the perfection of humanity itself. With men he is *primus inter pares*; that is his unique position. His Divinity does not consist in anything different from what is latent in all men. This can scarcely be regarded as an adequate expression of that place which Christian experience and devotion is forced to accord to its Lord and Saviour.

According to the first principle of the New Theology, the whole of nature is one with God, being the manifestation and expression of his being and will, and being suffused with his essence it may properly be described as divine. On this premise, whatever conceivable right has Campbell to restrict the word divine to life which self-consciously co-operates with God? Here we touch the fundamental thesis of the New Theology. It concerns the conception of Divinity. We are dealing with three conceptions of that term. There is first that view which we have called the traditional Christian conception of Divinity—that which belongs to God, as distinct from that which pertains to his creation which is outside himself. The other two conceptions of Divinity are both found inside the "New Theology", the third being a development out of the second. In this second view, therefore, which formed the first principle of the "New Theology", the whole universe is divine simply by being the self-manifestation of God; in other words, it is divine by nature, as existing as part of the being of God—his outward expression of himself. Divinity in this sense is generic, and it is physical. Being thus generic, the term Divine must include the whole of nature, irrespective of any teleological considerations attaching to any particular modes or parts of that nature. Such a view by itself is seen by the writers to be on the high-road to pantheism, and its tone is in any case of a quasi-materialistic tenor quite foreign to the thought of modern philosophy. When Campbell restricts the term "divine" to self-conscious nature, he is introducing a most significant modification. He has introduced the principle of value. Quite apart from the presumptuousness or otherwise of man deciding what parts of the universe are best fitted to display the nature and glory of God, there is a definite advance in the use of the term: it ceases to be thought of as a universal substance as it becomes a term of value or quality. Thus when Campbell states that General Booth is more divine than a crocodile he is not saying that General Booth is made out of different stuff from a crocodile—for in that case the crocodile would have no claim to be called divine at all—but that there is a difference of value between the two. Both are divine, since both manifest in varying degrees the character of God, but the General is more, much more, divine than the crocodile. This example illustrates the difference between this third, or qualitative, view of Divinity and both of the preceding views. For to speak of a being as "more" divine than another would be impossible for both the dualistic orthodox view and for the second, or quasi-materialistic view. The influence of idealistic philosophy, working over an old pantheistic conception is here clearly to be seen. According to such a manner of thought, the only ontological significance of a man or a crocodile is its reflexion or embodiment of ideas. In one passage of Campbell at least there is a note of pragmatism. When he declares that humanity is Divinity viewed from below, and vice versa, he shows quite clearly that his conception of Divinity is completely emancipated from the old categories of nature: it is an aspect and appreciation of value, appreciated and envisaged by the subject capable of apprehending it. Here again, the conception of Divinity, to say nothing of the possible ideas regarding the Deity himself that may underlie it, is one that belongs to a field of thought completely foreign to that which has ever been the vehicle of Christian truth. The Christian Gospel, to be sure, has passed through many variations in its intellectual expression—notably when as a purely Jewish way of thinking it was taken into the framework of Greek thought—but none of those systems or media through which it has passed contained elements fundamentally opposed to its main tenets. In the present instance, however, we are faced with an interpretation of Christian truth which renders it totally unrecognizable as the same religion, save in name and in its terminology—which is retained and employed in manners and meanings hitherto never applied to it.

Finally, it may be pointed out that the changes wrought by this system in the realm of soteriology are none the less startling. According to traditional theology, Christ came to reveal the character of God, his love, holiness and justice, and the nature of man, perfectible yet depraved. He came to reveal the wrath of God and the mercy of God. According to the New Theology, all that he can reveal is the nature of man, its perfectible character, and the avoidable character of sin—a poor consolation to those fettered by habit and passion. Thus the New Theology is completely Pelagian in outlook, and hence is saddled with all the inherent weaknesses of that heresy: to wit, its utter ignorance and lack of sympathy with the actual facts regarding human nature and human sinfulness. Christ, then, simply reveals a union which is already held to exist between God and men. Hence the word "Atonement" cannot possess any intelligible content in such a system. Neither can the word "Mediator" have any significant position; for God and man are already of a piece, and there is on their showing neither wrath nor guilt to be done away. The conception of Christ's death as a sacrifice of the unit to the whole is best understood as an attempt to find a place for traditional language within the system, but if it is seriously meant, then a vital principle of traditional Christian belief is at stake. The Christian doctrine of man, as a child of God, is that his personality, that is to say, every single human personality, is of infinite value in the sight of God. The language regarding the sacrifice of units for the whole belongs to a mode of thought utterly at variance with Christian thought; it belongs to the dim shades of pantheism, to the bestial horrors of nature-worship, to the savage lore of tribal and race superstition.

One or two final points of criticism will be advanced after the next writer has been considered.

*Edward Caird,* The Evolution of Religion. *The Gifford Lectures for* 1890–92.

Dr. Caird was noted as one of the most thoroughgoing of English Hegelians, and his treatment of the New Testament is probably the most radical application possible of the Hegelian method to the study of Christian origins. It goes even further than the theory proposed and developed by F. C. Baur and the Tübingen school; for Caird applies the method to the development of the ideas concerning the teaching and life—and hence the Person—of Christ, and not simply to the study of varying strains of thought within the early church.

To Dr. Caird, the Person of Christ is not significant as simply an observable, objective, fact in history; his existence is only consequential, only intelligible, in so far as he represents for the religious consciousness of mankind a stage in its upward development, not simply as himself a historical stage in the evolution of religion, but in virtue of the part which he plays for the mind of man at large, in whose sight he becomes the embodiment of certain moral ideals.

In the second volume of the lectures, the fifth to the ninth lectures deal with the subject in hand. Although these lectures were delivered nearly twenty years before the New Theology appeared, in many important respects they show striking affinities with that system; for the thoughts put forward by Dr. Caird could scarcely have won at so early a date more than a fleeting sympathy in English theological circles, whereas in the changed situation of twenty years later they could be seriously proposed as a tenable and acceptable system.

Lecture V is entitled "The distinctive Characteristics of Christianity as contrasted with Judaism". He writes that the thought of later Judaism had developed such a dualism between the real and the ideal as to make contact between them a practical impossibility; the difference that is, between heaven and earth was stretched so far, that intervention in the affairs of the latter could only take place by apocalyptic means, by cataclysmic irruption from without. It was essentially the work of Jesus to disabuse this view. He had to show men that God could work within them as well as from without: he had to substitute faith in present realities for hope in future cataclysms, and above all, he had to teach that evil must be conquered by love and not by external might: in other words, his revelation, his message, was a disclosure of God's immanence. He had to set aside the Jewish way of regarding the world of outward things as a mere instrument in the hands of God, teaching rather its continuity with the divine nature, in other words, Jesus substituted morality for religion.

It will be at once obvious how close is this starting-point of Dr. Caird to the basic thought of later radical liberalism—the unity of the world with God, and the evolutionary and immanentist view of revelation versus the cataclysmic view is reminiscent of Gardner as well as of Warschauer and Campbell.

The sixth lecture is entitled "The Religion of Jesus", in which Caird describes our Lord's teaching as primarily concerned with immediate reconciliation with God. The terms Jesus employs, "Father", "Son", do not exhibit any opposition, but rather the essential unity of God with man. This in fact is the sole attitude of consciousness in which a man can be at one not only with God but with himself. But this reconciliation with God, as Jesus preached it, was not negative like Buddhism—there was no negation of the finite. God was the God of the living, not of the dead: to Christ, this self-realisation was attained, not by sacrificing the finite to gain the infinite, but to lose the finite in order to realise oneself. Jesus' theory of life, then, was no dualist asceticism, but the sacrifice of immediate life to obtain a fuller life. This idea of divine immanence, realized by men in life through death, was the basic principle of Jesus' teaching. "Jesus was the most consistent of all idealists".[1] "Die to live",[2] that was Jesus' motto; man must die like the grain of wheat, he must seek first the kingdom of heaven, sell all that he has, for he that loseth his life shall gain it. The sufferings which the Jews thought were signs of hopelessness without apocalyptic intervention were in fact but the preludes to man's higher good. Unfortunately, Christianity ever since has been a religion of the other world, but as it came from the lips of Jesus it was nothing less than an absolute, practical idealism which weighed all the greatness of the world in the balances of the spirit, and which therefore, rejecting all the judgments of sense and immediate experience, all the fears and calculations of worldly prudence, regarded moral forces as practically omnipotent.[3]

Caird continues that Jesus had to struggle against the supernaturalism of his time; people were not to talk of his miracles, there was to be no miraculous sign except that of the prophet Jonah, i.e. his own life and teaching.[4] He was forced on occasions to express his teaching in apocalyptic language, though he himself knew "That it is only by a gradual process of evolution, and not by one sudden manifestation of divine omnipotence, that such a spiritual victory is to be gained".[5]

[1] *The Spirit and the Incarnation*, p. 151.  [2] *ibid.*, p. 152.
[3] *ibid.*, p. 167.   [4] *ibid.*, p. 169.   [5] *ibid.*, p. 170.

Caird would probably have found the conception of realized eschatology a great help in the elaboration of this interpretation of the Gospels.

In the seventh lecture, "The Lesson of Death and the Death of Jesus", Caird extracts and amplifies what he believes to be the central core of Jesus' message. Jesus clearly told Judaism that it must die to live; and his words were in fact themselves a touchstone by which the nobler and the baser elements and persons in Judaism were distinguished. But idyllic teaching in the fields of Galilee was not enough to inculcate the message of the Gospel: the principle of "Die to live" could be taught fully and convincingly only by one who made the last sacrifice himself. In other religions which teach the principle of "Die to live", either the death of the hero is only incidental and illustrative, as the use which Plato makes of the death of Socrates; or else it is mixed up with a dualism. But as Caird has already stated, in Jesus' thought, man's defect is not just the presence of natural life: nature is only an obstacle when it does not recognize the spiritual as its basis and end. In so far, then, as man seeks his ends, in which he desires the realization of himself, if not determined by the universal principle in relation to which all individuals are at one, they are ends for himself which are not ends for others; and hence he can carry them out only in conflict with others; only in a struggle for existence which he ultimately loses. Individuals can be infinitely egoistical, hence the war between good and evil. But Jesus inverts all self-seeking; he puts the general before the particular, God before man, the individual after the many. The Cross is therefore the highest revelation of the divine life in man in conflict with the evil of the world.[1] It is the culminating expression of Jesus' life work, which partially explains its exclusive pre-eminence for St. Paul. The Cross in fact is the bridge between the simple humanity of the Gospels and the theological idealism of Paul.

Of less importance for the present purpose, yet of absorbing interest, is the manner in which Caird traces the development of the basic idea through the New Testament writers.

Lecture VIII. "The Teaching of St. Paul". St. Paul was the first to grasp the lesson of Jesus' life and death in its full extent.[2] No one before him could see the wood for the trees; hence it was that he was able thoroughly to emancipate Christianity from

---

[1] *The Spirit and the Incarnation*, p. 191.     [2] *ibid.*, p. 196.

Judaism: he saw that Judaism had to die to live; hence his mission to the gentiles. In St. Paul, Christ is identified with the principle which he had taught, and therefore Christ is everything to him. Faith in Christ and in his Cross is the objective counterpart of that spirit; identification with Christ means yielding to that principle.[1] In Rom. 8 Paul shows how that principle which has been in all men striving for self-consciousness now in the Person of Christ has seen the light of day. In this chapter of Romans, salvation means the yielding of man to a power within and without himself. Commenting on the fact that Calvinists even deduced their doctrines from St. Paul's teaching, he writes: "Such a view is not St. Paul's, but it might be logically derived from certain of his utterances as to the opposition of grace and works, if we leave out of account the idea so vividly expressed in the Epistle to the Romans—the idea of a Divine Spirit immanent in nature and man, a spirit that from the beginning to the end is groaning and travailling for the complete 'Revelation of the sons of God', i.e. for the complete realisation of the divine sonship of humanity".[2]

The ninth lecture deals with the Gospel of St. John. Whereas St. Paul had abstracted from the tangle of the life and teaching of Jesus the great and overriding principle of "Life through death", and had realised that in Christ's own person and life was that essential law which might find new organs of expression in every human soul, St. John, by means of the Logos doctrine, brought back this idea into intimate contact with the actual historic life of Jesus. He thus completed the synthesis of the individual and the universal. He goes back to the flesh, but only as the Word made flesh. In him, the theory, abstracted from the teaching of Jesus by Paul and attached to the ideal Christ, reacts upon the historical life record. The memory of the Lord's life is interwoven with and interpreted by this principle. In John, therefore, the real and the ideal are stretched to their utmost tension, but faith is able to grasp what is intended.

The following remarks, specifically in comment upon Edward Caird, will serve to sum up the chapter.

1. Caird and his successors must be left to the tender mercies of the New Testament critics to decide whether theirs is anything approaching a fair representation of the teaching of Jesus and of Paul. Even to the superficial observer, their interpretation can

[1] *The Spirit and the Incarnation*, p. 209.   [2] *ibid.*, p. 213.

only be countenanced by ignoring considerable areas of New Testament teaching, which would appear to form an integral part of the whole outlook of Scripture, particularly in regard to wrath, judgment, evil and the utter holiness—or separateness—of God. Though it would appear that Caird has a more realistic view of evil than his successors, evil springing, as he sees it, from man's almost infinite capacity for selfishness.

2. For Caird, as for Campbell and Warschauer, Christ is our brother, placed on the side of man, as opposed to that of God. To them, this is natural, in view of the affinity—humanity cannot ever be more divine than man at his best. It is the reverse of traditional theology, in which he comes to us from the opposite side of an impassable gulf. Caird writes of this: "In St. Paul's teaching there begins a kind of separation of Christ from humanity and a kind of identification of him with God, which is practically a return to the Jewish opposition of God and man and a denial of the distinctive title which Christ gave himself as the Son of Man".[1] And again he writes: "There is a supreme reason why all generations of men should call him divine, not, indeed, as isolated from others, but as the first-born of many brethren".[2] His Divinity is clearly no more than is possible for other men to attain at their best.

3. Revelation, in Caird's thought as in the New Theology, means not the disclosure of something which man otherwise could not know, or of something done by God for man, but the appreciation by man of those faculties inherent in him, i.e. "Realization".[3]

4. Although, as already noted, Caird gives some place to a doctrine of sin; in general he bluntly ignores it or denies its power. Hence he describes Paul's thought as "poor" when the Apostle states that evil is intensified when men strive to do good—when actually, Caird protests, they are getting better. Again, pointing out that Augustine and Calvin derived their ideas from a misinterpretation of Paul—that man is under the sway of external forces of evil, only expellable by equally external forces of the divine spirit—he vigorously condemns this view. Naturally a confirmed idealist can scarcely be expected to countenance a view of evil as an objective power working from without.

5. These two following points are perhaps of the deepest

[1] *The Spirit and the Incarnation*, p. 213.
[2] *ibid.*, p. 230.
[3] *ibid.*, p. 213.

## IMMANENTISM AND "THE NEW THEOLOGY" 247

significance. Despite the attempt of these writers to do away with the so-called materialistic language of orthodox theology, they substitute a terminology that represents a depersonalization of God. Even from the point of view of the *Religionsgeschichtlich* school, this represents a grave retrogression in man's apprehension of God. For if the idea of the Deity evolved through the centuries to that of "personality"—a category which can be known and understood by man—it is surely a reversal of this process to revert to such terms as "principle", "force", "the universal", and so forth. If God is only comprehensible as an immanent force, he is more useless than the God of the Deists. The word "intercourse" connotes distinction—of persons. Only a madman can talk to himself—in a state when bits of his personality have broken loose and live separately within his brain. To be knowable, God must be two things—he must be a Personal Being, and he must be separate from us. The God of the immanentists is unknowable because he is a principle inside us, and not a Person outside us with whom we can speak.

6. In writers considered in the previous chapter, the distinction between kernel and husk, or between Christ and Jesus, sprang from critical research. In Caird, however, it sprang from his idealistic principles. In him, there is no question of Jesus as a person of history being accredited with divine honours: his merit derives from his place in the religious life of men. The Christ-ideal—which to Caird is an ideal and nothing more—derives from him, but his flesh is meaningless apart from the ideal.

Upon this movement in thought, Forsyth wrote the following grave words: "The present conflict in the church is more critical for Christianity than any that has arisen since the second century".[1]

As in the days of Gnosticism, so now the Christian religion was being offered the alternatives of forthright rejection or the reinterpretation of itself in terms of a system of thought with which it had nothing in common, and which proposed to dissolve in itself every recognizable trace of specifically Christian doctrine. The final attempt of liberal humanism to clothe itself in a Christian garb was itself the confession of its own nakedness—the husks had gone; so had the kernel.

---

[1] *The Old Faith and the New Theology*, p. 57.

To a considerable extent, the foregoing chapters have been concerned with the growth and the working out of liberalism in English theology with special reference to the central doctrine of the faith. We have watched the development of this movement in thought from the first beginnings of the acceptance of the principles of higher criticism and the casting asunder of the shackles of arbitrary dogmatism; we have noted how this new approach led to the belief in Christ's limited human intellect, and the consequent problems relating to his authority and sinlessness; we have observed how the introduction of still more incisive methods of criticism led to a further denuding of those supernatural and miraculous powers hitherto ascribed to Christ's Person; and we have witnessed how that humanism, incipient in the previous stages of the conflict, at length succeeded in divesting Christ, not only of the expressions of God's physical attributes, but also of his unique nature and character, and hence dethroned him from his place of pre-eminence for the religious life of mankind.

We have studied, moreover, at least four of the attempts which English liberal theology made to save itself from drowning in the waters of humanism and agnosticism—like some lost climber, slipping slowly yet inevitably down a precipitous cliff into the abyss below—clutching now at a boulder, and now at a clump of shrub, only to find that they cannot bear his weight.

The kenotic theory appeared for long to hold the balance between the ancient faith and a moderately critical exegesis of the Gospels; then the study of Christ's interior life—his Messianic consciousness—seemed to fill up the gap left by the disappearance of the miracles; the Ritschlian theory of value judgments was seized upon as furnishing a new apologetic and preserving the supremacy of our Lord; and finally the New Theology assayed to preserve the outward form of the Christian faith with an exclusively pagan essence.

It is a poor story that has no moral, and one or two suggestions may be offered in explanation of this apparent failure of the ancient faith to survive, once the bombardment had begun.

Perhaps the most easily discernible trait of liberalism that accounts for the tendencies above described was the rejection of the miraculous. We need not repeat the causes which led to the adoption of such an attitude. When once it be admitted that God does not operate save through the unchanging laws and categories

## IMMANENTISM AND "THE NEW THEOLOGY" 249

of the natural creation, then Christianity is lost: if it be granted that "God never does anything in particular in any other sense from that in which he does everything in general", as William Temple described the liberal view,[1] then the Christian faith dies; for at bottom, that religion rests upon the belief that the natural world as it stands is insufficient for man's needs, that it alone cannot save him—it is his graveyard, not his Olympus—and that consequently, God acted in Jesus Christ in an altogether unique and miraculous manner on man's behalf to secure his salvation. The anti-miraculous principle, then, at first a prejudice, but later a rule of thumb, marks the whole course of liberal theology: it prejudiced the interpretation of the evidence in the knowledge controversy; it expelled all external evidences for Christ's divine nature—such as the resurrection; and it ended by demanding the rejection of the concept of the Incarnation as an intervention from without. Once Christ ceases to be God the Son, the worker and the free and only giver of salvation, and is ranged alongside Socrates and the Buddha, his religion ceases to exist in any recognizable form

Again; the work of Christ was for all men in all ages. For this to be effective, men must have in all ages full access to the truth which he brought, taught, and was—truth, not so much in the sense of a collection of metaphysical data, as truths about his work for mankind, and truths, such as his Deity, which are indispensable for the understanding of his work. If he was God the Son, who entered this world for the salvation of all men, it is inconceivable that he should have ascended without leaving a perpetual guarantee of truth, and this he did in that living organism through which God now operates in the world, the Church—the body of Christ, the temple of the Holy Spirit. The tradition of that Church—not so much in the sense of hidden reminiscences or extra-Scriptural doctrines, but rather, the traditional consensus of belief within that body—is absolutely indispensable to the right apprehension of Christian truth. Liberal theology made the attempt to interpret the New Testament as it pleased, in the light of its own pre-conceived principles: some of the results of that attempt have been seen in this volume, others, even more grotesque, may be seen in a book such as Schweitzer's *von Reimarus zu Wrede*. For the New Testament, decisive though it ultimately is, is but the testimony of one

[1] *Christus Veritas*, Preface.

generation of Christian thought to the facts of redemption and revelation. But the Church, in Christ and the Holy Spirit, has lived many generations; and if the doctrine of the Incarnation and of the Church which flows from it be taken seriously, it is impossible to ignore the cumulative authority for Christian truth which those generations of faith and study possess and demand from the present age in the way of submission and active co-operation.

# 9

## PERSONALITY AND INDIVIDUALITY

IN the preceding chapters an attempt has been made to describe the steps which led up to the emergence of the typical Christologies of Britain and America, during the liberal era. The historical, philosophic, and scientific methods of the age, which had for long been playing a rôle of increasing importance, at length projected the idea of a Christ who was first and foremost a true subject of human psychological experiences. The birth-pains of the new Christology had been the controversy regarding Christ's limitation of knowledge: on its metaphysical side this had occasioned the kenotic theory, whilst on its apologetic side it had fostered the study of the Lord's inner consciousness. But these controversies and discussions were themselves of a very limited range of comprehension. The issues raised by the historical life of Jesus Christ were far deeper than the question of his human knowledge could plumb, and the gulf between his Divinity and humanity of such a kind as the kenotic theory could not adequately bridge. The interests which underlay these controversies were too narrow in scope, and too circumscribed by the needs of the moment, for any all-sufficing solution to emerge from them. For if there are two questions to which the mind of the time demanded a rational answer they are these—first, how can two natures so different as Divinity and humanity appear to be brought to accord in one single individual? This question the kenotic theories had been designed to answer. But just as the knowledge controversy dealt only with one attribute of the natures, so, too, the kenotic theory only provided for an approximation of the natures, by smoothing down the divine properties, but did not so much as touch the fringe of the second question, namely, how can two natures be united so as to form but one personality, or the converse, how can one single subject possess two such different modes of being and experience, and precisely *who* and *what* is this subject, this personality, who speaks to us from the pages of the Gospels? In the light of what the age had come to believe regarding the nature of personality, these questions were of the foremost importance, yet in the controversial atmosphere of the 'nineties they were recognised by scarcely any.

We turn too from the consideration of those more radical types of liberal Christology, in which the central figure is confessedly little related to the Christ of traditional Christian belief, to those in which an attempt was made to restate—rather than to reconstruct—to those writers who sought to preserve the classic doctrine of Christ's Divinity, not by stating a different doctrine, but by frankly facing the main difficulty which in modern times had become the central difficulty besetting the doctrine. We thus find ourselves once again discussing those questions relating to the conception of human personality which had become current.

It has been remarked upon more than one occasion that the most significant feature in the modern Christological crisis was the new attitude towards the nature of personality—not necessarily a wrong attitude, not altogether new, but an angle of approach hitherto never applied to the doctrine of the Incarnation. It is therefore necessary, before describing the types of restatement which were undertaken, to offer a few brief remarks in amplification of this contention. All that can here be offered are a few descriptive allusions to current tendencies: the questions themselves at issue are primarily a matter for the philosopher, and even in the scope of their application they concern the psychologist quite as much as the theologian.

It may at first appear strange, in view of the crucial importance and revolutionary change brought about, that the nature of personality was never during the period a subject of controversy. The reason for this indeed was that very few of the writers of the time were at all aware that any change had taken place—at least, if they were, they never said so; the great majority accepted the new attitude towards personality without question. This largely accounts for their failure to understand the Christologies of the past—the doctrine of Christ's impersonal manhood, the Definition of Chalcedon, and the diothelite formulary, to cite but three commonly misunderstood doctrinal utterances. They found these ancient systems of thought quite unsuited to their own circumstances, and were bewildered to think that they ever could have been regarded as satisfactory, for the simple reason that they had forgotten the foundations upon which they had been built, and forgotten the background of that orthodoxy which they themselves were nominally pledged to support and which occasioned them such embarrassment. It was a mere handful of conservative writers who were far-seeing enough to be able to point out how great a change had in fact taken place.

The ancient world, and hence the Fathers, had begun its approach to the question of personality from a view which may be described as substantial individuality. According to the realism of the time, just as material categories or substances subsist in particular representatives of the species, so the spiritual substance of which the soul is made as part of the human nature is represented in individual souls, this substantial soul giving individuality—i.e. personality—to that mental and bodily nature which it assumes. We are not concerned with a detailed examination of this system, but rather with those which superseded it; hence it is sufficient to point out how logically and completely the old system was applied by the Fathers to the subject of Christ's Person. Christ as a Divine Person was composed of the *ousia* essence, of Deity, of which he as God the Son was one hypostasis. As a divine Person, a spiritual substance, he possessed a divine nature—the sum of his attributes and faculties—which was inseparable from him. He united to himself a portion of the *ousia* of humanity, with its own human nature; naturally he did not unite himself to a human person, as that would have made two Christs, but his own substantial self became the personalizing principle in that portion of the human nature which he assumed— as much part of his own Person and individuality as the body is part of the soul of any man. Even if it were granted that nature or substance were only existent in particulars, yet nature and person are not synonymous terms, hence the Person of Christ did not simply possess one nature, a fusion of the two, but two separate and complete substances and natures. Hence his human nature possessed all those faculties which were attributed to human nature—as opposed to human individuality: human will, intellect, emotions, and everything else proper to that nature which Christ possessed in addition to his complete and unmodified Deity.

It is not possible to extract from the legacy of a writer or school an explanation or answer for questions which were not envisaged by him or it. Hence it is not possible to enquire what answer the Fathers would have given to the question of how the human and the divine consciousnesses were related within

Christ's Person, since such a matter never came within their ken; it would have been considered entirely subsidiary to those matters already alluded to in their system, and even if they had contemplated the question, they would not have dared to enquire into the workings of the Lord's mind and soul. They were solely interested in questions relating to the essence and nature possessed by individuals—the mental experiences of those individuals or natures scarcely entered into their picture.

Such then were the consequences of the application of a realist philosophy to the facts of revelation—to the doctrine that Christ is both God and man. On such premises and with such a philosophical background, the Creeds and dogmatic definitions of Christendom had been framed: the irrelevance—nay the utter inadequacy of these formularies to a totally new situation will now become apparent.

The post-Cartesian philosopher, on the other hand, begins his study of the nature of personality with himself, with subjectivity, with the first element of reality which we encounter—our own conscious experience. Hence the first question with which the idealist deals is man's knowledge of the outside world. These mental impressions and experiences which we receive—whatever relation they do or do not bear to the things outside ourselves—are found to fill the whole of our consciousness: apart from them, consciousness as a thing by itself cannot be conceived of; they constitute themselves our consciousness. This consciousness being all we know of self is also therefore only intelligible in relation to experience. We cannot conceive of ourselves apart from our experiences; the self exists in its experiences, in the mental impressions which it apprehends—the self is found to exist solely in consciousness, or rather, in those experiences which go to make up consciousness. Now the impressions have, in one sense, a transitory character; they appear to begin and end at particular moments in time; yet for the consciousness they possess a certain continuity and a certain relation to each other. This continuity and relationship is, in fact, the thing which constitutes continuous self-hood, and continued identity of the self with itself and with the selves outside it. This continuity is known in common speech as "memory", hence the radical empiricist definition of personality as a "chain of memories". Hume calls the self "a bundle or collection of different perceptions which succeed each other with an inconceivable rapidity, and are in a perpetual flux and movement".[1] It is argued by the opponents of this view that such is an altogether inadequate description of personality, since a chain of memories cannot possibly by itself have moral responsibility; and the fact that idealists and their successors generally added a doctrine which accounts for a morally-responsible self-hood is itself a demonstration of the inadequacy of their primary definition, as will appear proved to be the case. The continuity and relationship of the memories, even if not wholly of itself, helps us to understand much of how the continuous life of a person subsists, it is argued. It makes possible the idea of moral responsibility. Thus it is difficult to imagine that one can punish a dog intelligibly unless one is skilful enough to establish in its very restricted brain some definite connexion of memory between the offence committed and the punishment inflicted. In the case of the human being, the self, existing in its mental experiences and impressions, knows itself to be to-day that same subject and therefore the same person who underwent the experiences of yesterday—and this by virtue of its memory.

Here then is the new view of personality stated in its broadest form—personality equals self-consciousness. It has already been made abundantly clear how profound was the effect of this change upon Christology. No longer was it possible to approach the question of Christ's Person from the point of view of mere individuality, or of the duality of his natures: it must now be considered primarily from the point of view of the content of his consciousness. This had been the precipitate of the knowledge controversy: the unity of his Person being primarily conceived, by both liberal and conservative, as a oneness of consciousness, not of abstract or substantial individuality, it was necessary to show how omniscience and limitation were combined: the conservative virtually admitted that the omniscience was supreme, the liberal, that the omniscience was self-emptied.

It is now generally admitted that the idealistic definition as it stands is a very inadequate definition of human personality. As pointed out already, continuous memory may be one of the necessary prerequisites for moral responsibility, but memory without a subject independent of it can hardly play the part which moral personality does play. There are many other elements which will appear in due course which the definition

[1] *Treatise on Human Nature* I.4.6, quoted by F. J. Hall, *Dogmatic Theology*, vol. VI.

does not cover, and in fact certain modifications were, early in our period, being introduced into the idealistic framework to endow it with more adequacy; these modifications also in their several turn had an effect upon the development of Christology. Two of these developments will first be alluded to.

To begin with, there was the strong support given in certain circles to the idea of the "ego". This conception, drawn from contemporary psychology, was intended to take the place of the idea of the substantial soul, being fitted not altogether happily into the idealist scheme as a permanent and independent subject of mental experiences. Being more a figment of psychologists than of philosophers, it sat uneasily in its context and was eventually abandoned.[1] In the genuinely idealistic scheme, the ego, if such a thing is ever seriously conceived of, is inseparable from the conscious experience, it is simply the principle that connects the experiences together, the central point of reference for all the mind's activity; but without that activity, there is, strictly speaking, simply no ego at all. Yet on account of the sudden importance assumed in contemporary psychology by the human will, the idea of the ego was eulogized as though it virtually possessed a substantial existence, conceivable, that is, apart from the chain of experiences to which it refers itself. This conception of the ego was seized upon by one writer who may be mentioned as an example of its application, Mr. H. C. Powell,[2] as providing a modern rationale of Christ's Deity. It turns out, in fact, to be the ancient dogma in a modern dress. The oneness of Christ's Person, he writes, cannot imply oneness of consciousness. He had already argued with great force that the human and the divine manner of knowing are completely different in kind. If the union of the two natures meant that there was only one consciousness, then the human would be submerged, though, he argues, the contents of both must be in the absolute possession of the one Person.[3] But in the Incarnation, the ego of Christ comes to stand apart from everything that it represents, so as to become the subject of the manhood. "Apart it is, not only from other egos, but within its own personal sphere, apart from with which in that sphere it

---

[1] In the fourth chapter of *Christus Veritas*, 1924, Dr. Temple specifically repudiates the idea of a separable ego in the manner of a substantial soul, just as in his lectures on "The Nature of Personality" he had previously argued against the old realist conception of substantial individuality itself.
[2] *The Principle of the Incarnation.*
[3] *op. cit.*, p. 170.

is otherwise indissolubly associated and one".[1] It thus became the ego of true manhood, *but*—"It was not a homogeneous consciousness which extended over these two spheres". The most obvious criticism which this theory met with was that it tries to fit a realist idea—an ego stripped of every external reference—into an idealistic pattern in the realm of human personality. The view found little acceptance at the time, as it was found difficult to envisage a person, an ego, in the abstract, so completely divorced from conscious experience: and if conceivable, in what sense can a divine ego, thus dissociated from everything normally connected with it and become instead the subject of human experiences, be said to be personally God? If that consciousness contains no continuity of memory and experience with its divine life, in what sense can it still be recognized as the same Person as God the Son, since the content of consciousness virtually constitutes what a person is? The Christ so depicted is a human individual with a human consciousness, containing some abstraction which in another sphere is related to the conscious life of God—such a theory is little different from Martensen's kenotic theory, quite apart from the hybrid nature of the philosophical ideas therein involved. Powell himself virtually wipes out the whole implications of his theory in the third part of his book, where he admits that, despite the difference in kind between the divine and the human manner of knowing, there is a communication of omniscience to Christ's human mind. Hence, though his theory may help to elucidate the Christological problem by advancing certain ideas on the philosophical and psychological side, it flatly contradicts the picture of Christ drawn from the inductive study of the Gospels at that epoch.

A second development upon the bare idealistic view of personality as consisting in consciousness also took its impetus from contemporary psychology: this was a radically new attitude towards the human will. According to the ancients, the will was a faculty; it was like some automaton in control of the switch-board of a complex set of machinery, receiving its orders, the direction of its impulses, from the substantial self or ego. The will was, therefore, no more part of individuality than eyesight or the sense of smell.

The idealist philosophers themselves, it may be noted, had made but little advance in this particular region. They had continued

[1] *The Principle of the Incarnation*, p. 173.

to accept the old faculty psychology with but insignificant modifications. W. G. Shedd [1] discusses their psychology. The older psychology had divided up the mind into understanding and will; the idealists, into intellect, sensibility, and will. This, he argues, had been developed on the basis of Locke's dictum that man never desires anything contrary to his will. Shedd, expressing a preference for the former—with cognition and science on the one hand, which are stationary, and the volition on the other, points out that will is much more movable than the perceptive faculties; for desire, disinclination, and the like, are simply the turning of the will towards things which we do or do not like. He quotes Clement of Alexandria in illustration of this—"What is voluntary is either what is by desire or by choice".[2]

It took the modern thinker to apply the idealistic method to the scrutiny of this conception of will as a faculty. It became obvious that the old idea of the will as an automaton, motivated in its turn by other elements of the personality, is untenable, superfluous and meaningless, for the automaton turns out to be the man, the personality itself. It is superfluous to postulate an intermediary faculty between the conative impulses of the various parts of the human make-up and the actions themselves. Furthermore, when any human act, be it of thought, word or deed, is examined, it turns out that such a given act is produced by an instinct, or the emotions, or the intellect—generally a mixture of all the constituents of the personality. Therefore, just as in the examination of consciousness, all we can discover are the actual impressions themselves, so when an act of a person is examined, all that can be found is the act itself, and the inner motives of the self—be it emotional or intellectual which produced it: of some separate operational faculty of will there is not a trace. Hence all that we do, say, or think, we do with our whole personality, regarded as the active agent, and hence the whole personality regarded from that point of view may be described in terms of will—the word being used in a sense very different from its old meaning.

In a short series of lectures, Dr. Temple elaborates such a view of the human will. By illustration, he argues that just as plants and animals simply have appetitive desire, so to begin with, what we want, whether good or bad, we desire; for all the

[1] *Dogmatic Theology*, vol. II, p. 115 ff.
[2] *Miscellanies* II, 15.

## PERSONALITY AND INDIVIDUALITY

acts which make up conduct are reactions, not only of a conscious, but of an appetitive subject.[1] Therefore, a person's conscious desires, plus intellect and imagination, make up the substance of will. He urges that the invention of the idea of the faculty of will was occasioned by a failure on the part of man's imagination to apprehend activity apart from something which acts; which in turn was fostered by the materialistic demand for substances that may support attributes and activities; hence faculties were invented as constitutive parts of the substantial soul; and since purpose is different from any one chaotic idea, the will was invented.[2]

In a quite different setting we see the same principle at work where Percy Gardner, building on the work of William James, is attempting to discover a cosmical synthesis on the basis of will as the embodiment of the expression of personality. In the second lecture of his volume already discussed in another connection, *A Historic View of the New Testament*, he enlarges upon the idea that man's personality is chiefly will, rather than sensation or intellect; from which he leads on to his view of the universe as itself the expression of will. "In the nature of man the supreme element is will, which dominates alike feeling and thought. Man exists in virtue of the power which he puts forth amid his surroundings: he is a centre of force first, and only in the second place sentiment and intelligence."[3] He then cites the following passage from a paper of great importance by William James: "The willing department of our nature dominates both the conceiving department and the feeling department. And I am sure I am not wrong in stating this result as one of the fundamental conclusions to which the entire drift of modern psychological investigation sweeps us".[4] Upon which, Gardner comments: "Destroy the volitional nature, the definite subjective purposes, preferences, fondnesses for certain effects, forms, orders, and not the slightest motive would remain for the brute order of our experience to be remodelled at all".[5]

It will be clear at once that the introduction of such a new view of the place of the will in human personality into the framework of traditional Christology was like letting a bull loose in a

[1] *The Nature of Personality*, p. 24.
[2] *ibid.*, p. 25.
[3] *op. cit.* p. 37.
[4] *The Will to Believe*, p. 114, quoted by Gardner.
[5] *Historic View*, p. 38.

china shop. However much allowance modern writers might make in assessing the orthodox Christology of the Church for the old faculty psychology, they were quite unable to forget their own view-point, and this added its weight to the basic conception of personality as consciousness to make the Patristic definitions read as though two persons were united together in Christ. The will was now almost a synonym for person—not a portion of the nature as a whole—and hence to say that Christ possessed two wills was indeed to divide his Person. Fr. Tyrrell writes of the failure of theology on account of the current conception of personality, as distinct from that of the Creeds and orthodox theologians—"The latter was to a large extent shaped by controversial exigencies to explain how the supernatural being Incarnate in Jesus could be the Son of God, personally distinct from the Father, yet of identical and not merely similar substance, in such sort that the Son alone was made man, and not the Father or the Spirit. Outside theology, a person means, and always meant, a separate spiritual individual, a separaté mind, will, and energy. According to this use we must say there are two persons in Christ —two minds, two wills, two energies, human and divine; that in the Deity there is but one Person—one mind, will, and operation. For us there is no real distinction whatever between an individual spiritual nature and its personality".[1] This ill-humoured attack upon orthodox Christology none the less represents the impression created at the time stated in its clearest light. The formula of Chalcedon, and the later definition of two wills and operations— which is logically built upon it—are seen to be heretical, and utterly inadequate to account for the one personality of Christ; nay, as they stand, they appear to assert a duality of persons within Christ.

This, however, does not represent the full extent of the attack. For the orthodox Christology is at bottom based upon a distinction between the ideas of person and nature. Hence the possibility of the formula, "two natures in one Person". In the idealist scheme, the idea of nature practically vanishes: the only term left is conscious personality. One aspect of the central problem which this situation raised for Christology was the rejection of the doctrine of Christ's impersonal manhood. The will, and other such attributes of men, being no longer thought of as part of the nature, *qua* nature, but as the constituents of the individuals who

[1] *Jesus or Christ*, p. 9.

embody them, the idea of a non-personal manhood ceases to have any meaning. The idea of Christ's possession of the human nature had been regarded by the Fathers as one of the principal ways in which his redemption was effected—the uniting of that nature to the revivifying life of God. It was not so much that the term person had replaced the term nature—rather, the two had coalesced. The human person is seen, not so much as a distinct individual or ego, but as the total expression of all that goes to constitute his nature, being actively expressed by the content of his will, his purpose. Modern scientific investigation would appear to produce a similar attitude; for it regards the human individual as the expression of all that goes to make him what he is, heredity, environment, the instincts, the emotions, all playing their part to produce what we call the human personality, which is not something separable from the body or the mind, but the sum total of its operation, the life of that particular specimen of the human nature or species. It may be pointed out in passing that it is very difficult to find any place, in such a scheme—either idealistic or scientific—for the Christian doctrine of the soul, as a complete entity separable from the functioning of the human personality—for the human body and mind are now viewed as inextricably associated.

One immediate result of the new psychological verdict regarding the place of the will was a renewed fear of Nestorianism—a fear which for many was never far away during our period. It was felt by some theologians that under the new circumstances the preservation of a doctrine or formula in which two sets of psychological apparatus were attributed to Christ's Person, two wills, two consciousnesses even—after the manner of H. C. Powell—could lead only to a complete dividing up of his Person. Such a fear was quite justified, for certain writers faced with the new problem saw no solution to it except along the lines of Antiochene Christology (ch. XII). Accordingly, E. A. Litton, who will be discussed in another connexion in the eleventh chapter, and two American writers to be noted here, fell back upon a composite view of Christ's personality, "theanthropic" as they called it, stressing its complete internal unity and its uniqueness.

William Newton Clarke [1] urges that the greatest personalities are not exclusive; even though they exhibit the most perfect individuality. Christ was a genuine person *with one consciousness*

[1] *An Outline of Christian Doctrine.*

262     CONFLICT IN CHRISTOLOGY

*and one will.*[1] "If we ask whether this one consciousness in Jesus was divine or human, the answer is that strictly it was neither. It was unique, partaking of both qualities, human and divine. The unique Person that was constituted by the Incarnation must necessarily have been unique in his personal consciousness. His consciousness was neither that of God nor that of man exclusively, but was that of the unique God-man who was constituted by the Incarnation".[2]

The other writer is also one already alluded to, A. H. Strong.[3] He urges that there can be no "I" and "thou" between the natures in Christ, as there is between the Persons of the Trinity: nor do we in fact find such a distinction in the New Testament. He accepts the new psychology and proceeds: "Since consciousness and will belong to personality, as distinguished from nature, the hypothesis of a mutual, conscious, and voluntary appropriation of Divinity by humanity and of humanity by Divinity, during the earthly life of Christ, is but a more subtle form of the Nestorian doctrine of a double personality".[4] Yet no duality is ever to be seen in the Gospels—Christ does not say "I and the Logos are one". For self-consciousness and self-determination do not belong to nature as such but only to personality, hence Christ has not two consciousnesses and two wills but a single consciousness and a single will. This consciousness and will is never simply human, but is always theanthropic: an activity of the one personality which unites in itself the human and the divine.[5] This theory is interesting in the present context as a ready stop-gap in the face of the new psychology; it will be referred to again when it is grouped with the other restatements with which it may be classed.

But the question of personality was not one which merely presented itself as an enigma to be dealt with by the technical student of Christology. For the idea of the value of personality assumed at this epoch an importance which was almost overwhelming in every branch of theology. Personality was looked upon, and rightly too, as the highest category we know, and being such, every aspect of thought and reality must be related to it.[6] Personality in this new rôle—understood, it must be remembered, as will and self-consciousness—was applied as a

[1] *An Outline of Christian Doctrine*, p. 297.   [2] *ibid.*, p. 290.
[3] *Outlines of Systematic Theology*, 1908.   [4] *op. cit.*, p. 185.
[5] *ibid.*, p. 187.   [6] Mackintosh, *Person of Christ*, p. 417.

key to unlock the understanding of every doctrine: the Trinity, the being of God, the nature of man and his relation to God, the Atonement, and, of course, the doctrine of the Person of Christ. The range of its application may be gauged from the variety of the subjects dealt with in Moberly's *Atonement and Personality*, itself the classic example of the liberal approach to theology on the basis of a doctrine of personality. If there was little in the way of universal or lasting fruit to be gathered from this method it is surely due to the fact that the particular view of personality employed was too one-sided, being based solely upon the idealistic approach, to act as a permanent foundation for the whole of the theological structure. But it nevertheless remains true that the place accorded to the category of personality at this time had a radical effect upon theology, both dogmatic and apologetic. From some aspects, the emphasis upon personality was both needful and commendable, both then and now. The accession to its throne of natural science has banished the fickle gods of wind and storm, but in the minds of many it also banishes the idea of a personal God—and now, even, the idea of a personal man—as we understand the word "person". We are constantly hearing that Newton dispelled the possibility of purpose, i.e. personal activity, as we understand it, from the cosmical order; that Darwin has expelled the belief in design and purpose from the realm of natural life; and finally, in our own day, that the findings of the psycho-analysts disclose nothing within human mental processes but the blind working of predetermined forces. It was surely to meet such tendencies as these, which were for the first time raising their head in our period, that the doctrine of the value of personality, its dignity and superiority over every other category, was evoked. J. R. Illingworth's Bampton Lectures entitled *Personality Human and Divine* (1894) are a typical specimen of such an application of the doctrine.

It is not, however, for us to elaborate at any length the manner in which the idea of personality was developed during the period to meet the situation of the time; but simply to allude to several further modifications in the contemporary view of personality as they were to affect the study of Christology: for every new turn of elaboration or development in this field had an immediate repercussion in the restatement of the doctrine of Christ's Person.

As long as personality was primarily conceived of in the rudimentary, and narrow, idealistic manner related to consciousness regarded in an almost static manner, as had been done during the Knowledge and kenotic controversies, no fresh advance in Christology was possible. By the turn of the century, however, it was beginning to be seen that such a conception is far too narrow to account for the whole of human activities and possibilities. Attempts had already been made to modify it; by the reintroduction of the substantial idea, the ego, and the elaboration of a dynamic principle within the personality as its total expression, the will, in its new meaning. But much more than this was in fact needed.

We may see the original idealistic view being expanded, as far as that was possible within the given framework, in an essay by Rashdall in Sturt's *Personal Idealism* (1902), entitled "Personality Human and Divine". He begins with certain idealistic principles, such as that matter only exists in the mind, and for the mind, not for itself. This must also presuppose the reality of the individual souls who perceive the matter—an important admission. "First and most obviously, personality implies consciousness".[1] That is naturally Rashdall's starting-point. But, he points out, worms have consciousness, hence we must distinguish between thinking-consciousness, as opposed to merely feeling-consciousness. With feeling-consciousness alone there would only be a succession of unconnected experiences. Then again, the person can distinguish himself from the objects of his consciousness, even though these objects are themselves only experiences of the one consciousness. The person also has the knowledge of other minds which at the same time are existing for themselves, in their own right, as it were. But more characteristic of personality still is the will—self-determination, and the originating consciousness. Willing is not the same as thought and feeling, though all are bound up together. Between the blindest of instinct and the most deliberate of volitions there is every grade or degree of reflectiveness. Further, there is the characteristic of the capacity for morality, which divides up types of personality even more. None of these characteristics is satisfied below the human level; and even there, they are scarcely satisfied to any full degree, for only God satisfies every requisite for the perfect personality. And thus his argument unfolds itself. There is clearly much more involved here than in the bare assertions of many previous theologians.

[1] Sturt, *Personal Idealism*, 1902, p. 370.

## PERSONALITY AND INDIVIDUALITY

Of deeper moment, however, for the Christological question is the category of individuality. It must not be imagined that, because the new study began from consciousness and not from the distinction between individual and nature, that the question of individuality became blurred or ignored. On the contrary, the idea of consciousness as supreme touchstone emphasized quite as strongly as the idea of the substantial soul the fact of personal individuality: hence the acuteness of the Christological crisis.

Consciousness had become the most adamant substance ever conceived by man, the most indivisible unit ever envisaged. If human personality were conceived in this way, then nothing short of a complete metamorphic *kenosis* could satisfy the demand for a Christ possessing a human consciousness and individuality. But by degrees, this view of absolute exclusiveness of individuality in consciousness began to break up, from two directions, from within and from without.

The first of these eruptive forces, though itself a development from the idealistic basis, is a principle of revolutionary implications. It states that personality is not some substance or active principle *in vacuo*, but is only known, evaluated, evolved even, in relation to things outside itself—other personalities in particular. Just as continuous self-consciousness is thought to exist simply in relation to its experiences, without which it can scarcely be conceived of at all, so the personality as a whole exists solely in relation to its deeper experiences, in its relation to other personalities; in other words, the essence of personality is fellowship; without such relations with other beings, personality ceases to have any meaning whatsoever. A man who spends his days in a solitary cave can scarcely be said to possess any personality, since he holds no intercourse with others. Hence the human personality is thought to grow and be enriched as it comes more closely into communion with other human beings and *a fortiori* with God, who is the supreme personality. From this follows a further implication. Since personality exists in fellowship and increases by mutual assimilation and communion, there must follow the possibility of the mutual interpenetration of personalities, as they grow together, the individuality of each being enhanced rather than diminished by the assimilating process. This is possible since each exists in virtue of the other. Such a view is writ large in every page of *Atonement and Personality*, where it becomes the the basis of Moberly's whole theological outlook.

The line of argument above described is in part at any rate argued out in an essay on personality by Wilfrid Richmond,[1] who deals with the matter from a general philosophical angle, as opposed to the specific theological application in Moberly. Like Rashdall, this writer begins with certain idealistic principles. Experience, he holds, is the beginning and end of philosophy. Experience is the subject-matter, the test, and the method of enquiry. Philosophy begins with the experience of the common man, and its success is tested by that. In the second chapter, Richmond asks—what is the experience which itself gives the utmost meaning to experience: surely, personality, for it is the reality which is pre-eminently real. Personality is seen first of all as the outward aspect of a being as it presents itself; hence the first meaning of the word "person" was face, or physical appearance. Thence arose the idea of a person as the object of legal rights; hence it became used in connexion with the relations of persons. Hence it acquired the idea of the member of a family or citizen, while still meaning, however, simply a being with rights and duties. God, as we conceive of him, is a unity of Persons; this means, first, that we conceive of personality as the supreme reality, and secondly, that personality is most real when it is a fellowship of persons. Fellowship, love, and complete mutual communion, then, are the things which make personality most real and active. "His unity is a unity of Persons, and it is as a unity of Persons, and as a unity of Persons only, that Personality is conceived to be the supreme reality. Personality, in the form in which it is supposed to be most intensely and unmistakably real, is a communion, a fellowship of Persons, a communion of character and will, a communion of intelligence and mind, a communion of love, implying that each Person is, in these various phases or aspects of personal life, capable of complete communion with others".[2] He complains that in modern thought there is still a great deal of emphasis laid upon the personality, and the effect of this is to make it a mark of separation; for example the expression "Personal religion"—which makes for individuality simply, and not personality in its fullest sense; though even in the case of "Personal religion", what makes it personal is the intimate relation to God. This leads Richmond, in his third chapter, to enunciate his definition of personality as "the capacity for

[1] *An Essay on Personality and its Faculties*, 1900.
[2] *op. cit.*, p. 17.

fellowship". He illustrates this definition with examples drawn from almost every aspect of life: the knowledge gained by one person is shared by the whole society; language, even, is the creation and expression of collective intelligence; and our keenest pleasures are social ones. It is our environment, particularly the other persons in that environment, through which we learn to live and realise ourselves. On this view, illustrated by Richmond, it was thought possible to arrive at a satisfactory understanding of the union of God and man in Christ that would avoid all the pitfalls of the ancient materialistic terminology, and be couched in terms likely to appeal to the modern type of philosophy and outlook upon personal values.

A variant of the above view is the theory that personality equals the sum of its relationships. This too is idealistic in origin, since it takes its stand upon the content of experience. A person is what he is in virtue of his relation to those persons with whom he is in association; and the character and mode of that association and communion are naturally conditioned by the physical circumstances under which those persons exist. It is another way of stating that the whole personality—like the consciousness—is conditioned by the content of its experience, its relationships.

The above-described developments in the idea of the personality made possible the Christologies of Moberly and Weston; for on the one hand they made it possible to see how the elements of Christ's human personality, his human nature—which in any case were inseparable from his human body—could become one with the divine Son of God; and on the other hand, by defining the personality in terms of its relationships, they provided a basis for showing how God the Son could simultaneously act as a personal subject in two spheres of personality so different as the eternal and the Incarnate.

The belief in the exclusive individuality of consciousness as the be-all and end-all of personality also began to crumble from within. The psychological researches, particularly associated with the names of William James and F. W. H. Myers, had a profound and a lasting effect upon the doctrine of personality. It was shown beyond all doubt by this new research that consciousness, trumpeted hitherto as the whole essence of personality, was little more than a small fraction of the mental activities of the individual. If then the personality was so large and composite, it was not entirely justifiable to speak of the individuality as residing wholly or even primarily in the consciousness—the other parts of the personal activity might equally share this title. This particular approach will be discussed in ch. XI.

All of these modifications in the doctrine of personality opened up new fields for the Christologian. Yet, though these ideas were all derived from the same contemporary psychology, and based upon roughly the same philosophical presuppositions, they none the less produced diverse, and not altogether harmonious, theories in regard to the nature and content of personality. Their general upshot may, however, be summarized under three heads:

1. Regarded introspectively as a precise unit, the most obvious characteristic of personality is self-consciousness, which is continuous since its contents are related to a self which gives relationship and value, i.e. intelligible meaning, to every experience. But just as at any given moment we are conscious only of a minute fraction of what our memory contains, so in respect of every aspect of mental and spiritual activity there are vast regions of which we are not conscious, yet which constitute a vital part of our personality, at least on its active side, since they condition our every thought, word and deed.

2. Hence it was becoming difficult to regard individuality, whether as a principle or a substance, as vested exclusively in the consciousness. There was admitted by some, even if reluctantly, the idea of a self, or ego, which exists, even if rather abstractly, apart from the experiences which constitute the upper layer of consciousness; as the thing which binds together the whole of experience and the hidden workings of the personality; that which gives relevance, relationship and continuity to all man's activities, a central point of reference, the existence of which is as much part of our conscious experience as the impressions from without to which it is related. This principle, when viewed on its active side, is often designated by the term "will".

3. Regarded from without, the personality is seen as something which exists intelligibly only in a social context, personalities give light to one another, and the closer they approximate to one another, be it in intellect, love, or purpose, the more real and living does each become. The possibility of the complete relinquishing of the individuality of a person is not as a rule admitted—on the contrary, the individuality of each is thought to be heightened by communion.

It is the study of the application of these various developments of the idea of personality to the doctrine of the Person of Christ that will occupy the remainder of this volume. These developments did not together produce a homogeneous view even of personality considered at large; hence the proposed restatements undertaken on their behalf were of a diverse character.

The modern age had demanded a Christ who was an intelligible psychological unity (ch. I); ancient and venerable systems of Christology were discarded for failing to satisfy this demand (ch. II); and men had set themselves to assess the amount of knowledge possessed by Christ (ch. III), on the assumption, be it noted, that he who speaks in the Gospels is a human being intelligible to us, whose words are related to his mental content and processes in the same manner as ours are: and upon that same assumption, men had set themselves to describe the spiritual and moral growth of that same historic Person (ch. VI). Now the Jesus of history, to use their own phrase, had a personality which broadly speaking was like our own. On the one hand, his consciousness was made up of all those experiences and impressions which go to make up the consciousness—which make the consciousness, the idealist would say—of a normal man. This fact alone, on the idealistic principles, is tantamount to saying that Christ possessed a fully human personality. On the other hand, he sustained a fellowship, of human intercourse and love, with other men, and in the human manner of doing so: hence also the relationships, the content, of his personality was likewise human— whatever else it might be deemed to contain. With such premises, there were roughly four ways in which the dogma of Christ's Divinity might be elaborated. In the first place, it can be argued, assuming the possibility of an ego existing apart from its accidental experiences, that when the Son of God came down from heaven he became the subject or ego in a human personality. In this way he could truly be said to have assumed manhood, since what makes a human personality what it is—apart from its basic individuality—is the content of consciousness and even more its relationships and communion with others: the experiences and the relationships which were presented to the Logos through his human body and mind thus constituted within him truly human personality. The most eminent representative of this view will be dealt with in the following chapter.

Secondly, it may be contended that since being human largely consists in the content of our consciousness, which would be completely swamped if it were directly united to the divine consciousness, the most fitting seat for the indwelling of the Logos in Christ was in those regions of the personality outside the margin of consciousness: to be human one must have that completely human consciousness, but personality being a much wider thing, there is room for a complete personal union behind and beyond it: this will occupy the eleventh chapter.

Thirdly, if content of consciousness—including relationships—be the essence of personality, and if such a consciousness constitutes an indivisible individuality, and since, moreover, the historical Jesus without doubt possessed a human consciousness and hence an indivisible human individuality, the union between him and the Godhead must be one of spiritual accord, a coincidence of purpose, a communion of will and love.

Fourthly, there is that view suggested by Newton Clarke and A. H. Strong, already alluded to in this chapter, in which the personality of Christ is regarded as a composite entity. The most obvious criticism of this view is that it envisages a Christ who is proper to neither heaven nor earth; it is difficult to see how such a Christ can be properly regarded as true God and true man, when in fact he is neither—nor how he can truly represent God to man, and man to God. In fact, the view met with scant support at the time.

# 10

## THE THEOCENTRIC SOLUTION

### *Frank Weston* The One Christ, 1907

THE above-named work is not merely the clearest example of the attempt to assert the personal Divinity of Jesus Christ with the use of the ego alongside the idealistic view of personality, it is also one of the greatest theological monuments of the age. To begin with, it is practically the only full-length monograph upon the doctrine of Christ's Person produced during the period, from the point of view of dogmatic theology; it also contains great wealth of erudition and depth of reflection—coupled with a reverence and devotion, so conspicuous by their absence in many other books of the time of equal merit in other respects.

The book is a good peer to Principal Forsyth's *Person and Place of Jesus Christ*, and has this in common with it, that like Forsyth, Weston saw the doctrine of *kenosis*, not as some eagerly sought-for stop-gap in a pressing crisis, but as a part of the scheme of God's activities as a whole, as but one aspect of the Incarnation. This was because their starting-point was different; for neither of these writers began his enquiry from the point of view of certain troublesome questions arising out of the inductive exegesis of the New Testament. Principal Forsyth was to begin from the facts of the evangelical experience—the free gift of God, the certainty of salvation. Bishop Weston began his study from a certain conviction of the truth and infallibility of the Church's traditional teaching, attempting to elucidate this, not restate it, in the light of modern thought and modern interests. It is impossible in a few pages to give more than a passing glimpse of certain portions of the work.

Sufficient has already been said in the preceding chapter with regard to the developments in the idealistic view of personality, which to a large extent constitute the background of Bishop Weston's deductions, and need not be repeated here—such conceptions are never far from the surface at any stage in the writer's argument. In view of the fact that he is attempting to harmonize two systems so different as the Catholic theology based upon realism and the contemporary doctrine of personality based upon idealism, without detriment to either, it is necessary to mark his use of the relevant technical terms with care, as it is not always certain in which sense they are being employed.

Bishop Weston at the outset of his work frankly admits the limitation of Christ's human knowledge: on matters connected with the Old Testament his knowledge was no different from that of any other rabbi of his time. He also freely admits the rights of higher criticism.[1]

Weston would appear to accept in full the idealistic doctrine of personality—as may be seen in the six attributes of self-conscious personality which he elaborates in his fourteenth chapter. Added to this, he embraces two of the most significant developments upon the idea of personality. Personality, as seen in its perfection in the being of God, is not an exclusive but an inclusive term. "Here it is that personality passes from exclusiveness to inclusiveness, 'Three Persons in one God' not one Person distinct and separate from every other person".[2] Personality, too, he regards as the sum of its relationships—a view alluded to in the preceding chapter also. Speaking of the Incarnate Christ in this connexion, he writes: "The state of the Son of God at any one moment is merely the sum of his relationships".[3] In addition to this doctrine of personality, some would prefer to say "despite it", Bishop Weston assumes throughout his work the necessity of an ego to constitute not simply individuality but fully endowed personality as modern thought envisages it. This ego is a virtual equivalent of the idea of the substantial soul; it is not an essential part of that idealistic scheme of reality with which he is largely concerned, but to his own thought and the validity of his theory of the Incarnation it is vital. Without it, his Christology would cease to exist.

The central problem for Christology, as Weston sees it, is to provide an ego which may be the permanent subject for the human experiences of Christ. It is apparently not sufficient for him to state, as H. C. Powell had done, that the Divine Logos was the subject of Christ's humanity. This fact sheds a good deal of light upon Weston's thought; for it would therefore appear that he does not conceive the ego as being some abstract or colourless entity, conditioned solely by its relationships and experiences: it is much more than this; he speaks in one place

[1] *The One Christ*, 1907, p. 7.   [2] *ibid.*, p. 10.   [3] *ibid.*, p. 17.

## THE THEOCENTRIC SOLUTION

of the "content" of an ego, and he would certainly ascribe the property of self-determination to it. But the main difficulty in such a plain assertion would be that the ego who became thus Incarnate was no mere abstraction floating in a vacuum but God the Son, already replete with a set of relationships, perfect faculties, and an infinitely filled consciousness—an already perfected personality.

Weston examines and criticizes with very great care some of the attempts which had already been made by Christian thinkers of all the ages to provide a subject for the humanity of Christ.

The Alexandrines, for example, had regarded the unlimited Logos as the subject of the manhood of Christ. This was unsatisfactory, for at many times the unlimited Logos acts and undergoes experiences in a manner which is not strictly related to what is directly conditioned by the human experiences and relationships; and the humanity undergoes certain experiences which could scarcely be attributed to the unlimited Logos as subject—human weakness, suffering and ignorance; and, "My God, My God, why hast Thou forsaken me" seems to have no meaning if the Logos, its subject, was in full possession of divine powers.[1] Hence Weston concludes that the unlimited Logos could not serve as a *permanent* subject for Christ's humanity.

The monophysites, on the other hand, had produced a real subject for the manhood in the manner of a human consciousness, but they had virtually delineated a Christ who was neither properly God nor man.[2] Dorner's theory, which is a development from theirs, also errs because it assumes that the only possible subject of manhood is an individual human ego.[3] Such a theory only makes for an association of the Logos with an otherwise complete human person.

A contribution of some importance has been made by the kenoticists, for they have contrived to constitute the Logos as the permanent subject of the manhood by regarding him as depotentiated. Their theories, however, as they stand are quite untenable. It is impossible to conceive of the real abandonment of divine properties, for all God's attributes belong to him essentially.[4] The so-called physical attributes were not things which came into existence at the creation of the world—if they

[1] *The One Christ*, p. 75.
[2] *ibid.*, p. 91.
[3] *ibid.*, p. 90.
[4] *ibid.*, p. 120.

were, it would mean that God changed his nature at that moment. Nor are omnipotence and love antitheses, as Fairbairn thinks; for a child, for instance, ascribes omnipotence to its mother in proportion to its love. The physical attributes are God's love in action.[1] Weston returns to the question of the attributes in the fourteenth chapter, where, under the first property of personality which he lists—self-consciousness—he observes that this property means primarily knowledge of ourselves as we are, as we are in relation to other men and to God. Therefore, self-consciousness in God's own case equals his omniscience: we may never, then, speak of omniscience as a physical or external attribute of God.[2] Weston adds all the conventional logical arguments against the kenotic theories.[3]

The sixth chapter of *The One Christ* contains the gist of Bishop Weston's proposed solution. Stated briefly, the theory proposes that the Son of God in becoming Incarnate added to himself a human nature, of which he became the subject or ego. But his divine ego was self-restrained to the extent that within the personality of the Christ (a) on the passive side, he was the subject only of experiences (knowledge) which was mediated to him through the human body and mind; (b) as regards the content and development of that personality, his relationships and intercourse with other men and with God the Father were likewise conditioned by the capacities of the human nature; and (c) on the active side, he could only do, will, and reveal, what could be expressed by the whole human personality. The self-restraint was therefore always exactly proportionate to the measure of the development of the human personality: this is the cause of his complaint against writers such as Gore who appeared to postulate an act of self-emptying prior to, or not intrinsically related to, the actual conditions of the human personality. If human personality be indeed constituted by the content of its consciousness and the relationships which it sustains with others, and the divine ego could in fact become a subject within such a personality, then it could truly be said that the Son of God became true man.

He states his theological presuppositions with great care: The Person who became Incarnate was purely divine, that act in no way hindering his proper life within the Godhead. He remained truly the Word of God upholding all things. Moreover, he always

---

[1] *The One Christ*, p. 121.   [2] *ibid.*, p. 298.   [3] *ibid.*, pp. 121 ff.

remained in the absolute possession of his attributes and powers. Nor is the Divinity itself within the Incarnate modified so as to produce a Person neither properly divine nor human—"He is not to be conceived as a divine-human Person; he owes nothing to association with human individuality, nor is his self-consciousness in any the least degree composite, in part divine and in part human".[1] From this point of view, the Incarnation is a theophany, but it is also an anthropophany, exhibiting perfect manhood to God.[2] Nor did the Logos merely become morally united to a human individual—"He did not take a manhood in the sense that he associated with himself one human Person; ... but in Mary's womb he took human flesh which, with its own proper and complete soul, he constituted in himself so that he became truly man, living as the subject or ego of real manhood".[3] This is made possible by the fact that "he so limits his divine power that he can adequately serve as the proper subject or ego of his assumed manhood".[4]

The possibility of this is clearly Weston's major premise. It rests upon two conditions. First, it must be possible for an ego in certain portions of its activity to be dissociated from its conscious content and relationships enjoyed elsewhere; and secondly, it must be conceived possible for an ego to retain its self-identity, and yet be the subject of another set of relationships. The difficulty in all this, stated here in order that it may be kept in mind during the discussion, is that it either makes too much or too little of the idea of the ego. On the one hand, if the Logos can constitute himself the centre of a new personality, by adding to himself a new set of incidental relationships, it is difficult to see how that perfect self-identity fails to carry with it something of the divine omniscience which, according to Weston, is so integral a part of the divine personality. If, on the other hand, the idea be taken quite seriously that consciousness and hence personality can be and are constituted by their content, "the sum of relationships"; and that a personality so constituted can be united to the divine ego without sharing in the divine omniscience; if in other words, the idealist view of personality be taken quite literally, as Weston apparently does, since he conceives Christ to have had real and not merely superficial human consciousness—it is difficult to see how the divine ego in such a personality can or does play any

[1] *The One Christ*, p. 136.    [2] *ibid.*, p. 136.
[3] *ibid.*, p. 137.    [4] *ibid.*, p. 137.

greater part than a mere abstraction, which contributes nothing to the *content* of the personality save its identity—whatever that may mean by itself. The idea of the ego, then, tends to mean either more or less than Bishop Weston intends it to mean; such is the lot of one who attempts to join together elements from different systems of thought.

Weston continues that Christ's manhood was in all points like ours, except for sin. This entailed his living under all those limitations both mental and physical which properly belong to our state; therefore "The Incarnate Son must at every moment live under the law of self-restraint as to all his divine powers, in some real measure; while at the same time he must retain the ultimate possession of them so that he may communicate to manhood divine aid in the degree that it requires and is able to assimilate".[1] "The measure of the self-restraint is the capacity of the perfect manhood to receive, assimilate, and co-operate with divine power".[2] He must not say, do, or think anything beyond the human capacity. He expresses this in the strongest terms—"It is absolute putting out of action whatever of divine power that manhood cannot mediate".[3]

Weston proceeds to delineate the self-restraint further, showing how completely the human personality thus constituted serves as the vehicle of all the Incarnate Christ's activities. We cannot know *a priori* what man's capacities for receiving of the divine life are; we must go to the Gospels and see exactly what Christ did in fact do and know. It naturally follows that the degree of self-restraint was different at different ages of Christ's life. Christ, moreover, holds communion with the Father through his manhood.[4] Herein lies his mediatorship between God and man.

The idea of the self-limited Logos as the subject of the manhood, he concludes, is in every way to be preferred to the unlimited Logos or the kenoted Logos as subject. Personality equals the sum of relationships, and the Logos thus became the subject of two sets of relationships, those of the unlimited Son in heaven and those of the man Christ upon earth. Weston advances four pictorial illustrations of this fact. First, there is the instance of St. Francis of Sales, who at one period of his life acted as confessor to his father and mother. The saint was thus the subject of two quite different sets of relations to them. In the confessional, he

[1] *The One Christ*, p. 139.  
[2] *ibid.*, p. 139.  
[3] *ibid.*, p. 139.  
[4] *ibid.*, p. 141.

## THE THEOCENTRIC SOLUTION

was acting as judge and counsellor, unable to employ his filial love or his knowledge of their private lives.[1] Secondly, there is the example of the African king in slavery, thirdly, the son who is serving in his father's regiment, and fourthly, a king's son voluntarily living as one of the unemployed in his country: in all these instances we have either pairs of persons who have two sets of relationships with one another, definitely defined yet possessed by the same individuals, or persons who have two sets of relationships to the world at large. Weston admits the very inadequate character of these illustrations, and it is clear from his view of personality that his theory envisages something even more exclusive than appears in any of them. That the normal constitution of the humanity, filled and enriched by its experiences and relationships, is allowed fully and unreservedly to constitute Christ's personality is clear from Weston's treatment of the question of omniscience—always a touchstone, for terms such as "restraint" when used of omniscience always convey more than when used simply of omnipotence. He writes: "When God the Son became man, limiting the content of his self-consciousness within a certain sphere by freely accepting the conditions of manhood, he conditioned and limited his omniscience. To have abandoned it would have been to have abandoned self-consciousness; to have exercised it in its fullness would have required in him a second centre of self-consciousness as subject of manhood; but to limit and condition it as he did was to render himself the very true subject or personal ego of his manhood".[2]

The Incarnation was made possible, according to Weston, not only because of the kinship of human and divine personality, but because it was from the wider relationship that the limitation came, and because it was voluntary in its character. This limitation of the new sphere necessarily involves the fact that "the Son necessarily has a knowledge of himself, in his relations Godward and manward, that does not belong to his universal life as Logos".[3] What, then, did this man-conditioned consciousness of his contain with regard to his own identity? He did not know himself as God the Son exercising unlimited power, nor did he know himself as merely a man, nor as some composite divine-human personality, but he knew himself as God-in-manhood: for he knew himself as God just in so far as a perfect sinless God-assumed human soul

[1] *The One Christ*, p. 151.   [2] *ibid.*, p. 298.
[3] *ibid.*, p. 152.

could mediate the divine self-consciousness.[1] Neither was it the case that he knew himself to be the unlimited Logos, who had willed to respect the limitations of manhood: "He knew himself as Logos only in the measure that his human soul could be made to mediate that self-knowledge. But all the while in his universal state he was, nay is, the unlimited Logos who wills to be for evermore in such special relations of love to the redeemed that, in the sphere in which he meets with them, he is prepared to accept this limited content of self-consciousness".[2] This, he argues, implies no "forgetting" on the part of the Logos, but a will to have in one particular sphere no consciousness of himself that is not mediated by the human nature he assumed.

This emphasis upon Christ's consciousness of self is symptomatic of a change which had come over the Christological interests of the period. At the time of Gore's Dissertation, all attention was focused upon the question, how could Christ have possessed a limited knowledge of external events? Now, a decade later, the emphasis is upon the matter of the personality of Christ itself; and the question has become, in what sense could the Jesus of history have been conscious of himself as the universal Logos? It is indeed a measure of the *kenosis* which Weston envisages, a measure too of the seriousness with which he accepts the idealistic view of personality as constituted by its relationships, that he can speak of the Logos as undergoing, not merely an eclipse in his knowledge of outward things, but a modification even in the manner of his knowledge of himself. The species of kenotic theory proposed by Bishop Weston is popularly regarded as a mild and palatable form of the theory; in actual fact, like the theory of Forsyth described in the fifth chapter, it is more akin to the Christology of Gess than that of Thomasius—though Forsyth and Weston differ from the foreign schools in that they both allow for the continuance of Christ's cosmical activities. This seeming kinship with the more radical type of *kenosis* is due to the fact pointed out above that the interest now was not simply in questions relating to particular attributes such as omniscience, but in the real humanity of the Lord's personality itself.

Bishop Weston's insistence upon the necessity of postulating but one single consciousness within the personality of Christ is in full accord with the requirements of the age; it finds a place here as it further illustrates his view of the Incarnation. "The

[1] *The One Christ*, p. 152.   [2] *ibid.*, p. 153.

## THE THEOCENTRIC SOLUTION

importance of arriving at a conception of a single consciousness of the Christ cannot be over-estimated. The popular teaching that assumes in the Incarnate a full consciousness of divine glory side by side with a consciousness of certain occasional human limitations cannot be too strongly deprecated".[1] Such a view, he believes, would imply three states of the Logos—cosmic, occasionally limited, and limited. The kenotic theories are a slight improvement since they postulate but two states: "The kenotic theories are equally to be deplored. For they picture the Incarnate as of a dual consciousness in the sense that they require two centres of activity in the lower state: a centre of his self-abandonment, and a centre of his divine human or human activities".[2]

It is true that Weston contrives to unify the Person of Christ himself, but it still remains an open question whether he avoids postulating two consciousnesses in the life of the Logos. Strictly speaking, the Logos has but one "life centre" on Weston's view, since he is ego in both the human and the divine states; but it is difficult to see how he avoids postulating two personalities—as opposed to mere individualities—in the life of the Logos, so literally does he accept the view that personality is constituted by relationships—environment.

Weston also has something to say upon the subject of the Wills in Christ: he must have two wills, for his consciousness was not composite. We must not simply postulate one will—"The danger of so doing arises from the tendency to isolate the divine Person from the divine nature and functions; and so to think of the divine will as apart from his Person that we can conceive it either becoming associated with the human will by some kind of moral identity, or serving him as an instrument by which to subdue his human will".[3] The will, he continues, is not a function apart from the person: it is inseparable from it, a mode of its self-manifestation. Hence, Christ must exercise his Divinity and humanity through that proper mode of its expression, the human will.

Finally, it was observed in the fifth chapter that one objection to the popular kenotic theories was the difficulty of seeing, on their premises, how the manhood of Christ can continue intelligibly to exist as such after the Ascension. Weston has something to say even upon this point: "Therefore it is that in estimating the manner of the self-limitation of the Incarnate we must be most careful to predicate of him upon earth no mode of self-

[1] *The One Christ*, p. 157.   [2] *ibid.*, p. 158.   [3] *ibid.*, p. 169.

restraint that may not be equally predicated of him in heaven".[1]

The chapters in which the theory is applied to the life story of Christ are of great interest, but the acceptability of Bishop Weston's Christology must always rest primarily upon the compatibility of those elements in it which are drawn from the realist and idealist philosophies.

## W. P. DuBose

A few words should be said in the present connexion of the celebrated American theologian W. P. DuBose, one of the most outstanding figures of the liberal era. He was pre-eminently a thinker for his time; that is to say, he did not begin with what he himself believed to be a *philosophia perennis*, adopting a "take it or leave it" attitude towards the rest of mankind; he accepted the moral, philosophical, and psychological presuppositions of his age, and with their aid attempted to lead men to the Church's Faith, which, said he, is so true that if men can only be brought to accept one small piece of it they have received something of infinite value. It was observed in the sixth chapter that he was one of those who embraced whole-heartedly the new form of apologetic, beginning with man's evaluation of the human life of the Saviour: that was characteristic of his whole method. In the realm of Christology, as will be seen, he accepts as axiomatic: that God's revelation took place exclusively through the medium of the Lord's humanity, that Christ possessed a single intelligible consciousness, that the will is the expression of the whole person, and that personality is constituted by its content—i.e. environment, relationships, experiences, and the like. We begin our study at this point.

In the tenth chapter of his *Soteriology of the New Testament*, Dr. DuBose deals with the content and identity of Christ's human personality—that personality as men knew it. He advances no kenotic theory, specifically so-called, but certain of the observations which he advances bear a striking resemblance to the work of Frank Weston and, like the Bishop, he proposes a clearly theocentric solution.

"That Jesus Christ is the Incarnation of a divine Person; that he is not the union of a divine Person with a human person, i.e. with a particular or individual man with whom he united himself

[1] *The One Christ*, p. 177.

## THE THEOCENTRIC SOLUTION 281

later or in the womb of the Virgin, in a word, the Church's doctrine of the unity and the Deity of the Person of Jesus Christ is not only the doctrine of the New Testament and of Christianity, but is fully recognized and integrally and necessarily involved in the truth of Christ as I am endeavouring to present it, I hope is sufficiently apparent to all".[1] The nature of a person, he argues, is the mode of his personality or of his personal being or acting; here, it may be noted is yet another variant of the developed idealistic view; "mode" may be taken to mean much the same as Weston means by "relations", the total reference and hence the content of the consciousness. Christ, DuBose concludes, must therefore have assumed real human personality, since he assumed such a mode of living. The Incarnation, moreover, was a permanent union and complete from the first moment of the Virgin's Conception.

Since in the Incarnation the Son dwells as the personalising element in a human personality, his whole revelation, nay his whole personal activity is completely human as well as being completely divine. "We are not to find the Divinity of Christ in anything outside of his humanity, but in the divine perfection of his humanity".[2] Again: "Whatever of divine there was or is then in the knowledge, power, or any other function of Jesus Christ as man, it is the communicated Divinity of the Third Person of the Trinity, and not the original or underived Divinity of the Second Person".[3] It is nevertheless true that "he is the divine Logos realized in humanity, and we shall be humanity realized in the Logos, and between the He and the We there is all the difference between God and man".[4] In another place he points out that just as God's activity in us is also our own highest activity, so it is with Christ: "In this divine human life it is not part God and part we, but all God and all we, just as Jesus Christ himself is not God in some acts and man in others, but equally God and equally man in every act of his human life".[5]

"If then by personality we mean the subject of a personal mode of being and acting, Our Lord had no human personality; he was divine and not human. But if we mean the mode of being and acting of a personal subject, then he had a human personality; because as man he was and acted personally in that

[1] *Soteriology*, p. 138. [2] *ibid.*, p. 141.
[3] *ibid.*, p. 143. [4] *ibid.*, p. 144.
[5] *Gospel According to St. Paul*, p. 37.

mode which we call human".[1] Christ was not simply human in any impersonal functions such as the workings of his body, but as spiritual or morally we must be personal, so in this sense he had human personality: his personal faith, obedience, and knowledge, were human. Manhood was made and intended to know God, hence its capacities in that direction are practically infinite. Omniscience itself then is not necessarily a violation of pure humanity, but the way it is acquired, the mode in which it grows may be: "Between that knowledge which the man Christ Jesus had, or did not have, in the womb of his Mother or as an infant at her breast, and that omniscient divine knowledge which as man he now possesses, there was an infinite process and progress of growth in knowledge which, we may feel sure, violated in no degree or respect the nature and laws of the human mind".[2]

DuBose recognized a problem which at the time was not receiving the attention it deserved. Inherent in human consciousness is the free choice to obey or to disobey; if as God he were incapable of this, then Incarnation to him would have been impossible. Yet the admission of such a possibility would entail the admission that God's plan of revelation might have been wrecked. DuBose believes that as Christians we are bound to hold to both sides of the dilemma: we find antinomies everywhere; to say that Christ is both God and man is itself the greatest of antinomies.[3] What becomes, moreover, of our human bias towards sin; did Christ assume that also? Here DuBose states quite clearly that human nature only possesses a bias towards evil, no actual guilt being thereby incurred. Christ must really have assumed the flesh of sin, and not just something like it. Christ's sinlessness was not a fact of his nature, but his *work* in our nature. Nevertheless, the flesh is only called "sinful" because we sin in it.[4]

Ever since the recognition that the idealistic view of personality—in its crude or developed forms—has come to stay, as a permanent element in our intellectual outlook, attempts have been made to revivify the doctrine of Christ's generic manhood. This, almost more than any other Christian doctrine, obviously depended for its validity upon the realist philosophy, with its belief in human nature as a distinct entity, possessed and personalized by individual men, and assumed impersonally by

[1] *Soteriology*, p. 145.   [2] *ibid.*, p. 150.
[3] *ibid.*, p. 151.   [4] *Gospel According to St. Paul*.

## THE THEOCENTRIC SOLUTION 283

Christ, as the means by which the human race might be redeemed. There is therefore a soteriological as well as a purely Christological insistence behind the attempts to retain this doctrine in some form. Moberly had elaborated a doctrine of Christ's inclusive personality to meet this need; and in later years, in another context, Relton was to revive the ideas of the *enhypostasia*, and the archetypal manhood of Christ. In *The Gospel According to St. Paul*, p. 297, DuBose also makes an attempt to secure the acceptance of the old doctrines in a new setting. "The universality of our Lord's humanity is only explicable on the fact that his personality is a divine one". It is the Person of God living in it that makes it and its work applicable to all: humanity belongs to him not as concrete humanity, but as God in humanity.

Only long and careful criticism and disputation can show whether such a view of the representative character of the Lord's manhood can serve the same place in the scheme of Christian doctrine as did its forebear in the realist theology.

## 11

## THE ANTHROPOCENTRIC SOLUTION

FROM the consideration of those writers to whom the centre of the consciousness and personality of the Incarnate Lord is the divine ego, we pass to another group of scholars who adopt the second alternative, namely, that the point of individuation in the Lord's life upon earth is a human and not a divine ego. It has already been made abundantly clear that the postulation of *human* individuality in Christ is a reversal of the standard Christology both of East and West. In the Christology of the Nestorians there is indeed human individuality, but, as will be seen when the modern versions of this system are treated, the humanity is envisaged as living a life of its own; God and man are in as distinct a relation to one another as the elements in a chemical mixture—as opposed to a chemical compound to which the conception of the hypostatic union is more akin. Human individuality then had been of old postulated of a "mixture" Christ, but as an element in a "compound" Christ, as with the present writers, it was a novelty, and an experiment in Christological thinking well worth having been attempted.

This is not to suggest that these writers deposed the Divinity of Christ from being the all-important constituent in his personality. Their thesis appears to be that the transcendent Word of God Incarnates himself by working, speaking, thinking, and knowing through the medium of a human individual. Thus, considered from the manward side, when men spoke to Christ, loved him, knew him, had any dealings with him in fact, it was with his human ego that they so communed, behind which there stood the unknowable Deity itself. In an unusual sense of the word, this may be spoken of as the measure of God's *kenosis*, that he limits himself in his activity so as to operate only through the finite capacity and capabilities of human individuality. No absolute limitation is placed upon God's nature or attributes, but instead of speaking through earthquake, wind and fire, or any other manifestation of his transcendent power he choses rather to manifest himself through one single human being.

From this brief introduction we proceed to the consideration of two typical writers of this type—it can scarcely be called a school of thought. The first is a striking and original contribution to theology, the second is an English interpretation of the work of a celebrated German Christologian.

*William Sanday*

A most striking solution to the Christological problems of the day, and one which doubtless many liberal scholars were unwittingly moving towards, was proposed by the Lady Margaret Professor at Oxford in a course of lectures delivered during the winter of 1909–1910. They were published in 1910 under the title *Christologies Ancient and Modern*, and again in the following year with the addition of an appendix of some value as *Christology and Personality*. The original material is to be found in the sixth and seventh lectures of the series.

Allusion was made in an earlier chapter to the rapidity with which the study of psychology was brought to the notice of the general public at the beginning of the century. This topic again returns to our notice. The study of the human mind, for long the prerogative of philosopher and doctor, was suddenly thrown open to mankind at large. What had hitherto been a closed book, became the property of all thinking men; what had previously been the jargon of experts became the table-talk of multitudes. In particular, the attention of the public had been drawn to a recognition of the important part played in human mental processes by that sphere of activity in the brain which functions unknown to our normal waking consciousness. Originally known to researchers as "unconscious cerebration", it had recently come to be described in terms of the metaphor of a threshold. Hence our conscious thinking became known as supraliminal consciousness, whilst those motions of the brain which take place without our knowing about them were described as subliminal—in common speech the terminology was abridged and generally the newly explored region was spoken of as the subconscious mind, or self. This terminology must be applied with some care. To speak of the subliminal or sub-conscious *part* of the mind is in order, but when the psychologist, not always so accurate in his use of language as a philosopher would prefer, speaks of the "subliminal consciousness", he is simply uttering a contradiction in terms, since *ex hypothesi* the subliminal portion of the mind is *not* conscious. That such a region of mental activity exists is now established beyond all doubt as a scientific datum of the first importance. Its demonstration is patent to any man through the phenomena of everyday life, such as the sudden realization of the solution to a problem previously dismissed from the mind as insoluble, and the curious manner in which memories re-shape and arrange themselves, to reappear in strange combination especially in dreams. This is to say nothing of the wide and complex web of causation between the association of ideas within the mind, which forms the basis of modern psychoanalysis.

All of this and a great deal more is so much part of our common stock of knowledge at the present day that it would be tedious to enlarge upon it; but in the early years of the century it was a virtually new thing, and the toy of every educated speculator; it had passed out of the exclusive possession of elite bodies such as the Society for Psychical Research as it became patent to all.

It is a most remarkable fact that the two books which played the leading rôle in the introduction of modern psychology to the world should have had as their main interest and subject-matter the application of contemporary psychology to questions of a specifically religious character. This explains the fact of the material being already in so suitable a form for the Lady Margaret Professor to handle in a theological manner. The two books referred to are of course F. W. H. Myers' *Human Personality and Its Survival of Bodily Death*, 2 vols., 1893, and William James's *Varieties of Religious Experience*. The concept of the subliminal region of the mind, recognized for the first time fully in 1886,[1] is applied by these writers to specifically religious questions—the immortality of the soul, man's possible intercourse with the other world, and the facts regarding sudden religious conversions. With regard to the last point, for example, sudden religious conversions had hitherto been ascribed to the sudden and miraculous intervention of God; but James showed that such phenomena were the sudden manifestation of processes which had been going on in the lower regions of the subject's mind for some considerable time. That, for example, the undergraduate converted at three o'clock in the afternoon had not suddenly been moved by God, but that the flood-gates of his upper mind

[1] *Varieties of Religious Experience*, pp. 230 ff.

## THE ANTHROPOCENTRIC SOLUTION

had suddenly burst open letting through a torrent of new experiences, powers, and emotions, hitherto confined to regions of his personality outside the margin of his consciousness.

From these investigations, William James had been led to state the possibility that in general those regions of the personality which do not normally constitute part of our conscious self may in fact be the part of us, perhaps the only possible part of us, which can be in communion with the spiritual world, and hence come in contact with God. In two places he alludes quite definitely to this:

"Just as our primary wide-awake consciousness throws open our sense to the touch of things material, so it is logically conceivable that *if there be* higher spiritual agencies that can directly touch us, the psychological condition of their doing so *might be* our possession of a subconscious region which alone should yield access to them".[1] And again:

"In the religious life the control is felt as 'higher'; but since on our hypothesis it is primarily the higher faculties of our own hidden mind which are controlling, the sense of union with the power beyond us is a sense of something not merely apparently but literally true".[2]

In the light of these investigations, and in view of the prevailing perplexity regarding Christology, it was almost inevitable that sooner or later the new psychological knowledge should be applied in that sphere of religious truth also, and it was Dr. Sanday who made the attempt.

He had made as wide a study of the subject as was possible at that date, judging from the writers to whom he refers—Sir W. Hamilton, F. W. H. Myers, Joseph Jastrow, W. Wallace, B. P. Bowne, and G. F. Stout—though he himself made no claim to be a professional psychologist, but rather a theologian, seeking light from contemporary scientific knowledge; though some of his most eminent critics did challenge his view-point on philosophical grounds.

Sanday began his investigation at the point where William James left off. The subliminal consciousness, he asserts, is the proper *locus* for divine activity in the human soul. From it proceed those sudden upward rushes, produced by its contact with the Divine, which result in conversions and sudden ecstasies. From its depths are precipitated and realised those states of seeming

[1] *Varieties of Religious Experience*, p. 242.  [2] *ibid.*, p. 513.

union with the Divine which the mystics enjoy—the highest form of religious experience known to man; and from it surge those great impulses to devotion, self-sacrifice, and heroism, in which men feel themselves to be possessed by another self almost, which form the jewels of the active no less than the contemplative life of religious men. This region, then, is the seat of our highest ideals, and of our greatest potentialities, and hence that more limited region of our personality, the supraliminal consciousness, is like the dial-plate of some delicate instrument, with a finger flickering over it, which registers in summary manner those deeper motions of the personality that lie far below. Hence he concludes that "It is in these same subterranean regions, and by the same vitally reciprocating action, that whatever there is of divine in the soul of man passes into the roots of his being".[1]

It is thus that Sanday arrives at his first definite proposition, namely, that, "the proper seat or locus of all divine indwelling, or divine action upon the human soul, is the subliminal consciousness".[2]

That this is a most sweeping and therefore dangerous statement is plain to behold; and it has in fact received far more in the way of pointed criticism than his second proposition, which he bases upon it. In the first place, it assumes—although Sanday attempts to deny this[3]—that the subliminal consciousness is of a necessarily higher order than the supraliminal. Higher, that is to say, in the sense that by its constitution it is capable of direct communion with the divine, in a manner which is utterly debarred from the normal waking consciousness. Sanday's view, if pressed, would mean that the subliminal consciousness is the inner man, the spiritual side of the man, the heart and soul of the man, the part of him which is more his real self and abiding personality than is his waking consciousness. Is there then sufficient and sure evidence for a view so radical and revolutionary, so contrary to the accepted view of the location of the centre of personal activities? The majority of theologians replied in the negative.[4] It was pointed out on many sides that a superiority is ascribed to the subconscious which is quite out of all proportion to the actual evidence. It was pointed out that the subconscious is a

---

[1] *Christology and Personality*, p. 157.     [2] *ibid.*, p. 159.
[3] *Personality in Christ and in Ourselves*.
[4] E.g. D'Arcy, Hibbert Journ., Jan. 1911.

## THE ANTHROPOCENTRIC SOLUTION 289

rubbish-heap as well as a treasure-house.[1] The most that we know of it is that it is a dark region where instincts do their work, and where memories float about in grotesque forms to appear erratically in the upper consciousness at their own accord, or at the subject's conscious beck, or else to influence his volition in hidden ways. As Digges La Touche points out, the decisive area of the personality is the conscious self, which is the motor of men's greatest purposes, not the dial-plate of what is formed beneath the threshold. He adds that the subconscious is generally a good servant but a very poor master. Digges La Touche also urges that Sanday attempts to vindicate his theory by a conception of personality which is philosophically untenable, namely, by conceiving it as divided by boundaries in space.

Sanday would, however, have been the very first to repudiate such a notion stated in this way, that his conception was purely metaphorical—as he often repeats. The greatest opposition was nevertheless aroused in reference to the former criticism, that Sanday's view presupposes the belief that man's higher volitions and ideals take their rise in the subconscious mind. Such a theory was quite unacceptable to the intellectual world of the day—quite apart from the question whether or not Sanday's theory implies such a thesis (he himself denied it in part). It is very interesting to see, however, how the psychology of a later day completely shattered such a criticism as was levelled against Sanday. For according to the teaching of the schools of psychoanalysis, taken at its face value, the human consciousness is little more than a clearing-station in thought, receiving impressions from the outside world which are transmitted inwards, and receiving material from inside the personality which is transformed into word or action as the case may be. For we are given to understand by these thinkers that, far from our impulses originating in the upper consciousness, practically every single thought which enters it—apart from perceptions from without the person—is originated and predetermined by the lower regions of the mind: according to Freud, this even applies to a name or number which comes to mind—seemingly by chance. But in the days of Sanday's Christology, such researches were confined to a group of scholars on the continent.

Of equal importance in respect of Sanday's theory is the question, where, or in what part of the personality, in actual fact

[1] Myers, *Human Personality*, p. 72.

of experience does the divine influence impinge upon us—below, or above the threshold of consciousness? Dr. H. R. Mackintosh expresses the criticism thus—"The objection, as it appears to me, is not against your ascribing a higher value to processes in which the Divine is involved; that, probably, all would consent to. But the question rather is: In which processes is the divine most involved, and most valuably present? and to this I should answer, in conscious processes, as faith and love".[1] To this, Sanday replies that faith and love are the outcome of divine influence below the threshold. But other writers pressed the criticism that the major portion of the active life of communion with God—for communion with God is an active thing—takes place in our consciousness. We pray with our consciousness, whether it be with the intellect or the affections; and even the higher forms of prayer, such as the prayer of union, are in the first place connected with the activity of consciousness. Therefore, it is argued, we know God chiefly through our consciousness, just as we know those around us chiefly through it.

From this thesis, that the divine meets with the human preeminently in the subconscious mind, Dr. Sanday drew his second proposition, which we now proceed to consider. In the seventh lecture of the series, then, he brings his investigations into the field of Christology. "It is literal truth", he declares, "to say that the inner life of the spirit is 'Hid with Christ in God'; but the medium through which that inner life is manifested—so far as it is ever manifested—is the common workday life of men".[2]

"Now it seems to me that the analogy of our human selves can at least to this extent be transferred to the Incarnate Christ. If whatever we have of divine must needs pass through a strictly human medium, the same law would hold good even for him. *A priori* we should expect that it would be so; and *a posteriori* we find that as a matter of fact it was so".[3] Sanday's standpoint with regard to the Gospels would appear to have been a moderately liberal exegesis—full and ample recognition of the human limitations, with a minimising view of the miracles.

In an earlier lecture he had given a not very sympathetic description of Chalcedonian theology—as to many of his contemporaries it did not appear to convey the idea of a single personality.

---

[1] Quoted by Sanday in *Personality in Christ and in Ourselves*, p. 7
[2] *Christologies Ancient and Modern*, p. 165.     [3] *ibid.*, p. 165.

## THE ANTHROPOCENTRIC SOLUTION

"We have seen what difficulties are involved in the attempt to draw as it were a vertical line between the human nature and the divine nature of Christ, and to say that certain actions of his fall on one side of this line and certain other actions on the other. But these difficulties disappear if, instead of drawing a vertical line, we rather draw a horizontal line between the upper human medium, which is the proper and natural field of all active expression, and those lower deeps which are no less the proper and natural home of whatever is divine".[1]

Such, then, is the theory put forward by Dr. Sanday, that Christ's Divinity resided in the subconscious mind of the historic Jesus. Sanday believed that such a theory did justice to all the relevant religious interests. It left Jesus fully human, and yet since there is constant flow to and fro between the conscious and the subconscious, his two natures were in full harmony. Moreover, it left room for no problems such as that occasioned by the knowledge of Jesus, as the supraliminal consciousness was retained in its proper proportions: "Whatever there was of divine in him, on its way to outward expression whether in speech or act, passed through, and could not but pass through, the restricting and restraining medium of human consciousness. This consciousness was, as it were, the narrow neck through which alone the divine could come to expression. This involves that only so much of the divine could be expressed as was capable of expression within the forms of humanity".[2] On p. 175 he develops this bottle metaphor yet one stage further; imagining the narrow neck of it to be filled with porous material. Thus it comes about that in Christ the divine thoughts and impulses have to be transmuted into the often inadequate forms of human speech and thought. It is therefore possible for Sanday to indulge himself to the full in speculations regarding the growth of Christ's messianic consciousness and such-like topics—not so much as apologetic for his Divinity as illustration of the truly human character of the Lord's mind. One or two samples of such speculation may be given: "The most definite, comprehensive, and the most exalted of all the titles which our Lord took to himself was the Jewish title, Messiah. This title certainly included for our Lord himself, . . . the idea of vast dominion. . . . It included the idea of a vast restoration, redemption or salvation. . . . When our Lord assumes the right

---
[1] *Christologies Ancient and Modern*, pp. 165–6.
[2] *ibid.*, p. 167.

to forgive sins; when he lays down a new law like a second Moses; when he allows it to be seen that he thinks of himself as greater than Jonah or Solomon; . . . in all these cases his messianic consciousness is the moving cause. This messianic consciousness is central".[1] His theory also allowed for Christ's genuine moral growth: "Out of such constituent elements, physical, rational, moral, and spiritual, character was formed in him as in any one of ourselves, though with unwonted care and attention. . . . The forming of character is the unconscious automatic effect of particular decisions of judgment and acts of will. Conscience discriminates between right and wrong; in his case it invariably chose the right and eschewed the wrong. But out of the midst of all these moral decisions and actions, out of the interplay of social relations, under the guidance of observation and reflexion, there gradually grew up a sense of deliberate purpose, a consciousness of mission".[2]

Such human *media*, even human character at its best, were woefully inadequate to express the riches of divine truth: "Our Lord Jesus Christ when he became Incarnate, assumed such a disability as this. He could not—by his own deliberate act of self-restraint he could not—wear his Deity (as it were) upon his sleeve. He knew that the condition which he was assuming permitted only degrees of self-manifestation. He knowingly condemned himself, if the phrase may be allowed, to that inadequate expression of which I have spoken".[3] Sanday thus dresses up his theory, to suit the prevailing theological humour, to look almost like a kenotic theory; but such would be the very opposite to the facts of the case, for on Sanday's view, the Deity is left quite complete in himself and his nature, restricted, not in its own proper movements, but simply in the inadequacy of the human instrument.

It will now be apparent why this theory of Dr. Sanday has been labelled "anthropocentric". For the divine nature is conceived of as residing in Christ as an added gift to an already complete and sufficient human personality, it resides in him as a *donum superadditum*, as Digges La Touche puts it, which could be withdrawn from him without injury to any essential portion of his psychological constitution. We need to be shown, the same writer concludes, that Jesus was inextricably one with God in what passed

[1] *Christologies Ancient and Modern*, pp. 174–5.
[2] *ibid.*, p. 179–80.
[3] *ibid.*, p. 178.

above in his consciousness, not in what happened below it. For to be sure, it cannot truly be said that the "Word became flesh" if the Word came simply to reside as a subterranean influence in an already complete human personality; and resided in that personality, moreover, in a manner virtually unconscious, *ex hypothesi*, to that human personality. If personality is still to be defined in terms of self-consciousness—a view which in the light of tendencies noted in this chapter was at last beginning to crumble—then without doubt the personality of Christ, that part of him which men knew and loved, was human; its ego was human, its consciousness was human.

In the second place, if, as pointed out in the fifth chapter, one of the defects of the kenotic theory was that it concentrated upon the Incarnation as a veiling rather than a revealing of God's nature, the same criticism applied with surpassing poignancy to this theory. What would the Fathers have said if they had been told that in order for God to reveal himself to man his Divinity had to pass through a sieve or porous stopper, in order that it should be so restrained and restricted, like a wild animal, as only to allow so much of it to seep through as the natural man is able to bear? Speculations regarding our Lord's consciousness during the liberal era were often gross, but that the function of Christ's human personality was to act as a porous cork to keep back more of God's activity than man can take—like some piece of laboratory apparatus—verges upon the theologically obscene.

Hence thirdly, what right has Sanday to placard his theory as more spiritual and less materialistic than the Patristic theology set in terms of "substance". The Patristic terminology as applied to spiritual natures can scarcely be seriously envisaged as material; Sanday's theory, on the other hand, cannot be anything but materialistic, since the mode of union of the two natures and the communication from the one to the other is exclusively a process within the workings of a material brain.

Fourthly, Dr. Sanday's assertion that his theory in which a horizontal line may be drawn through the thoughts and acts of Christ is more satisfactory than one in which a vertical line is drawn, is one which can scarcely have received much enthusiastic support at the time. No line-drawing across the psychical or physical activities of Christ is ever satisfactory or possible, in whatever direction the line is drawn. That many liberal scholars did in fact assume that such a radical distinction between human and divine was the essence of Chalcedonian theology has been alluded to more than once; such a distinction is not Patristic orthodoxy but Nestorian heresy, and as such, utterly inadequate to express the facts relating to Christ's Person. No more, then, can a theory based upon a horizontal distinction present a satisfactory account of the Person of Christ; for where such a line exists there can be no real unity or union of personal activity, but only the activity of two separate centres of thought and action. This leads back to the fundamental point to be stressed in regard to this theory: it envisages the activity of a personal human subject, a completely constituted man, whose personality as shown to men is that of a human individual. "What there is of divine in him" resides in and is connected with the unconscious regions of his being. The overriding difficulty in the way of accepting the anthropocentric solution is this very fact—that a line can be drawn—that there can be a distinction within his being between the conscious activity of the personal manhood and the unconscious functioning of the divine nature. It is not helpful to criticize the theory on the ground that it merely depicts an inspired man—much more is both intended and provided for than that. But at its maximum even, it cannot portray one who was personally God the Son, speaking and acting as a knowable and recognisable human individuality.

Dr. Sanday hails with approval the eighth essay in the Hibbert Journal supplement *Jesus or Christ*, entitled "A Divine Incarnation", by Sir Oliver Lodge. In the view of this writer, every man alive is an Incarnation, having a soul with a transcendental existence, and a body with its physical life and heredity, a being in fact at whose conception part of the transcendental stuff comes into union with a fleshly body; which in the case of what we call inspired men grows into close union with it. This then must also be the process of The Incarnation—" 'A flower in a crannied wall' is an incarnation which is in intimate touch with the whole universe. And shall not the spirit of a man be larger and greater than that which animates his body and enters his consciousness"?[1] There is a larger self which except in the case of rare geniuses never enters the region of their normal consciousnesses. Yet— "Among all the lofty spirits which ever became incarnate on the earth, one supremely divine spirit entered our flesh and walked on

[1] *Jesus or Christ*, p. 117.

the planet for a time, was born, loved, suffered, and died, even as one of us".[1]

Such a theory as this naturally stands outside the general development of English Christology, but as a side-show it is most interesting. This, like the rest of Lodge's work is obviously intended to constitute a scientific rationale of spiritual truths, e.g. the existence of the soul.[2] It is difficult to see how the science of to-day could afford much ratification for his conclusions; e.g. the large fields within the personality occupied by the determinating forces of heredity and experience leave little room for a "scientific" demonstration of the existence of the soul.

Lodge's view has a superficial similarity to that of Sanday, but its differences are great, which when noted show both theories up in relief. Lodge's "larger self" is not the subconscious mind, which is a region of purely natural brain processes, but an ethereal substance which belongs to the world of spirit and not of flesh. To Lodge, Christ differs from men because he is a more noble spirit, and because that spirit was able to impart more to and through its body than is the case with us. He is no more specially divine than in the immanentist sense, whereas Sanday would hold that the divine nature pervading the subconsciousness of Christ was exclusively and personally God.

## A Disciple of I. A. Dorner

Whilst combing through the long lists of writers belonging to the period, it was often hoped to discover an English disciple of Dr. Dorner; and since one has in fact been found, it will be worth while describing his Christology, not owing to any celebrity on the part of the disciple himself, but on account of the system itself which has had so profound an influence upon the shape of modern Christology, English as well as continental, and not least because it provides a very clear illustration of the anthropocentric solution of the Christological problem as it was then apparent.

Mr. E. A. Litton's two-volume manual entitled *Introduction to Dogmatic Theology* (1892) takes the form of an exposition of the Thirty-Nine Articles.

The writer holds that Anglican theology finds its home not in Catholicism or in a via media but in Protestantism, and in the

[2] *Jesus or Christ*, p. 119.   [1] *Man and the Universe*, 1908.

Reformed rather than the Lutheran branch of Protestantism, and his exposition, therefore, moves from Holy Scripture, through some guarded references to the Fathers, to the description of Reformed theology, classical and modern.

Jesus Christ is truly and fully man. That, as usual, is the first axiom—here stressed with more than usual significance, as will appear. His body and soul underwent the normal development in the Virgin's womb, and he underwent a natural birth. Throughout his life, Christ exhibited properly human emotions, such as love and grief, possessed a natural understanding, passed through the ordinary stages of growth both physical and moral.[1]

In order to account for this human condition of Christ's life, two possible explanations are rejected as unsatisfactory: The Lutheran theory which suggests that the humanity which possessed the divine attributes kept them hidden during the life on earth is unsatisfactory because such a krypsis is a logical contradiction—having power, and yet restraining the use of it—and therefore introduces an air of unreality into the manhood.[2] To repress such divine powers would itself require a conscious act of will—even if it were possible—and it is difficult to see how a baby could exercise such an act of will.

Preference must therefore be given to the Reformed view—which he considers to be nearer the truth—which holds that the Logos, before the Incarnation (and not the manhood itself), suffered self-limitation. This made a union with true manhood possible. The Incarnation, therefore, irrespective of later humiliations was itself a *kenosis*. Thus there arises the second view, that in becoming man Christ suspended his own divine self-consciousness, gradually recovering it as the babe Christ grew to maturity. This, however, he argues, would tend to eclipse the Trinity, and is inconsistent with the formula of Chalcedon (it is curious to discover someone at this time allowing that fact to worry him). In any case, he argues, the Person of God the Son is indivisible from his nature. This leads him to state his own view, which he offers as a variant of the Reformed theory.

"The only other conceivable mode of self-limitation is that which leaves the Logos in full possession of his active Personality, but supposes that the fullness of the divine nature was not at once communicated to the human, but gradually accorded to the receptivity of the latter. That is, the union was not, as the

[1] *Loc cit.*, vol. I, p. 226.     [2] *ibid.*, p. 249.

Lutheran Divines teach, complete from the first, but was itself a process, involving successive acts; a continual efflux of the divine nature into the human, not an act perfected at once".[1]

One cannot resist a passing protest against the narrow perspective of a theologian whose Christendom consists of Lutherans and Reformed—quite ignoring the preponderating mass of Catholic scholarship of all ages. Such a contraction in outlook is calculated to convey a mistaken impression regarding the acceptation of his view. The universally accepted Catholic doctrine regarding the completeness of the act of Incarnation from the first is rejected as just Lutheran, whilst his own view, represented as the only sane interpretation of Reformed theology, is exalted to Œcumenical significance, when in reality it is, the speculation of a mere handful.

According to Litton, then, the manner, intensity, and intimacy, of the union of God and man in Christ kept pace with the development of the manhood, so that at no stage was there any incongruous or abnormal element present in the consciousness or the appearance of Christ. The following statement carries the argument still deeper:

"The Logos *inter carnem* was never during the earthly life present in his fullness as he is *extra carnem*; not because he abdicated his essential Godhead, but because he had not communicated it to the manhood in all its fullness, nor could do so until the manhood was *capax infiniti*".[2]

Surely it is a curious inversion of New Testament teaching to begin with the presupposition that the Logos is not as fully present within Christ as he is outside him!

Litton holds that this theory secures Christ's sinlessness and infallibility without his having to be omniscient: the knowledge of his origin and mission kept pace with his natural growth, and when the suggestion to evil arose, "It was instantly repelled through the power of the indwelling Logos".[3] "The indwelling Logos" is a favourite and significant expression of this type of anthropocentric Christology.

The first comment which may be offered with regard to this first portion of the theory is that, like Dr. Sanday's view, it is misleadingly presented as a kenotic theory, whereas in reality, despite some of its superficial aspects, it is nothing of the kind.

[1] *Introduction to Dogmatic Theology*, vol. I, p. 250.  [2] *ibid.*, p. 251.
[3] *ibid.*, p. 229.

According to this view, the divine Logos suffers no contraction, restriction, or diminution, in personality, nature, or attributes. The "limitation" is solely that in so far as he has willed to express himself to men *as a man*, he can therefore only reveal himself gradually, and in small doses. This is not what is usually meant by *kenosis*, a self-emptying on the part of God: There is no exinanition here even "within the sphere of the Incarnation" to use Gore's expression; the only limitation is that the Logos chose a manner of revelation which by its nature severely restricted the amount of revelation which could be given.

In the second place, the theory of gradual Incarnation—for such it is—begs far more questions than it answers. The union of God and man in Christ, the Incarnation, is conceived of as a gradual process, and yet it is not strictly correct on this view to assert that God gradually becomes man; what actually happens is that a man is gradually Deified—as he becomes more receptive of the divine Personality. At this point the theory makes perhaps its biggest assumption: that a man of thirty is more capable of union with God than is a child of twelve. On whatever grounds is such an assumption made when Christ himself distinctly informs us that the first prerequisite for entrance into the Kingdom of God is a possession of the child-like virtues? If God and man are akin—as we are told a thousand times—in nature, why does man need to grow in wisdom and stature to enter into closer union with God? Because, we may venture to suggest, the union conceived of in this theory is not one of two complete natures being united under one Person, but a union of two persons, or rather—as we shall see—the union of a human individual with the divine *nature*. A union which requires the intelligence, volition, and affections, of a human individual to accomplish it is obviously a different manner of union from that envisaged in Catholic theology—where God the Son assumes a human nature from the first—not a human person.

The theory goes on to assert that the union is completed when man becomes *capax infiniti*: this is simply meaningless. Man can never be *capax infiniti* in this life in any intelligible sense. In the traditional Christology, such heights of achievement on the part of the humanity are not necessary for the union as they evidently are in this theory where it is conceived as one of active co-operation. If the *capax infiniti* statement does not mean that by maturity the mind of our Lord was merged with the mind of

God—and it is difficult to imagine that it does mean this: then what it simply means is that in the mature Christ, there became present all that God could possibly convey and communicate to his human creatures, concentrated in the soul of this one man. This theory can be stated in such a way as to be no more than an inspiration of Jesus of Nazareth, culminating in the maximum inspiration which any man, the one perfect man, could receive. At this stage, therefore, we may conclude that here we have an anthropocentric Christology, in which Jesus is regarded as a man, truly and fully endowed with human personality, possessing the divine nature as a *donum superadditum*, an inspiration which kept pace with his moral development, without in any way coercing or deflecting that human development. The humanity was thus of so complete a character as could exist on the natural plane without this special inspiration—whose function—in so far as it modifies the actions of the humanity at all—is to preserve it from sin and error.

Litton also shares with Dorner certain other speculative theories of great importance for the understanding of the Christology. As the complicated reasonings leading up to them would be too lengthy, we present the conclusions in summary form. "Nature" cannot just be described by a complex of attributes as in the old Platonic sense; these must co-inhere in an individual or person. Nature, that is, only exists when it is individualised as a personality. Now in God there is but one nature and hence only one personality! The so-called Persons of the Trinity are simply relationships within the one personality of God. What is the Person of the Logos apart from his divine nature? Litton asks. Nothing but his filial relationship within the Godhead—just as a human father does not possess a personality *qua* father, but *qua* man.[1] Hence to ask, as St. Thomas does, whether the union took place within the Person or the nature of the Logos is meaningless. The Trinitarian *hypostasis*, therefore, without the connotation of his nature—the Godhead itself—does not seem capable of assuming a human nature. The union, therefore, was not just in one Person of the Trinity, but in the nature of God, the Incarnation being a work of the Trinity itself, terminating (to use scholastic language) in the Person of the Son. "Does it not seem to follow that if the Person of the Son is severed from his nature, while the two natures are to be considered as abstractions, not

[1] *Introduction to Dogmatic Theology*, p. 253.

living realities, little place is left for a true personal subject, a thinking and willing agent, in the Incarnate Logos".[1] Stated in plain language, what this theory means is that the Persons of the Trinity do not possess individuality, in the sense of anything approaching an ego, or self-acting principle, but are at most different faculties of the divine nature, or God looked at from different angles—the basic implication of "relationship". It would be out of place in a study on Christology to offer any detailed comment upon this novel doctrine of the Trinity. It may, however, be pointed out that behind the above-described reasoning lies the grave fallacy of *petitio principii*: on the recognized principle that a divine Person cannot be separated from his nature, the altogether baseless assumption is made that God's Person, or Persons, equal his nature; and since there is but one nature, then there can only be one Person, in the fullest sense of the word. The theory well illustrates that monophysite tendency alluded to more than once of equating "nature" and "person". Such a view reacts upon the doctrine of the Incarnation in two ways: as it minimizes the personality of God the Son, making him a mere aspect of God's nature-person on the one hand, it makes it necessary to suppose on the other hand that Christ's humanity being a complete nature was fully personal. The Person of the Son, then, in so far as he can be called a Person, becomes gradually united to a fully personal manhood: on this view, the divine nature thus present is the less personal of the two constituents. To outward knowledge, at any rate, Jesus Christ was a human individual, whatever lay beneath. In such a Christ, the ego of personality of the manhood is clearly the decisive and recognisable part of him; the indwelling Logos—only gratuitously called a Person—lies beneath the surface. Such is almost certainly the view of Dorner himself. Mr. Litton, on the other hand, lays more stress upon the Incarnation of the whole Trinity itself, focused, as it were, in that part of it which exhibits the filial relationship. Clearly, neither Litton, nor Dorner, nor anyone else in his right mind, would ever suggest that the whole personality of God, the Trinity, itself became the ego of the Incarnate Christ, the subject of the life-circumstances of Jesus of Nazareth; the idea would be preposterous. Hence in Mr. Litton's system, the divine side of the Incarnate Christ is reduced even more than ever to being a mere inspiration, an influence from on high. Such

---

[1] *Introduction to Dogmatic Theology*, vol. I, p. 254.

## THE ANTHROPOCENTRIC SOLUTION

must of necessity be the upshot of the system, in its God-ward aspect. What of the human element in Christ? Litton asserts quite frankly that there can be no such thing as a common human nature of us all, possessed by Christ impersonally—except in so far as the Logos himself personalizes it. This might have been deduced from his principles, had he not stated the belief. Litton asserts that an impersonal humanity—if such a thing could ever be conceived of—would simply not be humanity at all, if it did not possess that highest characteristic of humanity, the human ego and individuality; it would be just mutilated humanity without it. According to orthodox Christology, "Christ would seem to have a human nature defective in the property of personality on the summit of which, to supply the defect, is placed the divine personality of the Logos".[1] Such a view he rejects as not only philosophically untenable, but tending to destroy the true humanity of Christ.

In both of the theories considered under the heading of this chapter, the human individuality or personality of Christ is regarded as, not simply the focal point of Christ's person, but as that part of him which men held converse with. The two most obvious defects of such a system are, first, that it is virtually impossible to speak of such a one as personally God and Divine, since the Person we know and read about is personally man; and secondly, it is hardly possible to speak of God becoming man, living himself as a human, a human life from its centre, when he only dwells with a man as a hidden nature or influence beneath that otherwise complete human consciousness thus assumed. Yet these theories differ from those to be considered in the next chapter in that they do seek to account for a completely personal unity within Christ, whose very nature is composite to the core; they postulate real indwelling, and not merely external affinity.

[1] *Introduction to Dogmatic Theology*, p. 257.

# 12

## THE NEO-ANTIOCHENE SOLUTION

WE turn finally to a group of writers who sought for the solution to the problems relating to the personality of Christ along the lines of a school of thought marked out long ages ago. There was no attempt at conscious imitation, neither is any acknowledgement made regarding the source of the ideas thus put forward, though to the theological eye, the family kinship is plain to be seen. The theory represents the farthest reaction from the Patristic and scholastic approach with its Platonic and Aristotelean categories. Many were those who believed the language of substance, nature, form, etc., to be quite inadequate to express things which after all were realities of a higher order than material existences, higher even than the realms of human psychology. Terms such as essence and nature appeared to refer to static conditions rather than to active and vital relationships which characterise the world of spirits: hence expressions relating to will, power, energy, love, appeared to be far more suitable media for conveying truths regarding such living forces as the activities of God. Hence the tacit appeal was not made to the later theology of the school of Antioch, much though that system still appeared to guarantee Christ's real humanity. For the theology of Theodore of Mopsuestia, of Diodore, and of Theodoret, is just as much bound down with the materialistic terminology as that of their Alexandrian opponents. The appeal is rather made in the direction of the school of Antioch in its more youthful days, when the humanity of Christ and the union of the natures was sought for in an active principle of unity—generally known to the world under the label of Dynamic Monarchianism. Harnack regards as one of the greatest tragedies ever to have befallen Christian theology the condemnation of Paul of Samosata. It is without doubt the principle for which Paul stood that is what the writers presently to be considered apprehended as the only known basis for a satisfactory Christology.

## John Caird

In the very earliest years of our period, when many good men were wrangling over the interpretation of Mk. 10. 27 and 13. 32, a writer was putting forward suggestions of a far-reaching character with regard to the fundamental expression of the truth about Christ.

The Gifford lectures on natural theology were delivered in 1892–3 and 1895–6 by John Caird, Principal and Vice-chancellor of Glasgow University. In a memoir prefixed to the lectures, his brother Edward, in speaking of the lecturer's early preaching, notes that its emphasis was upon Christ's union with us rather than upon his atoning death. This approach, so different from the earlier evangelical outlook, may well have been the point from which Caird's Christology expanded. It is not fair to indict such an approach, as some have done, as treacherously ignoring the facts of soteriology. There is still a deep interest and concern with soteriology, but Christ is conceived of as saving in a rather different manner than heretofore emphasised. Even so great a mind as Forsyth is not free from the tendency to dub as un-evangelical any system that does not place the Cross in the forefront.

At the outset of the lectures on *The Fundamental Ideas of Christianity* Caird enunciates two presuppositions, already familiar to us in the theology of the day, upon which the Christology later to be described would be based. He writes:

"The Divinity of Christ, however we conceive it, was a Divinity that was capable of being expressed in a human life and through the words and acts of a human personality. Say that his was a perfect life, that it touched the supreme height of what is possible for a being made in God's image, yet whatever lay absolutely beyond the range of human nature, whatever of Divinity could not organically unite itself with and breathe through a human spirit, was not and could not be present in one who, whatever else he was, was really and truly human".[1]

Caird pleads for a re-defining of God in ethical terms, but the statement does mean that, absolutely speaking, the infinite divine Person cannot be united with manhood so as to constitute one living, thinking, organism. In the second place he writes:

"The Divinity of Christ was not that of a divine nature in local

[1] *The Fundamental Ideas of Christianity*, p. 14.

or mechanical juxtaposition with a human, but of a divine nature that suffused, blended, identified itself with the thoughts, feelings, volitions of a human individual".[1]

In the first place, he has stated that none of the divine glory is revealed which is not mediated through the human life, and that Christ's manhood was fully personal, "a human individual". There is a distinct hint of what later in the hands of Moberly, as above noted, became the idea of the interpenetration of personalities; but the thought, unfortunately, is not further alluded to or developed by this writer.

The Twelfth of the Lectures is entitled "The Possibility of Moral Restoration", in which the writer elaborates the grounds upon which man's dignity could be rehabilitated, and hence how the Incarnation fulfils this task. It was observed above that Caird's Christology was dependent upon his own soteriology just as much as any other theologian, hence it will serve well to begin at this point with him.

He writes that before the work of Christ on a man, he is faced with an unequal struggle, attacked from within and without, nor is conscience any help by itself to sin's abolition, so long as his temptations are too strong for him—the rather dull path of duty being more than offset by the allurements of the passions. Is there any means of turning the consciousness of sin to good effect, and disarming the passions of their power and bringing them "into subjection to that higher and better self which has in it the principle of a divine or infinite life"?[2] Christianity provides the answer by supplying the motive of love which reinforces dull duty, making it pleasant, and hence stronger than the lower inclinations. Such an ideal could be presented to man only in the form of loving self-conscious personality.[3] It must be truly human personality, for that is the highest we can know of God, being his image: "If therefore the moral ideal is to be identified in our thought with a living, self-conscious personality, it can only be with that of a perfect humanity, and, in the first instance, at least, of a perfect individual human life".[4] Such conditions are fulfilled by Christ who not only left a perfect example for us to follow but an abiding personal influence upon his followers.

Such an approach could well be accepted by the traditional apologist, as far as it goes, though as a view of atonement it is

[1] *The Fundamental Ideas of Christianity*, p. 14.
[2] ibid., II. 89.   [3] ibid., II. 89.   [4] ibid., II. 89.

## THE NEO-ANTIOCHENE SOLUTION

perfectly useless: To supply a man with good and attractive motives cannot save him from sin—the instincts, and consequently in our fallen state the misuse of the instincts, are the most powerful forces within him. Man can know the good; that does not mean he can do it; the fault lies in the will itself.

One must generally make some allowances in any strictly theological arguments which appear in Gifford lectures, for the lecturer will argue upwards from the natural to the supernatural; hence the argument of this chapter cannot be taken as Principal Caird's ultimate rationale of the Incarnation. But it is not without significance that the argument thus described only reaches the conclusion that Jesus Christ must be truly man, without suggesting any good reasons why he must also in the same sense be truly God. The apologetic of the time was always hesitant on the matter of God coming in the flesh.

The three following lectures are exclusively Christological. The method employed is virtually that of the *reductio ad absurdum* proposition—eliminating one by one the various attempts made in the past to arrive at a solution, and after closing every by-way, to state his own conclusions.

In the thirteenth lecture, for example, which bears the sub-title "Theories that exclude or modify the divine element in the nature of Christ" (note, incidentally, that the word "nature" is used of Christ in the singular), he disposes of two such systems. First, he deals with the obvious physical difficulties in the way of the Incarnation:

"Do not the attributes we commonly ascribe to God, such as omnipresence, omnipotence, eternity, immutability, express ideas which are essential to his nature, without which he would cease to be divine: and can we conceive of these as belonging to a being who exists in time and space, who is mortal and mutable, who begins to be and passes away, and who, at least from one side of his nature, is but a transient link in a vast system of material causes and effects by which his individuality is infinitely transcended"?[1]

"To obviate this difficulty of uniting incompatible attributes in a single self-conscious subject, popular thought has sometimes had recourse to the too obvious expedient of separating in time the seemingly contradictory elements, and of ascribing some of the acts and experiences of Christ to the divine, and others to the

[1] *The Fundamental Ideas of Christianity*, II. 105.

human, side of his composite nature. As man, he passed through the changeful experiences of human life, its physical and mental growth, its gradually expanding knowledge, its moral temptations and conflicts, its manifold sorrows and sufferings, and especially the physical pain and mental agony of his passion, and the death with which it terminated. These were experiences which it is impossible that an omnipotent, immutable being should undergo. On the other hand, in his miraculous works, his power over nature, his arresting of disease, and restoring life to the dead, his transfiguration, resurrection and ascension—in these a superhuman glory flashed forth from beneath the veil of his humanity, and the presence in him of a divine nature was disclosed".[1]

Against this view, Caird advances, first, that it destroys the unity of Christ's Person and life—"It virtually asserts that he was not always throughout his whole life the God-man, but only now the God and now the man".[2] And secondly, that it militates against his views regarding the atonement, since "For many minds, the sufferings and death of Christ would be deprived of their atoning value and efficacy, if there were nothing more in them than the sufferings and death of a merely human hero, or of a human personality".[3]

The above is the criticism of a caricature of Chalcedonian Christology: it is the old method of crying "Wolf, wolf", for no council or universally accredited doctor of the church has ever taught such a doctrine. In the last quotation, the atonement is seen as something which exclusively concerns man—it is never for one moment considered what may atone in the sight of God for man's sin.

The second view which Caird refutes is styled the Unitarian or Deistic view, whereby the difficulty of uniting Deity with real humanity "has been met by reducing the divine element in his person simply to a divine or superhuman influence analogous to that of prophetic inspiration, perpetually operating on his human consciousness and bringing it into unbroken harmony with the mind and will of God".[4] Caird's reply to this line of thought on pp. 117 ff. should be noted carefully, in view of the conclusions which he himself will ultimately arrive at. Caird replies that the Deistic theory is based upon the presupposition of the impassibility of God, his inability to participate in the feelings of a human soul;

[1] *The Fundamental Ideas of Christianity*, II. 107.
[2] *ibid.*, II. 108.   [3] *ibid.*, II. 109.   [4] *ibid.*, II. 112.

## THE NEO-ANTIOCHENE SOLUTION

whereas the Christian mind can be satisfied with nothing less than God himself actually participating in our sorrows, thus providing us with not a mere finite but an infinite example.

Caird therefore does not condemn this view *qua* moral union, but simply because the view of God envisaged is not sufficiently ethical to permit of such a completely ethical and sympathetic union.

The fourteenth lecture, bearing the same sub-title as the previous one, is devoted entirely to a criticism of the kenotic theory, that theory, as he puts it, "according to which the higher principle in the Person of Christ is not absolute Deity, but Deity by an act of infinite condescension so divesting itself of its essential glory as to be capable of taking on itself the nature of man".[1] This theory is shown to be untenable, (a) for as a matter of sheer fact it is a logical contradiction of itself. "Can we attach any meaning to the notion of a self-limiting, self-emptying God—the notion, that is, of omnipotence causing itself to become powerless, of omniscience resolving to be ignorant of what it knows, of an infinite will voluntarily determining itself to be incapable of willing? Does not such a notion involve the obvious contradiction of a nature which at once is and is not, which asserts itself in the very act of denying itself"?[2] (b) This act of humiliation, moreover, would not only have to be, as some have imagined, a single act of abandonment, but would have to continue throughout the whole period of the Incarnation which is even more incredible—infinite power remains infinite in the very act of repressing itself. (c) It is, even if conceivable, difficult to see how such a depotentiated God would differ in any practical degree from a mere man, hence (d) His experiences and sufferings would only be those of a mere man not those of true God. (e) What becomes of the governance of the world during the Incarnation? And (f) the modification of the theory in which the humiliation is spoken of as "veiling" is equally unsatisfactory, since by it Christ becomes a concealment of God's nature, a travesty of the idea of revelation. Caird shows that he has considerable sympathies with the religious aims which lie behind the kenotic theory. He admits the strong appeal made by the divine self-sacrifice idea, but protests that God does not need to become finite in order to suffer with us, since the wider our own knowledge and

[1] *The Fundamental Ideas of Christianity*, II. 124.
[2] *ibid.*, II. 127.

understanding, the greater our sympathy and compassion becomes.

Caird's criticisms of the kenotic theory throw this much light upon his own view: by denying the necessity, as well as the possibility, of God's modification of his attributes, he makes it clear that he regards the mode of union as one which in no way necessitates the participation of the Deity in the incidental bodily or mental restrictions of Christ's life, but a sharing of his feelings, his love and his sufferings; nothing is done to modify the physical or metaphysical constitution proper to God or man.

All this becomes even more apparent in the fifteenth lecture, sub-headed "Theories that exclude or modify the human element in the nature of Christ", of which he takes Apollinarianism as a typical example. But before doing so, he makes an excursus of great importance. He asks—"Is it possible to conceive of two complete spiritual natures, two self-consciousnesses, self-determining beings, as losing their separate individuality and becoming so blended as to constitute one self-conscious personality? . . . Can we think of one conscious being as dropping its independent identity and passing into that of another, or of two such beings as abandoning each its own independent consciousness and spiritual life, and being so transformed as to constitute a new personality which is both in one? . . . The wildest imagination has never attempted to represent a single personality as, all through its career and at every moment of it, possessed of a double consciousness, or a single self which was the combined result of two selves reduced to one".[1] According to this passage, to reduce it to more manageable proportions, three possibilities are being excluded: the first is the case of two personalities coalescing to form one new or composite personality; secondly, the case of one personality being absorbed into another, the latter retaining its proper identity; and thirdly, a single personality consisting of two self-consciousnesses. Such a rejection Caird bases upon the following considerations: "Is it not the essential characteristic of a spiritual subject—that which raises it above the unconscious existence of nature, above the life of the animal, in which the race is all, the individual nothing—that it possesses an individuality, an isolated identity, in virtue of which it is for itself to the exclusion of every other, which can be invaded or shared by no other, and the moral life and acts of which are inalienably and unalterably its own".[2]

[1] *The Fundamental Ideas of Christianity*, II, 149.  [2] *ibid.*, II. 150.

## THE NEO-ANTIOCHENE SOLUTION

Only material substances, he points out, can combine in such a way as to lose each its separate identity. "Even if it be possible", Caird continues, "to think of two human beings as so closely alike in their intellectual and moral natures that their ideas should be perfectly coincident, their feelings and affections absolutely sympathetic, their wills in every volition and action, all through life completely concurrent, they would still be, not one mind and will, but two: the intelligence of each its own intelligence, the process by which its opinions are reached a process going on in its own mind and not in the other's, the moral acts of each involving a personal responsibility intransferable to the other".[1] Such a total union or absorption would be even more inconceivable in the case of an infinite and a finite personality; for, "Can an omnipotent will be conceived to reside in the same spirit with a limited human will without dominating and suppressing it? In such a coalition, would not all real activity on the part of the latter be suspended, and its moral independence, its very existence, be virtually extinguished"?[2]

Caird took his stand upon the belief in a moral and spiritual unity between Christ and God; yet here he explicitly robs himself of the one line which could ensure the totality of such a union—a course of action which the next writer to be considered certainly avoids at all costs. Caird flatly refuses to have any dealings with that view of personality which conceives of the possibility of interpenetration. "The wildest imaginations" were as a matter of fact busily engaged in conceiving of such a view as he scorns, for only a few years were to elapse before *Atonement and Personality* and Wilfrid Richmond's essay were to see the light of day. Caird resolutely maintains the exclusive view of personality, that view in which it is conceived of as an absolute and indivisible, and even uncombinable unit, as the atom was originally intended to stand in relation to the physical world.

Caird's immediate purpose was to criticize the heresy of Apollinarius, to whom it had seemed impossible that two wills could exist side by side within the same person. He criticizes Apollinarius along the conventional lines—that his view provides no real union between God and man but only between God and an animal; and gives no remedy against sin at its source, within the human spirit—and then proceeds at once to his own reconstruction: First, a passage which appears to be more rhetorical

[1] *The Fundamental Ideas of Christianity*, II. 151.  [2] *ibid.*, II. 152.

than dogmatic in character—"Instead of the presence and action of God in the human spirit involving an impossible dualism, or a suppressing of human individuality, the true conception is rather that the divine life is the condition of the human, the atmosphere in which alone all spiritual life can exist; and that it is only in union with God that the individual spirit can realize itself and become possessor of the latent wealth of intelligence and goodness that pertains to it. It is true indeed, that there is something unique in the Person of Christ, and that a participation in the being and life of God can be predicated of him as distinguished from all other members of the human race. But, however true it be that the relation of the divine and human in the Person of Christ transcends, in one sense, all earthly parallel, it must yet be a union of which by its very structure and essence humanity is capable".[1] Absolutely speaking, then, Caird would admit that the union is of a type into which any man could enter under given conditions.

What type of union then is possible between spiritual beings, seeing that the possibility of total submergence is ruled out? "The highest kind of unity is not that which is repelled but which is created and conditioned by moral and spiritual individuality; that in other words the oneness which is most real and absolute is not that which is attained by the absence or suppression of individual distinctions, but that which involves yet transcends them".[2] The parts of a stone, he points out, are all alike, and hence have a certain unity together. So too the parts of a machine have a unity, but because they are all different, their unity is of a higher order. This is even more true of the parts of a living organism—a stage higher. Hence, he concludes, the relation of self-conscious beings when brought into union makes them even more individual still. This is shown by the fact that as our range of sympathy or fellowship with others increases, we enoble ourselves also, as is seen in the fact that the highest human virtues are self-sacrifice, devotion to duty, and love. Hence we have each to find our complement in others—*a fortiori*, in God. It is "that absolute surrender of thought and will which no man can yield to another, it is the supreme ideal of man's intellectual and moral nature to be capable of yielding to God. . . . It is the very glory of our nature to surrender our intelligence to the infinite wisdom, our will to the all-perfect will: to abandon all

[1] *The Fundamental Ideas of Christianity*, II. 158.   [2] *ibid.*, II. 159.

## THE NEO-ANTIOCHENE SOLUTION

opinions, to suppress every volition that pertains to us as mere individuals, and to let the infinite and eternal life flow into and dominate our whole life and being".[1]

It must be by now clear to any student of these three lectures that somehow or other Principal Caird has bitten his own tail. He has forged a rationale of the Incarnation either aspect of which leads into the postulation of views which he has previously condemned in the most rigorous terms. He has offered a theory of moral union between Christ and God. Taken at its face value, that is to say, on its minimum side, how can such a theory possibly be said to differ essentially from that Christology described and condemned in Lecture XIII, as the Unitarian and Deistic view? According to that view, as Caird himself describes it, the human person of Christ is in complete harmony and accord with the Deity through unbroken communion and inspiration: this is precisely what Caird's own view amounts to, except that he introduces a doctrine of the divine compassion.

A maximum view, on the other hand, in which the union involves a complete and organic junction of human and divine is ruled out by the statements in the opening section of Lecture XV that however close two persons may approach one another in mind and intent they still remain two separate persons.[2] Caird would have replied to this that the two separate persons—realising their individuality more and more as they came closer together—by possessing a coincident will, would become as perfectly united as beings of a spiritual nature can be, that is infinitely more united than the parts of a stone, machine or physical body: "It is not two wills but one will, at once human and divine".[3] In the following section of the chapter, the difficulties involved in assigning the union to a coincidence of wills will be discussed. But in any case it is difficult to see how such a union of wills as he envisages at the close of his treatment can escape his own very shrewd criticism of such a union on p. 152. In such a union, he argues there, the divine will would completely dominate the human, so that all moral and intellectual activity on the part of the human person would virtually cease. "When eternal truth discloses itself to the mind, it dissipates all mere individual opinion, it subjects thought with an absolute,

---

[1] *The Fundamental Ideas of Christianity*, II. 166.
[2] See p. 151, II. ibid.
[3] *The Fundamental Ideas of Christianity*, II. 168.

irresistible authority; but it is not an authority which is external to me, but one which utters itself in and through my own mind".[1] It is still possible to urge that Caird has somewhat contradicted himself in this respect.

How does it then come about that Principal Caird has arrived in this predicament? He complains a good many times that the failure alike of old-fashioned orthodoxy, and heresies too, was due to the fact that Divinity and humanity had been defined in such a way as to render them mutually incompatible, e.g. II., p. 111: "Divinity and humanity being conceived of as reciprocally exclusive . . ." He means by this, always defined in metaphysical or physical rather than ethical terms. Yet by his own principles he has done exactly the same thing, he has reared up an insuperable barrier, and his theory crumbles in his own hands. He has so defined personality as to make any such union as he proposes distressingly inconclusive. In the ancient definition of personality, where a substantial soul, or ego—to give it its modern dress—is envisaged, there is no difficulty in positing the possession of two natures—even if that term includes consciousness—of one single person. Similarly, according to one of the modern theories, where room is found within the subliminal self, or in the mutual interpenetration theory, it is not impossible to define the doctrine of Christ's Person in terms of coalition of personality. But where the word is taken to imply a rigid unit, no such perfect accord or oneness can be proposed. Such a union is bound to be an inadequate expression of Christ's Deity, definable only in terms of what each has in common with the other—exactly parallel purpose, identical emotions, etc. It can never be a union but only a perfect similitude. It is true that Dr. Caird twice gives a hint of a non-exclusive view which might have saved the situation: as the sentence on p. 14, already cited, and again, at the very close of Lecture XV he writes—that the mind, heart, will, and consciousness of Christ are "possessed and suffused by the very spirit and life of the living God".[2] But this cannot weigh much against his other explicit statements.

In the terms stated by this author it must be concluded that the Christological solution presents itself as an improved unitarianism. That this is the case is borne out by the very terminology which Caird employs: The divine element is described as "God",

[1] *The Fundamental Ideas of Christianity*, II. 167.
[2] *ibid.*, II. 171.

the human element is regularly described as "Christ". Hence there is no thought of the divine in Christ, in the orthodox sense, being designated God the Son, a divine Person possessing a human nature which bears his own name and title. To this writer there are two Persons involved—God, and a man, Jesus Christ, a perfect man in moral union with God the Father. It is impossible to see how such a view can serve as an adequate intellectual expression of the assertion of Christian faith, "Jesus is personally God". On such a view as Principal Caird's, Christ can only be described as "personally man"; he cannot, on the writer's explicit principles, be designated "personally God".

## William Temple [1]

A view which bears striking similarities to the above, was proposed by Dr. Temple in his contribution to *Foundations* (1912). It resembles Caird's Christology in that it begins with the assumption of the completeness of the personalities, human and divine, constituting the Christ, and seeks a dynamic rather than a physical or hypostatic union of the two: it is perhaps the clearest known exposition of the modern Antiochene interpretation of Christ's Person.

B. H. Streeter had begun his contribution to the volume, entitled "the Historic Christ", with the observation that the question of Christ's limited human knowledge was now no longer a controverted fact but was a *sine qua non* of practically all modern theologians for the last twenty years.[2] That is, of course, an exaggeration of the spread of liberal theology—even to-day, the scholar shut in his study tends to forget that the man in the street is generally either an agnostic or a fundamentalist. But the point serves to illustrate the changed theological atmosphere. It is at the same juncture as Streeter that Dr. Temple takes up his task of explaining the relation of God and man in Christ. Alluding to the intrinsic difficulties in the way of accepting a dogma of Incarnation, he writes—"Thus, for example, the word 'divine' suggests omniscience; then where is the evidence that Jesus of Nazareth was omniscient? He suffered surprise and disappointment and openly stated that he did not know the hour

[1] It should be clearly understood that no criticism is being offered with regard to this writer's later theological opinions, but only in regard to the particular essay under review.
[2] *Foundations*, p. 75.

of the judgment".[1] The liberal victory of the 'nineties is therefore regarded as complete, and we have now moved on to fresh ground, where speculative reconstruction has succeeded a merely destructive exegesis.

In 1857, Frederick [Archbishop] Temple had written: "Our theology has been cast in a scholastic mould, i.e. all based on logic. We are in need of and we are being gradually forced into a theology based on psychology".[2] It was the purpose of this essay to assist in the transformation. To-day it appears curious that men should have so yearned for a theology based upon the language and thought of a merely empirical science—and a very inexact one at that—rather than upon pure reason applied to the data of revelation. In any case, reason and logic would have to be retained even for the elucidation of psychological data and theories—the antithesis is quite false. But as we have more than once observed, the first two decades of the century was a time when psychology was looked upon as a key to unlock every problem.

Dr. Temple begins by attempting to show how inadequate had been the categories of the older theology. The Fathers, for example, had only a logical realm to draw from: Paul of Samossata, he points out, had been the only Father to draw upon psychology. Normally, they dealt with a purely abstract realm of thought; their apparatus was Aristotelean; they envisaged the Incarnation of the Son of God as the union of two substances in one Person, the assumption of impersonal manhood—this was possible, he urges, since sufficient importance was not accorded to the will. But such a conception as that based upon the idea of substances possessing attributes and represented in hypostases could never serve as a permanent basis for theology—"The whole of Greek theology, noble as it is, suffers from a latent materialism".[3] The *reductio ad absurdum* of the whole system was reached in the events of the year 451, in the definition of the council of Chalcedon, which, although it purports to be an exposition of the Faith, merely states the two sides of the problem without offering any solution: it is therefore unscientific, and "is, in fact, a confession of the bankruptcy of Greek Patristic theology".[4] Something has already been said in the second chapter of this charge brought

---

[1] *Foundations*, p. 213.
[2] *ibid.*, p. 226, cited from *Memoirs*, vol. II, p. 517.
[3] *ibid.*, p. 231.  [4] *ibid.*, p. 230.

## THE NEO-ANTIOCHENE SOLUTION

against the formula of Chalcedon and need not be repeated in the present context.

Dr. Temple, therefore, opens his reconstruction by quitting the realms of logic for the categories of politics—for he shows how often the language of theology has been influenced by the prevailing political ideology. Thus the system of monarchy inculcated the idea of a cosmical emperor as Deity, ruling his creation by arbitrary laws. Constitutional and impotent monarchy, on the other hand, produced Deism: "But now that democracy is established", the members of society will only obey the will of the body politic itself, i.e. compulsion from within, and thus to-day the soil was fertile to produce a theology based upon the idea of the indwelling will of God.

The Greek theology based upon the concept of substance had been first applied to the question of the relation of the two natures in Christ, and afterwards, in a slightly differing manner, to the union of the believer with Christ; and Dr. Temple follows much the same method with his own categories, applying them first to Christology itself and then in a similar manner to the union of believer and Lord.

An isolated attempt had been made in ancient times to explain the Incarnation psychologically, by Paul of Samossata, deposed from the see of Antioch in 268. This writer, true to later Antiochene type, had sought to establish a doctrine of the Incarnation in the terms of a union of two wills—that of Jesus of Nazareth united to that of the Godhead. This attempt, so much acclaimed by liberal theologians since it gave full scope for the human personality of Christ, had broken down in its own day owing to the nature of the prevailing psychology, in which the will was looked upon merely as an attribute of the human substance, possessed as a mere faculty by each individual, and not, as it were, the expression of the total personality itself. Dr. Temple was not going to make an idle repetition of Paul's system, and be stifled by the same weakness, for he would not make any attempt to distinguish between will and substance.

"For, after all", he writes, "will is the only substance there is in a man; it is not a part of him, it is just himself as a moral (or indeed 'active') being".[1] No other words than these could serve to express more clearly the difference between the new psychology—or rather, the psychology of that time—and the old:

[1] *Foundations*, p. 247.

the will has ceased to be thought of as a faculty, it has become another name for personality itself. Instead, however, of this new view making heresy and nonsense of the diothelite formula, a Christology based upon the union of two wills—naturally in a rather different context from the old formula—appeared to Dr. Temple to be the only possible basis for an intelligible reconstruction.

With this in view, therefore, he posits the key question: "What then is the relation of the will—that is, the entire active personality of Christ to the Father? It is clear that no final answer can be given until philosophy has provided us with a final account of Personality, both human and divine".[1] Thus, reiterating his emphasis on the term Will, he proceeds to the core of his argument, as follows: "Christ's will, as a subjective function, is of course not the Father's will; but the content of the wills—the purpose—is the same. Christ is not the Father; but Christ and the Father are one. What we see Christ doing and desiring, that we thereby know the Father does and desires. He is the man whose will is united with God's. He is thus the first-fruits of the Creation—the first response from the creation to the love of the creator. But because he is this, he is the perfect expression of the divine in terms of human life. There are not two Gods, but in Christ we see God. Christ is identically God; the whole content of his being—his thought, feeling, and purpose—is also that of God. This is the only 'substance' of a spiritual being, for it is all there is of him at all. Thus, in the language of logicians, formally (as pure subjects) God and Christ are distinct; materially (that is, in the content of the two consciousnesses) God and Christ are one and the same. The human affections of Christ are God's affections; his suffering is God's; his love is God's; his glory is God's".[2] A little further he writes:

"In all our experience there is a subject and object; but in the last resort they are not separable. At any rate the subject is nothing apart from the object. Will is distinguishable from purpose, but apart from purpose, there can be no will: the activity of thinking is distinguishable from any thought, but apart from thoughts there is no thinking. We easily fall into the notion of a self which 'has' various thoughts and purposes; but in truth the self exists in thinking its thoughts and willing its purposes, and apart from its thoughts, purposes and the like, it is just nothing at all. When,

[1] *Foundations*, p. 248.      [2] *ibid.*, pp. 248-9.

therefore, we say that in 'subjective function' Christ is distinct from God, we are speaking of something which, while distinguishable in thought, is not in fact a separate 'thing' from that 'content' which was said to be the whole 'substance' of Christ, and in which Christ and the Father are one".[1]

A similarity between these passages and the writing of John Caird is at once apparent, in the rather special use of terminology. The use of the terms "Christ" and "The Father" in apposition to one another suggests at first sight the relationship of two of the Persons within the Blessed Trinity. But later in the passage, "Christ" becomes "the man", and "the Father" becomes "the divine"; and it therefore becomes apparent that as elsewhere in *Foundations*, terms are being used in a sense readily understandable by the people. Quite clearly then, Dr. Temple has cleared his ground by reducing his whole problem to the relation of two terms—God, and the man, Christ. Such a treatment immediately by-passes all questions posited in terms of the classical theology—of the Persons of the Trinity, or of the natures in Christ.

Serious objection may be taken to such a view as is here advanced in which the idea of personality is entirely connoted by conation—like the view which restricts it to consciousness, it is far too narrow a concept to account for the manifold activity of a spiritual subject; but the chief characteristic of Dr. Temple's theory, without which it cannot be understood, is the idealistic conception of the person as existing in the experiences through which he passes, the view that the person, the mind, the subject, does not exist save in his experiences, thoughts and volitions. It is upon such a basis as this that the writer would build his Christology. Since the subject only subsists in all that goes to make up his active mental life, then two such subjects who share such feelings and volitions can be said to be one—since they only exist separately in the subjective identity, which itself is only separable from the common feelings and volitions in an abstract sense. Such is the bold view erected upon the premises of idealistic philosophy which this writer purposes; a view in which, he would argue, there is to be found the only intelligible type of unity which can pertain between two spiritual subjects.

Assuming that Dr. Temple avoids the pitfall of the absorption of one personality by another as assiduously as Principal Caird,

[1] *Foundations*, pp. 249–50.

there remain many difficulties involved in either asserting a maximum or a minimum interpretation of the theory of the union of two wills, divine and human.

Take first the maximum that the theory can mean. In 1913 there appeared a full-length criticism of *Foundations* by R. A. Knox, under the satirical title *Some Loose Stones*, which is as sparkling as *Foundations* is tedious. In the eighth chapter of his book, Mr. Knox makes one or two criticisms of great value on Dr. Temple's essay.

Dr. Temple had previously condemned the Fathers' theology on the grounds that they had worked upon a purely artificial distinction between substance or essence and hypostasis: For said he in effect, the idea of a substance which could exist apart from, or even be intelligibly thought of apart from, the individualizations of it was an academic refinement which to an age steeped in a totally different philosophy, could have little meaning. But, points out Knox, Dr. Temple immediately proceeds to base his own Christology upon a distinction of a precisely analogous type, namely between the form or subject of a will or purpose and its matter or content—which on his own principles is a distinction only possible in the refinements of logic. God and man, he holds, are united in will—which to him connotes the whole active personality: personally and formally they are distinct, the Person of the one is God, the person of the other is a man; yet the content or purpose of their wills is identical and therefore, on his own showing, in all that matters to us, they can be considered together as one single organic operation. Dr. Temple admits quite frankly that whilst the two subjects are distinguishable in thought, the one is not a separate "thing" from the other. The two are therefore only distinguishable in thought and not in practice: this union he therefore presents to us as the only appropriate union for two spiritual beings. Naturally, it is not a sufficient criticism of the writer to point out that he has based his reconstruction upon an intellectual refinement similar to that which it is intended to replace; it is, however, relevant to point out that the union of God and man thus conceived is at least as closely dependent upon the maintenance of an idealistic philosophy as was ever the Patristic theology linked up with realism. There are, however, objections of a theological character which we would stress in preference to merely philosophical considerations.

## THE NEO-ANTIOCHENE SOLUTION

According to Dr. Temple, the will exists not as a faculty or substantial soul but in the things that are willed, in the content of the purposes. Therefore, for a perfect union of two persons—two wills—a given content of purpose must be shared completely by two individuals. However can it be imagined that God and a man can share an identical content of purpose? In the formation of purpose, the whole of the personality surely co-operates: there is a moral judgment and an intellectual judgment involved in any act of conation—and the intellectual is intrinsically bound up with the moral, as the psychology upon which Temple based his theory plainly teaches. Consequently, in order freely to express the same purposes as God—to say nothing of experiencing the same feelings as God—the man Christ would of necessity have had to be endowed with a personality like that of God, otherwise he could never have thought the thoughts of God and willed the purposes of God. Dr. Temple does in fact confess a difficulty in the way of his theory arising out of Christ's limitation of knowledge, but attempts to overcome this by yet another distinction. He points out that in the world of spiritual realities, the element of quantity does not apply, concepts such as "whole" and "part" are irrelevant; what matters is quality. Even this distinction still leaves room for the objection that finitude and the creaturely status do not simply imply diminuity in size, but a spiritual outlook of an altogether diminutive type—it is mere arrogance on man's part to imagine that if he were hypothetically as pure as his unfallen nature had been he could then think the thoughts of God. Furthermore, although it may be true that moral law and hence moral judgment can exist and be formed without any circumstantial knowledge or empirical circumstance, yet the idealist would surely admit that not only does man's will manifest itself and exist solely in the thousand and one decisions of everyday life, but even in those cases where an almost purely "qualitative" or moral judgment is required, it is specifically determined by the empirical circumstances.

Now the content of Christ's will, as of every man, was filled with the affairs of human life in its every aspect: how then can its content be said to be coincident with the divine mind? Furthermore, the moral judgments of such a human person together with the intellectual, were formed through the manifold influences of circumstance, emotion, inhibition, heredity, and everything which goes to make up our mental state at any given moment of life:

such a mode of purpose-forming is totally different from that which pertains to God, formed as it is within the divine omniscience, and unless it be conceded that the human Christ were illuminated or coerced, it is difficult to see how his purpose would always circumstantially coincide with that of God—even though his conscience and moral integrity were always flawless. If then the Person of Christ is not to be thought of as an automaton, it is not easy to see how his mental content can intelligibly be conceived as totally coincident with the mind of God.

It must be of even greater importance to insist upon the absolute fixity of the human will of Christ to a theology wholly based upon a psychological union than it was, say, to the ancient diothelites, whose formula was merely ancillary to a doctrine of the hypostatic union of the two natures.

To provide for such a fixity of direction, it might be argued that the human will would have to be reduced to impotence by divine coercion, and would in fact cease to be a free will. Dr. Temple frankly faces this point, by insisting that "a man's will is most 'free', not when he may do anything and no one can count on him, but just when he is quite dependable, and *must* do this, or *can't* do that".[1] This, of course, is one of the classic arguments in justification of Christian freedom, and in the present instance is very pertinent; but Dr. Temple's use of it demonstrates the fact that his view is not meant to imply that maximum interpretation discussed above—for if Christ's human will, entirely by the workings of its own personality, conceived purposes which in fact were coincident with the purpose and mind of God, then such a reply would be pointless, since there would then be no question of Christ's will ever doing anything which had not the full support of its intellectual and moral background.

Assuming therefore that Dr. Temple does not mean us to understand by his theory that the two minds, purposes, or "wills" as he terms it, have all things in common—which would be the only sufficient foundation for such a union as is conceived to exist; then it must be intended that we should understand that the human Christ in all that he did and thought conformed in his limited sphere to that portion of the divine will which was relevant to himself. Here there are difficulties too. Let the proposition be stated in its barest form: Every volition of Christ is in

[1] *Foundations*, p. 247.

## THE NEO-ANTIOCHENE SOLUTION 321

complete harmony with the will of God. Then, quite apart from the question already alluded to as to whether this could itself be achieved without the pressure of coercing grace, the situation can best be represented by a figure, elsewhere employed by Dr. Temple, of a small circle—representing the area of the human volition of Christ—inside a larger circle—representing the total divine will. If this is what is meant, and there seems little doubt that it is so, two cardinal objections at once present themselves. In the first place, and this would apply equally to a maximum interpretation, a union of active will or purpose is in reality only one of coincidence of purpose. To suggest that the content of will, which is supposed to furnish the individual with real existence, is itself of such a stuff as to make of two individuals one unit, is to give to thoughts a materialized content which defies imagination. God and man would simply be united by an abstraction, which is all that purpose is; they might agree in that purpose, but they would still be separate individuals.

In the second place, and this was made clear when discussing the theory of John Caird, it is quite impossible to designate Jesus as God or even divine, simply because in all things he does God's will.[1] If it only requires perfect conformity with God's will for a man for him to be divine, how can Christ's condition be said to differ from that of one of the saints—from the Virgin Mary, for instance, who is traditionally represented as being actually sinless, or from a newly baptized baby which dies before having committed any sin?

Surely under such conditions, Christ is only called divine by a figure of speech or as a courtesy title. In this sense, then, God may be said to have become man, become Incarnate, in that a given human individual, Jesus Christ, lived a human life thoroughly attuned to the divine will, that in and through this man, the perfect will and character of God became manifest to men—in so far as men are capable of understanding it. That this is what the Christian church has *never* meant by its teaching with regard to the Incarnation is obvious; yet, as was seen in the eighth chapter, it is possible to employ traditional language on a lavish scale without any apparent indication that the underlying meaning has vanished. Again we may draw attention to the nomenclature, clearly chosen with great deliberation. To the writers considered in this chapter there are but two terms, God and

[1] See Knox, *Loose Stones*, pp. 151–5.

Jesus, called Christ, and by courtesy called divine: it is a Christology to which no sincere Unitarian could take exception.

In view of Dr. Temple's allusions to the "indwelling will of God", it may be surmised that the theory thus outlined is intended to be a variant of the immanentist Christology, in this case the special manifestation of the divine presence being manifested in the expression by Christ of the divine will.

Thus too, Dr. Temple, like Principal Caird, is not a kenoticist; for he posits no abandonment on the part of the Deity, but only a restriction in the mode of expression adopted by him.

Dr. Temple extends his method, as the Fathers had done with theirs, to the matter of the union of the believer with Christ. He had taken as his starting-point Moberly's dictum "Christ is not generically but inclusively man", upon which he comments: "Christ's inclusiveness is not substantial, but spiritual, not quantitative but qualitative—that is, it is accomplished through personal influence".[1] As spiritual substance to Dr. Temple is represented by personality, i.e. will, then Christ is representative of man, not as mankind now is but as all men will become—which, on his own showing must mean that all men will one day become quasi-divine.

R. A. Knox here objects that such a doctrine of the union of believer to Christ through personal influence, cemented in the union of purpose either means a suppression of individuality or a mere metaphorical association conveying no ingrafting in nature. It may be replied, however, that such a criticism would apply equally to the Patristic theology, in which the believer is conceived of as united to Christ in a substantial manner—the work of his regeneration of human nature being effected in this way. The analogy is not, however, quite so accurate, since in Greek theology, the believer through the sacraments partakes of the Sacred Humanity of Christ and hence of the saving benefits which belong to it; there is no question of the believer's hypostatic union with the Godhead: whereas in Dr. Temple's thought the union of believer and Christ is exactly similar to that pertaining between Christ and God.

We may conclude our survey of the neo-Antiochene type of Christology with the tentative reconstruction along the same lines offered by the ubiquitous Dr. Garvie, who writes as follows:

[1] *Foundations*, p. 253.

## THE NEO-ANTIOCHENE SOLUTION 323

"1. The perfect moral ideal (God) is the absolute metaphysical reality; 2. The metaphysical relations of the universe must be expressed not in terms of physics (nature) but in terms of ethics (personality); 3. The highest ethical term is personality, which is eternally realised in God, but only being progressively realised in an ethical process in man; 4. Accordingly the metaphysical reality of the union of God and man in Christ is most adequately and satisfactorily expressed as a personal union realised progressively in an ethical process".[1]

Two final observations upon this type of Christology require to be made.

It was the claim of scholars at this time to base not only their primary investigations but also their final conclusions, not upon a set of given metaphysical principles, but upon a candid interpretation of the New Testament. It is therefore not unfair to assess their theories on their own principle, judging to what extent they account for the plain meaning of the Scriptures.

When we turn to the New Testament, the Apostolic witness, we do not simply find a man, Christ, who lives a completely human life in a completely human manner—a primarily moral man living a life in harmony with the will of God: in fact, as pointed out in the seventh chapter, we are told singularly little about Christ's thoughts or the relationships of everyday life, in which a man's moral character is most clearly displayed. We are presented with a figure who, in the first place, possesses and exercises divine powers—he performs miracles of healing, control over nature, and superhuman vision: above all, he enters and leaves the world in a manner in which other men cannot. This figure, moreover, makes far-reaching claims for himself: he can remit the eternal guilt of sin, he proclaims himself equal with God, and foretells that he himself will sit as judge over all men at the grand assize. All these things, and more, do not and cannot pertain to one who was merely a man, perfectly fulfilling God's will, or even suffused with God's life—they pertain only to God himself. The modern Antiochene theory, therefore, is inadequate if only for this, that it does not, as a scientific hypothesis should, account for all the relevant data.

Finally, it may be urged that such a predicament in Christology is arrived at because the wrong starting-point has been chosen.

[1] Garvie, *Studies*, p. 520.

For the apologetic of the day—and *Foundations* was, of course, primarily a manual of apologetics—it may have been necessary to begin with Christ's humanity and human life, and thence to work upwards, as DuBose does, to the confession of his Deity. But in the realm of pure Christology, such a method is inexcusable. Those who do not begin with the fundamental Christian assumption that "The Word was made flesh", but with the postulate that Christ was a complete man, and then attempt to show how such a complete man as they suppose Christ to have been was united to God, cannot but end in some such speculation as those considered in this chapter.

# BIBLIOGRAPHY

ABBOTT, E. A.: "The Son of Man: or Contributions to the study of the thoughts of Jesus", pp. 873, 1910.
ADAMSON, T.: "Studies of the Mind in Christ", 1898.
ADENEY, W. F.: "The Divinity of Christ", 1907.
ALEXANDER, W.: "The Johannine Epistles", 1889.
ANDERSON, SIR R.: "The Lord from Heaven", 1910.
ANDREWS, S. J.: "The Life of Our Lord upon Earth".

BALFOUR, LORD: "The Foundations of Belief", 1894.
BALLARD, F.: "Christian Essentials", 1907.
BEATTIE, A.: "The New Theology and the Old", 1910.
BEEBY, A. E.: "Doctrinal Significance of a Miraculous Birth", Hibb. Journ., October 1903.
BENSON, R. M.: "The Virgin Birth of Our Lord and Saviour Jesus Christ", paper, 1904.
BETHUNE-BAKER, J. F.: "Introduction to the Early History of Christian Doctrine", 1903.
BOUGAUD, E.: "The Divinity of Christ".
BOWNE, B. P.: "Personalism", 1908.
BRIERLEY, J.: "Religion and To-day", 1913.
BRIGHT, W.: "The Incarnation as a Motive Power", 1889.
BRIGHT, W.: "Waymarks in Church History", 1894.
BROOKE, A. E.: "Johannine Epistles", I.C.C., 1912.
BROWN, W. ADAMS: "The Essence of Christianity".
BRUCE, A. B.: "Humiliation of Christ", 1881.
BRUCE, A. B.: "Jesus", Encyc. Bibl.

CAIRD, E.: "The Evolution of Religion", Giff. Lecs., 1890–2.
CAIRD, J.: "Fundamental Ideas of Christianity", Giff. Lecs., 1895–6.
CAIRD, J.: "Christianity and the Modern World", 1899.
CAMPBELL, R. J.: "The New Theology", 1907: withdrawn from publication 1915.
CAMPBELL, R. J.: "Faith for To-day", 1900.
CARPENTER, J. ESTLIN: "The First Three Gospels".
CHASE, F. H.: "The Supernatural Element in Our Lord's Earthly Life . . ." paper, 1902.
CHEYNEY, T. K.: "The Origin and Religious Content of the Psalter", Bampton Lectures, 1889.
CLARION, THE . . . CONTROVERSY: Inc. C. T. Gorham, J. M. Robertson, etc., 1904.
CLARKE, W. NEWTON: "An Outline of Christian Theology", New York, 1899.
CHURCH QUARTERLY REVIEW: relevant articles in—

April 1890, "Lux Mundi".
October, 1891, "W. S. Swayne—Our Lord's Knowledge as Man".
Jan. 1892, "C. Gore—Incarnation of the Son of God".
Jan. 1893, "T. B. Strong—Manual of Theology".
July 1894, "W. Sanday—Biblical Inspiration".
Jan. 1896, "C. Gore—Dissertations".
Oct. 1896, "R. L. Ottley—Doctrine of the Incarnation".
July 1897, "H. C. Powell—Principle of the Incarnation".
Oct. 1897, "E. H. Gifford—The Incarnation; A. S. Hawkesworth on the De Incarnatione; and Hort's Christian Ecclesia".
April 1898, "Moberly—Ministerial Priesthood; A. D. White—History of the Warfare of Science and Theology; J. R. Illingworth—Divine Immanence".
Jan. 1899, "F. J. Hall—Kenotic Theory".
Jan. 1900, "Two Books by Henry Van Dyke".
July 1900, "Twenty-Five Years of C.Q.R.", esp. p. 274.
Oct. 1900, "Some books on Ritschlianism: J. Orr, A. E. Garvie, H. M. Scott".
Oct. 1900, "J. Caird—Fundamental Ideas . . .".
Oct. 1900,. "On 'The Atonement in Modern Religious Thought' Symposium—Forsyth, Campbell, F. W. Farrar, W. F. Adeney, etc.".
April 1901, "Moberly—Atonement and Personality".
Jan. 1903, "Contentio Veritatis—Six Oxford Tutors".
Oct. 1910, "W. Sanday—Christologies A. and M.".

DALE, R. W.: "The Atonement", 1890.
DALE, R. W.: "Christian Theology", 1894.
DALE, R. W.: "The Living Christ and the Four Gospels", 1896.
D'ARCY, G. J. A.: "The Human Mind of Our Lord".
D'ARCY, BISHOP C. F.: Hibb. Journ., Jan. 1911, Theology and the Subconscious; Jan. 1912, Is Personality in Space?
D'ARCY, C. F.: "Christianity and the Supernatural".
DENNEY, J.: "Studies in Theology", 1895.
DENNEY, J.: "Death of Christ", 1902.
DENNEY, J.: "Jesus and the Gospel", 1908.
DIGGES LA TOUCHE, E.: "The Person of Christ in Modern Thought", Donnellan Lecs., 1911–12.
DORNER, I. A.: "History of the Doctrine of the Person of Christ", 1839.
DORNER, I. A.: "System of Christian Doctrine",
DRUMOND, J.: "Via Veritas Vita", Hibbert Lectures.
DRUMOND, J.: "The Fourth Gospel", 1903.
DRUMOND, J.: "Studies in Christian Doctrine", 1908.
DRUMOND, J.: "Thoughts on Christology", 1902.
DUBOSE, W. P.: "Soteriology of the N.T.", 1892.
DUBOSE, W. P.: "The Œcumenical Councils", 1896.
DUBOSE, W. P.: "The Gospel According to St. Paul", 1906.
DUBOSE, W. P.: "The Gospel within the Gospels", 1906.

# BIBLIOGRAPHY

Du Bose, W. P.: "High Priesthood and Sacrifice", 1908.
Durrell, J. C. V.: "The Self-Revelation of Our Lord", 1910.
Durrell, J. C. V.: "The Word of Jesus".

Eck, H. V. S.: "The Incarnation", Oxford Lib. of Practical Theology, 1902.
Edwards, T. C.: "The God-Man", 1895.
Emmett, C. W.: "The Eschatological Question in the Gospels", 1911.

Fairbairn, A. M.: "Studies in the Life of Christ", 1880.
Fairbairn, A. M.: "Christ in Modern Theology", 1893.
Ferries, G.: "The Growth of Christian Faith".
Forrest, D. W.: "The Christ of History and Experience", 1897.
Forsyth, P. T.: "Immanence and Incarnation", in C. H. Vine, "The Old Faith and the New Theology", 1907.
Forsyth, P. T.: "Person and Place of Jesus Christ", 1909.
Fundamentals: Chicago, undated. B. B. Warfield, etc.
Foundations, Ed. B. H. Streeter, 1912.

Gardner, P.: "Exploratio Evangelica", 1899.
Gardner, P.: "Historic View of the N.T.", 1901.
Garrod, H. W.: "Religion of all God Men", 1906.
Garvie, A. E.: "The Ritschlian Theology", 1899.
Garvie, A. E.: "Studies in the Inner Life of Jesus", 1907.
Gifford, E. H.: "The Incarnation: Phil. 2. 5 ff.", 1897.
Godet, F.: "Studies on the N.T.", 1873.
Goodrich, A.: "The Immanence of God and the Divinity of Christ", in C. H. Vine, "The Old Faith . . .", 1907.
Gordon, G. A.: "The Christ of To-day", Boston, 1895.
Gore, C., Ed. "Lux Mundi", 1889.
Gore, C.: "The Incarnation of the Son of God", Bampton Lectures, 1891.
Gore, C.: "Dissertations on Subjects Connected with the Incarnation", 1895.
Gore, C.: "Reconstruction of Belief", pp. 521 ff.
Gwatkin, H. M.: "The Knowledge of God and its Historical Development", 1906.

Hall, A. C. A.: "Christ's Temptation and Ours", 1897.
Hall, F. J.: "Theological Outlines", 2 vols., 1892, 4.
Hall, F. J.: "The Kenotic Theory", 1898.
Hall, F. J.: "Dogmatic Theology", 10 vols., Vol. 6—"The Incarnation", 1915.
Hastings' Dictionary of Christ and The Gospels.
Hawkesworth, A. S.: "De Incarnatione Verbi Dei", N.Y., 1897.
Headlam, A. C.: "The Miracles of the N.T.".
Heurtley C. A.: "Faith and the Creed", 3rd ed., 1899.
Hibbert Journal Supplement for 1909, "Jesus or Christ".

HOBSON, W. F.: Letter to W. Bright on the *Kenosis*, Phil. 2. 5 ff., 1891.
HOBSON, W. F.: "Some Aspects of the Incarnation, chiefly in reference to Lux Mundi." Paper.
HODGE, A. A.: "Outlines of Theology", N.Y., 1863.
HODGE, C.: "Systematic Theology", 3 vols., N.Y., 1871.
HORTON, R. F.: "Miracles", 1892.
HORTON, R. F.: "My Belief", 1908.
HORTON, R. F.: "The Incarnation", paper, 1894.
HUGEL, BARON F. VON: "The Mystical Element in Religion . . .".
HUTCHINGS, W. H.: "The Mystery of Temptation".
HUTCHINGS, VEN. W. H.: "Life and Letters of T. T. Carter", 1903.
HUTTON, R. H.: "Theological Essays", 1871.

ILLINGWORTH, J. R.: "Personality Human and Divine", Bampton Lectures, 1894.
ILLINGWORTH, J. R.: "The Gospel Miracles".
ILLINGWORTH, J. R.: "Divine Immanence", 1898.
ILLINGWORTH, J. R.: "Doctrine of the Trinity", 1907.
INGE, W. R.: "Christian Mysticism", 1899.
INGE, W. R.: "Personal Idealism and Mysticism", 1907.

JAMES, W.: "Varieties of Religious Experience", 1901.
JAMES, W.: "The Will to Believe", 1913.
JASTROW, J.: "The Subconscious", 1906.
JONES, E. G.: "The Ascent Through Christ".

KEDNEY, J. S.: "Mens Christi", 1891.
KNOX, R. A.: "Some Loose Stones", 1913.

LACEY, T. A.: "The Historical Christ", 1905.
LANG, C. G.: "The Miracles of Jesus", 1905.
LANG, C. G.: "The Parables of Jesus", 1907.
LIDDON, H. P.: "The Divinity of Our Lord and Saviour Jesus Christ", Bampton Lectures, 1866.
LIGHTFOOT, J. B.: "Epistle to the Philippians", 1868.
LITTON, E. A.: "Introduction to Dogmatic Theology", 1892.
LODGE, SIR O.: "Man and the Universe", 1908.
LYTTELTON, A. T.: "The Place of Miracles in Religion", 1899.

MACKINTOSH, H. R.: "Person of Jesus Christ", 1912.
MACPHERSON, J.: "Christian Dogmatics", 1898.
MARSHALL, H. R.: "Evolution and Religion", N.Y., 1898.
MARTENSEN, H.: "Christian Dogmatics".
MARTINEAU, J.: "The Seat of Authority in Religion", 1890.
MASON, A. J.: "The Faith of the Gospels", 1887.
MASON, A. J.: "Conditions of Our Lord's Life on Earth", 1896.
MEYRICK, CANON: "The Bishop of Manchester (Moorhouse) on Our Lord's Limitation of Knowledge", paper.
MEDD, P. G.: "The One Mediator".

MILL, W. H.: "The Temptation of Christ".
MILLIGAN, G.: "Theology of the Epistle to the Hebrews".
MILLIGAN, W.: "Ascension and Heavenly Priesthood of Our Lord", 1892.
MOBERLY, R. C.: "Atonement and Personality", 1901.
MOORHOUSE, J.: "The Teaching of Christ", 1891.
MORTIMER, A.: "Catholic Faith and Practice", 2 vols., 1896.
MOULE, H. C. G.: "Outlines of Christian Doctrine", 1889.
MOULE, H. C. G.: "Philippian Studies", 1897.
MOZLEY, J. B.: "Augustinian Doctrine of Predestination".
MYERS, F. W. H.: "Human Personality and its Survival of Bodily Death", 2 vols., 1903.

NARSAI—Liturgical Homilies of c. 502. Ed. Dom. R. Connolly.
NOLLOTH, C. F.: "The Person of Our Lord", 1908.

ORD, A. C.: "The Blessedness of the Person of Christ", paper.
ORR, J.: "Christian View of God and The World", 1893.
ORR, J.: "The Progress of Dogma".
OTTLEY, R. L.: "Doctrine of the Incarnation", 1896.
OULTON, R. C.: "On Gore's Essay in Lux Mundi", paper, 1891.

PARKER, T.: "The Transient and Permanent in Christianity", 1908.
PASCENDI GREGIS: Encyc. Pius X, 1907.
POWELL, H. C.: "Principle of the Incarnation", 1896.
PROVIDENTISSIMUS DEUS: Encyc. Leo X, 1899.

RAGG, L.: "Aspects of the Atonement".
RASHDALL, H.: "Doctrine and Development", 1898.
RASHDALL, H.: "Personality Human and Divine" in Sturt—"Personal Idealism".
RASHDALL, H.: "The Idea of Atonement", Bampton Lectures, 1915.
RAVEN, C. E.: "What think ye of Christ?" 1916.
RICHEY, A.: "The Incarnation and the *Kenosis*", 1898.
RICHMOND, W.: "An Essay on Personality", 1900.
ROBERTSON, J. M.: "Christianity and Mythology", 1900.
ROBINSON, A. F.: "Self-Limitation of the Word of God".
ROBINSON ARMITAGE: "Some Thoughts on the Incarnation", 1905.
ROBINSON, C. H.: "Studies in the Character of Christ".
ROMESTIN, H. DE: "Letter to T. T. Carter: 'How Knoweth This Man Letters'"? 1891.
ROSS, J.: J. T. S., July 1909, p. 573.
ROSTRON, S. N.: "The Christology of St. Paul".

SADLER, M. F.: "The One Offering".
SALMON, G.: "Evolution", etc., 1906.
SALMON, G.: "The Human Element in the Gospels", 1907.

SANDAY, W.: "Biblical Inspiration," Bampton Lectures, 1893.
SANDAY, W.: "The Criticism of the Fourth Gospel", 1905.
SANDAY, W.: "Outlines of the Life of Christ", 1906.
SANDAY, W.: "The Life of Christ in Recent Research", 1907.
SANDAY, W.: "Christologies Ancient and Modern", 1910.
SANDAY, W.: "Personality in Christ and in Ourselves", 1911.
SANDAY, W.: Expos. Times, July 1913, p. 438.
SCHWEITZER, A.: "Quest of the Historical Jesus", tr. 1910.
SCOTT, E. F.: "Purpose and Theology of the Fourth Gospel", 1906.
SEAVER, J.: "The Authority of Christ in the Criticism of the O.T.", paper, 1891.
SEAVER, R. W.: "Through Criticism to Christ", Donnellan Lectures, 1905.
SEELEY, J. R.: "Ecce Homo", 1866.
SHEDD, W. G. T.: "Dogmatic Theology", 2 vols., 1889, N.Y.
SHEDD, W. G. T.: "History of Christian Doctrine", 2 vols.
SIMPSON, P. C.: "Fact of Christ", 1906.
SMITH, D.: "The Days of His Flesh", 1905.
STALKER, J.: "The Teaching of Jesus Concerning Himself", 1899.
STANLEY, DEAN, A. P.: "Christian Institutions", p. 48.
STEARNS, L. F.: "The Evidence of Christian Experience", 1890.
STEARNS, L. F.: "Present-Day Theology", N.Y., 1893.
STONE, DARWELL: "Outlines of Christian Dogma", 1913.
STOUT, G. F.: "Manual of Psychology", 2nd Ed., 1907.
STREATFIELD, G.: "The Incarnation".
STRONG, A. H.: "Systematic Theology", N.Y., 1886.
STRONG, A. H.: "Outlines of Systematic Theology", N.Y., 1908.
STRONG, T. B.: "Manual of Theology", 1892.
STRONG, T. B.: "The Miraculous in Gospels and Creeds".
STUBBS, W., BISHOP: "Diocesan Charges", June 1890, and April and May 1893, at Oxford.
STUBBS, "Ordination Addresses", pp. 173-82.
STURT, H.: "Personal Idealism", 1902.
SWAYNE, W. S.: "Our Lord's Knowledge as Man", 1891.
SWETE, H. B.: "Apocalypse of John", 1906.
SYMONDS, J. A.: "The Idea of God".

TEMPLE, W.: "The Nature of Personality", 1911.
TEMPLE, W.: Essay in "Foundations", 1912.
TENNANT, F. R.: "Origin and Propagation of Sin".
THOMASIUS, G.: "Christi Person und Werk", 1853-61.
THOMPSON, J. M.: "Jesus According to St. Mark", 1909.
THOMPSON, J. M.: "Miracles in the N.T.", 1911.
THOMPSON, J. M.: "Through Facts to Faith", 1912.
THORBURN, T. J.: "Jesus the Christ".
TREMENHEERE, G. H.: "The Consciousness of the Incarnate Lord: the Knowledge of the Incarnate Lord", 1934.
TYRRELL, G.: "Lex Credendi", 1906.
TYRRELL, G.: "Christianity at the Crossroads", 1909.

VAN DYKE, H.: "Gospel for an Age of Doubt", 1896.
VAN DYKE, H.: "Gospel for a World of Sin", 1899.
VARIOUS: "The New Theology and Applied Religion", 1908.
VIDLER, A. R., and KNOX, W. L.: "The Development of Modern Catholicism", 1933.
VIDLER, A. R.: "The Modernist Movement in the Roman Church", 1934.
VINE, C. H.: "The Old Faith and the New Theology", 1907.
VIVIAN, P.: "The Churches and Modern Thought", 1906.

WACE, H.: "On Inspiration and N.T. Criticism", paper, 1894.
WALKER, W. L.: "The Spirit and the Incarnation", 1899.
WALKER, W. L.: "The Cross and the Kingdom: as viewed by Christ Himself and in the Light of Evolution", 1902.
WALLACE, W.: "Lectures and Essays", 1898.
WARFIELD, B. B.: "Incarnate Truth", 1892.
WARFIELD, B. B.: "The Right of Systematic Theology", 1897.
WARFIELD, B. B.: "The Emotional Life of Our Lord" in Biblical and Theological Studies" by members of faculty of Princetown Theol. Seminary, 1912.
WARFIELD, B. B.: "Saviour of the World", 1913.
WARREN, W.: J.T.S., April 1911, p. 461, on *kenosis*.
WARSCHAUER, J.: "Antinunquam", 1906.
WARSCHAUER, J.: "The New Evangel", 1907.
WARSCHAUER, J.: "Jesus: Seven Questions", 1908.
WARSCHAUER, J.: "Jesus or Christ", 1909.
WARSCHAUER, J.: "Problems of Immanence", 1909.
WESTCOTT, B. F.: "Christus Consumator".
WESTCOTT, B. F.: "Epistle to the Hebrews", 1889.
WESTON, F.: "The One Christ", 1907.

YOUNG, J.: "The Christ of History . . .", paper, 1906.

www.ingramcontent.com/pod-product-compliance
Lightning Source LLC
Chambersburg PA
CBHW070838020526
44114CB00041B/2022